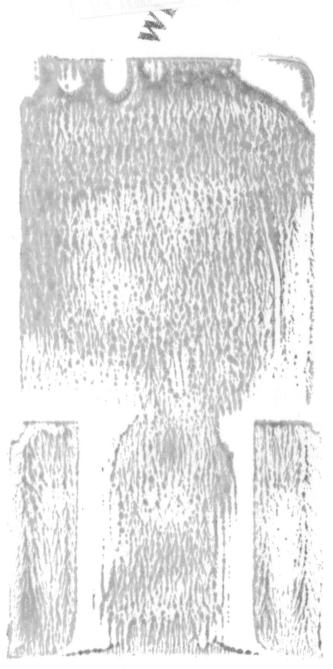

LAFAYETTE IN
THE FRENCH REVOLUTION

Through the October Days

LAFAYETTE IN THE FRENCH REVOLUTION

Through the October Days

By

LOUIS GOTTSCHALK

and

MARGARET MADDOX

THE UNIVERSITY OF CHICAGO PRESS

CHICAGO & LONDON

Library of Congress Catalog Card Number: 69–12572

THE UNIVERSITY OF CHICAGO PRESS, CHICAGO 60637
The University of Chicago Press, Ltd., London W.C. 1

TO

THE ASSISTANTS AND SEMINAR STUDENTS
(too numerous to mention singly)
*who have helped to prepare this volume, its predecessors,
and its projected successors*

PREFACE

THIS IS the fifth in a series of studies of General Lafayette and his times to be published by the University of Chicago Press. The first four dealt with his role in the American Revolution and its consequences (to 1789). This one and the next three are intended to deal with his role in the French Revolution (to August 1792). If it be asked why so much time and space should be devoted to somewhat less than four years of one man's life, the answer is that that one man during those four years not only represented the ups and downs of what has long been considered the classic revolution of modern times but, already famous before it began, continued until his death in 1834 to be a leading advocate of orderly revolution in every significant political crisis of the western world (though only to be regularly frustrated, since *orderliness* and *revolution* tend to be contradictory terms). As a famous man he was watched; his acts were recorded and commented upon, and they can be amply retold by his biographer, for his papers were scrupulously preserved or, when deliberately destroyed by his enemies, are in essence frequently reconstructable. Thus the biographer faces no dearth of evidence about a career which is both interesting as a prominent individual's life story and engaging as a case study of the moderate revolutionary type.

This volume deals with approximately the first nine months of Lafayette's career in 1789—up to the climax of October 5 and 6. It begins with his hard-won campaign to get elected to the Second Estate—that of the Nobility—in the Estates General of 1789, destined to become the Constituent Assembly and the major agency of the first phase of the French Revolution. It ends with his becoming the principal guardian of the king's person, the real power behind the toppling Bourbon throne. The story it tells is not unfamiliar, but that story has never been told in detail before nor, we think, placed in proper perspective. We consider Lafayette neither a scheming, ambitious *arriviste* nor a simple, undeserving *niais* but a competent, well-meaning, patriotic soldier and statesman who, at this stage at least, generally managed to control events, even if they sometimes got out of hand, and in so doing was thrust into a position of leadership, a position he neither diligently conspired to achieve nor earnestly shunned.

A word about the composition of this book. Since *Lafayette between the French and the American Revolution, 1783–1789* was published in 1950, the series on the French Revolution has been, off and on, in preparation. During this interval the pressure of other writings and obligations left me with little time to devote to the series, but Margaret Maddox continued to work on it. Adding to the materials collected since 1927, she composed a huge manuscript on the career of Lafayette from January 1789 to August 1792, when he fled from France and became a prisoner of the Austro-Prussian alliance. I reworked the manuscript covering the period of this volume into a second draft, which she then criticized and corrected. That process continued until a subsequent draft (which, not counting the intermediary steps, was draft no. 5) finally went to press. Our collaboration, although discontinuous on my part, has required long, arduous attention from both of us. The generosity of the Guggenheim, Rockefeller, and Fulbright Foundations, of the University of Chicago's Social Science Research Committee, and of the Center for the Advanced Study of the Behavioral Sciences has provided us with time and resources, which might otherwise have been less readily accessible, abroad and in the United States.

In the course of nearly two decades that this volume has been in preparation many students and assistants (to say nothing of librarians, collectors, publishers, scholars, and other well-wishers) have had a hand in it. One of the rewards of a professor's labors is that he learns while teaching, and some of these cooperators perhaps would be astonished if they were to discover how much I have learned from them. If I dedicate this volume to them, it is not merely to do them whatever honor cooperation in the production of this study can convey, but rather to express to them the gratitude of one who, though he thinks the two are interdependent, considers good students rather than learned books the major product and the chief reward of a humanist professor's efforts.

Louis Gottschalk

Chicago, 1968

TABLE OF CONTENTS

CHAPTER I

The Prelude

W HEN William Wordsworth, looking back to his youth, recalled the early years of the French Revolution, his mind probably was not on the Marquis de Lafayette. Yet the poet's oft-quoted sentiment that "Bliss was it in that dawn/to be alive, but to be young was very heaven!" applied with a special fitness to his French contemporary. In January 1789 Lafayette was still young and sanguine enough to envision a better world to come. He hoped for a civic paradise for his compatriots in which duty and rights, responsibility and power, would fall into proper balance and all would prosper in the state of France.

Yet this young French nobleman was no poetic stripling unused to the ways of the political world. He was thirty-two years of age. He had fought in the American War of Independence, gaining honors, well-merited glory, and the lasting friendship of George Washington and other American statesmen of world renown, and he could boast the rank of major general in both the American army and the army of King Louis XVI of France. His high rank among the royal officers had come to him in recognition of his distinguished service at Yorktown and earlier battles of the American War, at an age that made older men whom he outranked feel also outraged. He had played an enviable role too in the councils of the French ministers of foreign affairs and of finance, advising them on trade and cooperation with the new American confederation, and he was looked upon in both countries as the most acceptable interpreter of the needs and preferences of the one people to the other. Recently, when Louis XVI had assembled the Notables of the realm to advise him on the ever precarious questions of revenue and reform, Lafayette had stood forth as a champion of change—change not merely of personnel or of decrees but of the very method of making laws, change in the fundamental constitution of France. He could hardly consider himself the outstanding advocate of the rights of man and of a national representative body to share in the government of the people, since several generations of illustrious *philosophes* and other critics had preceded him, making at least as cogent demands as he, but he had a good claim to being one of the foremost among the ruling class to pronounce such ideas resoundingly and in a milieu where they were not considered good form and were rarely given voice. In addition, personal charities, a reputation for generosity in good causes, a long list of friends or admirers in all walks of life, and some eloquent speeches in the Council of Notables and in the provincial assembly of his native Auvergne had given him a nationwide reputation as a champion of the poor.

High birth and practical, even hard, experience had made this young man a veteran in the fields of war and politics. What distinguished him from most other veterans of high rank was not his youth alone but also his liberalism. Very few among his colleagues in military and political circles were, as he, liberal in several senses of the word—seeking freedom for the oppressed, giving generously of his resources, granting to others and reserving for himself liberty of personal thought and action, and though in his adolescent years inclined toward diffidence, now at ease among men and women of both high and low station in his own country and in the several foreign countries which he had visited.

Such a veteran should perhaps have recognized that good will in high places alone (if indeed good will existed) was no guarantee of success in great political ventures. He should have foreseen that the deep and incrusted wrongs of which he, along with thousands of others, had complained could not speedily be uprooted and replaced with just and lasting institutions merely by the wave of a scepter. And so he should have been skeptical when Louis XVI finally called upon the Estates of his kingdom—the Clergy, the Nobility, and the Third Estate (or Commoners)—to choose representatives to an Estates General and send them to Versailles, there to advise him on matters pertaining to tax reform and other problems of state. In so doing, Louis yielded to the pressure created in part by his own good will but also by a crisis generated by his need for a better balanced budget, the widespread demand for reform, and the desire among various groups in his realm for a share of his power. The upshot was revolution, for which Lafayette was prepared, to which indeed he was committed. The young general's vague knowledge of the ups and downs of the Dutch War of Independence of the sixteenth century and of the English Civil War and Revolution of the seventeenth century and his intimate personal association with the American Revolution in his own day ought to have taught him that revolutions are likely to succeed only if they emerge from a fairly universal conviction that sweeping change is both desirable and unavoidable and that they are likely to encounter faction, counterrevolution, terror, and reaction if opinions are divided on what should be changed and how far.

If, at the beginning of 1789, the Marquis de Lafayette was more hopeful than events were to justify, the reason was not to be sought alone in the fact, though fact it was, that he was by nature optimistic. Success, rewards, prestige, and popularity had been his lot since his adolescent frustrations, and he had yet to encounter a serious personal defeat in his public life. He had good grounds for confidence in himself, but he also had reason to believe in the rapid triumph of his cause. The king himself appeared ready to share his power as absolute monarch with some kind of representative body. Many of Lafayette's friends, both at court and elsewhere, seemed prepared to approve a new regime based on the more liberal principles of the contemporary Enlightenment. A number of influential clergymen and aristocrats agreed with *philosophes* and lawyers, financiers and merchants that France needed a new governmental organization which not only would correct the more obvious deficiencies in the legislative process and in the administrative system but also would inaugurate a greater equilibrium of political power and social privilege among the three estates.

In principle so many celebrated persons were in accord on so many important issues that even a more cautious observer than the young, energetic, ambitious, and enthusiastic Lafayette might have felt sanguine. Not only Wordsworth but some of the best political minds of the day—Thomas Jefferson, Mallet du Pan, Friedrich von Gentz—visualized a new day for France, and even Edmund Burke was as yet willing to wait and see. Some of the most astute commentators failed to raise the always annoying but all-important questions that reveal the frightening gap between the practical details and the general principles. The marquis was not the only one who, while recognizing the prestige and power of the likely opponents of change and the stubbornness of the vested interests, underestimated their following and their pertinacity. And the whole glad spirit of the day contributed to his failure to fathom the passion and the strength of those who, once the doors were opened, would strive to sweep on to more thoroughgoing change than even he had envisaged.

These miscalculations were to prove fatal to the marquis' program by 1792. But the pages that follow will show that his earlier hopes were not entirely unfounded. At the beginning he had good grounds for confidence in his cause and in his own leadership of it and some right to count upon the loyal support of men from all ranks of society. He had ample reason to share the general persuasion that the provisions of an enlightened constitution would readily be found and widely accepted and that the opposition from those on the one hand who resented their loss of privileges thereby and from those on the other hand who complained that they had been deceived in their rightful anticipation would be outweighed by a patriotic and altruistic public opinion.

The first nine months of the year 1789 were by themselves a longer span than many, including Lafayette, at first considered necessary for the successful termination of the revolution for which Louis XVI had given the starting signal when he consented to convoke the Estates General. Although in that period moments of crisis and reaction occurred, it was a time of almost steadily mounting public confidence and patriotic devotion, with Lafayette always prominent, at times foremost, among those who inspired an expectant people. The story of those nine months is a story of triumph interrupted only now and then by temporary setbacks for the cause of constitutional monarchy and for Lafayette. And there was even greater triumph to come before, as in a Greek tragedy, unpopularity, defeat, military defection, and exile ensued. But those are the themes of later volumes.

On the eve of the French Revolution, J.-P. Brissot de Warville, introduced by Lafayette, visited Washington at Mount Vernon.[1] Washington spoke of Lafayette "with the greatest tenderness" and left Brissot with the impression that he regarded his young companion in arms as his own child. As Brissot afterward described his visit:

Washington foresaw, with a joy mixed with inquietude, the part that this pupil was going to act in the approaching revolution of France. He could not predict with clearness the event of this revolution. If, on the one side, he acknowledged the ardor and enthusiasm of the French character, on the other he saw an astonishing veneration for their ancient government and for those monarchs whose inviolability appeared to him a strange idea.[2]

Washington's foresight (or was it, rather, Brissot's hindsight?) was correct, and he had good reason for "inquietude." His "pupil" was to be impaled on the horns of a dilemma—ardor and enthusiasm for reform offset by veneration for the old forms—but not until after October 1789.

[1] Lafayette to Washington, May 25, 1788, Louis Gottschalk (ed.), *The Letters of Lafayette to Washington, 1777–1799* (New York, 1944), p. 344.

[2] Quoted (with slight changes in punctuation and verb tenses) from Gilbert Chinard (ed.), *George Washington as the French Knew Him* (Princeton, 1940), p. 87.

CHAPTER II

"Too Republican"?

ALTHOUGH the expectations of a magnanimous young man might well have run high at the beginning of 1789, the political situation in France was neither intrinsically simple nor intentionally free of ambiguity. To be sure, the king had finally summoned the Estates General, thus giving some reason to hope that he contemplated a significant change of government. Yet the hope might still have proven illusory, for before its long lapse into limbo the Estates General had been a body that only advised the king, who might disregard its advice if he chose, and in the old days the Estates General had been dominated by the Clergy and the Nobility, frequently without serious opposition from the Commoners. Hence arose uncertainty that the revived Estates General could effect significant change. This time, however, control by the upper orders seemed forestalled by a recent decision of King Louis XVI; the previous December, prompted by his popular finance minister, Jacques Necker, he had issued a decree doubling the size of the Third Estate for the forthcoming meeting so that the Commoners would have as many deputies as the other two orders combined. Hope arose, but what this *doublement du Tiers*, as it was called, portended was not at all clear.

One thing doubling the size of the Third Estate *might* mean was that the king proposed to give it the decisive voice in the Estates General. If that, however, were in fact the royal intention, as Lafayette and his liberal political friends—the self-styled "Patriots"—preferred to believe, why did not the king also specify how votes were to be counted in the Estates General? Obviously, if, as previously, each of the three orders was to have no more than one vote, determined by its majority, the greater size of that majority was of dubious advantage, but if individual votes were to be counted, each having equal value, then the 600 votes of the Third Estate might readily counterbalance the 300 of each of the other two orders.

This issue was not a matter of mere prestige. It was not simply whether the nobles, who would make up the Second Estate and could expect as prelates to dominate the First, would be able to outvote the lawyers, writers, and other bourgeois who, with few exceptions, would make up the Third Estate; it was, rather, part of the corollary but more basic question whether France would have a new constitution and, if so, of what kind. Generations of discussion among *philosophes*, a continuing flood of pamphlets, and recent debates in the law courts known as parlements, in the Councils of Notables, and in the provincial assemblies had made clear a deep division in the nation on that score. The conservatives, composed largely of nobles, insisted that "reform" must be in keeping with the traditional institutions of France, that the absolutism developed by the Bourbon kings of the seventeenth and eighteenth centuries should be tempered by a restoration of some of the aristocracy's political power. The more liberal reformers countered this appeal to history and tradition by an appeal to reason and to the recent experience of America. Reason required, or so at least its champions contended, that the institutions of France be based upon the ancient concepts of "natural law," "the rights of man," and "the social contract" which had been aired nowhere more eloquently than in France in recent generations and at no time more repeatedly than in France's current literature upon the American Declaration of Independence, the constitutions of the American states, the new Constitution of the United States, and the forthcoming meeting of the Estates General.

Among the foremost of the advocates of natural rights and reason were the Patriots, and prominent among them was Lafayette. The defender of liberty in America, the friend of George Washington, Benjamin Franklin, and Thomas Jefferson, the host sooner or later of nearly every American official, merchant, or tourist who came to France, he had made no secret of his devotion to the principles of natural rights and reason. Conspicuous in his home on the Rue de Bourbon in Paris, inserted in one panel of a double frame, hung a copy of the Declaration of Independence, which boldly proclaimed that among the "unalienable Rights" with which the Creator had endowed "all men" were "Life, Liberty, and the pursuit of Happiness." To those who troubled to ask, he answered that he was reserving the empty panel for the French counterpart of the American document.[1]

While waiting for that French counterpart, Lafayette had not been idle. After his return from America in 1784, he had espoused several liberal causes. His memoirs urging freer trade with the United States, his almost daily contacts with the liberals of France and the United States, his speeches in French political assemblies and his voluminous letters urging reform, his efforts on behalf of Negroes and Protestants, and his private charities had all pointed in the direction of greater justice for the underprivileged—sometimes bringing upon him the displeasure of the privileged. Recently, together with some liberal men of letters like Brissot de Warville and the Abbé Sieyès he had helped to organize the French Society of the Friends of the Negroes,[2] and in 1789 he proposed his wife, Adrienne, the *philosophe* Marquis de Condorcet, and other cherished friends for membership.[3] Likewise, together with some other nobles and some professional men he had formed a "committee" or "society" for the express purpose of prodding public opinion in a liberal direction. Among them were personages who, if they were not already closely associated with him, were to become so in the ensuing months—Condorcet, the Duc de La Rochefoucauld, the Vicomte de Noailles, the Comte de Latour-Maubourg, the publicist Comte de Mirabeau, the parlementarian Adrien Duport, Bishop Talleyrand of Autun, the Abbé Sieyès, and the lawyers Guy-Jean-Baptiste Target and Henri Bergasse. This society had come to be known as "the Thirty," and its activity soon earned for it both contemporaneously and subsequently

[1] Louis Gottschalk, *Lafayette between the American and the French Revolution* (Chicago: University of Chicago Press, 1950), pp. 53–54 (hereafter cited as *Between*).

[2] *Ibid.*, pp. 369–70; C. Perroud, "La société française des Amis des Noirs," *Révolution française*, LXIX (1916), 125–26; "Règlements de la Société des Amis des Noirs, année 1789," Bibliothèque de l'Arsenal, Paris Ms. 2867 (56 bis. S.A.F.).

[3] Perroud, pp. 130–35.

perhaps more credit or blame than it deserved for the course of the reform movement then under way.[4] The members of the Thirty had favored the *doublement du Tiers*, and now that the king had "doubled" the Third Estate, they intended to exert their influence in favor of "vote by head" (decisions by a majority of all the deputies) rather than "vote by order" (decisions by a majority of two out of the three estates). Vote by head would enable the Third Estate with the support of liberals among the Clergy and the Nobility to carry a program of profound constitutional reform based upon reason, natural rights, and social contract.

Events were to show that Necker and the court meant to keep control of the Estates General in their own hands if they could. It would obviously be to the royal advantage if the court could decide when the conservative upper orders or the reformist Commoners should have the determining voice, and that advantage might be won if the Estates General were to meet as a rule in three separate rooms, each order voting as an independent body, but on occasion jointly in a single room—as a "National Assembly," to use a not altogether unfamiliar phrase which Lafayette had recently pronounced[5]—each member having an equal vote. Lafayette had committed himself to regular voting by head long before the idea had gained general currency.[6]

On the principle of vote by head the Thirty were in full accord. On a question of tactics, however, they were not at first agreed. Lafayette thought that it would be better for nobles who were committed to the popular cause to seek election by the Third Estate. That procedure might mean that a greater number of liberal-noble candidates would succeed in getting elected, with fewer unwelcome conservative pressures upon the successful ones.

---

[4] Gottschalk, *Between*, pp. 412–13, 416, 418, 424. The Society of the Thirty is frequently portrayed as a conspiratorial group that took control of the early stages of the French Revolution, but we see no reason to consider it anything other than an active and influential body of Patriots. A detailed study of it is contained in C. A. McClelland, "The Lameths and Lafayette: The Politics of Moderation in the French Revolution, 1789–1791" (Ph.D. diss., University of California, Berkeley, 1942).

[5] Gottschalk, *Between*, p. 314.

[6] For an account of these events by Lafayette see *Mémoires, correspondance et manuscrits du général Lafayette publié par sa famille* (Paris, 1837–38), II, 177, and VI, 802 (hereafter cited as *Mémoires*).

Mirabeau, however, thought it wiser for the liberal nobles to leaven the hard conservative lump of the Second Estate—to bore from within the ranks of the nobles. At meetings held three times a week, usually at Duport's home in Paris, questions like these were debated. In the end Mirabeau won on this issue, and Lafayette agreed with the others to seek election by the nobility of his own bailiwick.[7] He was to prove more successful than Mirabeau, who would be obliged by the distrust of his fellow nobles to seek election by the Third Estate.

The role of an illustrious young general and court noble as a leader of the popular cause won the approval of the Comte de Rochambeau, who had commanded the French expeditionary force at Yorktown. Rochambeau wrote to Washington that he himself and "your pupil Lafayette" were among the few Notables who had favored equal representation for the Third Estate.[8] But such views as theirs naturally excited apprehension in more conservative minds. That the American minister in Paris, Thomas Jefferson, should be concerned about Lafayette was to be expected, since Washington's "pupil" was a popular American hero and Jefferson's close personal friend and disciple as well. But crowned heads like Tsarina Catherine II of Russia[9] and King Stanislas Poniatowski of Poland[10] were also kept informed about him through their correspondents in Paris. Influential persons were so aroused by the young man's political program that Jefferson had feared at one time that his friend might yet end his shining career in the Bastille, but nothing more serious than a temporary removal from active military command had ensued.[11] The mildness of this punishment was, if anything, a political blunder, for it had

[7] *Ibid.*, II, 249, 360. Cf. *Mémoires biographiques, littéraires et politiques de Mirabeau écrits par lui-meme, par son père, son oncle et son fils adoptif* [ed. Gabriel Lucas de Montigny] (Paris, 1841), V, 195 n. (hereafter cited as *Mémoires de Mirabeau*).

[8] January 31, 1789, George Washington Papers, Library of Congress (hereafter abbreviated LC), Series 4, Microfilm reel no. 98.

[9] Catherine to Baron de Grimm, January 27, ed. Ya. K. Grot, in *Sbornik imperatorskago ruskago istoricheskago obshchestva*, XIII (1878), 473.

[10] Filippo Mazzei to King Stanislas, January 2, *Lettere di Filippo Mazzei alla corte di Polonia*, ed. Raffaeli Ciampini (Bologna, 1937), I, 72.

[11] Jefferson to James Madison, January 12, Julian P. Boyd (ed.), *The Papers of Thomas Jefferson* (Princeton, 1950———), XIV, 436–37 (hereafter cited as Boyd), and Gottschalk, *Between*, p. 391.

no chastening effect upon the marquis, who continued to count upon his influence at court to rectify complaints that came to his attention,[12] and it left him freer after mid-summer 1788, just when all of France was in ferment over the forthcoming election, to attend the frequent meetings of the Thirty. The aristocratic Comte de Bouillé long afterward recalled with somewhat of a shock that on New Year's Day 1789, when he congratulated Lafayette on the king's *doublement* of the Third Estate, the marquis replied, "Oh, we'll take him farther than that."[13] About this time, the elder of the king's two brothers, the Comte de Provence, meaning to rebuke the liberal marquis semi-publicly, said to him at the king's dinner table, "I hope, M. de Lafayette, that, quite republican though you are, you do not approve the murder of Charles I [of England]."[14]

Of course Lafayette did not approve of regicide. He was not in fact even a *republican* if that word were meant to convey opposition to hereditary monarchy in France. He did not believe that the French people wanted a government without King Louis XVI or that a vast, ancient country like France with its deep-rooted institutions, its vested interests, and its traditional complications could safely adopt the simpler forms of government that so admirably suited a new, sparsely settled country like his beloved America. Besides, he greatly respected the king and the royal minister Necker, counting upon them, despite the conservative influences that surrounded them at court, to lead the French people toward a new regime where, among other liberal institutions, constitutional checks and balances would restrain royal absolutism, "the natural rights of man" would replace aristocratic privilege, and religious toleration would flourish alongside an established church. His reply to Provence, therefore, condemned Charles I's execution as an act of iniquity, but since it failed to repudiate his liberal principles, it still must have sounded extreme to his royalist table companions.[15]

Lafayette did not lack more appreciative listeners, however.

---

[12] Lafayette to unknown, January 1, courtesy of Dr. Max Thorek, Chicago.

[13] Louis-Joseph-Amour, marquis de Bouillé, *Souvenirs et fragments pour servir aux mémoires de ma vie et de mon temps, 1769-1812* (Paris, 1906), I, 96.

[14] *Mémoires*, III, 198.

[15] *Ibid.*

Censorship had relaxed, where indeed it had not collapsed, under the strain of the current electoral excitement, and with the unconcealed purpose of influencing local opinion on the questions of the day, pamphlets now circulated freely in metropolis and provinces. At least two of doubtful authorship were attributed to Lafayette by contemporaries or later bibliographers—*Idées sur les États-généraux par M. le M. D. L. F.* and *Voeu patriotique d'un américain sur la prochaine assemblée des États généraux*. But they probably were not his. Though sharing his convictions in general, they departed from them in certain details.

Besides, no reason suggests itself why Lafayette should have preferred to conceal his authorship if he were in fact the author of these pamphlets. He had expressed their more dangerous views, sometimes publicly, on more than one occasion. His call for a national assembly in the very stronghold of aristocrats, the Council of Notables of 1787, and for the *doublement* in the Council of Notables of 1788 had already acquired a legendary aura. When the Provincial Assembly of Dauphiny defiantly decided that its members should be chosen by all the voters regardless of estate at a ratio of one for the Clergy, two for the Nobility, and three for the Commoners, he had come out openly for such a radical procedure, which, if applied to the forthcoming Estates General, would tend to make every member responsible to all his constituents, not of his order alone, and, in any case, would give the Commoners a voting power equal to that of the other orders combined.[16] In acknowledging a bold *Discours* by Bergasse on the best way to limit legislative and executive power in a monarchy, Lafayette went even further than its author; he disagreed with Bergasse's proposal to follow the British constitutional model, for he did not approve of a chamber of hereditary peers; inheritance of office was harmful where it was not necessary, and it was necessary, he thought, for the royal office alone.[17]

---

[16] *Copie d'une lettre de M. le Marquis de La Fayette au syndic des trois orders des Cevennes* (January 3), Collection of Stuart W. Jackson, Yale University Library, New Haven. See also *Mémoires,* II, 202 n., and III, 226, and *Idées sur les États-généraux par M. le M. D. L. F.* (which probably was not by Lafayette, however), p. 5.

[17] *Mémoires,* III, 200–201.

To reconfirm his already widely known views Lafayette put them in print for easier circulation, unmistakably signed with his own name. The occasion for this publication was a letter from the syndic of the region known as the Cevennes, where a controversy had arisen over the rightful place of the Third Estate. Speaking in the name of the inhabitants of the Cevennes, the syndic had expressed approbation of Lafayette's espousal of the *doublement du Tiers*. Lafayette gave his reply the form of a brief pamphlet. Thanking his correspondent for the expression of confidence, he affirmed that he looked upon the recent decision of the king to double the Third Estate's membership as a popular victory; while short of "the excellent proportion of Dauphiny," it would give to the Commoners "that equality which will enable the national assembly to deliberate by head." The regulation of further procedure, he believed, lay in the hands of the national assembly, which now had the power "to erect the great edifice of French liberty, of which several basic points are already recognized by the government, which deliberation by head ought to accelerate, and toward which the king promises in advance to make common cause with the national sovereignty" (meaning "the nation as sovereign"). This happy prospect, he wrote, might well eliminate any lingering doubts. "We should feel content that the big issue is won; everything should now tend toward harmony among the orders and to the union of hearts and minds toward the great goal that concerns all citizens equally."[18] He made a similar plea for patience and expressed a similar confidence in the future in a private letter to the officers of the city of Bayonne.[19]

In the France of January 1789 only the bolder spirits used phrases like *national assembly* and *national sovereignty*, and Lafayette at first directed his major attention toward the elaboration of daring political principles like those rather than toward the practical politics of electioneering. He shared Jefferson's disappointment that the recently adopted Constitution of the United States con-

---

[18] *Copie d'une lettre de M. le Marquis de La Fayette* (January 3). See also M. B. Garrett, *The Estates General of 1789* (New York, [1935]), p. 163.

[19] January 24, Municipal Archives of Bayonne, AA50, No. 37, courtesy of Professor Beatrice Hyslop, New York.

tained no declaration of rights.[20] The time was near, he now felt, for a resounding French declaration to take its place beside Jefferson's Declaration of Independence—for Europe's first true proclamation, "matching the principles of the American Era" and "not just a concession or a petition of rights"[21] like those which in the seventeenth century had set forth the rights of Englishmen. Once principles that were at the same time indispensable and sufficient for liberty were enunciated and their observance assured, the detail of government, he held, would be but "secondary variations."[22]

In the meantime Lafayette worked quietly on a declaration of rights that should be ready when the time came. Even the Comtesse Adélaïde de Simiane, his confidante and (if a widely held opinion was correct) his mistress,[23] learned about this "catechism of France"[24] only months later. But Jefferson knew about it earlier. Whether he helped his young French admirer to write the first version of this manifesto, destined in a later draft to become world famous, no one, it seems, was allowed to learn. But when it was done, Jefferson sent a copy of it to his friend James Madison, intended eventually for the eyes of Washington—or so Lafayette thought.[25] Meanwhile, its author waited for the proper moment to disclose his pronunciamento to France and to the world. Jefferson believed that it was a good draft; it contained, he declared, "the essential principles of ours accomodated [*sic*] as much as could be to the actual state of things here" and "adapted to the existing abuses."[26] He apparently thought that Madison, who was soon to become engaged in an effort to add a bill of rights to the new American constitution, might profit from French cogitation on the same subject. "Everybody here is trying their hand at forming declarations of rights."

---

[20] Gottschalk, *Between*, p. 366.

[21] *Mémoires*, II, 251.

[22] *Ibid.*, III, 202. See also *ibid.*, p. 227.

[23] *See* Chap. IV, pp. 62–63, and Appendix I.

[24] Lafayette to [Mme de Simiane?], [*ca.* June 23], *Mémoires*, II, 309.

[25] *Ibid.*

[26] Jefferson to Madison, January 12, Boyd, XIV, 437.

Lafayette was one day to describe his document as the culmination of his career—"fruit of my past, gage of my future."[27] The select few who knew about it at this stage learned, if they did not already know, that in his political philosophy nature had made men equal, distinctions among them, though required by monarchy, being acceptable only if commensurate with benefit to the general welfare.[28] Subsequently, he himself described his attitude at this time as centered upon "an ardent wish and hearty undertaking that a Revolution might take place in this country founded on our American principles of Liberty and Equality."[29]

Gouverneur Morris, an old American acquaintance, whose duty and honor it had recently been to play a leading role in polishing the final draft of the American constitution,[30] became one of the few who were allowed to learn early of Lafayette's proposed declaration of rights. Morris arrived in Paris as a representative of some American business concerns on February 3. His first calls were on Jefferson and Lafayette, and so he found himself almost immediately in the main stream of French political affairs. Taking upon himself the role of adviser, he suggested several amendments to Lafayette's declaration, "tending to soften the high colored expressions of freedom," for, he added, "It is not by sounding words that revolutions are produced." In his opinion Lafayette appeared "too republican for the genius of his country."[31]

Obviously Lafayette's two leading American friends in Paris were not equally enthusiastic about his political philosophy. How could they have been, since one held as a major premise that *all* men were equally endowed with inalienable rights and the other emphasized the need of adapting one's political convictions to the *genius* of one's country? At this stage of France's history Lafayette preferred to adapt to his country's needs the broad

[27] Lafayette to M. d'Hennings, January 15, 1799, *Mémoires*, III, 227.

[28] Boyd, XIV, 438–39. For a brief but comprehensive statement of the part of Jefferson in drafting Lafayette's declaration of rights see the editorial note *ibid.*, pp. 231–33. The variations in Lafayette's drafts are analyzed below, pp. 82–90 and 93–97.

[29] Lafayette to Short, November 16, 1791, William Short Papers, LC.

[30] Madison to Sparks, April 8, 1831, Jared Sparks, *Life of Gouverneur Morris* (Boston, 1832), I, 284–85.

[31] *Ibid.*, pp. 294–95.

humanitarian propositions by which the American Declaration of Independence sought to justify a revolution rather than to borrow from the endemic phraseology of the Constitution of the United States, which sought to provide stable institutions for a particular people recovering from a revolution. If less favorably impressed than Jefferson by Lafayette, Morris was, on the other hand, less "astonished at the Grossness of his Ignorance of Goverment [*sic*] and History" than John Adams, who, however, apparently was hard to impress since he was shocked also by the "gross Ideology" of "Turgot, Rochefaucault [*sic*], Condorcet and Franklin."[32]

In those days, when mutual friends were the best letter-carriers between residents in distant lands, Morris brought to Lafayette a letter from Washington. It referred to a report received in the United States in late September 1788: "We were first in doubt and then under great anxiety about your personal liberty, as an ugly story prevailed respecting your having broken into the Bastille. Since that time I have been made happy by hearing that public affairs have taken a more favorable turn in France."[33] Mentioning French visitors who had recently come to see him, Washington added a touch which revealed his warm attachment to his devoted young friend: "You will not forget, my dear Sir, that I have your promise for bringing Madame la Fayette to America, whenever you shall gratify it with another visit."[34]

Morris also carried a letter to Jefferson from John Jay, the American secretary of foreign affairs. It spoke of a minor crisis in Franco-American relations. The Comte de Moustier, French minister in New York, had become *persona non grata*. His elaborate establishment, his relations with his sister-in-law, who acted as his hostess, and his insistence upon the prompt payment of America's debt to France had combined with a haughty manner to alienate the country to which he was assigned, and Jefferson was instructed

---

[32] Adams to Jefferson, July 13, 1813, Lester J. Cappon (ed.), *The Adams-Jefferson Letters: The Complete Correspondence between Thomas Jefferson and Abigail and John Adams* (Chapel Hill, 1959), II, 355.

[33] November 27, 1788, J. C. Fitzpatrick (ed.), *The Writings of George Washington* (Washington, 1931–44), XXX, 139 (hereafter cited as Fitzpatrick).

[34] *Ibid.*, p. 140.

to ask for his recall. In delicate matters like this Jefferson had learned, since his arrival in France in 1784, to move by indirection, using the willing Lafayette as a go-between. He decided in this matter to call again on "the invaluable mediation of our friend." Lafayette thereupon went to see the Comte de Montmorin, the French minister of foreign affairs, who was "sensibly impressed," and Moustier soon received a leave of absence designed to bring him back to France immediately.[35]

Other men had recently come to count upon the intercession of Lafayette in high places, and among them were the authorities of his native province, Auvergne. As had happened several times before,[36] they appealed to him to intercede in a dispute. This time it involved the prestige of certain cities in Auvergne. The election of deputies to the Estates General was to take place, according to an almost forgotten precedent, in the principal cities of the subdivisions of the realm known as *bailliages* ("bailiwicks") or *sénéchaussées* ("seneschalsies") instead of in those of the provinces. The capital of the *bailliage* that comprised Auvergne was Riom, but the capital of the province of Auvergne was Clermont. For generations the two cities had been rivals, with Clermont steadily gaining in population and standing. To lose to an ancient rival the prestige of being the seat of local elections that were to bring a new era to France seemed unjust to the citizens of Clermont. They sent a deputation to the capital to plead that an exception to the general rule be made for the province of Auvergne, and they instructed this deputation to invite the "seigniors of the country" who lived in Paris to join in their plea.

Lafayette was one of those seigniors, and he complied, thereby becoming involved in electioneering in the two rival communities and a third as well. His intercession brought him the thanks of one of Auvergne's towns, but it was neither Clermont nor Riom; it was St. Flour, the ancient capital of Haute Auvergne, near which Lafayette had recently bought some property.[37] St. Flour conferred

[35] Jefferson to Jay, February 4, 1789, Boyd, XIV, 520–21.

[36] Gottschalk, *Between*, pp. 406, 409, 413–14.

[37] See p. 19 and n. 42.

upon him a greatly coveted honor, for the royal council, in attempting to mediate the dispute, had decided to divide Auvergne into three parts—the seneschalsy of Auvergne (with Riom as its capital), the seneschalsy of Clermont, and the bailliage of Haute Auvergne (with St. Flour as its capital). Thanking him for his graciousness, all three orders of St. Flour invited him to take part in the elections in their town.[38] He gained few friends in either Riom, Clermont, or Basse Auvergne by his intercession, but he felt rewarded by "the pleasure of having brought peace to a little city that is my neighbor and where everyone had been eating his heart out."[39]

Being a rich and illustrious member of the highest court circles in France, Lafayette was conspicuous as a leader in the demand for popular rights, but he was not unique among the rich or illustrious—as was once more illustrated when he became a member of the Club de Valois. The Abbé Sieyès, famous as a publicist, was the prime founder of the club (in February 1789), and among its first members were other conspicuously liberal nobles—such as the Duc d'Orléans, La Rochefoucauld, the Duc de Liancourt, Talleyrand, Duport, Condorcet, and Charles de Lameth, who had distinguished himself at the Battle of Yorktown, as well as other members of the Society of the Thirty like Target and Bergasse; and its rolls were soon to include other liberal nobles as well as several liberal bankers and merchants of Paris. But not all of its members were liberals; some more conservative French nobles, magistrates, savants, soldiers, and bourgeois, and some eminent foreigners also gathered at its handsome quarters in the Palais Royal—to talk, dine, play cards or billiards, and read the latest periodicals. The Club de Valois reflected the prevalent accord among the social, intellectual, and economic elite in the early weeks of 1789. It was not primarily a political club, though much political

---

[38] The city corporation of St. Flour to Lafayette, February 25, cited in Francisque Mége, *Les Elections de 1789, la dernière année de la province d'Auvergne* (Clermont-Ferrand, 1904), p. 163. See also *ibid.*, pp. 19–20, 34, 82, 163, and the same author's *Gaultier de Biauzat, député du Tiers-état aux États-généraux de 1789: sa vie et sa correspondance* (Paris, 1890), II, 301–6.

[39] Lafayette to [Mme de Simiane?], March 8, *Mémoires*, II, 240–41.

discussion took place there, and it was never to cultivate or to acquire the influence of the Thirty, even after it welcomed to membership free of dues all those who were elected deputies to the Estates General.[40]

As the time for the election of deputies to the Estates General drew close, Lafayette undertook to influence the selections in and around his province of Auvergne as much as he could. Since his boyhood friend Latour-Maubourg intended to stand for election in nearby Puy-en-Velay (today's Le Puy), they planned to help each other. Both of them approached the Chevalier de La Colombe, who had gone to America in 1777 with Lafayette and had served as his aide-de-camp there. Lafayette invited his neighbor (using the English phrase) into *the family* to serve once more as his aide,[41] and La Colombe accepted.

The Marquis de Lafayette was a landowner in several provinces of France. His possessions in Auvergne provided only about one seventh of his income of 108,000 livres and comprised but part of the old towns and other lands of which he had inherited or otherwise acquired the seignorial rights—the most recent, bought the previous December, being Clavière, near St. Flour.[42] Since the king had decreed that every noble might take direct part in the choice of the representatives of his order from his bailiwick, Lafayette now intended to go where he was most likely to achieve his own election and carry the most weight in the choice of others. He decided to go to Riom first and then, if there were time, to St. Flour. Toward the end of February his carriage was on its

---

[40] Gouverneur Morris, *Diary of the French Revolution*, ed. B. C. Davenport (Boston, 1939), I, 94 n. (hereafter cited as Davenport); Augustin Challamel, *Les Clubs contre-révolutionnaires* (Paris, 1895), p. 51; J. H. Clapham, *The Abbé Sieyès: An Essay in the Politics of the French Revolution* (London, 1912), p. 62; and G. Lacour-Gayet, *Talleyrand, 1754–1836* (Paris, 1928–31), I, 106.

[41] February 1, Ulysse Rouchon, *Un Ami de La Fayette, le chevalier de La Colombe* (Paris, 1924), p. 28. See also *Mémoires*, III, 404 n.

[42] "Etats des contrats, titres et papiers remis par le C^{en} Morizot pour La Fayette, émigré," Archives Nationales (hereafter abbreviated AN), T1640, No. 61. See also Mège, *Elections de 1789*, p. 54; Henry Mosnier, *Le Château de Chavaniac-Lafayette: description, histoire, souvenirs* (Le Puy, 1883), p. 56; and Bibliothèque de Clermont-Ferrand, Mss. du comte d'Espinchal, E, I, 27, Ms. 360, Tome VI, pp. 231–39.

wintry way to Auvergne.[43] There, for the first time in his life, he was to stand for an elective office, and his political theory was to have its first encounter with practical vote-gathering politics.

BIBLIOGRAPHICAL NOTES

The studies by Francisque Mège of the history of Auvergne in the eighteenth century are still unsurpassed.

Julian Boyd's footnotes to the *Papers of Thomas Jefferson* are extraordinarily detailed and informative. He and his staff have sent us, besides, several helpful communications relative to Lafayette in this period.

The collection of the late Stuart W. Jackson is now the property of the Yale University Library. His *Lafayette: A Bibliography* (New York, 1930), though inadequate and occasionally inaccurate, is still the best bibliography available on the subject.

The letter of Lafayette to Lautor-Maubourg cited below (n. 43) from the Archives Nationales has been published, but not accurately, along with other letters of the same to the same, by L. Mortimer-Ternaux in *Histoire de la Terreur* (Paris, 1863), I, 426–28, and by Charles Nauroy in *Le Curieux*, I (1884), 92–93.

[43] Lafayette to Baron de Gallifit (requesting that he be informed in Auvergne whether the Comte de Pons could be placed in the Noailles Regiment), [February 22?], Bibliothèque de Rouen, Collection Blosseville; Lafayette to Baron de [Gallifit?], Chavagnac [*sic*], March 8 (thanking him for kindness to the Comte de Pons), Cornell University Rare Book Room, Blancheteau Catalogue, typed supplement, p. 38; Morris to William Carmichael, February 25, Davenport (ed.), I, xxxix; Jefferson to Short, February 28, Boyd, XIV, 598; and Lafayette to Maubourg, April 1, AN, F^7 4767.

CHAPTER III

Politics Provincial and Metropolitan

A WEEK or more on the carriage route to Auvergne, which part of the time was little more than frozen mud or slushy clay, brought Lafayette early in March to his native château in the village of Chavaniac. Here, his ancestors had been the lords, and here he was respected and beloved. Though he had rarely returned since as a boy he had gone off to complete his education and embark upon a military career in Paris, the château's four plain round turrets were in some ways more familiar to him than the mansions of his wife's family (the Noailles) in Paris and Versailles or his own home in Paris.

No sooner did neighboring nobles hear of Lafayette's return than they began to sound him out. He quickly discovered—if indeed he had not already realized—that liberals like the Thirty were not alone in trying to influence opinion and swing elections. A conservative, high-born clique was at work as well and had made many proselytes in Auvergne; Lafayette called it "the Princes,"[1] for several princes of the blood had recently demanded that "the ancient constitution and forms be maintained in their entirety."[2] The Princes wanted to preserve the monarchy as it was, granting few concessions to the common people, and the local aristocrats, he learned, had been "forewarned and prepared against" his radical opinions.[3] Some of them indicated that if he made certain conces-

[1] Lafayette to Rabaut, March 10, [1789], Bibliothèque de la Ville de Nantes, Ms. 667, pièce 244.

[2] Gottschalk, *Between*, pp. 4, 9 and n.

[3] Lafayette to [Mme de Simiane?], March 8, *Mémoires*, II, 240. Morris diary, March 16, Davenport (ed.), I, 13, indicates that a report was current in Paris that Lafayette "is like to loose [*sic*] his Election in Auvergne." This report suggests that this letter may have

sions, he would be unanimously elected, but otherwise not at all. He replied that he wanted "to convince and not to delude." Although he felt certain that he could find support and "a chance for celebrity" in the Third Estate, he feared that that order "wanted to go far." The unyielding character of the demands he encountered on all sides shocked him, but "I shall do my duty," he decided, "and shall be moderate," even if moderation might cost him his election.[4]

One of Lafayette's friends was Rabaut St. Etienne, a Huguenot minister with whom he had recently collaborated in the successful effort to win toleration for France's Protestants. Since their political views were much the same, he could afford to be explicit about his plans when writing to Rabaut about the situation in Auvergne. While they were certainly far from preserving "the ancient constitution and forms," as the Princes wished, neither did they "go far." "I believe that it is necessary to conciliate all the orders and to unite them for a common goal," he explained. "My personal conduct will be guided by my guess of the means best suited to delimit the revolution, but if the nobility want to monopolize liberty, they ought not to give me any responsibility for their interests." Hence he intended to make his sentiments clear before the election at Riom.

The king's instructions had asked every electoral assembly for a *cahier de doléances* ("memorandum of grievances"), leaving each order's electoral assembly free to draw up a separate *cahier* or to join with the other local orders in a common statement. What Lafayette advocated, now as previously in the case of Dauphiny, was that all *cahiers* be written and all deputies chosen jointly by the three estates "so that each member of the sovereign assembly may be deputed by the entirety of the citizens of his canton," for all three orders ought to recognize that "their welfare is in union." While this program, as he apprehended, might jeopardize his election, he saw in it a way to preserve the principles essential

---

been addressed to Mme de Lafayette rather than to Mme de Simiane, who would perhaps have been less disposed to spread abroad that she had received news from Lafayette, but we think it more likely to have been Mme de Simiane. See below, Appendix I.

[4] Lafayette to [Mme de Simiane?], March 8, *Mémoires*, II, 240.

to a good monarchical government—namely, "the executive power of the monarchy, the pre-eminence of the nobles, and the rights of property." Those principles, however, he was persuaded, would be assured "only under the shelter of a free constitution permitting all citizens to share in the advantages which nature has granted to all men, which common sense ought to guarantee to all societies, and which all Frenchmen will enjoy within six months unless despotism and aristocratic abuses, backed to win the race against the good patriots of all the orders, carry off a victory which is not probable." Realizing that his insistence upon this program would be "a little disturbing, especially to the assembly at Riom," he asked Rabaut not to speak of it and to communicate with him only indirectly, through La Colombe at Le Puy, since he had detected "little accidents in the mails."[5]

Meanwhile, Lafayette maintained a brisk correspondence with his supporters in Velay. La Colombe was kept busy electioneering and acting as his intermediary at Le Puy, forwarding letters to and from Chavaniac (sometimes by special courier) and sending election bulletins.[6] Having learned that Latour-Maubourg's election was opposed at Le Puy by the local bishop and the Polignac family (the Duc de Polignac being a favorite of Queen Marie Antoinette and perhaps the most powerful landlord in Velay), Lafayette determined to make a special effort to achieve his friend's success.[7]

On March 11, well ahead of the elections, Lafayette left Chavaniac. He was unhappy, he confessed, about his colleagues' biases in favor of retaining their privileges, the consequent discord among the Auvergne estates, and the intrigues directed against Latour-Maubourg. He arrived the next day at Riom.[8] The Third Estate of the seneschalsy of Auvergne was already in session there, under the able leadership of a former naval functionary named

[5] Lafayette to Rabaut, March 10, *loc cit.*

[6] Lafayette to La Colombe, March 11, Rouchon, p. 29.

[7] Same to same, March 8, 11, April 1, *ibid.*, pp. 29–31, and Lafayette to Maubourg, March 11, April 1, Mortimer-Ternaux, I, 426–28.

[8] Lafayette to La Colombe, March 11, Rouchon, p. 29, and Lafayette to Maubourg, March 11, Mortimer-Ternaux, I, 426.

Pierre-Victor Malouet. Since the king's instructions permitted an electoral assembly to draw up a separate *cahier* if it preferred, Malouet and his colleagues saw a chance to steal a march upon the other two estates; they planned to prepare a draft to present to the Clergy and the Nobility as the basis for a common *cahier,* and the Third Estate was already at work upon it. The political atmosphere of Riom thus was strained, in a manner Lafayette could hardly have approved, even before the upper two orders had convened. The great national issue of vote by head versus vote by order was here going to be faced in microcosm.

The first meeting of all three orders of the Auvergne seneschalsy did not take place until the morning of March 14. It was filled with formalities and produced no crisis. Clergy, Nobility, and Third Estate attended Mass together and then in the main hall of the Palais de Justice listened to speeches by the king's procurator, by the Comte de Langhac, who as the seneschal of Auvergne spoke for the Nobility, and by Malouet, who spoke for the Commoners. The keynote of all three speeches was the need for harmony among the orders. Nevertheless, the probability of disharmony was fore-shadowed in the speeches of the spokesmen for the Second and Third Estates. Langhac indicated that the nobles were ready to give up their exemptions from certain taxes, but certain other prerogatives, he insisted, in phrases reminiscent of Montesquieu and other apologists for the aristocratic tradition, ought to be pre-served as a means of ensuring to the nobility sufficient authority to protect the people from the potentially arbitrary power of the king. Malouet, on the other hand, describing the Third Estate's preliminary *cahier,* appealed to the Nobility to make sacrifices in the interest of unity.[9] Thus from the outset two probably irrecon-cilable policies stood revealed.

The speeches over, the delegates took an oath "to proceed in honor and in conscience," and then they separated, to meet as three distinct orders.[10] The Nobility did no more that day than confirm Langhac as their presiding officer. The next morning they turned

[9] *Procès-verbal des séances de l'assemblée de l'ordre de la Noblesse de la sénéchaussée d'Auvergne, tenues à Riom dans le mois de mars 1789* (Riom, 1789), pp. 19–20.

[10] *Ibid.,* p. 11, and Mège, *Elections de 1789,* pp. 102–5.

to consideration of their own *cahier*, but before they could take any action, a deputation from the Third Estate asked permission to address them. The seneschal appointed four gentlemen, including Lafayette, to escort the deputation into the hall, where, formally presenting a copy of the Third Estate's preliminary *cahier*, it asked the Nobility to cooperate in drawing up a common *cahier*. When its spokesman had finished, the four gentlemen escorted the deputation back to the door. The Clergy had meanwhile received a similar request.[11]

The Third Estate, under Malouet's leadership, thus confronted the other two orders at Riom with a dilemma. If they agreed to joint sessions of the three orders, even if for no other purpose than to draw up a common *cahier,* the Third Estate might win enough support in the First Estate from parish priests and other lower clergy to include in a joint statement the current demands for the elimination of more privileges than most of them were ready to concede, and if they did not agree to joint sessions, they ran the risk of alienating the Third Estate. The Nobility decided that the second risk was the lesser; they would deal with the Third Estate through deputations.[12]

If Lafayette disapproved of this decision, nowhere is his disapproval (or approval) recorded. Probably he said nothing, for he was caught in a dilemma. If his previously announced position was in favor of joint *cahiers*, it also seemed to posit joint action by good will rather than by manipulation. Langhac appointed a committee of four to take to the Third Estate the Nobility's reply to its request, and Lafayette was named one of that committee. The Marquis de Lacqueuille, the committee's chairman, notified the Third Estate that his order would always be ready to send commissioners to confer with them on all matters pertaining to the public welfare and would always give earnest attention to the interests of the Third Estate. And Lafayette's "moderation" (if moderation it was) received further open recognition, but recognition that was a private setback. His was the second

[11] *Procès-verbal . . . de la Noblesse . . . à Riom,* pp. 12–13.

[12] *Ibid.,* p. 13. See also Mège, *Elections de 1789,* pp. 94–133, and Baron Malouet (ed.), *Mémoires de Malouet* (Paris, 1868), I, 255–56, 268, 278.

name (after Lacqueuille's) to be selected by vote of the whole order for membership on a committee (eventually of twelve) to draw up the Nobility's separate *cahier*.[13]

Only the third member of that committee had been designated when another deputation of the Third Estate requested to be heard. This deputation, announcing that their order was nearly done with its business and that several of its members wished to return home soon to attend to their spring farming, submitted a resolution which that estate had passed in favor of naming representatives to the Estates General "in common." The implication of their announcement was clear; the Third Estate hoped that the Nobility would proceed to joint selections as rapidly as possible. Again Langhac tried with a soft answer to turn away the wrath that the Nobility's probable decision might stir up. The Second Estate, he declared, could not choose its deputies until its *cahier* was completed, but as soon as its *cahier* committee was selected, it would consider and report upon the proposals of the Third Estate's *cahier* and upon its own, and then steps would be taken to enable the farmers to return to their work. The implication of this answer also was clear: although the Second Estate meant to be polite in its insistence upon its independence, it firmly intended not to be rushed into joint action.

The election of the remaining members of the Nobility's committee on the *cahier* was completed only the following morning (March 16), and the committee was empowered to confer with the other two orders on whatever it judged proper and useful. Then Langhac brought up the question of joining with the Third Estate, and the Second Estate voted, "in keeping with the ancient practices of the realm," to deliberate as a separate body but to continue to confer with the other two orders through commissioners. The proposal of joint election of deputies was disposed of the next day (March 17) by a vote which practically repudiated joint elections by declaring the Third Estate free to go ahead with its own elections if it chose.[14] The First Estate was equally uncom-

---

[13] *Procès-verbal . . . de la Noblesse . . . à Riom*, p. 14, and Mège, *Elections de 1789*, pp. 118–19 and nn.

[14] *Procès-verbal . . de la Noblesse . . . à Riom*, pp. 16, 18.

promising. Thus frustrated, the Third Estate drew up a resolution which, after recounting its effort to bring about "a genuine and national union of the citizens of all ranks," attested that since the majority of its members could no longer stay away from their farms, it would proceed to separate elections.[15] So Lafayette's preference for joint *cahiers* and joint elections was defeated, and apparently without any stalwart resistance on his part.

One of the chief demands in the Commoner's *cahier* was that taxes be distributed among "orders, corporations, and individuals according to their financial ability,"[16] and the Nobility had left the question of tax reform for its *cahier* committee to consider.[17] Lafayette, rich, generous by nature, and long accustomed to making sacrifices for the general welfare, was prepared to renounce the tax exemptions of his order. He found, however, only a small minority of his colleagues prepared to go that far. On March 17, when the Nobility took up its *cahier* committee's report, debate centered first upon the proposal that "taxes to be levied by the Estates General should be assessed proportionally upon all the provinces of France." Since a national decision to that effect would wipe out the advantages accorded certain provinces, of which Auvergne was not one, the nobles of Riom accepted that proposal by acclamation.

The next issue was crucial. It concerned the placing of the tax burden proportionally upon all three estates, and the committee proposed that the nobles be made responsible for taxes proportionate to their shares of the country's wealth. The debate that followed was bitter; the committee's proposal was attacked by several speakers, and Lafayette made a speech in its defense.[18] It finally passed, but only with two reservations. The first stipulated that the nobles' liability to taxation should apply alone to new taxes

---

[15] *Ibid.*, p. 19.

[16] "Instructions pour les députés du Tiers-état aux États-généraux, proposés par les députés de la ville de Riom," *Archives parlementaires de 1787 à 1860*, ed. J. Mavidal and E. Laurent, 1st ser., V (Paris, 1879), 570 (hereafter cited as *AP*).

[17] *Procès-verbal . . . de la Noblesse . . . à Riom*, pp. 16–17.

[18] *Mémoires*, II, 249–50. See also *Procès-verbal . . . de la Noblesse . . . à Riom*, pp. 21–22; Henry Mosnier, *Les Elections de 1789 dans la sénéchaussée d'Auvergne* (Clermont-Ferrand, 1898), pp. 34–35; and Mège, *Elections de 1789*, p. 119.

to be levied by the Estates General, and the second that since distinction of the orders was necessary in a monarchy, the nobility ought to retain at least one privilege, which for Auvergne ought to be exemption from taxes for an extent of property locally known as "the capon's flight" (*vol du chapon*). "The capon's flight" was understood to encompass no more than a nobleman's house when actually occupied by him, its court, and its garden.[19]

Having reached this decision, the Nobility went in a body to announce their "pecuniary sacrifice"[20] (as Lafayette ironically called it) to the Third Estate. The nobles' willingness to surrender any of their privileges, even if with reservations, was an act of generosity which the Third Estate greeted with shouts of approval: "Long live the king! Long live the Nobility!" And the nobles answered, "Long live the Third Estate! Long live our brothers!" Equality and fraternity seemed for a moment on the march.[21]

Lafayette probably did not share in the general display of enthusiasm. According to local tradition, when "the capon's flight" was under discussion, he remarked that the capon's wings ought to be clipped close in order to cut its flight short.[22] Whether fiction or not, the tradition correctly reflected his sentiments: the capon's flight, he subsequently complained, "means nothing but is in bad taste."[23] The victory seemed real, however, to the majority of the Third Estate, and when the meeting adjourned, the Commoners together with the Nobility escorted the Seneschal de Langhac to his home in a gesture of esteem and approval.[24] Next morning the Third Estate presented to the Second a resolution expressing appreciation of the renunciation of pecuniary privileges; the nobles, it said, "would always find an honorable compensation in the affection and gratitude of the people."[25]

[19] Lafayette to Maubourg, April 1, Mortimer-Ternaux, I, 426–27, and *Procès-verbal . . . de la Noblesse . . . à Riom*, pp. 21–22.

[20] Lafayette to Maubourg, April 1, Mortimer-Ternaux, I, 426.

[21] *Procès-verbal . . . de la Noblesse . . . à Riom*, p. 22.

[22] Mosnier, *Elections de 1789*, pp. 34–35, and Mège, *Elections de 1789*, p. 119, n. 2.

[23] Lafayette to Maubourg, April 1, Mortimer-Ternaux, I, 427.

[24] *Procès-verbal . . . de la Noblesse . . . à Riom*, p. 22.

[25] *Ibid.*, p. 25.

For over a week thereafter Lafayette and the other members of the Nobility's *cahier* committee held long meetings, consulted with the committees of the other two estates, and defended their recommendations before their colleagues. The chief subject of debate among the Nobility continued to be the renunciation of pecuniary privileges. Upon sober reconsideration, several selfish, conservative, or practical men regretted the resolution passed in a flush of *noblesse oblige* and made repeated efforts to rescind it. "We had as much trouble keeping it," Lafayette afterward estimated, "as we had getting it in the first place," and the more liberal nobles had to rally "time after time" to repel the attack. When the opposition seemed about to override them, Langhac, Lacqueuille, and Lafayette resigned from the committee stating that they could not serve if this clause were stricken from the *cahier*. The nobles refused to accept their resignations, however, and voted finally to retain the disputed article.[26] Thus the risk of losing the good will of the Third Estate was averted. Throughout the entire discussion of the *cahiers* the Second Estate had paid considerably more attention to the Third Estate than to the First. "We treated the Clergy very casually," Lafayette reported.[27]

When finally completed, some parts of the *cahier* of the Riom Nobility showed signs of being Lafayette's handiwork, but it is hard to tell which parts he formulated alone or was primarily responsible for elaborating.[28] The statement that taxes ought to be "proportionate to true needs . . . and to true capacity to pay" could be found in almost the same words in the draft of a declaration of rights which he had recently prepared.[29] And the injunction upon deputies to remember that "nature has made men equal and distinctions among them, particularly in a monarchy, are

[26] Lafayette to Maubourg, April 1, Mortimer-Ternaux, I, 427, and Mège, *Elections de 1789*, pp. 120–21.

[27] Lafayette to Maubourg, April 1, Mortimer-Ternaux, I, 427.

[28] Lafayette sent to Maubourg a copy of the *cahier* underlining the passages he himself had written ([April 3], *ibid.*, p. 428), but we have not been able to find this copy. See below, p. 38 and n. 63.

[29] Cf. "Instructions pour les députés de la Noblesse aux États-généraux, arrêtés dans l'assemblée de la sénéchaussée d'Auvergne, séant à Riom," *AP*, V, 564, with Lafayette's draft in Boyd, XIV, 438.

founded upon the general welfare" was also contained almost *verbatim* in Lafayette's document. But whereas the latter posited that equality among men despite occasional justifiable distinctions was a single fundamental principle, the *cahier* specified first equality and then distinctions as "two truths" which form "the basis of our constitution."[30]

Other parts of the *cahier* presumably also had Lafayette's approval, since they were in keeping with ideas he had already expressed or soon was to express. Among them was a scheme for constitutional reform. The *cahier* advocated that the forthcoming Estates General draw up a new constitution before it attended to the finances of the realm. This constitution should entrust the executive power to the king (whose ministers were, however, to be responsible to the Estates General), the legislative power to the Estates General, and the judicial power to an independent judiciary. The *cahier* urged that the law courts and the law codes be reformed to provide equality before the law, freedom from arbitrary arrest, counsel for the accused, and judgment by one's peers. It approved freedom of opinion and disapproved taxes not sanctioned by the Estates General. It called for frequent meetings of the provincial assemblies, which were to have a good share of authority in local affairs, and requested national aid for Auvergne's schools, health services, and charities.[31] On points like these a liberal noble like Lafayette could agree with more conservative nobles, since the extent and the manner of their realization depended largely upon whether the royal court, the aristocracy, or the Third Estate would control the Estates General, and that issue, as each group still had reason to hope, might yet be decided in its favor.

With certain provisions of the Riom Nobility's *cahier*, however, Lafayette could not have sympathized. Its exclusion of "the capon's flight" from the nobles' renunciation of their pecuniary privileges was foremost among them, but its prohibiting *roturiers* ("commoners") to carry arms seemed to him also markedly inconsistent

[30] Cf. Boyd, XIV, 438, with "Instructions pour les députés de la Noblesse," *AP*, V, 563.

[31] "Instructions pour les députés de la Noblesse," *AP*, V, 564–66.

with its lip-service to the ideal of equality, and its taxing of industry with its demand for the abolition of burdensome taxes.[32] And he must also have found obnoxious its insistence upon the prior claim of nobles to military commissions. Such preferments hardly fell within the category of distinctions that Lafayette was prepared to tolerate because they were "founded upon the general welfare."

Some of the provisions of the *cahier* were debated by the assembly of the order only after they were submitted by the committee. Hence they were accepted piecemeal. Since the Second Estate felt that it was not free to elect its deputies until it had formally approved its *cahier* as a whole, this procedure gave the conservative faction ample opportunity to air its views before any of the Auvergne Nobility were designated as representatives to Versailles. To make clear their stand that the revived Estates General should be controlled by the aristocracy, they moved on March 23 that their representatives in the Estates General should demand vote by order and, if outvoted, should withdraw.[33] To head off this uncompromising proposal, which would have made it incongruous for Lafayette to accept election as a deputy, he made a long speech. He cited "some great English and American principles,"[34] perhaps derived from the literature reflecting the current American constitutional controversy, particularly *The Federalist,* in which he—afterwards, at least—found "more practicable and essential political philosophy than in any other work preceding the Revolution."[35] When he spoke thus in favor of vote by head, he found himself "almost alone,"[36] not only because his views seemed extreme but also, he thought, because a deliberate campaign was afoot to isolate him as a dangerous conspirator.[37] The overwhelming majority of the Riom Nobility, however, sought to avoid ex-

[32] Lafayette to Maubourg, April 1, Mortimer-Ternaux, I, 427.

[33] *Procès-verbal . . . de la Noblesse . . . à Riom*, p. 30.

[34] Lafayette to Maubourg, [April 3], Mortimer-Ternaux, I, 428.

[35] "Quelques idées sur les institutions de la France, des États-Unis, et de l'Angleterre," [*ca.* 1829], *Mémoires*, VI, 800.

[36] Lafayette to Maubourg, April 1, 1789, Mortimer-Ternaux, I, 427. Mège thinks that Lafayette twice pleaded in favor of vote by head: *Elections de 1789*, pp. 122–23.

[37] Malouet, I, 277 and Lafayette to Maubourg, [April 5], Mortimer-Ternaux, I, 429–30.

tremes on either side, and when the ballot was taken on the motion
that there be no compromise at all on vote by order, only three
were counted in its favor.[38]

The conservatives then tried another tack. They moved that if
a plurality of the Estates General were to decide to vote by head,
the deputies of the Riom Nobility should ask permission to insert
in the record a formal protest to the effect that their constituents
regarded deliberation and vote by order as a constitutional right.
This motion was adopted,[39] and the record does not indicate any
open opposition to it on Lafayette's part. Obviously such a protest
by the deputies of the Riom Nobility, if it became necessary, would
be a mere statement of fact (for such was indeed the opinion of
their constituents), and since it would then leave him free to act,
he could honorably accept a post as deputy even under this unwelcome condition.

The *cahier* thus supplemented appeared acceptable, but formal
acceptance, article by article, was left for the morrow. The Nobility
passed on, instead, to the business of at last opting its representatives to the Estates General. Langhac was chosen on the first ballot,
with only fifteen votes for others. Lafayette, having regularly been
among the first picked by the Provincial Assembly (and so far
even by the Nobility's electoral assembly) for membership in
groups selected by ballot, had good reason to believe that, under
normal circumstances, he would be elected a deputy early. But the
circumstances were not normal. Rumors had begun to circulate in
Riom that he was a dangerous conspirator, and they crystallized
around an imputation that he had plotted an armed insurrection
during the political crises of 1787 and 1788. The rumor-mongers
produced a letter, alleged to be his, stating that he was "sure of
Velay and Vivarais" and that it "would be better to fight than to
be slaves."[40] Lafayette did not deny that he might have written

[38] *Procès-verbal . . . de la Noblesse . . . à Riom*, p. 30.

[39] *Ibid.*

[40] Lafayette to Maubourg, [April 5], Mortimer-Ternaux, I, 429–30. See also *Mémoires*,
IV, 73; "Lafayette jugé par le comte d'Espinchal," *Revue retrospective*, nouvelle série, XX
(1894), 295–96; Ernest d'Hauterive (ed.), *Journal of the Comte d'Espinchal* (London,
1912), p. 1; and A.-F. Bertrand de Moleville, *Histoire de la Révolution en France* (Paris,
1801–3), I, 380.

some such letter. He certainly believed it better to fight than to remain a slave, but the reference to neighboring provinces, he supposed, could have meant only to apply to a movement of public
opinion, not to an armed insurrection. He stoutly disclaimed ever
having been "criminal enough to want the horrors of a civil war";
and it was "abominable," he charged, "to say that on the eve of the
meeting of the Estates General, the man who had first demanded
it, who has taken no step that did not tend to the conciliation of the
Nobility and the Third Estate has the infamous intention to rouse
the kingdom and set it on fire at a time when we have before us a
chance of becoming free and happy in the most peaceful way
possible."[41]

The smear campaign seemed to have respectable backers, however—Queen Marie Antoinette and the Prince de Condé among
others, Lafayette understood—and they were believed to be sending more evidence to incriminate him. His friends wanted him
to stand for election immediately, but he preferred to postpone his
nomination until the cabal against him might burn itself out.[42]
Meanwhile, Malouet prepared to have him elected by the Third
Estate, if necessary,[43] although Lafayette felt that now more than
ever it behooved him to triumph over the cabal and win election by
his own order. Not only would he thereby be somewhat vindicated,
but also he would be more useful to the popular cause, for "the
people will have friends enough in its own chamber"[44]—which
seemed unlikely to be true of the Second Estate.

Partly at least because Lafayette insisted upon waiting and
would not allow his friends to present his name,[45] elections were
not resumed until March 25. The intervening day was given to a
new sally of the conservative nobles intended to shore up the
threatened institution of vote by order. The *cahier* committee had
proposed a mandate requiring each deputy to bear in mind the
principles of those who had elected him and to make of those prin-

---

[41] Lafayette to Maubourg, [April 5], Mortimer-Ternaux, I, 430.

[42] *Ibid.*

[43] Malouet, I, 277.

[44] Lafayette to Maubourg, April 1, Mortimer-Ternaux, I, 428.

[45] Same to same, [April 5], *ibid.,* p. 430.

ciples "the foundations on which will rest forever the true grandeur
of the monarchy and the well-being of all French citizens." The
proposed mandate seemed thus to bind every candidate for election
to a set of principles assumed to be recognized in advance, one of
the most explicit of which was opposition to voting by head even
if a plurality of the Estates General should favor it. Nevertheless,
the mandate contained immediately after this injunction the
words: "Follow your conscience; the instructions which you are
given contain our views and your powers. We are certain that you
will never forget that the distinctive characteristic of the French
nobility must ever be patriotism and honor."[46] These words seemed
to imply that the deputy might be permitted to observe his own
standards of conduct.

The Riom Nobility had not yet modified this ambiguous wording. Now, however with a liberal noble like Langhac already
elected and Lafayette presumably soon to be elected as deputies to
the Estates General, the conservative members wanted a firmer
hedging of their deputies' freedom of action. They wished to make
certain that no deputy of theirs would think he was free to take
part in any movement within the Second Estate at Versailles to
renounce its prerogative to vote as a separate order. The way to do
that seemed to be to oblige their deputation to protest against vote
by head even beyond the point where all other authorities might
yield. The last order to reach that point presumably would be the
Second Estate. Hence, the conservative nobles called for a small
change in the most recent version of the Riom mandate—a change
from the words "plurality of the Estate General" to the words
"plurality of the Second Estate." The proposed amendment seemed
simple, but it would in fact make a considerable difference. When
the Estates General met at Versailles, the Third Estate doubtless
would want vote by head and might receive the support of the
First Estate, which would be composed largely of lower clergy who
could be expected to be sympathetic with the Third Estate. In that
case, the plurality of the Estates General would favor vote by head,
but by the proposed wording the nobles' deputies from Riom

---

[46] "Instructions pour les députés de la Noblesse," *AP*, V, 567.

would still be bound to protest even if the Second Estate, acting as a separate order, also consented to voting by head. The Riom Nobility approved the new wording of their mandate.

The next day on the first ballot Lafayette was elected deputy— the second so designated. But he received only one vote more than the barest majority—198 out of 393[47]—in vivid contrast to the huge margin of Langhac's victory. Lacqueuille was chosen next, and two other deputies as well as two alternates were chosen in the course of the next two days.[48] Obviously, Lafayette retained his popularity among his peers only with difficulty and only after they had bound him not to use his representative capacity to bring about a "national assembly." But he had a right to feel that in winning election by his own order he had acted in keeping with the wishes of the Thirty and some other good friends[49] and had vindicated his own good name. "If I had raised anew the question *by order*," he subsequently apologized, "they would have returned [unconditionally] to the plan to withdraw or to protest. I preferred to sacrifice myself—so much the more since, with everyone knowing that the Third Estate was daily offering me election, I cannot be suspected of self-interested compliance."[50]

One of Lafayette's most bitter critics, the Comte d'Espinchal, who himself was chosen the second of the two alternate deputies, afterward claimed that Lafayette, upon his election, made a speech of conciliation. In this alleged speech the suspect marquis was supposed to have formally accepted the obligation to perform "what could rightfully be expected of him" and to uphold the *cahier* entrusted to him.[51] But Espinchal's testimony, written down only

[47] *Procès-verbal . . . de la Noblesse . . . à Riom*, p. 33. Lafayette (*Mémoires*, II, 250) claims that the election of deputies took place before they were required not to join the Third Estate until the majority of the Second Estate had agreed to do so, but his memory (1829) was at fault.

[48] *Procès-verbal . . . de la Noblesse . . . à Riom*, pp. 34–37, and Mège, *Elections de 1789*, pp. 117–18.

[49] Lafayette to Maubourg, [April 3], Mortimer-Ternaux, I, 428. Cf. Morris to William Carmichael, February 25, 1789, Davenport (ed.), I, xl.

[50] Lafayette to Maubourg, [April 3], Mortimer-Ternaux, I, 428–29.

[51] "Lafayette jugé par le comte d'Espinchal," *loc. cit.* See also Mège, *Elections de 1789*, pp. 117–18. Lafayette (*Mémoires*, VI, 6) firmly repudiated the imputations (of which he apparently knew) that he had concealed his popular sentiments.

long after the event, is full of inaccuracies, partisan in tone, and uncorroborated by other evidence. Moreover, the imputed gesture seems highly uncharacteristic of Lafayette, and in view of his well-known record it would have been an idle, unconvincing one. Nevertheless, when Lafayette signed his *mandat* as representative of the Nobility of the seneschalsy of Auvergne,[52] whether he pronounced this public profession of faith or not, he had made at least one significant concession that bade fair to hamstring his future conduct. He presumably was honor-bound not to advocate vote by head in the Second Estate at Versailles, and to join his colleagues in registering the protest of their constituents if vote by head were approved by his order.

The closing hours of the Riom electoral assemblies were spent in speeches by deputations from the several estates to each other expressing gratification with the results achieved. Lafayette was a member of the Nobles' deputation to the Third Estate.[53] The Second Estate adjourned its meeting on March 28.

Since the debates at St. Flour had not been so protracted as those at Riom (and possibly, as Lafayette thought, because the Nobility of Haute Auvergne had hurried to finish before he could come to disturb their equanimity),[54] the St. Flour electoral assembly had already adjourned, and so he returned to his château in Chavaniac. There he set to work to assure Latour-Maubourg's election at Puy-en-Velay, where the Nobility were divided between the Polignac influence and the liberal principles for which Maubourg stood. While still in Riom, Lafayette had authorized La Colombe, if necessary, to buy a fief (and hence the right to vote) from one of Maubourg's opponents, "who will be delighted to make some money" (and La Colombe probably could guess who that was, though Lafayette, always fearful that his letters would be intercepted, gave no name); he would then send La Colombe his proxy or go himself to vote. "In short, make use of all I am and all I can

[52] *AP*, V, 567.

[53] *Procès-verbal . . . de la Noblesse . . . à Riom*, pp. 39–40.

[54] Lafayette to Maubourg, April 1, Mortimer-Terneaux, I, 428. See also Mège, *Elections de 1789*, p. 164.

do to get Maubourg elected," he instructed La Colombe.[55] He himself was soliciting proxies for Maubourg, and by the time he returned to Chavaniac he had sent three of them. His messages went by courier since he wanted none but Maubourg and La Colombe to see them, "for I do not say a word without someone taking a mean advantage of it."[56]

In the quiet of his country château the new Auvergne deputy took stock of his anomalous position. He had some reason to feel apologetic about it and perplexed about his future obligations. Nevertheless, he thought the opposition recognized that he had won a victory at Riom, and he was himself "pleased that we got out of it so well."[57] He took some consolation from the recognition of his right to act as deputy according to his conscience and from a suggestion that his colleagues favored a bicameral legislature. Still, he confessed, "that *cahier* oppresses me";[58] he called it "our salmagundi of a *cahier*"[59] and conceded that "no matter how difficult what we have done has been, it comes to very little."[60] It was filled with inconsistencies: "It is a composite of great principles and petty details, of popular ideas and feudal ideas. . . . We lay down imperative instructions, and we tell our deputies to follow their consciences. There are two hundred years between one provision and another."[61]

When, however, he learned what the Second Estate of St. Flour had done in his absence, Lafayette felt somewhat better about his work at Riom. The Nobility of Haute Auvergne had bound their

[55] Lafayette to La Colombe, [March 24], AN, 359, dossier 1901, pièce 13. Etienne Charavay, *Le général La Fayette, 1757–1834* (Paris, 1898), pp. 166–67, and Rouchon, p. 30, date this letter April 1, 1789, assuming it to have been written from Chavaniac, but Lafayette's promise to go to Le Puy directly from Riom or by way of St. Flour makes clear that it was written in Riom. La Colombe seems to have become involved in some kind of dispute which further induced Lafayette to consider going to Le Puy if necessary: see Lafayette to Maubourg, [April 3], in *Le Curieux,* I (1884), 92.

[56] Lafayette to Maubourg, April 1, AN, F[7] 4767. The version of this letter in Mortimer-Ternaux, I, 428, omits this passage.

[57] Lafayette to Maubourg, [April 3], Mortimer-Ternaux, I, 429.

[58] Same to same, April 1, *ibid.,* p. 428.

[59] Same to same, [April 3], *ibid.*

[60] Same to same, April 1, *ibid.,* p. 426.

[61] *Ibid.,* p. 427.

deputies to insist upon vote by order and to renounce none of their pecuniary privileges.[62] He took upon himself a large share of credit for the differences in the two *cahiers* and, not concealing the pride he took in being accused "of seducing the assembly at Riom," he sent Maubourg a copy of the Riom *cahier*, underlying the parts he himself had written: "You will see that several bad articles are canceled by those that follow and particularly by the mandate which gives liberty to act according to our consciences." That saving clause and his conviction that his friends, including Maubourg, had wanted him to seek election by the Nobility rather than by the Third Estate seemed to console him for having bound himself to abide by the Riom Nobility's *cahier*.[63]

Not being given to crying over spilled milk, Lafayette prepared to return home. He undertook to keep several political appointments on the way and then to hasten to Paris, where the elections had not yet taken place, in order "to be of service to [i.e., help elect] those of our friends whom intrigue has left stranded in the provinces."[64] On April 4[65] he began his journey. He stopped at Brioude that day,[66] and the next he was at Clermont. By that time he had received the welcome news that Maubourg had been elected at Puy-en-Velay on April 3. Expressing his most lively joy, he urged his newly elected colleague to join him quickly in Paris, "where we shall have much to do and say, for men are pretty cowardly and pretty malicious." He had read Maubourg's *cahier* and found it excellent. "But ours tells us: 'Follow your conscience,' and that is

---

[62] Mège, *Elections de 1789*, p. 164.

[63] Lafayette to Maubourg, [April 3], Mortimer-Ternaux, I, 429.

[64] *Ibid.*, p. 430.

[65] Charavay's date of April 11 (p. 167) is a miscalculation based on the last sentence of the letter dated "Chavaniac, le vendredi soir" (Mortimer-Ternaux, I, 430), which would seem to indicate that it was written after Lafayette learned of Maubourg's election) i.e., after April 3), but Mortimer-Ternaux has garbled the text of this letter, and the last sentence of his version is not complete (nor is it in fact the last sentence of the letter). It should read (italics ours): *"Prêchés un peu la sagesse à notre chevalier,* car à present que vous êtes nommé, *du moins il n'en doute pas,* nous devons commencer. . . ." The italic passages were omitted by Mortimer-Ternaux. The original of this letter is in AN, F⁷ 4767, and its date must be April 3.

[66] Hauterive (ed.), *Journal of Espinchal*, p. 2, and Mège, *Elections de 1789*, p. 116 n.

a good deal."[67] From Clermont he resumed his journey northward. On April 6 he was again at Riom and from there made his way to Paris, which apparently he reached on the 13th.[68] Gouverneur Morris informed Washington shortly afterward that their mutual friend had returned "crowned with success," despite an imposing array of prejudices and personages lined up against him; he had proved "too able for his Opponents," having "played the Orator with as much Eclat as ever he acted the Soldier."[69]

Lafayette was just in time for a political tempest in Paris. The problem of electing representatives to the long-disused Estates-General from a city of about half a million inhabitants had presented so many complications that only on April 13 did the royal government issue a *Règlement* definitely indicating how the city's deputies were to be chosen. Elections were to be indirect even for nobles, of whom there were many in the city. The voters of each order were to assemble separately in the various localities into which Paris was divided for the occasion, the Nobility in twenty departments on April 20, and the Third Estate in sixty districts on April 21. These primary assemblies were to choose electors, who would then assemble to draw up *cahiers* and select the deputies of their respective orders. Hence, Paris would not be represented as a unified commune or corporate body, which the more liberal held to be its traditional right. Commoners were incensed because they had hoped for joint action and a common *cahier*. Even conservative nobles were displeased; not only were they denied the privilege enjoyed elsewhere of electing their representatives and writing their *cahiers* directly but also their domination of the city government might be jeopardized. Advocates of the reform movement in general suspected that indirect election by three distinct orders was intended to keep the liberal spirit of Paris scattered and ineffective. The widespread resentment against the *Règlement* added to the impatience of a population already made restless by months of

---

[67] Lafayette to Maubourg, [April 5], Mortimer-Ternaux, I, 429.

[68] Jefferson to William Short, April 13, Boyd, XV, 51.

[69] Morris to Washington, April 29, Davenport (ed.), I, 59–60.

political activity, an unusually long and severe winter, food shortages, high prices, and unemployment.

Lafayette gave considerable thought to his part in the forthcoming meetings, which, as a Paris nobleman and property-holder,
he had the right to attend. Some concerned nobles had agreed to
meet informally on April 17.[70] That morning Morris called on
Lafayette, and they had a long conversation about the current
unrest.[71] Morris had so consistently urged caution and respect for
realities that the devoted Adrienne de Lafayette had called him an
"aristocrat" both to his face and in a letter to her husband during
his absence.[72] Morris once more recommended caution, and Lafayette conceded that revolt "might occasion much Mischief but
would not produce any Good." The best thing to do, they agreed,
would be, while protesting against the *Règlement*, to elect the
deputies as required and "to go on with the Business." For that reason Lafayette intended to give support to the Comte de Clermont-
Tonnerre, also one of the Thirty, who was expected to talk in that
vein at the meeting. Morris found it "a whimsical Part of the
Drama" that Lafayette, "who is hated both by King and Queen,"
was not in sympathy with a movement to declare Marie Antoinette
ineligible to become regent "in Case of Accidents," while the constituents of the Duc de Coigny, whom Morris described as "one of
the Queen's Lovers," required the duke to support it. For the moment Morris approved of his host—"I find his Mind is getting right
as to the Business he has in Hand"—although he had considerable
doubt about Lafayette's general philosophy: "His Principles accord
best with those of a Republic, mine are drawn only from human
Nature and ought not therefore to have much Respect in this Age
of Refinement. It would indeed be ridiculous for those to believe in
Man who affect not to believe in God."[73]

Later that day Lafayette attended a meeting of about a hundred

---

[70] Lafayette to Maubourg, [April 18], Mortimer-Ternaux, I, 42.

[71] Morris diary, April 17, Davenport (ed.), I, 42.

[72] March 10, *ibid.*, p. 9.

[73] April 17, *ibid.*, pp. 42–43.

gentlemen of Paris at the home of the Duc d'Aumont.[74] Among them were several members of the Thirty. As expected, a proposal to ask for a different set of electoral regulations was presented. Clermont-Tonnerre opposed it, and Lafayette supported him with "a few words which were very well."[75] The proposal was lost, and the meeting adopted, instead, a resolution which, while calling the *Règlement* "illegal and unconstitutional," announced readiness to go ahead in order not to delay the opening of the Estates General. Clermont-Tonnerre then presented a model *cahier*, and his proposal that all twenty of the Nobility's primary assemblies be asked to adopt it was unanimously adopted. The meeting ended on a note of cooperation and accord. "We must not toy with so large a population as that of Paris," Lafayette the next day explained to Latour-Maubourg, and he again exhorted his friend to hasten his arrival in Paris, "where the slightest trouble may lead further than we think." Even though "the prospects of insurrection do not terrify everybody," he himself, he wrote, was opposed to disorder. "It would certainly be the height of folly or ill will to risk the slightest fuss without purpose or coherent program on the eve of the Estates General." He preferred to wait and see whether the duly chosen electors would unite the three orders of the city, difficult though that might prove to be.[76]

Lafayette hoped for cooperation of the three orders also in drawing up "a little *cahier* containing the constitutional principles,"[77] to which should be added a protest of the nobles and bourgeoisie of Paris against the *Règlement*. That was the procedure recommended by the Thirty at their next meeting (April 19), which presumably Lafayette attended. The Thirty thereupon published a pamphlet which urged every primary assembly, while protesting

[74] *Ibid.*, p. 43; Lafayette to Maubourg, [April] 18, Mortimer-Ternaux, I, 431; *Gazette de Leide*, April 28, and *Gazette de Leide, supplément*, May 6. Ch.-L. Chassin, *Les Élections et les cahiers de Paris en 1789* (Paris, 1888–89), I, 457–58, puts this meeting on April 16, but his source does not necessarily contradict Morris' testimony that it took place on April 17.

[75] Morris diary, April 17, Davenport (ed.), I, 42.

[76] Lafayette to Maubourg, [April] 18, Mortimer-Ternaux, I, 431–32.

[77] *Ibid.*, p. 431.

formally against the "illegalities" of the *Règlement*, nevertheless to choose its electors as prescribed and to draw up a short *cahier*. The pamphlet contained a model *cahier*, affirming that all power was derived from the people and advocating equality of rights, consent of the governed to legislation, freedom of thought, freedom from arbitrary arrest, regular meetings of the Estates General, and a number of similar political principles to which Lafayette and other liberal nobles openly subscribed and which were already well known and widely approved throughout the realm.[78]

The location of Lafayette's residence put him in the eighteenth department of the Paris Nobility. When on the morning of April 20 the department came together to choose its electors, the forty-three gentlemen present began as the pamphlet of the Thirty had suggested. While declaring their intention to comply with the *Règlement* in order not to impede the elections, they protested against the denial to the electors of Paris of the right to meet in one body and to the Nobility of the right to name its representatives directly. Then they sent delegations to the other nineteen departments to inform them of this action and to ask for their opinions. By the time an evening session met, nine other departments had sent deputies to attend it. Thereupon, the eighteenth department decided to send a deputation to the Marquis de Boulainvillers, who as "Prévôt de Paris" was the nobility's principal local royal officer, to voice a protest. Lafayette was the third of the four delegates chosen for that purpose. The four set off immediately only to return shortly and report that several other departments had sent similar deputations to the prévôt and hence a lengthy conference was expected for that night. At 10 o'clock delegates from nearly all the departments assembled at the prévôt's. Lafayette was not among them although other liberal nobles—La Rochefoucauld, Condorcet, and Clermont-Tonnerre—were. The debate dragged on until four o'clock in the morning of the twenty-first, and again undisguised dissatisfaction with the *Règlement* gave way to mere protests which, though energetic enough, were discreetly worded so as not to delay the opening of the Estates General.[79]

[78] Chassin, I, 470–72.

[79] *Ibid.*, II, 160–62, 165–67.

On April 21, the delegates of Lafayette's department reported to their constituents that the joint delegations had accepted the department's principles. The department then drew up its suggestions for articles to be inserted in the *cahier* of the Paris Nobility. In addition to restating the principles pronounced the day before, it enlarged upon the demand for frequent and regular meetings of a legislative assembly that would share with the government the power to make fiscal arrangements, but at the same time it instructed its deputies to support voting by order in the forthcoming Estates General and to get the desired constitutional changes before dealing with the government's financial problems. It thus betrayed that the major purpose behind its statement of principles was less to promote justice and equality than to make certain that the Nobility would share constitutional authority with the king.[80] No testimony records whether Lafayette openly opposed the less liberal of these suggestions, but his opposition could be taken for granted, and when the department chose its five electors and their five alternates neither Lafayette nor any other prominent liberal was among them.[81]

The elections were not yet over for Lafayette, however. He kept busy—so "engaged in Politics" that on April 22 he did not go home to freshen up but, somewhat disheveled, went late in the afternoon to an appointment with Jefferson and Morris at Jefferson's house on the Champs-Élysées. His report induced Morris to believe that "the Business . . . is going well," and they discussed Lafayette's future conduct in the Estates General. With a practical eye to the role of military power in times of stress, Morris counseled that the Estates General reorganize the royal bodyguard, reducing the number of mercenaries and increasing that of the native troops. While Jefferson thought that matter unimportant in itself, they all agreed that Lafayette ought to speak only on important issues.[82] Morris evidently took seriously his role as wire-puller behind the scenes of a revolution, for he called on Lafayette three times that

[80] *Ibid.*, pp. 200–201. For the suggested articles of the *cahier* see *ibid.*, pp. 285–86.

[81] See the list of electors and alternates *ibid.*, p. 201.

[82] Morris diary, April 22, Davenport (ed.), I, 49.

week—but only to find him out each time.[83] The marquis apparently was busy earning the description which, only a few days before the Estates General was to convene, Morris gave Washington of him: "He . . . is at this Moment as much envied and hated as his Heart could wish. He is also much beloved by the Nation for he stands forward as one of the principal champions of her Rights."[84] Lafayette would probably not have described himself otherwise. At this juncture he was merely one of several outstanding champions of the liberal cause in France. Yet, for all his desire to appear modest and for all his "ambition . . . to rise above ambition,"[85] he could not have been so blind to his own popularity, wealth, position, and ability as to overlook his own good chance of becoming the top leader of the liberals. He was not the only one to appreciate that his living model was George Washington,[86] who that month had been chosen president of the newly reorganized United States. But he also knew that he had enemies who hated and envied him and suspected his motives. Besides, his hands were tied, for he was under obligation to give voice to the opposition of the Auvergne Nobility to vote by head.

BIBLIOGRAPHICAL NOTES

See the comments above, p. 20, regarding the letters of Lafayette to Maubourg in Mortimer -Ternaux's *Histoire de la Terreur*. For this period the best biography of Lafayette still is Charavay's, but also see Brand Whitlock, *La Fayette* (New York, 1929). The best studies of the Auvergne elections are those of Mège and Mosnier, and the best study of the Paris elections is that of Chassin. Vol. I of the latter work is entitled *La Convocation de Paris aux derniers États généraux* (1888); Vol. II, *Les assemblées primaires et les*

---

[83] April 25, 26, 29, *ibid.*, pp. 54–55, 58.

[84] April 29, *ibid.*, p. 60.

[85] Lafayette to Mme de T[essé], March 25, 1797 [*sic*, for 1798], *Mémoires*, IV, 406.

[86] See Lafayette, Talleyrand, Mazzei, Mme de Staël, and Augustin Barruel as cited in Louis Gottschalk, *Lafayette and the Close of the American Revolution* (Chicago: University of Chicago Press, 1942), pp. 391, 421–22 (hereafter cited as *Close*); Gottschalk, *Between*, p. 340; and Gottschalk (ed.), *Letters of Lafayette to Washington*, pp. xi–xx. See also Alphonse Aulard, *Histoire politique de la Révolution française* (Paris, 1921), p. 5 n.; Marquis de Clermont-Gallerande, *Mémoires particuliers pour servir à l'histoire de la Révolution qui s'est opérée en France en 1789* (Paris, 1826), III, 295; Etienne Dumont, *Recollections of Mirabeau and of the Two First Legislative Assemblies of France* (London, 1832), p. 30; and A.-F. de Bertrand Moleville, *Mémoires particuliers pour servir à l'histoire de la fin du règne de Louis XVI* (Paris, 1816), II, 80.

cahiers primitifs (1888); Vol. III, *L'assemblée des trois ordres et l'assemblée générale des électeurs au 14 juillet* (1889); and Vol. IV, *Paris hors les murs* (1889).

André Bouton, *Les Francs-maçons et la Révolution française, 1741–1815* (Le Mans, 1958), p. 56, says that Lafayette was initiated on December 27, 1779, in the "Loge militaire no. 9 du Rite d'York" in the United States (which is hardly likely since Lafayette had already been initiated in France [see Gottschalk, *Close*, pp. 433–44] and was on that date in France) and was affiliated on June 24, 1782, with the Loge Saint-Jean d'Ecosse du Contract Social in Paris (which is correct; see Gottschalk, *Close*, pp. 368–69) and again in 1789 with the Loge Saint-Amable dite ,les Amis de la Vertu in Riom (which was physically possible in March–April 1789 but is corroborated nowhere else that we know). Bouton does not give his source of information, and André Lebey, *Lafayette ou le militant Franc-maçon* (Paris, 1937), which in our opinion overemphasizes the Masonic associations of Lafayette, says nothing about such an affiliation at Riom at this time.

CHAPTER IV

Estates General or National Assembly?

W EEKS before May 1, the delegates of the Estates General converged upon Versailles from every corner of France. Some of them came with their families. Enthusiasts and quidnuncs, patriots and would-be journalists flocked in, adding to the excitement and the housing shortage. In several cities—Marseilles in March, Paris at the end of April, and elsewhere—disorder had already lent an air of violence to the election of deputies and the composition of *cahiers*, as a people that for nearly a century and three quarters had lost its voice found it again. How would it use its revived power of expression? Could it speak in unison? And if so, who would lead it—the privileged orders or the Third Estate or the king? Would it return to "the ancient constitution and forms" or would it provide new ones or could the king keep change within the limits he preferred?

These questions, not always clearly formulated, were nevertheless present in the mind of many a deputy as he prepared for the initial meeting of the Estates General. They were all necessary corollaries of a question clear in everyone's mind: vote by order or vote by head? To that question the elections had produced three disparate answers. Vote by order, demanded the great majority of the Nobility in unmistakable terms; vote by head, demanded the Third Estate in almost a single voice; and the court seemed to wish to determine when vote should be by head and when by order. On the final answer seemed to hinge the outcome of the daring decision to revive the Estates General. Vote by order would probably once more give a decisive share in government to the privileged orders, enabling them, as in the days before "the grand monarch," Louis XIV, to arrest the growth of royal absolutism. Vote by head could be expected to push France toward experiment with liberal institutions based upon the dazzling concepts of the rights of man. And if vote by head or by order were left to the court to decide, it would doubtless try to enhance the Bourbon pretensions to paternalism without surrendering any essential part of the king's absolute power.

Lafayette's preference was already well known: he was for the rights of man. He left Paris for Versailles at the end of April and put up at the home of his wife's family, the Noailles. Adrienne followed shortly afterward.[1] The Noailles were not only among the most honorable and ancient families around the king; some of them were also at this juncture among the most liberal. Long rivals of the conservative Polignacs for the favor of the court, they gathered around them the Patriots, of whom not only Adrienne's husband but also her cousins, the Prince de Poix and the Vicomte de Noailles, were leaders. And Adrienne's aunt, the Comtesse de Tessé—a lady astute and bold enough to observe in her "Petites Pensées" that "kings and pretty women have to be dethroned to take the measure of their intelligence"[2]—was a close friend of Thomas Jefferson. At her table the *lumières* of the world gathered[3] —at least so far as they were to be found in Versailles.

On May 2 the king formally inaugurated the Estates General with a reception of the delegates at the Château of Versailles, the royal palace. Each order was received separately, and the turn of the Second Estate came early in the afternoon. Dressed, as prescribed, in the style of Henry IV's day (black costume with gold

[1] Morris diary, May 2, Davenport (ed.), I, 63. *Assemblée nationale, liste de bailliages et sénéchaussées* (Paris, 1789), p. 11, gives Lafayette's address as "hôtel de Noailles, rue de la Pompe, no. 24." See also Lafayette to Monsieur Savary, no date, but obviously between May and July, Indiana University, Ball Collection, XI, 21–22: "Le Mis de L.F. demeure à Versailles chès M. de Tessé, ou chès M. le mal de Noailles." See also Alphonse Roserot (ed.), *Mémoires de Madame de Chasteney, 1771–1815* (Paris, 1896), I, 105, and Morris diary, May 14, Davenport (ed.), I, 77–78. Mme de Tessé, the sister of Adrienne's father, was the marshal's daughter.

[2] Château de Chavaniac (Haute Loire), Ms. No. 12.

[3] H. R. Marraro (trans.), *Memoirs of the Life and Peregrinations of the Florentine Philip Mazzei (1730–1816)* (New York, 1942), p. 309; Gilbert Chinard, *Trois amitiés françaises de Jefferson d'après sa correspondance inédite avec Mme de Bréhan, Mme de Tessé et Mme de Corny* (Paris, 1927), pp. 65–68; and Jean Egret, *La révolution des notables: Mounier et les monarchiens, 1789* (Paris, 1950), p. 54.

trimmings, white lace cravat, and white plumed hat) they entered
the king's cabinet without distinction of rank. Lafayette was presented with his colleagues from the seneschalsy of Riom. The
Third Estate, more simply garbed, was received last and with
noticeably less cordiality.

The next day was Sunday, and Lafayette dined with Jefferson
in Paris. Morris, too, was Jefferson's guest, and again he gave his
French friend what he considered shrewd advice: Make the most
of the great names on your side; see that the Duc d'Orléans is
elected to the Estates General from Paris (where the elections
were not yet over); and place Necker "advantageously." Lafayette
was sure that Paris would elect the duke and agreed that Morris'
suggestion regarding Necker would be "very useful."[4] Morris may
not have known, nor for that matter Lafayette either, that Orléans
and Necker had plans of their own, but the advice was both valid
and obvious.

On May 4 the Estates General assembled as a single body for
the first time. Its purpose that day was to ask for divine guidance.
King, court, and deputies, clothed in the costumes prescribed by
tradition and regulations, went in procession from the Church of
Notre Dame to the Church of St. Louis while Versailles' population and hundreds of visitors from Paris watched from pavement, doorways, and windows. Houses and spectators were dressed
in their best, and Gobelins borrowed from the Château hung from
the balconies. Lafayette marched with the Second Estate, behind
the Third and ahead of the First, which was followed by the king
and his court, riding in carriages. Swiss Guards and French Guards
held the onlookers in line. Bands played, trumpets sounded, and
the crowd cheered: "Vive le Tiers Etat!" "Vive le roi!" But no
shouts for the privileged orders. Only one incident distinguished
the services in the church. When the bishop who preached the
sermon, tracing the history of the Estates General from the time
of Clovis, appealed for reform in the name of Christian ethics,
many of the deputies broke into applause even though they were
at a divine service in the king's presence.

[4] Morris diary, May 3, 1789, Davenport (ed.), I, 65.

On May 5 the three estates assembled, in keeping with the revived tradition, to hear an address from the throne. The only available room in Versailles large enough to accommodate approximately 1,200 deputies was the assembly hall of the Hôtel des Menus Plaisirs, and there the king, with the leading court dignitaries gathered around him under a baldachin, faced the Estates General, the Clergy seated on his right, the Nobility on his left, and the Third Estate far to the rear. The king indicated that his major concern was for fiscal reform, deplored the radical notions that were currently threatening to mislead public opinion, and expressed his desire for the happiness and prosperity of his realm. Chancellor Barentin, then, in a scarcely audible voice indicated that His Majesty, once fiscal affairs were adjusted, would consider certain reforms such as freedom of the press and a more modern law code. Next, Necker read his speech, until his voice gave out and a clerk took over. For three hours fiscal details and suggestions for reform poured forth, but they dealt ambivalently with the issue that interested Lafayette and his colleagues the most. Disagreement over vote by head or vote by order, Necker warned, might create a schism and postpone France's regeneration; hence he proposed that the three estates first meet separately, thereby giving the upper orders a chance to win "merit for a generous sacrifice" by surrendering their pecuniary privileges of their own free will; then other matters might be assigned to joint or discrete consideration. When Necker's speech was over, the assembly, "somewhat fatigued," adjourned, presumably to meet as three distinct bodies the next day.[5]

To Lafayette and the Patriots this revelation of the throne's intentions could have been only a profound disappointment. Where was the king whom they had expected to lead the nation to a quick and glorious revolution? What of the "new constitution"—an idea which had almost been overlooked in the hours of speech-making? Were all the hopefulness and agitation of past

[5] The speeches are given in *AP*, VIII, 1–26. The quoted phrases are on pages 24 and 25. A story that Lafayette and other "anti-royalists" opposed the queen's presence and intended to halt her party rests on extremely feeble testimony; see *Secret Memoirs of the Royal Family of France . . . from the Journal . . . of the Princess Lamballe . . .* (London, 1826), 335–61, and *National Intelligencer* (Washington), October 25, 1826.

months to end merely in a few fiscal reforms and paternalistic concessions by an absolute monarch hearkening to the petitions of the estates of his realm?

On May 6 the Nobility met in the hall assigned to them. Under the oldest member as provisional president, they proceeded to the matter which a legislative body must initially consider—verification of its members' credentials, and immediately the dissensions beneath the surface became overt. Verification of credentials by the Nobility as a separate estate would underline its acceptance of the trisection of the estates. Most of those present must have anticipated that the Third Estate would refuse to organize as a separate body and would, as the representatives of all but about 4 per cent of the population, expect of the other estates a respectful consideration of its attitude. They must also have anticipated that the Clergy, because of the large number of parish priests among them, would split nearly in half on the issues. The nobles could less easily have conjectured how their own order would split, divided as it was by tensions between court nobles and country nobles, rich nobles and poor nobles, nobles of ancient lineage and newly ennobled, nobles of the sword (military) and nobles of the gown (civil service), nobles who thought France should return to the pre-Bourbon "constitution" and nobles who thought France's constitution should rest upon universal principles of right.

In the Noblesse two points of view appeared in quick succession. The first advocated that credentials be verified by the order alone, the second that they be verified by a joint commission of all three orders. Lafayette was one of several who spoke in favor of verification by a joint commission, but only 46 of his colleagues voted for it, 188 favoring separate verification. Thereupon a committee was named to verify the credentials of members of the Noblesse alone.[6] For the liberal nobles this first vote of their order was a disheartening defeat. For Lafayette, bound by the instructions of his constituents to uphold vote by order, it was a conspicuous

---

[6] AP, VIII, 28; Mémoires, IV, 88–89, 191, n.2; Gazette de Leide, May 29; Gaultier to Monestir, May 5–6, 1789, Mège, Gaultier de Biauzat, II, 36; [Bertrand Barère de Vieuzac], Le Point du jour, ou résultat de ce qui s'est passé aux États-généraux, 27 avril–17 juin 1789 (Paris, 1790), p. 67 (hereafter cited as Point du jour).

setback; he had been the only one of the Riom delegation to advocate a joint commission.

Jefferson recognized the marquis' quandary at once. If Lafayette remained loyal to his instructions, he would lose his popular following. If then, as was conceivable, civil war came, he would not easily win the trust of the popular side, while his position in the Second Estate would become unbearable. If he supported the Nobility on some occasions and the Commoners on others, he would look like a trimmer and lose the confidence of both sides. Jefferson could see only two possible solutions for his friend's difficulties: Either Lafayette must "go over wholly to the Tiers Etat" or he must effect a compromise by which the three estates would become a bicameral legislature, the privileged classes in one house and the unprivileged in the other. If he chose the first solution, Jefferson advised him to do so soon, since the time had already come for "that honest and manly stand . . . which your own principles dictate"; a firm alliance with the Commoners "will win their hearts for ever, be approved by the world which marks and honours you as the man of the people, and will be an eternal consolation to yourself," and if once he broke his instructions, they could never embarrass him again, whereas "an acquiescence under them will reproduce greater difficulties every day and without end," requiring "a constant sacrifice of your own sentiments to the prejudices of the Noblesse." But if Lafayette preferred the compromise of a bicameral legislature, Jefferson reasoned, and succeeded in getting it, he would thereby not violate his instructions (for a bicameral legislature would not mean vote by head), and if he failed, his siding with the people would seem justified, "even to those who think instructions are laws of conduct."[7]

Jefferson knowingly departed from the unwritten code of diplomatic conduct in giving this advice. Even if only in a private letter to an old friend, he was taking an active part in the domestic affairs of the country to which he was accredited, urging a member of its legislature to disregard his instructions or to circumvent them by compromise in order to feel free in the event of civil con-

---

[7] Jefferson to Lafayette, May 6, 1789, Boyd, XV, 97–98.

flict to take the popular side. To Lafayette he apologized for presuming to offer advice; friendly anxiety had led him to express his uneasiness and to "talk of things I know nothing about."[8] Yet no matter how sincere his modest assurances of a private concern might have been, he was soon to reveal himself also as "an international extraterritorial universal Whig."[9] A few days later as the American minister in France he wrote to Washington (who was already president of the United States, though this fact was not yet officially known in Paris) about his "great pain" for their mutual friend. Admitting that he had "not hesitated to press on him to burn his instructions," he predicted that "if he cannot effect a conciliatory plan, he will surely take his stand manfully at once with the tiers etat."[10] Actually, whether Jefferson knew it or not, Lafayette had no real choice between compromise and defiance, for he had already committed himself against a hereditary upper house.[11] Jefferson himself obviously preferred the defiant alternative, that of burning the instructions, for he estimated Lafayette's prestige in the Third Estate to be so great that he could "be what he pleases with them." Nor did he believe such a course would incur any grave personal risk: "I am in hopes that the base is now too solid to render it dangerous to be mounted on it."[12]

The French revolutionary was not yet prepared, however, to take the American revolutionary's advice, for he felt honor-bound to respect his constituents' wishes.[13] Moreover, the liberal nobles, unwilling to admit defeat, were rapidly building up an esprit de corps. Not only Mme de Tessé but also other sympathetic noblewomen and noblemen of Versailles or nearby welcomed them to their homes. A favorite meeting place was the mansion of the Duchesse d'Enville, mother of La Rochefoucauld, whom Lafayette was one day to describe as "the best citizen, the most virtuous man,

---

[8] *Ibid.*, p. 98.

[9] The phrase is Lord Acton's: *Lectures on the French Revolution* [London, 1910], p. 20.

[10] Jefferson to Washington, May 10, 1789, Boyd, XV, 118–19.

[11] See above, p. 12.

[12] Jefferson to Washington, May 10, 1789, Boyd, XV, 119.

[13] *Mémoires*, II, 250.

without exception, that I have ever known and whose most intimate friend I had long been."[14] After a while the liberal nobles came to be thought of as forming a sort of club, which at first was called the Club du Potager.[15] In gatherings like these they laid plans to push verification of credentials in common. Jefferson soon learned that a minority of the Noblesse were contemplating, "should reconciliation be impracticable," joining the Third Estate, to be followed perhaps by some others of their own order and most of the Clergy.[16] Reconciliation became increasingly unlikely, however. On May 11, although a deputation from the Third Estate expressly requested joint verification, the Second decided that, despite incomplete returns, enough of its members were already duly accredited to justify declaring itself legally (and separately) constituted. Lafayette again was one of the minority of nobles, smaller than that of May 6, who voted against this decision.[17]

In the Clergy, on the other hand, the acceptability of reconciliation was general enough to make a compromise seem desirable. To break the impasse between the other two orders the Clergy proposed a joint committee to consider some method of verification that might be acceptable to all three. Since neither of the antagonists cared to risk the onus of refusing, they accepted the plan. The Noblesse proceeded to choose its "conciliatory commissioners" on May 19, permitting each deputy to vote for his own list of candidates but requiring that no one be chosen by less than a third of the votes cast. This cumbersome method of voting, as Lafayette discerned and as one of the supporters of the motion frankly admitted, was intended to keep the minority from electing any candidates. When another of the conservative leaders began to

---

[14] *Ibid.*, III, 262. See also Alexandre Lameth, *Histoire de l'Assemblée constituante* (Paris 1828), I, 34–37 nn., 421; Comte d'Allonville, *Mémoires secrets de 1770 à 1830* (Paris, 1838–45), II, 149; Espinchal, *Journal*, p. 5; and L.-F.-S. La Rochefoucauld, *Mémoires de M. de la Rochefoucauld, duc de Doudeauville*, IV (Paris, 1862), 364–65. The belief that Lafayette attended meetings in Mme de Staël's salon this early is not implausible, but it rests on suspect evidence, such as Duchesse d'Abrantès, *Histoire des salons de Paris* (Paris, [1893]), II, 148.

[15] The Potager was the king's vegetable garden, close to the Château of Versailles. See La Rochefoucauld, IV, 364 and Allonville, II, 149.

[16] Jefferson to Jay, May 12, 1789, Boyd, XV, 126.

[17] *Gazette de Leide, supplément*, May 22. Cf. *AP*, VIII, 32–34.

attack the Third Estate for using the expression "commons" to describe itself, Lafayette found the atmosphere "suffocating." "The foul air of prejudices is no good for my chest," he wrote Mme de Simiane[18] (who doubtless remembered that he had once had tuberculosis).[19] He left the session abruptly and went to Paris.

That day and the next Jefferson wrote to three friends who were also friends of France's Third Estate revealing that he had recently learned of the plans of the Nobility's minority. Though he called his description of these plans "conjectures"[20] and "hypothesis,"[21] his correspondents might easily have guessed that at least one of his sources was Lafayette (whom he had seen at Mme de Tessé's only recently,[22] if not in Paris still more recently). In his letters he made some predictions—with a degree of accuracy which suggests that he had inside information. The Clergy's attempt at conciliation, he forecast, would fail; the Third Estate would then invite the other two orders to join it in a common chamber; a majority of the Clergy and a minority of the Nobility would accept this invitation; and the chamber thus constituted would declare itself the Estates General. If the king should refuse to cooperate, Jefferson further predicted, the reconstituted chamber would declare an end to taxes, issue a declaration of rights, "do such other acts as the circumstances will permit, and go home."[23] In that case, tax collectors would be resisted, and civil war would follow, but Jefferson thought it more likely that the king would "agree to do business with the States general so constituted."[24]

Whether Jefferson's guess was independent or had been prompted by Lafayette and others, events were to show that it

[18] Lafayette to [Mme de Simiane], [May 20?], *Mémoires*, II, 307. The editor of the *Mémoires* (*ibid.*, n.1) assigns the date May 6 to this letter, but it obviously refers to the events of May 19. Cf. Robespierre to Buissart, May 24, Georges Michon (ed.), *Oeuvres complètes de Maximilien Robespierre*, III (Paris, 1910), 41.

[19] See Gottschalk, *Between*, pp. 294, 301, 325.

[20] Jefferson to Richard Price, May 19, 1789, Boyd, XV, 138.

[21] Jefferson to St. John de Crèvecoeur, May 20, 1789, *ibid.*, p. 140.

[22] Morris diary, May 14, Davenport (ed.), I, 77–78. Chinard (p. 108) dates a letter of Mme de Tessé to Jefferson May 22, 1789, but it is of May 22, 1788; see Boyd, XII, 187.

[23] Jefferson to Thomas Paine, May 19, 1789, Boyd, XV, 136.

[24] *Ibid.* See also letters cited in nn. 20 and 21 above.

correctly divined the program of the Patriots. None of the joint commissioners chosen by the Nobility was in favor of union with the other orders.[25] Even after the king's ministers tried their hands at effecting a compromise, neither the Second nor the Third Estate would yield, and each meanwhile maneuvered to win the Clergy to its side. Thousands of excited spectators from Paris added to the ferment. On May 28 the Nobility by a vote of 197 to 44 resolved that its respect for the "constitution" of the realm obliged it to maintain that "deliberation by order and the right of veto, which belonged to each of the orders separately" was one of "those conservative principles of the throne and of liberty" which were "constitutive of the monarchy."[26]

An otherwise pleasant episode revealed the strain which these political wrangles wrought in social relations. The Comte de Montlosier, an Auvergnat deputy hostile to Lafayette's views, was embarrassed when he was asked by some Auvergne fruit merchants to introduce them to the marquis; they wanted the two men to share an ample shipment from their native province. Montlosier hesitated for a time to carry out this friendly assignment (although, when he did, the Lafayettes received him in affable fashion).[27] Lafayette's critics persuaded themselves either that he was a mediocrity who had somehow managed so far to cover up his inadequacy[28] or that he had a strange, impractical philosophy imported from Boston.[29]

A month had gone by without any solution of the problem confronting the Estates General when on June 2 Jefferson, this time accompanied by his secretary, William Short, visited Versailles. There they sat down with Lafayette and Rabaut St. Etienne, who

[25] *Gazette de Leide, supplément,* June 2.

[26] *Ibid.,* June 12; *Procès-verbal des séances de la chambre de l'ordre de la Noblesse aux États-généraux, tenues à Versailles en mil sept cent quatre-vingt-neuf* (Paris, 1792), pp. 118, 122.

[27] *Mémoires de M. le comte de Montlosier sur la Révolution française* . . . (Paris, 1830), II, 300–301 (hereafter cited as Montlosier).

[28] Manuscrits du Comte d'Espinchal, Bibliothèque de Clermont-Ferrand, E.I. 27, Ms. 306, T. VI, 240–41; [P.-A.-F. Choderlos de Laclos *et al.*?], *La galérie des États-généraux* ([Paris], 1789), pp. 60–62, gives a sketch of Lafayette under the name of Philarete.

[29] Montlosier, I, 214.

was one of the Third Estate's conciliation commissioners, to discuss the impasse that threatened to thwart all the fine prospects of a few weeks before. The four men conversed earnestly about the crisis until Rabaut had to leave, and then the three others continued, wondering whether the best way out of the blind alley might not be for the king to use his personal influence. Apparently the idea had been broached before among the Americans in France, for Morris that very day propounded a strikingly similar idea to a liberal member of the Clergy.[30] As Jefferson elaborated the idea after a further day's cogitation, it ran: The king should call the Estates General together in (and Jefferson used the French phrase) a *séance royale*—that is, as a single body convened to hear the royal will—and lay before it "a Charter of Rights" all ready "in his hand, to be signed by himself and every member of the three orders," whereupon the Estates General should adjourn until its first regular annual meeting.[31]

After Jefferson returned to Paris, he found he liked the idea "more and more." Again disregarding the convention that frowned upon direct participation by foreign diplomats in the domestic affairs of the countries to which they were accredited, he began to compose a charter "containing all the good in which all parties agree."[32] The minister of the United States in Paris, a paladin of the American Revolution, could hardly remain inactive in the face of prospective civil war in the realm of his country's ally. And so the author of the American Declaration of Independence now composed a charter for France. He offered to Frenchmen as excuse for his "presumption" "an unmeasurable love for your nation and a painful anxiety lest Despotism, after an unaccepted offer to bind it's [*sic*] own hands, should seize you again with tenfold fury."[33] On June 3 he had copies of his proposed charter made, and he sent one to Lafayette and another to Rabaut, each a potential advocate of compromise by the two unbending orders. Its ten points called for regular annual meetings of the Estates

[30] Morris diary, June 2, Davenport (ed.), I, 103.

[31] Jefferson to Rabaut St. Etienne, June 3, Boyd, XV, 166–68.

[32] Jefferson to Lafayette, June 3, *ibid.,* p. 165.

[33] Jefferson to Rabaut St. Etienne, June 3, *ibid.,* p. 167.

General, which should have control of the budget and should participate with the king in the making of laws; for freedom from arbitrary arrest, subordination of military to civil authority, liberty of the press, and abolition of tax privileges; and for a fiscal arrangement that would tide over the current emergency until the first of the regular annual meetings of the Estates. The author intended this charter to comprise the major reforms which Louis XVI's ministers had already offered, reinforced on the one hand by the sacrifice of pecuniary privileges by the privileged orders and on the other by a fiscal concession to the crown by the nation as a whole.[34] If Rabaut and his colleagues could produce such a charter, Jefferson assured him, "You will carry back to your constituents more good than ever was effected before without violence, and you will stop exactly at the point where violence would otherwise begin" but with the prospect that more might be gained at future meetings of the Estates General.[35] Talking to Morris that day, however, Jefferson felt less sanguine "of anything being done to Purpose by the States General" than he seemed to be in his appeals to Lafayette and Rabaut.[36]

When Lafayette acknowledged receipt of his copy of Jefferson's "Excellent ideas," he too was discouraged. A royal charter granted by a paternalistic king was a far cry from the resounding European Declaration of the Rights of Man that he had already prepared for the representatives of the French nation to proclaim. Moreover, whether or not he was now willing to compromise on those principles, events of that day showed that Jefferson's charter was hardly likely to be acceptable to all the Second Estate. Things had happened that made Lafayette exclaim, "What will become of the States Generals [sic] God knows."[37] That morning the presumption of the Third Estate in calling itself the "Commons" again was aired by the Nobility. Lafayette (among others) defended the practice, arguing that a number of ordinances and other royal documents, as well as recent political tracts, had used that expres-

[34] *Ibid.*, pp. 167–68.

[35] *Ibid.*, p. 167.

[36] Morris diary, June 3, Davenport (ed.), I, 104.

[37] Lafayette to Jefferson, [June 3], Boyd, XV, 166.

sion and its derivatives. Despite the largest vote (99 to 116) the minority had so far been able to muster, the majority of the Noblesse,
considering the term loaded in favor of the Third Estate's pretensions, voted to permit its commission to sign the minutes of the
joint commission's conferences only if they did not describe the
Third Estate as the "Commons."[38] Upon reporting this caviling
proviso to Jefferson, Lafayette mentioned another captious issue:
"The Commons have said that there must be no *intermediaire* between them and the king"—words which, though probably meant
to refer to the king's ministers, the Nobles regarded as a direct, unfriendly reference to themselves. The king and the queen, he
added, "are on the aristocratical side." Nevertheless, in his Gallic
English he showed that he did not despair: "I will endeavour to
bring matters to the issue you point out—less even than that for the
present. But it is very hard to navigate in such a whirling."[39] Lafayette obviously did not consider the time ripe for reason to prevail.

The cool reception his plan received ended the effort of the author of the American Declaration of Independence to become also
the author of a French Charter of Rights. Twenty-five years later
Jefferson admitted that his earnest endeavor to get Lafayette and
"the patriots of my acquaintance to enter into a compact with the
king" was misguided. At that later date Jefferson had come to believe that in 1789 he had thought of his proposed charter as em-
bodying the most that the people of France were then "able to bear
soberly and usefully for themselves," while Lafayette had thought
(in Jefferson's words) that "the dose might be still larger." Subsequent events, Jefferson's hindsight led him to infer, had shown that
his friend had been right and himself wrong.[40] But Jefferson was

[38] The bulletins of the Noblesse are in AN, C 26, 178³. The debate of June 3 is reported
ibid., pièce 24. See also Georges Michon, *Essai sur l'histoire du parti feuillant: Adrien
Duport (1789–1792)* (Paris, 1924), p. 49; *Gazette de Leide, supplément,* June 19;
Procès-verbal de la Noblesse, p. 156; and *AP,* VIII, 64.

[39] Lafayette to Jefferson, [June 3], LC, Jefferson Papers, 8480. We have departed from
Boyd, XV, 166, slightly, reading *even* instead of *corn.* We have used (and hereafter shall
use) modern capitalization for Lafayette's letters in English; often it is hard to tell
whether he meant a capital or a lowercase letter.

[40] Jefferson to Lafayette, February 14, 1815, A. A. Lipscomb and A. E. Bergh (eds.),
The Writings of Thomas Jefferson (Washington, 1905), XIV, 246–47 (translated into
French in *Mémoires,* V, 492–93).

perhaps, long after the event, doing his friend more than justice, for he seemed to forget that Lafayette too had been willing to settle for less and that part of his own purpose in June 1789 had been to forestall violence (and if the people of France afterward proved able to swallow a larger dose of liberty than he had prescribed, they were not to do so without several violent convulsions).

Meanwhile, the stalemate of the Second and the Third Estate defied all efforts to break it. On June 6, for a variety of reasons in which politics and charity were mingled, the Clergy asked the other two orders to cooperate with it in creating a joint committee to consider ways of relieving the patent "misery of the people,"[41] for whom the unsettled political conditions had aggravated the ill effects of a hard winter, food shortage, mounting prices, and unemployment. And on June 10 the self-styled Commons issued what it called a "final invitation"[42] to the others to join with it in verifying credentials, threatening to recognize no credentials not verified in common. It behooved the Nobility now to make a decision on these invitations. Acceptance of the Clergy's would underline the readiness to act as a separate body before the problem of verification was disposed of, and refusal to act would imply indifference to the misery of the people. Acceptance of the Third Estate's ultimatum by a majority of the Nobility was inconceivable.

Lafayette wondered what the English Parliament would have done with regard to relief of the people's misery. He also wondered whether the liberal minority of the Nobility, defying the majority, should accede to the Third Estate's demand. He asked Jefferson for his opinion. Directly approached in this fashion, Jefferson proved unexpectedly coy. Perhaps he had begun to feel, since the cool reception of his proposed charter, that he had gone too far.[43] Perhaps he had begun to be apprehensive that violence was now the more rather than the less likely outcome of the quarrel among the orders and that Lafayette was less fearful of violence than he. In any case, he replied cautiously. The British Parliament, he sup-

---

[41] *AP*, VIII, 72.

[42] *Ibid.*, pp. 85–86.

[43] Cf. Dumas Malone, *Jefferson and His Time*, Vol. II: *Jefferson and the Rights of Man* (Boston, 1951), p. 217.

posed, would, under analogous circumstances, vote a sum of money
to relieve scarcity, asking the king to spend it for that purpose; and
he added, "If I see you at Versailles today, I can be more particular."
And "with respect to the utility or inutility of your minority's
joining the Commons . . . I know too little of the subject to see
what may be it's [*sic*] consequences."[44]

About this time Lafayette received from the English writer
Jeremy Bentham a copy of "part of a series of essays on Political
Tactics undertaken originally with no other view than in the hope
that something may be picked out of them that may be of use in
the Etats Généraux." The English theorist was less cautious than
the American diplomat at this juncture: "When you have obliged
the two privileged orders to break up their particular assemblies in
order to come and help make up the General Assembly and have
declared that all other Assemblies than the General one and its
committees are but assemblies of individuals destitute of all binding force, you have gone as far as you ought."[45] If the Jeffersons and
Benthams were not agreed, although both seemed to fear excess,
how was a young marquis, torn between loyalties of class and of
principle, to feel certain what his next step should be? One thing
was certain: no matter how he decided, he was not likely to
persuade the majority of his fellows, as was made readily clear
when the Noblesse balloted for its president. Of the votes
cast for ten different persons, Lafayette received 1, the Duc de
Montmorency-Luxembourg being elected with 145.[46]

The persistent demand of the Nobility's minority for cooperation with the Third Estate made the majority more and more stubbornly loyal to an alliance with the Clergy and the court. The majority took advantage of a conciliatory plan submitted by the king's
ministers to underscore the separateness of the Noblesse once more.
They proposed that the three estates verify credentials separately
but endeavor to settle disputed elections by conference, leaving to

---

[44] Jefferson to Lafayette, June 12, Boyd, XV, 179–80. *Le curieux,* I (1894), 94, dates
a letter of Lafayette to Maubourg June 12, [1789], but it is most likely of 1788.

[45] Bentham Papers, 1789–1790, University College, London. Another copy went to
Mirabeau.

[46] AN, C 26, 178³, pièce 32 (June 12).

the king the resolution of disputes that could not otherwise be resolved. The majority of the Nobility accepted this plan, with reservations that once more affirmed its insistence upon separately verifying the credentials of those deputies elected exclusively by the nobles of their bailiwicks.[47] In the same uncompromising spirit the Noblesse turned down by more than a 2-to-1 vote the equally uncompromising demand that it join the Third Estate (June 13).

Despite expectations in some quarters, the minority did not immediately secede to the Third Estate. For some of them this apparent inconsistency was due, as Jefferson learned, to the thought that "they could do more good in their own chamber by endeavouring to increase their numbers and bettering the measures of the majority."[48] Certainly several of Lafayette's colleagues, both friendly and unfriendly, suspected him of such Trojan-horse tactics,[49] but Lafayette insisted that only his instructions kept him from joining the Third Estate.[50] Meanwhile, he took a small but clearcut part in the sometimes hot debates of the Noblesse, intervening on June 13 and 15 briefly to decry the tactics of "those who sought to barricade themselves" by getting the king to intercede on behalf of the Nobility against the "less powerful."[51] Those speeches perhaps had some influence upon a vote of June 15 which enabled the minority of the Nobility to register a victory that was brilliant though not substantial. It prevented the passage of a motion to petition the king, when he was notified of the Second Estate's resolution rejecting the Third Estate's ultimatum, to support the Second Estate in its conflict with the Third. Instead, an overwhelming vote favored reporting the resolution "purely and simply."[52] That vote, however, as Jefferson advised his government, was due to no liberal principle but rather to the desire of the "very great majority" of the

[47] *AP*, VIII, 67–68, 72–73, 94, and *Procès-verbal de la Noblesse*, pp. 186–87, 189–90.

[48] Jefferson to Jay, June 17, Boyd, XV, 188.

[49] M. de Lescure (ed.), *Mémoires du marquis de Ferrières* (Paris, 1880), p. 46n.; Lameth, I, xi 37, n.1; and Gaultier to his constituents, June 25, Mège, *Gaultier de Biauzat*, II, 143–44.

[50] *Mémoires*, II, 250; IV, 146 and n.

[51] AN, C 26, 1783, pièces 33vo. and 34vo.

[52] *Procès-verbal de la Noblesse*, p. 231.

Noblesse as a party in a three-cornered contest to avoid "throwing themselves into the arms of despotism"[53]—not to yield to royal prerogative in the struggle to hold off the underprivileged.

On June 17 the Third Estate, having verified the credentials of those deputies who had presented them, took a bold step in the direction of revolution. It declared that, despite the absence of other deputies, as representatives of 96 percent of the nation it was "the National Assembly," that to it alone belonged the power to "express and represent the general will of the nation, and that all existing taxes were null and void unless freely accorded by the National Assembly."[54] The majority of the Nobility were, as Jefferson put it, "absolutely out of their senses"—"so furious" that they were most unlikely to accept this outgrowth of the debates with the Third Estate, now over a month long.[55] When an outraged member in the chamber of the Noblesse vehemently insisted that existing taxes were still legal because they had been decreed by the king and registered by the parlements, Lafayette questioned whether those who now advanced that view genuinely held that registration by the parlements made a tax perpetual.[56]

Pressure was exerted on Louis XVI to take a definite stand in the controversy. Necker had all along been one of those who had hoped that the impasse could be breached by conciliation. He now joined those who sought to persuade the king to hold a *séance royale* (along the lines suggested to Lafayette and Rabaut St. Etienne by Jefferson on June 3), propounding a program which, he hoped, would meet with the approval of all three orders and under royal leadership would give a single direction to their efforts. The king thereupon suspended the meetings of the Estates General for a few days until he should be ready to express his will.

Lafayette found all this maneuvering extremely trying. Even before he knew whether the king would act at all or what the royal proposal would be, Necker's readiness to compromise made him feel uneasy. He sought reassurance from Adélaïde de Simiane,

---

[53] Jefferson to Jay, June 17, Boyd, XV, 188–89.

[54] *AP*, VIII, 127.

[55] Jefferson to Madison, June 18, Boyd, XV, 196.

[56] AN, C 26, 178³, page 2 (June 19).

to whom he poured out the anxieties "of a tender heart and of a mind occupied perhaps uselessly but at least vigorously."[57] Reflecting the atmosphere of the aristocratic circles in which she moved, Adélaïde, despite her devotion to him, did not share his political philosophy. Though she showed a sympathetic interest, he detected a note of blame, and he responded with an impatience which upon leaving her he repented. He expressed his repentence in a lengthy, semi-apologetic, semi-boastful letter. Detailing (with forgivable exaggeration) his truly remarkable career as a champion of liberty since he was nineteen years old, he revealed how long he had waited and how hard he had worked to bring "the liberty of man and the destruction of despotism" to his own country. He had tried everything but civil war, which he could have started, he claimed, but had not, because he dreaded its horror. "For a year now I have had a plan whose simplest points used to seem extravagances but which six months from now will be carried out in its entirety—yes, its entirety without changing a single word"; and his proposed declaration of rights, or something very close to it, "will become France's catechism." Mme de Simiane therefore ought now to understand why, "having drawn the sword and thrown away the scabbard," he rejoiced in "whatever advances the revolution" and fretted over "everything that might prevent reaching the point where I want us to stop." Recalling sardonically that in previous revolutionary efforts, as in Ireland and Holland,[58] the "wisdom of our ministers" had prevented his success, he now worried about Necker's plans. If he confided to Adélaïde all these "fatuities," it was not, he explained, because he expected her to approve of them but because he knew that she would keep them secret. "I assure you that in the twelve years of my public life, if I have made many mistakes, I have not had a moment of which I am not proud, and among the mistakes I have made there are many that I owe to the prudence of others."[59]

---

[57] Lafayette to [Mme de Simiane], [June 19], *Mémoires*, II, 308. See also below, Appendix I.

[58] Cf. Gottschalk, *Between*, pp. 75, 89–90, 170, 264 (for Ireland), and pp. 152–53, 191, 229–30, 264, 326, 338–41, 370, 375 (for Holland).

[59] Lafayette to [Mme de Simiane], [June 19], *Mémoires*, II, 309–10.

No minister's prudence this time upset Lafayette's calculations. By a series of unexpected incidents Necker's compromise plan only made matters worse. The Third Estate, believing that the king's order to suspend its sessions was a deliberate scheme to keep it from carrying out its purpose, openly defied what it mistakenly took to be the king's will by meeting in a tennis court close by the Château and taking an audacious "Tennis Court Oath" not to disband but to draw up a new constitution wherever it might be able to meet (June 20). This was but the culminating defiance in a series of acts that had angered and frightened the more conservative advisers of the court, who now induced the king to disregard Necker's conciliatory opinion and to give to his proposed announcement a turn that favored the Second Estate and distinctly rebuked the Third.

When Necker realized that his plans had gone awry, he decided not to attend the royal session. Very little happened in court circles that was not quickly known among the elite, and Lafayette was soon apprised of Necker's new decision. He was thoroughly upset. His friends had begun to feel that Necker's reputation was inflated, and his own impatience now convinced him that they were right. "No worn-out machine," he complained, "runs down in a shorter time than M. Necker"; the minister had allowed the opposition in the king's council to tamper with his plan to the point where he had achieved the "worst possible situation—enough bad and enough good to embarrass everybody and to put the Third in the wrong."[60]

The marquis' disgust proved premature, for victory smiled upon the Third Estate just as defeat seemed to stare it in the face. On the eve of the *séance royale* the majority of the Clergy joined the Third in a temporary meeting place. On the morning of June 23 the three estates assembled once more in the Salle des Menus Plaisirs and in royal session heard the king sternly declare that he wanted them to consider in separate meetings of their respective orders a program of reform which he outlined, and he threatened to enact those reforms by himself if they failed to cooperate as he

---

[60] Lafayette to [Mme de Simiane?] [June 22?], *ibid.,* p. 310. See also Morris diary, May 31, Davenport (ed.), I, 101, and Jefferson to Jay, June 17–18, Boyd, XV, 190, 191–93.

indicated. He then ordered them to adjourn immediately and to meet separately thereafter. The privileged orders left the meeting hall accordingly, but the self-styled National Assembly refused to follow. On the contrary, it reaffirmed its status as National Assembly and defied the king's grand master of ceremonies when he asked it to obey the royal behest. This defiance was open rebellion, and a better prepared, more vigorous, or more ill-intentioned king would have used force to suppress it. In fact, the king's bodyguard was recalled to enforce the royal will, but "the minority nobles rallied near the Salle to defend the Commons or to perish with them."[61] Because the king's officers were not yet indignant enough over the audacity of the Third Estate and its noble sympathizers to risk the bloodshed and civil war which thereupon might ensue, no force was used, and the National Assembly remained, despite an explicit royal command, what it had been before—a self-appointed representative body whose courage and intentions were clear but whose authority was still uncertain since it lacked the monarch's sanction.

No doubt, however, could long exist regarding the wishes of the people—at least of those who milled around the palace grounds and made their wishes heard. When they learned that Necker had not attended the royal session, they concluded that he had offered the king his resignation. They made plain their confidence in him, crying out that he be retained. An unfriendly contemporary accused Lafayette of being, along with Necker himself, one of a group of willful men who deliberately instigated this popular demonstration in order to thwart the king's intentions,[62] but the demonstration was, more likely, an entirely spontaneous manifestation of the wants and fears of partisans of the Third Estate. Again a baffled but well-meaning king yielded, reassuring Necker of his

---

[61] *Mémoires*, IV, 5, which is corroborated by *Mémories de Larevillière-Lépaux* (Paris, 1895), I, 82–83; [E.-L.-A. Dubois de Crancé], *Contre-poison, ou compte rendu des travaux de l'Assemblée nationale depuis le 27 avril 1789 jusqu'au 15 avril 1790 par un député patriote à ses commetans* [Paris, 1792], p. 8; and F.-G. de la Rochefoucauld-Liancourt (ed.), *Mémoires de Condorcet sur la Révolution française* (Paris, [1893]), II, 69–70. See also *Mémoires*, II, 310, n. 2.

[62] Archives du Château de Chatillon, quoted by Paul Filleul, *Le Duc de Montmorency-Luxembourg* (Paris, [1939]), p. 117.

confidence. Whether or not Necker had contemplated resignation, his unmistakable popularity had won him a distinct political triumph.[63]

On the afternoon of June 23 Morris had dinner at Mme de Tessé's, and Lafayette was there too. Lafayette, as his wife had previously done, now chided his American friend for aristocratic leanings. Morris' sentiments were injuring "the good Party," the marquis charged, because they were continually being quoted against the Patriot cause. Morris justified himself by drawing a distinction between democracy and liberty; he was opposed to the one, he said, out of regard for the other. The Patriots, however, were "going Headlong to Destruction" because their democratic views were "totally inconsistent with the Materials" of which France was composed, and "the worst Thing which could happen would be to grant their Wishes." Lafayette, if Morris recorded him correctly, replied that he was aware that "his Party are mad, and [he] tells them so"; nevertheless, he was determined, if need be, "to die with them." Morris' rejoinder was that it would be "quite as well to bring them to their Senses and live with them." Lafayette, apparently unimpressed by Morris' apprehensions of violence, then announced his intention to resign his seat in the Nobility, and Morris, despite his fear of Patriotic madness, approved, for he recognized that the instructions by which Lafayette was bound went "contrary to his Conscience."[64]

Later that day the liberal minority of the Nobility gathered at the Marquis de Montesquiou's home. They decided that those of them who were permitted by their mandates to join the Third Estate should now prepare to do so, announcing their intention at the next meeting of the Noblesse. Fear of violence and, more effectively, the tactics of the presiding officer kept them from making that announcement at the day's session on June 24, but that evening they gathered again at Montesquiou's to draw up a letter to the president of their order making their intention known in black and white.[65]

[63] Ibid., and Gazette de Leide, July 3.

[64] Morris diary, June 23, Davenport (ed.), I, 121.

[65] Lameth, I, 411–15, and Procès-verbal de la Noblesse, pp. 272–73.

Lafayette appears to have played no part in these meetings. Bound as he was by his mandate, he could hardly take an overt step in favor of the union of the three orders. He recognized, however, that the open defiance of the self-styled National Assembly and the vehement reaction of the Second Estate made a decision imperative, for, as Jefferson had warned, he found himself increasingly embarrassed by being committed to neither side. He finally made up his mind to resign his seat,[66] but, as things turned out, he did not have to do so.

The defiance of the National Assembly made decisions imperative for others, too. On the twenty-fourth a majority of the Clergy, also defying the king, rejoined the National Assembly in the Salle des Menus Plaisirs. The next day the liberal nobles, their letter having been delivered to their disconcerted colleagues, likewise seceded to the National Assembly. Forty-seven of them, with Clermont-Tonnerre as spokesman, went over, but Lafayette was conspicuously absent from among them. He "could not be of the number, being restrained by his instructions," Jefferson reported, but was "writing to his constituents to change his instructions or to accept his resignation."[67] Clermont-Tonnerre explained to a jubilant National Assembly that a number of their "brothers," acting from "a motive as respectable as ours," had refrained from joining them only because of their mandates. To spread the good news of the National Assembly's victory an illustrious representative from each of the orders was sent to address the huge crowd that waited outside the Hôtel des Menus Plaisirs, and whenever these messengers had occasion to mention "names particularly dear to the country like those of the Duc d'Orléans, Marquis de La Fayette, and many others" they evoked rounds of applause.[68]

By this time the public was generally aware that Lafayette, accustomed to occupying the front rank and champing to be active, might try to join the Third Estate.[69] Not only was he being disloyal

[66] Morris diary, June 23, Davenport (ed.), I, 121.

[67] Jefferson to Jay, June 25, Boyd, XV, 208.

[68] *Point du jour,* June 26, p. 50.

[69] Cf. Gaultier to his constituents, June 25, 1789, Mège, *Gaultier de Biauzat,* II, 143–44, and *Gazette de Leide, supplément,* July 7.

to his political creed but, perhaps no less important, he was obliged to appear uninvolved, and hence inconspicuous as a leader, in events which he had done so much to prepare. Mme de Simiane, torn between her royalist sympathies and her personal loyalty to him, was distressed by his intentions, and in a lengthy explanation, which could have given her little reassurance, he revealed how his mind was running. "The incalculable, although unforeseen, misfortune of having been chosen by the Nobility," he confessed, "leaves me only a choice among difficulties." The king at the recent *séance royale* had authorized deputies who felt restrained by their mandates to ask their constituents for new ones, though without leaving their posts. Lafayette presumed that he could, without going to Auvergne, break with the nobles of his province and resign, but such a course would produce complications. Still worse complications would result if he were to go to Auvergne and put up a fight for his cause, for he would then be "going to lose a battle while displeasing the whole National Assembly, which does not look with favor on departures for the provinces." Moreover, he did not want to be absent for any length of time because "the National Assembly is threatened with several dangers that it behooves me to share" and because "it is going to take up a declaration of rights, on which I can be useful to it." Hence, he planned to go to Auvergne as late as possible and stay only long enough to resign in person. Then, hoping that some member of the Third Estate would withdraw in order to make room for him, he would stand for election to the vacant post. Recognizing that Mme de Simiane would find some difficulty in approving his running for election to the Third Estate, he tried to justify it:

It is natural that when twelve hundred Frenchmen are at work on a constitution I should be and should want to be one of them. A country accustomed to shady court intrigues at first confuses the ambition to win from the people the privilege of defending it with those solicitations for which one sometimes blushes, which one almost always keeps secret, and which place a man temporarily in a position of dependence upon his fellowmen of which he is by natural impulse a little ashamed. But at Rome votes were sought in the public forum; in England, in America they are sought in the press; and Frenchmen soon will grow used to the same customs.

Since, however, everything was at the moment uncertain—within a week or two "we shall probably be driven away or firmly rooted." —he was not going to act immediately. Meanwhile, "I cannot limit myself to being the man of the seneschalsy of Auvergne after having contributed to the liberty of another world. Remember that I cannot stop in the middle of the race without falling off and that with the greatest desire to be at my post, that post must be in the political breach."[70]

The denouement came much faster than Lafayette expected. Torn between the intention to be an absolute monarch and the desire to be a father to his people, between unwillingness to use force and the fear that force would be unavailing, Louis XVI temporized once more. Without recognizing the National Assembly as such, he nevertheless requested the Nobility and the Clergy to join the Third Estate, deputies whose *cahiers* forbade them to vote by head being permitted to abstain from voting until they received new instructions. Despite some diehard opposition the Nobility decided to comply. Following their instructions to the last, the Riom deputation, among others, requested permission to put on the record the protest that their constituents required of them:

The deputies of the Seneschalsy of Auvergne ask that the minutes of the Nobility record the efforts they have continually made since the opening of the Estates General to win approval for the opinion which expresses their constituents' wishes and that in keeping with the said wishes they now have consented to pass to the chamber of the Third Estate only because such has been the decision of the plurality.

Lafayette signed this statement with his colleagues.[71]

About five o'clock in the afternoon of June 27 the majority of the Nobility and the hitherto unyielding rump of the Clergy, marching in two parallel columns, entered the Salle des Menus Plaisirs amid an impressive silence. Lafayette was among them. The Duc de Montmorency-Luxembourg, president of the Second

---

[70] Lafayette to [Mme de Simiane], [June 25], *Mémoires,* II, 310–12. See also *ibid.,* p. 250.

[71] *Procès-Verbal de la Noblesse,* p. 320.

Estate, declared that his colleagues had decided to come over "in order to give to the king the token of their respect and to the nation the proof of their patriotism." The president of the National Assembly, the illustrious scientist Jean-Sylvain Bailly, answered: "This day will be celebrated in our annals. It makes the family complete. It ends forever the divisions which have mutually afflicted us. . . . The National Assembly will now occupy itself, without distraction or relaxation, with the regeneration of the realm and the public welfare." That night there were "illuminations" in Versailles, almost every window gleaming with lamps and candles, and almost every thoroughfare aflame with bonfires and torches, and the royal couple appeared upon the palace balcony to share in the public rejoicing.[72]

The verification of the credentials of the latecomers proceeded forthwith. On July 1, two months after the inauguration of the Estates General, Lafayette was at length duly accredited a member of that National Assembly[73] which he had been one of the first to demand but which Louis XVI had not yet fully sanctioned. Absolutism seemed on the point of surrender, but there were those who meant to keep on fighting for its survival. Some of the Noblesse, refusing to admit defeat, continued to assemble as a separate body,[74] and few could tell to which side the king eventually would rally.

BIBLIOGRAPHICAL NOTES

Maurice de La Fuye and E. A. Babeau, *Lafayette, soldat de deux patries* (Paris, 1953) says (p. 71) that upon arriving in Versailles in May 1789, Lafayette informed Adrienne that when in 1785 he had visited Prussia, Frederick the Great had warned him about a young man who, having advocated ideas of liberty, had been hanged. According to La Fuye, Lafayette thought the episode funny, but Adrienne did not. The remark of Frederick in 1785 rests upon *Mémoires*, III, 199 (cf. Gottschalk, *Between*, p. 186), but we know of no evidence for Lafayette's telling Adrienne about it in 1789.

The Ball Collection at Indiana University was formerly the collection of the late Judge Walter Gardner of Jersey City, New Jersey.

[72] *Point du jour*, June 28, p. 66. See also Lameth, I, 37, and n. 1.

[73] *AP*, VIII, 180.

[74] Until the emigration of its president, the Duc de Montmorency-Luxembourg, on July 15: see *Procès-verbal de la Noblesse*, pp. 359–77.

The so-called *Mémoires de Condorcet* are spurious, having been compiled according to the subtitle, from *"extraits de sa correspondance et de celles de ses amis."* The work is at times well informed.

The volume of *Le Point du jour* which deals with the events from April 27 to June 17 was subsequently made up by Barère and so has the value only of a memoir rather than of a daily newspaper.

The early phases of the French Revolution have been carefully narrated in *La Prise de la Bastille, 14 juillet 1789* by Jacques Godechot (Paris, 1965).

CHAPTER V

"The First European Declaration of Rights"

ALTHOUGH Louis XVI, with as much grace as he could summon to the occasion, had tentatively yielded to the demands of the National Assembly, his defeat was obvious. Even if he himself were too good-natured or apathetic to be resentful, those nearest to him—particularly his queen and his brother the Comte d'Artois—felt that the king's dignity had been wounded and his power jeopardized, and they wanted redress. In their indignation they found sympathizers among a hard core of conservative clerics and nobles who, for reasons of their own and not altogether out of royalism, were determined to turn the clock back. Convinced that force would be required to overawe the National Assembly and to contain its allies among the populations of Versailles and Paris, they prevailed upon Louis to bring to the two cities foreign mercenaries whose loyalty to those who paid them presumably could be taken for granted. A ready pretext was found in the necessity for added precautions to preserve order in the face of rising fermentation.

Hence, whether the "aristocrats" or the "patriots" would ultimately triumph was far from settled by the provisional creation of a National Assembly out of the Estates General. The issue was discussed at a dinner to celebrate the Fourth of July to which Jefferson invited Lafayette and his wife along with a large Party of Americans."[1] Here, after dinner, Morris had "some political conversation," in which Morris again aired his doubts that French-

---

[1] Morris diary, June 30 and July 4, Davenport (ed.), I, 128, 134. See also Jefferson to John Paradise, July 5, Boyd, XV, 242 and n.; A. B. Shepperson, *John Paradise and Lucy Ludwell, of London and Williamsburg* (Richmond, 1942), pp. 381–84; and Malone, pp. 212–13.

men were equal to the responsibilities of democratic government. Without feeling any profound confidence in the French nobility,[2] he urged Lafayette "to preserve if possible some constitutional Authority to the Body of Nobles as the only Means of preserving any Liberty for the People." Morris did not explicitly record Lafayette's reaction, but the Frenchman does not seem to have shared the American's conviction that the French were incapable of preserving liberty without a house of lords, for when Morris left Jefferson's he apprehended that "the Current is setting so strong against the Noblesse" that it was doomed.[3]

Two days afterward the American minister became involuntarily involved in an awkward political tangle in the National Assembly. The shortage of food in Paris threatened to bring actual starvation to that large part of the city's inhabitants which lived continually on the verge of destitution, and Jefferson, approached by the French minister of foreign affairs and intending to promote American commerce while alleviating French hunger, had called the attention of Americans to the high prices for breadstuffs on the French market. For all that, the distress of Paris continued into July and beyond, providing a humanitarian cause to those who for good or other reasons chose to censure the government. Outstanding among them was Mirabeau, whose reputation as an eloquent defender of the people had grown every day since he had first stood forth as a defiant leader of the Third Estate, although he was never able to free himself of the suspicion of seeking personal advantage.

Necker was one of the most popular figures of the moment, but Mirabeau, having recently aligned himself with another popular hero, the Duc d'Orléans, now sought to discredit the still powerful minister. A good opportunity came on July 6, when the National Assembly, having appointed a Committee on Subsistence to consider the food shortage, took up the committee's report. It included a letter from Necker describing the efforts of the ministry to bring an adequate supply of food into the hungry city. Mirabeau thought

---

[2] See Morris to William Carmichael, July 4, Davenport (ed.), I, 136–37.

[3] Morris diary, July 4, *ibid.*, p. 134.

he had information which showed that the minister had been extraordinarily inept in meeting the emergency, and so he rose to inquire whether the committee was aware that Jefferson had offered to have abundant food sent in from America—"propositions" which Necker had declined. The committee admitted having no knowledge of such transactions, and Mirabeau asked for twenty-four hours to produce the evidence. If Mirabeau was right, Necker would be justly exposed to public rebuke for failure to take advantage of the American offer, and Mirabeau would have earned the people's gratitude.

At a time of mounting strain between the royal court and the National Assembly Lafayette could not remain indifferent to a charge made by a Patriot leader but directed at a minister assumed to be friendly to the Patriot cause. Moreover, having himself at the close of 1788, engaged in an effort to relieve Paris' hunger with American foodstuffs, he must have found it hard to believe that Jefferson had made an offer to a French minister on so important a matter without his knowledge.[4] Feeling called upon to confirm or deny Mirabeau's allegation, he asked Jefferson for his version of the story: "I don't care much about it in general, ... but ... we must not quarrel with our party in the [king's] council, at least for the present." If Jefferson wished, Lafayette would undertake to try to call off Mirabeau, "but he is not easily stopped." Lafayette himself thought it "well enough" to censure the ministry for exporting flour from France to the West Indies in times of need without compensating imports from the United States,[5] but he did not share Mirabeau's readiness to discredit Necker entirely.

Jefferson, recognizing that "it would be disagreeable and perhaps mischievous" if Necker suspected him of encouraging Mirabeau, undertook to forestall any such impression. His reply to Lafayette took the form of a personal letter stating that while he had informed his government of France's flour shortage, he had "never made an offer to anybody to have corn or flour brought here from America";[6] he might, however, have been confused with an

---

[4] Editorial note, Boyd, XV, 243–47. See also *Mémoires*, II, 360–61.

[5] Lafayette to Jefferson, July 6, Boyd, XV, 249.

[6] Jefferson to Lafayette, July 6, *ibid.*, p. 250.

American merchant who he believed had "offered to Mr. Necker to bring a large supply." Even before receiving this exculpation of Necker, Lafayette spoke to Mirabeau and received from him a promise to make a retraction of his error in the Assembly.[7] Jefferson, going himself on July 7 to Versailles, met Lafayette at the home of the Duchesse d'Enville,[8] and Mirabeau's attack upon Necker entered their conversation.[9] They agreed that Jefferson should make a formal denial for the National Assembly's records of any *propositions* (the word Mirabeau had used) to Necker to have American foodstuffs shipped to France. Accordingly (and without mentioning the American merchant who had made an offer of "a large supply" to Necker), Jefferson wrote to Lafayette: "I never in my life made any proposition to Mr. Necker on the subject; I never said I had made such a proposition," and he begged leave to avail himself "of your friendship and of your position to have a communication of these facts made to the honorable assembly of the nation of which you are a member."[10] Jefferson submitted copies of this more tactful letter to Necker and to Foreign Minister Montmorin,[11] and he also provided Lafayette with some statistics showing the relative paucity of American importations of foodstuffs into France's Atlantic ports.[12] This more formal letter made a better case for Necker than Jefferson's previous reference to "a large supply" offered by an American merchant would have permitted.

When Jefferson's more formal letter came to hand, Mirabeau proved willing to give the gist of it to the Assembly (obviously Lafayette might otherwise have felt constrained to read it), but the next day, while admitting in the Assembly that Necker had tried to encourage American shipments to France, he insisted

---

[7] Jefferson to Necker, July 8, *ibid.*, p. 253, and Lafayette to Jefferson, [July 8], *ibid.*, p. 254.

[8] Lafayette to Jefferson, July 6, *ibid.*, p. 250.

[9] Jefferson to Montmorin and to Necker, July 8, 1789, *ibid.*, p. 253. The declaration of rights was another subject of conversation. See below, p. 81.

[10] Jefferson to Lafayette, July 7, Boyd, XV, 252.

[11] July 8, *ibid.*, p. 253.

[12] July 7, *ibid.*, pp. 251–52.

that everything he had said was essentially correct except for his use of the word *propositions*. He then deposited Jefferson's letter with the secretariat, without actually reading it. Necker's friends in their turn now tried to embarrass Mirabeau. Evidently distrusting Mirabeau's interpretation of Jefferson's words, they asked that a French translation (which had been prepared presumably from Necker's copy of the letter) be read.[13]

Until that time Lafayette had felt bound by the still unmodified instructions of his constituents to take only a limited part in the National Assembly's proceedings. While awaiting release from those instructions, he considered himself free to attend the Assembly's meetings but not to speak or to vote.[14] At this point, however, Lafayette thought it "indelicate if not for Mirabeau's feelings at least for my own,"[15] and "not convenient" for Jefferson either,[16] that Mirabeau be subjected to further stress upon Jefferson's repudiation of his statement. He felt called upon, therefore, to intervene in the debate, thus making his first public remarks in the National Assembly. Being careful to speak from his seat and not from the tribune, he commented that Mirabeau "had litterally [*sic*] translated" Jefferson's "expressions" and "a second reading" would be "useless."[17] Lafayette was far too generous about the literalness of Mirabeau's paraphrase, but he had no desire, while exculpating Necker, to humiliate Mirabeau, and he won his point. His endorsement of Mirabeau's résumé of Jefferson's letter seemed to satisfy the Assembly.

Mirabeau was duly grateful, but Lafayette soon learned that both Necker and Montmorin were angry with him because they were dissatisfied with Mirabeau's questionable qualification of his retraction. To vent their anger Lafayette thought they might

[13] Lafayette to Jefferson, [July 8], *ibid.*, p. 254; *Mémoires*, II, 360–61; and *AP*, VIII, 208.

[14] *Motion de M. de La Fayette sur les droits de l'homme, et de l'homme vivant en société* ([Paris], 1789), p. 3, and *Mémoires*, II, 250.

[15] Lafayette to Jefferson, [July 8], Boyd, XV, 254.

[16] Same to same, [July 9], *ibid.*, p. 255.

[17] Lafayette to Jefferson, [July 8], *ibid.*, p. 254. See also the letter of [July 9], *ibid.*, p. 255. These letters seem to state that Mirabeau actually "read" Jefferson's letter, but it appears that what Lafayette really meant was that Mirabeau had told "everything that was in it" (p. 254) or had said "every word which [it] contained" (p. 255). Cf. *AP*, VIII, 208.

want to publish Jefferson's letter exculpating Necker, and he did not object.[18] The original, however, had passed out of his hands into Mirabeau's,[19] and Lafayette did not know where to find it. So he asked Jefferson for a copy which he might send to the press.[20] He also requested Jefferson to "accomodate [sic]" the letter containing the statistics of American importations into French Atlantic ports "as writen [sic] today" (i.e., to rewrite it under today's date) so that he could "deliver both [letters] tomorrow morning to Mr. Necker, who is very anxious about them."[21] Jefferson, having learned that "scandalous versions" of his formal letter had been made public, believed that in fairness to Mirabeau as well as to Necker it should be made public.[22] So he obliged Lafayette on both counts; he "accommodated" the letter with the statistics, dating it the ninth, leaving out the reference to Lafayette's intervention in the Mirabeau episode as his reason for writing it, and adding an explanation of the paucity of American imports into France as due to competitive demand elsewhere;[23] and he gave permission to publish the formal letter, which was given to the press shortly afterward.[24] The matter seems to have ended there, but it had added no luster to the reputation of either Mirabeau or Necker. Nor did it improve relations between Necker and Lafayette. Though Montmorin thanked Jefferson for his copy of the formal letter to Lafayette,[25] Necker apparently never did, perhaps because

[18] *Mémoires*, II, 361, and Lafayette to Jefferson, [July 8], Boyd, XV, 254.

[19] One would assume that it is the autograph copy now in the papers of the National Assembly in the Archives Nationales of Paris (C 28, liasse 224, pièce 3), but Boyd (V, 249, n. 23, and *ibid.*, p. 252) thinks that another autograph copy was the original, the one in the Archives Nationales being the copy subsequently provided to Lafayette (see below, nn. 23 and 24).

[20] Lafayette to Jefferson, [July 9], Boyd, XV, 255. Why Lafayette (or Necker and Montmorin) did not use the copies which Jefferson had sent to the ministers is not clear.

[21] *Ibid.*

[22] Jefferson to Lafayette, July 10, *ibid.*, p. 256. Cf. Morris diary, July 9, Davenport (ed.), I, 141.

[23] Editorial note, Boyd, XV, 248, and Jefferson to Lafayette, July 9 and 10, *ibid.*, pp. 255–56.

[24] See *Journal de Paris*, July 11, pp. 872–73, where it is published in both French and English. Boyd (XV, 48) thinks Lafayette may have prepared the introductory remarks to this published version, but we doubt it; they contain errors which he was unlikely to have made.

[25] July 8, Boyd, XV, 254.

he believed that Lafayette was seconding Mirabeau in the sparring with him and that Jefferson was in their corner.

Jefferson afterward described the episode as "of little consequence in itself,"[26] but he perhaps underestimated its importance. Future events were to show that Necker was marked for dismissal from the royal council soon, and if Mirabeau had succeeded in painting him as a minister who had turned down a good chance to lower the price of bread, his dismissal probably would have been no less welcome to the populace than to aristocrats. By clearing the minister of a popular orator's charge of rejecting "propositions" of food shipments, Jefferson and Lafayette had blunted Mirabeau's attack, which otherwise might have obliterated the people's confidence in Necker.

Against hostility at court, however, Necker had no such mediators. The concentration of mercenary troops in and around Paris and Versailles by this time had reached into the tens of thousands, and doubt grew whether even in a period of tension so many armed men were needed merely for the preservation of order. On July 7 several Patriot deputies—Lafayette and Mirabeau among them —happened to meet at the Hôtel des Menus Plaisirs. Mirabeau suggested that the National Assembly send an address to the king asking for the troops' withdrawal since their presence threatened rather than guaranteed public order. The deputies all agreed that Mirabeau should present some such proposal to the Assembly. That happened to be the day already mentioned when Jefferson was visiting Versailles, and Lafayette left to keep his appointment with Jefferson.[27] Mirabeau then more or less confidentially raised the question whether the Duc d'Orléans might not have to be made lieutenant-general of the realm, the real power behind the throne, intimating that Orléans himself favored such a step.[28]

The next day Mirabeau addressed the National Assembly on the imprudence of massing soldiers in an excited city. He ended

---

[26] Jefferson to Jay, July 18, *ibid.*, p. 285.

[27] Testimony of Bergasse in *Procédure criminelle instruite au Châtelet de Paris sur la dénonciation des faits arrivés à Versailles dans la journée du 6 Octobre 1789* (Paris, 1790), I, 20 (hereafter cited as *Procédure au Châtelet*), and J.-J. Mounier, *Appel au tribunal de l'opinion publique* . . . (London, 1791), p. 11 n. See also Nicholas Bergasse, *Un défenseur des principes traditionnels sous la Révolution* (Paris, 1910), p. 117.

[28] Mounier, *Appel*, pp. 11–12 n.

a masterful speech by moving a formal address to the king requesting the withdrawal of the menacing army. This motion was designed to take the bull by the horns, but the Assembly, less fearful
as a whole than Mirabeau, was disinclined to take vigorous action.
It seemed to be on the point of referring the matter to its subdivisions (known as *bureaux*) when some Patriot colleagues urged
Lafayette, perhaps the country's most beloved general, to speak
in favor of an immediate decision; since he had not yet formally
addressed the Assembly, his maiden speech, they were persuaded,
would have greater weight than the repetition of familiar sentiments by other members.[29] Lafayette conceded and went to the
tribune for the first time. There were only two reasons, he declared,
for sending a proposal to the *bureaux*—because the relevant facts
were in doubt or because the course to follow was unclear. "But
the presence of troops brought up around this assembly is a fact
clear to everyone of us," and "as for the course to follow in such
a case, I will not insult the Assembly by supposing any of us can
hesitate." Hence, he not only supported Mirabeau's motion; he
asked that the chamber vote on it immediately. After some debate
Mirabeau's motion passed.[30]

It was now incumbent upon Mirabeau to propose the proper
wording for the Assembly's address to the king. Accordingly, a
group of Patriot deputies agreed to gather that night at Lafayette's
house to consider the draft of an address which Mirabeau would
bring. At that gathering Mirabeau again made remarks in favor
of giving special emergency powers to the Duc d'Orléans,[31] but

[29] *Mémoires*, II, 361. In the Lafayette Archives, Cornell University Library, Carton V
(microfilm) there is the original of the comments by Lafayette on the first edition of
Adolphe Thiers' *Histoire de la Révolution française* (Paris, 1823–27.) It is more complete
than the version in *Mémoires* (IV, 196–214), the editors having sometimes omitted
passages or transferred them as footnotes to other sections. The original gives some
additional details dealing with Mirabeau's address on July 8 that confirm the account
given above.

[30] *Mémoires*, II, 250. See also *AP*, VIII, 210; Boyd, XV, 254; and *Point du jour*, July 9,
pp. 142–43.

[31] *Mémoires*, II, 361, and see "Bibliographical Notes," below, p. 99. Jean Egret (*La
Révolution des notables*, p. 92) says that Mounier was among those present, but Lafayette
says only that Mounier was shocked by the remarks of Mirabeau, and Mounier's detailed
statement (*Appel*, pp. 11–14 n.) indicates that the remark which particularly shocked him
(and which Lafayette quoted: *Mémoires*, II, 361 n.) was made at a different time and
place. See also the testimony of J. M. J. Regnier in *Procédure au Châtelet*, I, 21.

the group approved only of the draft of an address asking for the removal of troops. The next day (July 9) the Assembly accepted it and sent it to the king.[32] Thus, the Patriot party's most eloquent orator and its most popular soldier joined forces once more, this time against the strong-arm policy of the court and its ministers, none of whom—not even Necker—had publicly disavowed that policy.

Lafayette was certain that his support of Mirabeau's motion only added "a new subject" to the ministers' "quarrel" with him. The ministers, he informed Jefferson, "wish us never to show our noses," preferring that the Assembly delay action until they ironed out their own differences, but "it is impossible to go on so."[33] He soon began to feel that the government was displeased enough to put him under arrest, and he wrote to the American minister: "If they take me up, you must claim me as an American citizen"[34] (as indeed, by special act of several states of the United States, he was).[35]

While the court was thus suspected of planning to crush opposition, the National Assembly continued along its defiant course. A committee had recently been appointed to prepare a new constitution, with Jean-Joseph Mounier, famous as a leader in the fight for the *doublement* in Dauphiny's Provincial Assembly, as spokesman. Despite repeated alarms, this committee had persevered and on July 9 it submitted a preliminary report. Mounier, describing the general structure of the proposed constitution, listed as its first requirement a declaration of rights which, serving as its preamble, would enumerate briefly but precisely the principles upon which the rest of the constitution would be based. The committee presented no such declaration itself, however, recommending instead that one be prepared tentatively and slowly elaborated.[36]

For Lafayette Mounier's report served as the long-awaited signal

---

[32] *AP*, VIII, 210–11.

[33] Lafayette to Jefferson, [July 8], Boyd, XV, 254. The original (LC, Jefferson Papers, Vol. 53, fol. 9049) reads *nozes* for *noses*.

[34] Lafayette to Jefferson, [July 9], Boyd, XV, 255.

[35] Gottschalk, *Between*, pp. 435–36.

[36] *AP*, VIII, 214–17.

to launch his "catechism of France." As he later explained to his Anglo-American friend Thomas Paine, his "particular reason" for choosing that juncture to present a declaration of rights was that "if the National Assembly should fail in the threatened destruction that then surrounded it, some trace of its principles might have a chance of surviving the wreck."[37] In preparation for the strategic moment Lafayette had recently submitted his declaration a second time for Jefferson's consideration, and on July 6 he had asked him: "Will you send me the Bill of Rights with your notes?"[38] In reply Jefferson promised to bring it to the Duchesse d'Enville's house,[39] and when they had met on July 7, though primarily concerned with Mirabeau's attack upon Necker, they probably found some time to talk also about the projected declaration of rights. At any rate, two days later the marquis wrote again about it, and this time he was more persistent: "Tomorrow I present my Bill of Rights about the middle of the sitting. Be pleased to consider it again, and make your observations." This letter was the same one that reminded the American minister of Lafayette's claim to diplomatic protection "as an American citizen."[40] It ended on a note of urgency: "I beg you to answer as soon as you get up and wish to hear from you about eight or nine at last [i.e., at the latest]. God bless you."

Although his correspondent was a French subject who had incurred the French court's displeasure and possible arrest, Jefferson gave Lafayette's proposed declaration of rights serious attention. Three versions of it are known. The first (the January draft) is the one which Jefferson sent to Madison with his approval.[41] The second is the one which he promised to bring to the Duchesse d'En-

---

[37] Thomas Paine, *Rights of Man,* in P. S. Foner (ed.), *The Complete Writings of Thomas Paine* (New York, 1945) (hereafter cited as Foner), I, 262. This assertion by Paine was scoffed at by M. Robespierre, *Oeuvres complètes* IV (Nancy, 1939), 171 n., but on the unconvincing ground that Lafayette's subsequent behavior belied his patriotic motives.

[38] Lafayette to Jefferson, July 6, Boyd, XV, 249.

[39] Jefferson to Lafayette, July 6, *ibid.,* p. 250.

[40] Lafayette to Jefferson, [July 9], *ibid.,* p. 255, and see above, p. 80 and n. 34.

[41] Boyd, XIV, 438–39, and see above, pp. 14–15. We have here followed the punctuation of the original (LC, Jefferson Papers, Vol. 36, fols. 6250–6251).

ville's house on July 7.[42] The third is the one which Lafayette was soon to present to the National Assembly and, through it, to the world.[43] He and Jefferson were now concerned with the second version.

France had been moving so fast and so far that a project for a declaration of rights which might have seemed highly satisfactory in January seemed much less so in July. In fact, as early as June 19, when Lafayette had informed Mme de Simiane of its existence, he had intimated that he was considering a revision of it. It "or something very close to it," he had predicted, would become "France's catechism."[44] When the first version had been written, the major political controversy centered on the structure and role of a representative chamber in an absolute if patriarchal monarchy, but by July the major issue had become the extent of the limitations to be placed upon the monarch and the nobles in a constitutional regime.

The intellectual background behind Lafayette's proposed declaration of rights was the philosophy of "natural law" and social contract. That philosophy was in the literary tradition and the political atmosphere of the France and the America of his day, and he had encountered it at every turn, particularly through his American experience and associations.[45] The first version of his project for a declaration of rights, as Jefferson had said of it, "contains the essential principles of ours accomodated [sic] as much as could be to the actual state of things here."[46] It was based on two major premises—a sovereign people (one of America's "essential principles") and a strong monarchy ("the actual state of things here"). "All sovereignty," it declared, "resides essentially in the nation." "Nature has made men equal" and given them certain rights.

---

[42] This version is in LC, Jefferson Papers, Vol. 36, fols. 6252–6253. The date July 6, 1789, has been assigned to it in another hand, neither Lafayette's nor Jefferson's. Boyd (XV, 231 n.) places it at the end of June or the beginning of July.

[43] See below, pp. 93–97.

[44] Mémoires, II, 309, and see above, p. 63.

[45] See Louis Gottschalk, Lafayette Comes to America (Chicago: University of Chicago Press, 1935), esp. pp. 136–38; Lafayette Joins the American Army (Chicago: University of Chicago Press, 1937), esp. pp. 328–31; Close, esp. pp. 419–25; and Between, esp. pp. 1–11, 366–78.

[46] Jefferson to Madison, January 12, Boyd, XIV, 437, and see above, p. 14.

Those rights of man were "his property, his liberty, his honor, his life," and "no impairment [of these rights] may be permitted except by laws consented to by him or his representatives, previously published and [to be] applied by legally constituted courts." Nature had also endowed man with speech and thought, and he "may not rightfully be molested either for his opinions or the communication of his ideas unless he has done violence to the social order or individual honor, in which case he is subject to the law." And "since the spread of enlightenment and the development of abuses make necessary from time to time a revision of the constitution," there ought to be provided "at distant though fixed intervals an assembly of deputies whose sole object shall be to restore to the nation all its rights by enabling it to revise its government." This idea of amendment of the constitution by regular periodical conventions was obviously an elaboration upon recent American experience with constitutions, which Lafayette had watched with loyal concern.[47]

Although he was an adopted citizen of several American states, Lafayette was also by birth a subject of the French king. He did not wish to abolish the monarchy of the still beloved Louis XVI, but he did envisage a government of a sovereign people through a monarch with genuine though constitutionally limited authority. He favored a tripartite separation of governmental authority—the legislative power, "exercised principally by a large representative assembly, freely and frequently elected," the executive power, belonging "exclusively to the King, whose person is sacred and whose ministers are responsible," and the judiciary, "vested in tribunals whose only function should be to act as guardians of the law and to apply it literally in the cases submitted to them, and whose structure and administration assure to the judges their independence, to the public their impartiality, to the litigants the means of presenting their case [*justification*] and a ready distribution of justice."

In Lafayette's political philosophy, since the king was to be vested with an exclusive executive authority, it followed that "the

47 See Gottschalk, *Between*, pp. 324, 328–29, 347, 364–68, 377–78, 398–99.

command of the troops belongs to the king alone, their allegiance having no limits other than those needed to guarantee public liberty." Obviously, such a king would be no *fainéant*, yet his power would have marked boundaries. By implication he was placed under the obligation to respect public liberty, the rights of man, and the independence of the legislature and the judiciary, but Lafayette also counted on the power of the purse to restrain the royal urge toward absolutism: "Taxes should be consented to for a short term and be proportionate to actual needs when granted and to actual capacity to pay when distributed"—in short, no taxation by royal decree and no tax-exempt, privileged classes.

Despite these restrictions upon royal prerogative and noble privilege, one concession to the vested interests of France seemed unavoidable in January 1789. No matter how loudly *philosophes* or American political manifestos might proclaim the equality of man, in France, at least, inequalities existed which were not only socially accepted but also legally sanctioned, and at this stage Lafayette did not consider it practical to ask for their elimination. Hence, in the very first sentence, the one which proclaimed that "Nature has made men equal," he went on to concede that social inequalities nevertheless did exist among Frenchmen and might have some justification: "Distinctions among them necessitated by the monarchical form of government are based upon and ought to be measured by [their contribution to] the general utility." Thus, by implication, a hereditary nobility along with other privileged groups was suffered to exist as a practical necessity, and in consequence Lafayette's January document placed not only property but also honor among the "natural rights"; and the equally implied acceptance of an established Catholic Church probably explains why it made no specific mention of religious freedom.

Lafayette's draft of a declaration of rights in January revealed him as a child of the eighteenth-century Enlightenment. He might easily have picked up the ideas expressed in it from a knowledge of English history or of Montesquieu and Rousseau, from the French law courts' remonstrances in recent struggles over arbitrary royal decrees, or from discussions with his friend Condorcet and other *philosophes*, but probably he was more directly under the influence of the American Declaration of Independence, the constitutions of the several American states, and recent conversations with Americans like Washington, Alexander Hamilton, Franklin, Paine, Jefferson, and Morris, all of whom were personal friends.[48] He himself (in words which incidentally reveal how little acquainted he was with the lengthy tradition of natural law before the American Declaration of Independence) subsequently insisted upon this indebtedness: "The era of the American Revolution, which may be regarded as the beginning of a new social order for the whole world, is properly speaking the era of the declaration of rights. . . . Only after the beginning of the American era did the question arise of defining, independently of any preexistent order, the rights that nature had imparted to every man, rights so inherent in his being that society as a whole has no right to deprive him of them."[49]

Although Lafayette's document might have seemed radical in January 1789, it must have seemed fairly moderate by July 1789, when vote by head appeared to have been victorious, when the upper estates seemed divided and defeated in their quest for greater political power, and when the king, though wavering as an ally, might yet prove ready to yield to eloquent defiance. Hence Lafayette had prepared a revised draft of his projected declaration of rights, and presumably Jefferson saw it for the first time at the beginning of July.[50] The new version was somewhat lengthier than that of January despite the perceptibly greater pithiness of its separate parts, and it was considerably less favorable to the monarchical-aristocratic form of government.

The tenor of the changes was revealed in the opening sentences.

[48] See *Mémoires*, II, 303–6, and IV, 198–99. These passages show a knowledge of the English precedent and of Rousseau's doctrine of the "general will" but are critical of them and enthusiastic about the American example. Moreover, they were written after 1797, and that in Vol. IV not before 1827.

[49] "Sur la déclaration des droits," *Mémoires*, II, 303–4.

[50] See above, n. 42. This copy is in the same hand—neither Jefferson's nor Lafayette's—as that of the January draft. It is endorsed by Jefferson, "Fayette. his declt of rights."

Nature now was said to have made men not merely "equal" but "free and equal"; and though distinctions among them were again recognized if "based upon general utility," nothing was said about such distinctions being "necessitated by the monarchical form of government." The second paragraph of the second draft did not merely list the rights of man, it attempted to speak of them with greater precision. While stating that "every man is born with inalienable rights," retaining among them, undefined, "property" and "life," the idea of "liberty" now was spelled out as "the complete disposition of his person, of his labor, of all his talents," and the idea of "honor" now became "concern for his honor" (which did not imply, as the simple word *honor* might, that honor was born in every man and was inalienable from him). In addition, two new rights appeared as native and inalienable—"the pursuit of well-being [*recherche du bien être*]" and (particularly pointed at a time when the court was assembling an army) "resistance to oppression." These new phrases together spelled out a more meaningful measure of economic and political freedom than the word "liberty" alone might have connoted. And whereas the rights of man had in the previous draft been declared limitable by laws properly passed and properly applied, they were now said to have only those limits which assured equal regard for the rights of society as a whole.

After these opening paragraphs the order of the subjects of the second draft diverged from that of the first. Where the earlier draft had gone on to speak of the powers of governments, the new draft continued to speak of the rights of man. The later one mentioned the right of free speech sooner and defined it in more explicit terms: "No man may be disturbed either for his religion, his opinions, or the communication of his thoughts by speech, writing, or print unless he has disturbed the civic peace by slander"; and only in this connection recurred, with some apparently studied changes in wording, the precept about the proper application of law. This time it ran: "No man may be placed in subjection except by laws consented to by him or his representatives, previously promulgated and legally applied." The changes in wording seem intended to take the precept out of the realm of generality and to make it specifically applicable to the exercise of police power.

Then came a statement regarding sovereignty, "the source" of which now was said to be not "essentially" (as before) but "imprescriptibly" in the nation. Consideration of the tripartite division of political authority followed, with greater emphasis upon keeping legislative, executive, and judicial powers "distinct and definite." The new draft sounded more democratic than the first, declaring that "all government has as its exclusive purpose the common welfare, . . . no corporation or individual being permitted to have any authority which does not emanate expressly from the nation." Whereas the first draft stipulated that the legislative power was to be "exercised principally by a large representative assembly, freely and frequently elected," the second again was more precise, requiring it to be "exercised essentially by deputies chosen in all the districts by free, regular, and frequent elections"—thus not "principally" by deputies widely representative of the people but "essentially" by deputies chosen throughout the country as a whole, and chosen regularly as well as freely and frequently. The difference in wording appears to reflect the difference between January's aspirations for a still unrealized Estates General and July's program for a National Assembly already hard at work. The executive authority was still vested in a sacrosanct king, but whereas in the earlier draft his ministers were called "responsible" without stating to whom, now "all his agents individually or collectively are accountable and responsible to the nation for whatever authorization they have received." And whereas the judiciary had been vested earlier with the guardianship of the law (which Montesquieu and the parlements had played up as one of the chief honors of the nobility), now the judicial power was succinctly "limited to the application of the law," which should be "clear, precise and uniform for all citizens" and applied through public procedure with a "ready and impartial distribution of justice."

Finally came a revised statement on taxation and another on constitutional conventions. The first was without essential change, though the word for "taxes" now was *subsides* ("subsidies") in place of *impôt* ("imposts"), implying a *voluntary grant* rather than *levied tribute*. The statement on conventions foresaw the possibility of changes in the constitution not only, as before, because of "the spread of enlightenment and the development of abuses" but also because of "the right of succeeding generations"—all three circumstances being said to necessitate the revision not of political institutions alone but "of every human establishment." Constitutional revisions had been required in the first draft "at fixed though distant intervals," but here the requirement that they be at fixed intervals was omitted; instead, revision was called for by "constitutional means which assure in certain instances an extraordinary convention of representatives whose sole object shall be to examine and, if need be, modify the form of government." Apparently Lafayette was less anxious for regular constitutional conventions in July, when a commendable and lasting constitution for France seemed probable, than he had been in January when it had seemed an overdrawn if widespread objective.

Also revealing the wide gap between the aspirations of the winter and the intentions of the summer of 1789 was the omission from draft no. 2 of two propositions that he laid down in draft no. 1. These were that the courts were the guardians of the law (a point which the hereditary magistracy advocated) and, more conspicuously absent, that the king was exclusive commander of the army, which owed him allegiance in all matters that did not violate public liberty. The latter omission, together with the promulgation of "resistance to oppression" as one of the rights of man, suggests that draft no. 2 was prepared about the first days of July, when the king's mercenaries began threateningly to mobilize around Versailles and Paris.[51]

Perhaps we shall never know how far the changes in the several drafts were influenced by Lafayette's conversations with Jefferson. The direct evidence of that influence is suggestive but not conclusive. No marginal comments appear on draft no. 1, but there are at least two, and in Jefferson's hand, on draft no. 2. The first of them seems to query whether property and honor are correctly enumer-

---

[51] Its earliest possible date must be after June 19, when Lafayette described draft no. 1 to Mme de Simiane. See *Mémoires*, II, 309, and above, p. 63.

ated among the natural and inalienable rights of man.[52] The second one suggests (in English) a change in Lafayette's passage dealing with the tripartite separation of governmental powers. Lafayette's wording was: "Every government has as its exclusive purpose the common welfare; the Legislative, Executive and Judicial powers ought to be distinct and definite." Jefferson advised (apparently for better transition and greater clarity) the insertion, between these two rather disconnected thoughts, of the words: "This [i.e., 'the common welfare'] is best promoted by a division of its powers into Legislative, Judiciary, and Executive."[53] His insertion (perhaps studiedly) varied Lafayette's ordering of the three governmental powers, putting the executive power last, whereas Lafayette had put it second.

One suggestion and one query do not establish that Jefferson's influence on Lafayette was decisive. Yet copies of the drafts under examination were retained by Jefferson and still are among his papers, and if there were any other copies which he returned to Lafayette but which were lost with many other papers of Lafayette during the troubled days that were to follow, conceivably the comments on those copies were less sparse. Much more probably, in their personal conversations they talked about desirable changes in the two drafts. The direct, documentary evidence, in short, permits the assumption (but does not require the conclusion) that Jefferson had a hand in more than one modification in the second draft of Lafayette's proposed declaration of rights.

The indirect, circumstantial evidence fortifies that assumption.

[52] See Boyd, XV, 230–33. Gilbert Chinard in several works—see esp. *The Letters of Lafayette and Jefferson* (Baltimore, 1929), p. 82; *La Déclaration des droits de l'homme et du citoyen et ses antécédents américains* (Washington, 1945), p. 16; and *Thomas Jefferson, the Apostle of Americanism* (Boston, 1929), pp. 232–33—assumes that Jefferson suggested the deletion of *property* and *honor* from the enumeration of natural rights. The assumption is based on two sets of brackets inserted by Jefferson—an opening bracket (followed by no closing bracket) before the words *le droit de propriété* and a complete pair around the words *de son honneur* and by the mark *qu?* (which Professor Boyd informs us was "Jefferson's habitual formula for querying a passage": Boyd to Gottschalk, February 10, 1966) in the margin at this point. It is unclear exactly what words Jefferson meant to include in his query, but he undoubtedly had reservations about property and honor being natural and inalienable rights.

[53] Above *division* Jefferson wrote *separn* (abbreviating *separation*), above *separn* he wrote *distribn* (abbreviating *distribution*), and above *powers* he wrote *magistracy*.

A philosophy which posits that "every man is born with inalienable rights," including "the pursuit of well-being" seems to restate the preamble of the Declaration of Independence ("All men are created equal" and "endowed by their Creator with certain unalienable rights" among which is "the pursuit of happiness"). Lafayette's inclusion of "resistance to oppression" among the natural rights is reminiscent of the Declaration's contention that "a long train of abuses and usurpations . . . under absolute Despotism" makes it a people's "right . . . to throw off such government." That "no man may be disturbed . . . for his religion" was an idea that re-echoed Jefferson's words in the Virginia Act for Establishing Religious Freedom: "No man shall . . . suffer on account of his religious opinions."[54] And the dictum that it is "the right of succeeding generations" to revise a constitution leads to wonder whether Jefferson did not, because of his discussions in July with Lafayette, ponder a question that he raised the next September: "Whether one generation of men has a right to bind another."[55] These principles were, of course, commonplace among some French *philosophes* and were current in the air that Lafayette breathed, and he might have borrowed them not from Jefferson alone (or at all) but from Jefferson's own sources or still others. But then why were they not present in the January version of his declaration of rights, which it seems Jefferson did not see until it was finished, but were present in the version of July, which was submitted for Jefferson's approval?

"Tomorrow" (July 10) passed without Lafayette presenting his "catechism" for the approval of the National Assembly, but he did so the next day. He must have spent some of the intervening time revising the second draft of his proposed declaration of rights, for what finally was presented to his colleagues was a third version. But another matter also claimed his most serious attention that day.

---

[54] See Chinard, *Jefferson*, pp. 103–3, and Boyd, II, 546.

[55] Jefferson to Madison, September 6, Boyd, XV, 392. On the speculations of Jefferson (as well as Mounier and Condorcet) on this question see "The Earth Belongs in Usufruct to the Living," editorial note, *ibid.*, pp. 384–98. For other possible resemblances of Lafayette's words to possible American sources, see Chinard, *Déclaration des droits de l'homme,* pp. 10–11, 35–38. On the other hand, Jefferson found that "a majority [of the National Assembly] cannot be induced to adopt trial by jury": Jefferson to Paine, July 11, Boyd, XV, 269; cf. *ibid.*, pp. 232–33, n. 16.

Since Mirabeau, on July 8, had revealed his interest in Orléans' becoming lieutenant general of the realm, Lafayette had begun to
recognize that some of the seemingly warmest advocates of the
Revolution entertained notions that went "beyond the achievement
of the constitution." To make matters worse, rumors began to circulate of a counterrevolutionary coup; the king's brothers and
some close advisers were said to have drawn up a proscription list,
on which Lafayette's name was prominent. The ministry, he had
heard, had become desperate, and even the Comte de Saint Priest,
minister of state without portfolio, who had hitherto been friendly
to the Patriots, had spoken disapprovingly of him.[56] As the sense
of danger grew, some of the more exposed thought of self-defense.

Lafayette and the Patriots were indeed charting a dangerous
course. Mirabeau seemed to have concluded from the cooperation
of recent days that Lafayette might be ready to go so far as to join
forces with him on behalf of Orléans. On July 10 Mirabeau himself or some other partisans of Orléans (or both)[57] told Lafayette
that he was already considered an enemy of the court and "proscribed" because he was the only known "member of the minority"
who was capable of commanding an army. They proposed that he
and Orléans unite their efforts. As Lafayette described their proposition, "he [Orléans] would be my captain of the guards and I
his." Lafayette was uncertain whether the duke was aware of this
"plan to create confusion" or it was only a scheme of "the people
who push him on,"[58] but in future years he recollected that his
reaction to these "adroit approaches" was that of one interested only
in establishing liberty: "Since we correctly wanted to keep a king,
the actual incumbent seemed better than any other."[59] And so he
replied "coolly" to his interlocutors somewhat as follows: "Orléans

---

[56] Lafayette to [Mme de Simiane?], July 11, *Mémoires*, II, 312 and Rigby to his
family, August 11, [Elizabeth] Eastlake (ed.), *Dr. Rigby's Letters from France, etc., in
1789* (London, 1860) (hereafter cited as Eastlake), pp. 39–40.

[57] That it was probably Mirabeau himself appears from *Mémoires*, II 361.

[58] Lafayette to [Mme de Simiane?], July 11, *ibid.*, p. 313.

[59] *Ibid.*, p. 356. See also *ibid.*, III, 229. Lafayette sometimes gives the impression that
he believed the Orléanists meant to have Orléans succeed to Louis XVI directly and immediately, but their immediate goal seems to have been that he become *de facto* rather
than *de nomine* ruler.

is in my eyes only a private individual, richer than I, whose future is no more important than that of other members of the minority. ... It is useless to form a party if you are on the side of the whole nation. ... We must move ahead without bothering ourselves about consequences and build an edifice or leave the materials behind us."[60]

Mirabeau never raised the subject again with Lafayette,[61] but he made similar advances to Mounier. Shortly afterward Mirabeau and Mounier had a particularly heated discussion, during which Mounier expressed his horror at such treasonable maneuvers. Happening to meet Lafayette and some friends on leaving, he told them of his exchange with Mirabeau and was led to understand that Lafayette was perhaps better informed than he about Mirabeau's intentions.[62]

If Lafayette thought treason was afoot, why didn't he immediately denounce the conspirators? Aside from possible scruples about violating a confidence and the probable conflict between his loyalty to a fellow Patriot and his loyalty to the monarch, he evidently considered the conspiracy as yet too amorphous to take seriously or to prove convincingly. "But," he decided, " I shall for the present keep an eye on M. le Duc d'Orléans, and perhaps I shall be in a position to denounce at the same time M. le Comte d'Artois as a factious aristocrat and M. le Duc d'Orléans as factious in more popular ways. All these trouble-making schemes will be thwarted by the force of circumstances just as surely as the despotic schemes."[63]

Meanwhile, the king delayed replying to the Assembly's request that he withdraw his troops, and a sense of impending disaster spread. In the streets of Versailles the local companies of the French Guard, fraternizing with the people no less openly than their comrades in Paris, fought with royalist troops, and several combatants were hurt. Finally, on July 11 the king replied: the troops were needed to keep order, but if the Assembly was concerned over their

[60] Lafayette to [Mme de Simiane?], July 11, *ibid.*, II, 313.

[61] *Ibid.*, p. 361.

[62] Mounier, *Appel*, pp. 13–14 n.

[63] Lafayette to [Mme de Simiane?], July 11, *Mémoires*, II, 313.

presence, he was willing to go with it to some quieter town. In the debate that followed, Mirabeau voiced the opinion that the answer was unsatisfactory, and the house generally agreed with him. But what to do? Conform, and thereby abandon the seat of popular demand for a new constitution? Or resist, and thereby run the risk of civil defiance, defeat, and proscription?

In these "terrible moments"[64] Lafayette decided to present his declaration of rights.[65] His introductory remarks were "short but animated and expressive," an English observer reported;[66] a French colleague described them as having "the noble simplicity of a hero-philosopher";[67] another said that they had "nobility and vigor";[68] and to still another "it seemed as if we were listening to Wazington [sic] speak to the people on a square in Philadelphia."[69]

His constituents' instructions, Lafayette began, still deprived him of the privilege of voting in the Assembly, but that was all the more reason why he should at least "offer the tribute" of his opinions. The justly appreciated report of the Committee on the Constitution had proposed that the Assembly give its attention first to a declaration of rights. Whether the Assembly offered the nation such a "manifesto of indisputable truths" immediately or only as a preamble to the "great work" of a completed constitution, it should, he declared, give primary consideration to stating the basic principles of any constitution, of any system of laws, no matter how simple and commonplace such principles might be. Such a statement would have two practical purposes: it would serve as a re-

---

[64] Larevellière-Lépeaux, I, 79.

[65] Paine, *Rights of Man*, in Foner, I, 262, says: "It was hastily drawn up," but he apparently knew nothing of the earlier drafts. For Abbé Sabatier's statement that J.-F. Marmontel helped Lafayette to prepare his project (*Journal politique national des États-généraux et de la Révolution de 1789* [Paris? 1790], No. 9, p. 96 n.) we have no corroboration.

[66] Rigby to his family, August 11, Eastlake, p. 39.

[67] *Point de jour*, July 12, p. 170.

[68] *Journal d'Adrien Duquesnoy, député du Tiers états de Bar-le Duc sur l'Assemblée constituante, 3 mai 1789–3 avril 1790*, ed. Robert de Crèvecoeur (Paris, 1894) (hereafter cited as *Journal de Duquesnoy*), I, 189.

[69] D. Ligou (ed.), "Documents sur les premiers mois de la Révolution . . . papiers de Poncet-Delpech," *Annales historiques de la Révolution française* (hereafter cited as *AHRF*), XXXVIII (1966), 446.

minder of "the sentiments which nature has implanted in the hearts of every man," and it would "express those verities from which all institutions should derive," providing "an unerring guide" for the nation's representatives, "constantly sending them back to the source of natural and social right." The universal recognition of these eternal verities was all the more engaging because "for a nation to love freedom, it need only know it," and "for it to be free, it need only wish to be."

A declaration of rights, Lafayette went on, ought to come at the moment that the form of the government had been clearly fixed, as was true of monarchy in France, leaving to future decision such matters as the organization of the legislature and the royal prerogative, though proclaiming in advance the principle of the separation of powers. The value of a declaration of rights lay in its truth and precision; it ought to state what everyone knew, what all the world felt. With that idea alone in mind he had drawn up the outline of a proposal which, "far from asking that it be adopted," he requested the Assembly only to send to its different *bureaux* "in the hope that this first attempt of mine will induce other members to present other projects which will better meet the Assembly's intentions" and which, in that case, "I shall be glad to prefer to my own." A burst of applause interrupted the speaker at this point.[70]

Lafayette then read his proposed "catechism of France." The few who were familiar with either of the two earlier drafts would have recognized that it had again undergone some changes. The distinctions among men, which the last draft had said were "based upon general utility," were now called "distinctions necessary to the social order" (i.e., presumably not necessary in the state of nature) and were to be "based only on the general utility." The "inalienable rights" previously attributed to "every man" at birth had now become "inalienable and imprescriptible rights." Furthermore, their number had grown, and the order of their listing had changed somewhat. The present draft stated: "Every man is born with inalienable and imprescriptible rights. Such are the liberty of all his opinions, concern for his honor and his life, the right of

[70] *Motion de M. de La Fayette sur les droits de l'homme*, pp. 3–5. See also *Point du jour*, July 12, pp. 170–72; *Mémoires*, II, 251–52; and *AP*, VIII, 221–22.

property, the full disposal of his person, of his labor, [and] of all his talents, the communication of his thoughts by all possible means, the pursuit of his well-being, and resistance to oppression." Thus at the head of the list a new phrase, "liberty of all his opinions," had displaced "the right of property," which dropped to third place; and before the list was brought to a close (as previously) by "the pursuit of well-being and resistance to oppression" the right of "communication of his thoughts by all possible means" had been inserted. The five separate phrases enumerating the rights of man in draft no. 2 thus had grown to seven in draft no. 3, the two new ones dealing with the liberty and dissemination of thought. The reason for this new emphasis upon liberty of thought became clear with the next significant change (not counting the mere clarification of wording in the intervening paragraph). That change was the entire omission of the separate paragraph in draft no. 2 on liberty of thought. Even though the central idea in the omitted paragraph was expressed in the two newly enumerated "inalienable and imprescriptible rights," the absence of one specific injunction in the omitted paragraph was especially conspicuous—that on behalf of religious toleration—the omitted paragraph having begun with the words "No man may be disturbed . . . for his religion." Despite Jefferson's preferences, Lafayette, one may well presume, was being careful not to alienate the nobles by excluding property and honor from his list of natural rights or the clergy by explicitly including free thought.

After this striking omission came some changes that were mere differences in wording or order until draft no. 3 took up the division of governmental powers. Draft no. 2 had devoted a paragraph of one sentence each to essential principles guiding the exercise of legislative power by elected deputies and of executive power by the king, as well as of judiciary power, but now in the place of these three paragraphs was inserted a single one (which read somewhat as Jefferson had suggested): "All government has as its exclusive purpose the common welfare. This concern requires that the legislative, executive and judicial powers be distinct and definite and that they be so organized as to assure the free representation of citizens, the responsibility of their agents and the impartiality of their judges." Not only was this statement more general and more succinct than that of draft no. 2, it also studiously avoided mentioning king or elected deputies and specifying their powers.

The final changes occurred in the last paragraph, whose subject was the desirability of periodic re-examination of the constitution. "The spread of enlightenment" now dropped out as one of the possible causes for revision (again to assuage the clergy?), leaving "the development of abuses and the right of succeeding generations." Other words of the paragraph were changed, but only the final ones implied a new train of thought. In draft no. 2 the concluding sentence had stipulated that "there be indicated constitutional means which assure in certain cases an extraordinary convention of representatives whose sole object shall be to examine and if need be, modify the form of government." Possibly with "troublemaking schemes" in mind, Lafayette changed this wording in the final draft to stipulate that "it be possible for the nation to have in certain cases an extraordinary convention of deputies whose sole object shall be to examine and to correct, if necessary, the flaws of the constitution." He apparently now wished to avoid any implication that the fundamental "form of government" of France once fixed by the National Assembly, was subject to modification by specified constitutional means, although correction of "the flaws of the constitution" should be permissible.[71]

Lafayette long afterward said of his declaration of rights that it was his "profession of faith, fruit of my past, pledge of my future" and that it "was at the same time a manifesto and an ultimatum."[72] That the National Assembly, which at that very moment was engaged in asking the court to withdraw its forces, should boldly proclaim the rights of man struck a responsive chord among his colleagues. On the other hand, the dictum that resistance to oppression was one of the inalienable and imprescriptible rights of man must have sounded like a challenge to the supporters of a

[71] This comparison has been made by collation with the draft in the papers of the National Assembly (AN, C 27, 200), which was probably the one read by Lafayette on July 11. It has crossings-out and writings-over which show it to have been a rough draft. What was left differs only in negligible details from the version given in the *Motion de M. de La Fayette sur les droits de l'homme* (see above, n. 14) and in *Mémoires*, II, 252–53. There were many other contemporary versions (without serious variations).

[72] *Mémoires*, III, 227.

court which was planning to dismiss its more popular ministers and resort to arms, if necessary, in order to forestall further defiance.

When Lafayette finished reading his "profession of faith," applause again filled the room.[73] The Comte de Lally-Tollendal went to the tribune to second Lafayette's proposal. It was fitting, he declared, that Lafayette be the first to offer a declaration of rights: "He speaks of liberty as he has defended it." (More applause.) Some such declaration, Lally agreed, ought to guide the work of the Assembly and become the preamble to the constitution, but reflecting the doubt of many of his countrymen where Lafayette had no doubts at all, he wondered whether the American experience provided France with the model Lafayette saw in it. Moreover, the proclamation of a general bill of rights before fixing the relationship of man to citizen, subject to monarch, might become, Lally feared, an invitation to extravagant expectations and possible disorder. Hence he proposed that while Lafayette's manifesto should be considered by the *bureaux*, no declaration of rights be formally adopted until after the rest of the constitution had been completed.[74] This reaction was exactly what Lafayette had expected,[75] and so, without further debate, his "manifesto" went to the *bureaux*.

The public impact was nevertheless enormous. Old journals, new journals, deputies in reports to their constituents and in diaries, and fly-by-night sheets that had sprung up amid the reigning political excitement all mentioned, and some reported at length, the speeches of Lafayette and Lally-Tollendal and quoted the proposed declaration of rights.[76] Lafayette's speech and declaration were widely circulated in Paris the next morning (July 12).[77] The

[73] *Journal de Duquesnoy*, I, 189; C. F. Beaulieu, *Essais historiques sur la Révolution de France* (Paris, 1801), I, 516; J.-S. Bailly, *Mémoires* (Paris, 1821), I, 315; and *AP*, VIII, 222.

[74] *Mémoire de M. le comte de Lally-Tollendal ou lettre à ses commettans* (Paris, 1790), pp. 55–57, and *AP*, VIII, 222–23.

[75] Lafayette to [Mme de Simiane?], July 11, 1789, *Mémoires*, II, 313.

[76] In addition to the references cited above, see, among others, *Courrier de Provence*, No. 19, July 9–24, pp. 415–16; *Journal de Paris*, July 13, p. 875; *Courrier national*, session of July 11, p. 5; *Courrier de Versailles à Paris et de Paris à Versailles*, July 12 and 13, pp. 110–11, 125–26; *Procès-verbal de l'Assemblée nationale*, session of July 11; and *Le Declin du jour, du samedi 11 juillet*, No. 5, pp. 3–4.

[77] See above, n. 76, and *Mémoires*, II, 253–54.

electors of Paris (still meeting although their official task was ended), having listened as their secretary read Lafayette's words, agreed that they should be printed as part of the official minutes.[78] From that day on, the proposed declaration of the rights of man was a subject of discussion in wider precincts than the *bureaux* of the National Assembly.

As Lafayette had asked, other projects were soon presented. Sieyès, Target, Mounier, Rabaut St. Etienne, Mirabeau, Duport, La Rochefoucauld, and the Sixth Bureau as a whole were among those who tried a hand at composing at least parts of a declaration of rights, and the study of these suggestions was to go on until late August. Finally there emerged the Declaration of the Rights of Man and of the Citizen that was to become the preamble of the Constitution of 1791 and to make its way around the world and through the centuries as a token of the aspirations of the French Revolution, as an expression of the "Spirit of 1789." Only parts of the final Declaration were to resemble the project that Lafayette had elaborated in the early half of 1789 and had hopefully and daringly placed before his troubled colleagues on July 11. The accumulating dangers of the ensuing months were to require all his attention and keep him from helping in its further elaboration. Nevertheless, when as a septuagenarian he came to write an account of the early career of the National Assembly, he quoted his third draft in full under the proud heading "First European Declaration of the Rights of Man and of Citizens."[79] By that time, however, he had long recognized that "amidst darkness and storms" a declaration of rights, though it may keep alive "the knowledge of liberty," does not always guarantee its practice.[80] He had not (to adapt his own metaphor) built an edifice, but he had left some usable building materials behind.[81]

[78] J.-S. Bailly and H.-N.-M. Duveyrier (eds.), *Procès-verbal des séances et délibérations de l'Assemblée général des Electeurs de Paris* (Paris, 1790), I, 164–67.

[79] *Mémoires*, II, 252.

[80] Lafayette to Thomas Pinckney, July 4, 1793, Jules Thomas (ed.), *Correspondance inédite de La Fayette (1793–1801)* (Paris, [1903]), p. 207.

[81] For Lafayette's influence upon the Declaration of the Rights of Man and the Citizen of August 1789 see below, pp. 220–26.

The editorial notes in J. P. Boyd's edition of the papers of Jefferson are veritable mines of information on many matters that arise in the text of those papers. If in rare instances we have presumed to depart from his readings on interpretations of the documents, it is only on details and usually only with his cooperation.

Mounier's *Appel* has a long footnote on pages 11–14 which was written largely to correct the testimony in the *Procédure au Châtelet* (I, 19–20) of Bergasse (who Mounier thought had confused a remark of Mirabeau which he had heard on July 7 with one he had not heard but Mounier had told him about) and of Regnier (who [*ibid.*, p. 21] was reporting at second hand what Mounier had told him). Lafayette's quoting (*Mémoires*, II, 361 n.) of Mounier is obviously from memory of the latter's statement in the *Appel*. The account of Mounier is in keeping with the known circumstances and, if taken as the basic testimony, coincides in essentials with the testimony of the others (Bergasse, Regnier, and Lafayette) on Mirabeau's campaign in favor of the Duc d'Orléans. Lafayette's faulty recollection of Mounier's quotation of Mirabeau's remark suggests that Mirabeau wanted to replace Louis XVI on the throne with Orléans, but the other witnesses suggest that he meant Orléans to be only lieutenant general with the dauphin as King Louis XVII. Lafayette himself in 1789 did not consider the maneuvers of the Orléanists anything but serious (*Mémoires*, II, 313), and neither did any of the other witnesses, but in his later recollection of Mirabeau's remark to Mounier (*ibid.*, p. 361 n.) he thought "Mirabeau pouvait s'amuser à lui faire peur." We accept the more immediate evidence of Lafayette and Mounier.

Some doubt has been raised regarding the genuineness of the *Journal de Duquesnoy*, but see F. M. Fling, "The Authorship of the *Journal d'Adrien Duquesnoy*," *American Historical Review* (hereafter cited as *AHR*), VIII (1903), 70–77, which argues convincingly that at least the first forty bulletins were in fact by Duquesnoy, who was a member of the National Assembly.

CHAPTER VI

Paris Captures Its King

O N THE very day that Lafayette presented his declaration of rights (Saturday, July 11) the court precipitated the crisis which the National Assembly had dreaded. The king dismissed Necker and his supporters in the ministry and named conservative or reactionary ministers in their stead, ordering Necker to leave the country at once. The National Assembly did not meet on Sundays, but if the court calculated that the partisans of the Revolution would not rally if the Assembly was not in session, it miscalculated once again. It overlooked the solidarity that had come to Versailles and Paris since the preceding year. Paris now had its press, its meetings (especially in the garden of the Duc d'Orléans' Palais Royal), its leaders, and an embryonic revolutionary government in its Assembly of Electors.

The news of Necker's dismissal and exile reached Paris shortly after noon on July 12, when, for the very reason that it was Sunday, the gardens and squares of Paris were crowded. Soon thousands were milling in protest in the streets, undaunted by the royal cavalry, and blood spotted the garden of the Tuileries Palace. Before nightfall fear of looters and of repression by royal troops led householders and shopkeepers to barricade their doors, and frightened or angry people thronged into the Hôtel de Ville. They surged into the meeting place of the Assembly of Electors, demanding the means of defense from "brigands" on the one hand and royal cohorts on the other.

Faced with the threat of disorder from the homeless and the lawless, of force from the military, and of panic among its people, the unofficial but representative Assembly of Electors took extraordinary measures for the defense of Paris. Thus, in the attempt to dominate the National Assembly and control the Revolution, the court had succeeded in bringing into play a new revolutionary instrument, a popularly supported municipal authority. The Electors ordered the distribution of the arms stored in the city hall and asked the sixty electoral districts of the city to take steps to restore order within their respective precincts. Tumult continued, however.

Summoned the next morning (Monday, July 13) to help reassure the people, the royal city officials agreed to cooperate with the Electors, and the two groups created a Permanent Committee, a joint executive body to remain in session as long as the crisis lasted. One of its first acts was to approve a plan for a voluntary citizens' guard of eight hundred men for each of the city's sixty electoral districts. As agitated Electors and citizens moved around in the Grande Salle of the Hôtel de Ville, they could not help noticing the Houdon bust of Lafayette, the gift of the State of Virginia to the City of Paris,[1] which stood out conspicuously on the mantel, and some were heard to say that they wanted Lafayette to be their military leader.[2]

At Versailles all that morning the National Assembly heatedly debated what its policy should be in the face of the king's dismissal of a ministry which had its confidence. About mid-day harrowing details arrived of unrest and terror in Paris—mobs, fires, threats of attack on soldiers, prison releases, and the seizure of arms. However harrowing such violence might seem, it justified Mirabeau's prediction, endorsed by the Assembly, that the threat of military force might promote rather than prevent revolt. The Assembly decided to send a deputation headed by the Assembly's president, the Archbishop of Vienne, to ask the king again to remove the principal cause of the people's disaffection, the royal troops. If the king consented, the Assembly was prepared to send a committee to Paris to bear the good news and to help quiet the city. Lafayette was designated as a member of that committee.[3]

The Assembly then recessed to await the return of its deputation

---

[1] Gottschalk, *Between*, pp. 250–52.

[2] Bailly and Duveyrier, I, 186; Ch. Duveyrier (ed.), *Histoire des premiers Electeurs de Paris en 1789* (Paris, 1828), p. 14; and Chassin, III, 493, n. 3.

[3] *Journal de Paris*, July 15, pp. 883–84, and Lafayette to [Mme de Simiane], July 13, *Mémoires*, II, 314.

from the Château. In the interval Lafayette sent a message to Mme de Simiane telling her not to worry; the post of deputy of the people was "a safeguard against everyone and at the same time an obligation not to compromise." The Assembly's deputation would ask for measures needed to calm the people, which, he expected, would include the dismissal of the new ministers, the recall of the old ones, the withdrawal of the troops, and the approval of a bourgeois guard in Paris. Also, probably with Mirabeau's recent maneuvers in mind, he speculated on the possibility that the disorders in Paris were the work of a faction: "If the king appreciates the danger to which he has been exposed, if he leaves us free to act, we shall restore complete calm, and even in the event that there be a faction, we shall destroy it. But if the ministers recover from the fear which they have at this moment, if their outrageousness reasserts itself, great misfortune may befall the state."[4]

When the deputation returned from the palace, the Archbishop of Vienne gave a sobering report. The king, it appeared, held that he alone was the judge of what to do in the present crisis, contemplated no change in his plans, and advised the Assembly to attend more earnestly to its own business. The Assembly stood rebuked and uncertain of its next step. To act in defiance of a king who had thousands of troops at his beck and call might expose the members of the Assembly to grave personal danger; not to act would be surrender, after a series of heartening moral victories, to the first determined show of force by the party of reaction.

Uncertainty vanished, however, when for the second time in his career as a deputy Lafayette went to the tribune. Personal safety, even the making of the constitution, he declared, was a less exigent consideration than the danger immediately menacing the nation. The king's advisers—"perifidious councilors" he had called them[5] —must be held responsible for the current pandemonium and for all that might yet happen. That morning he recalled, Clermont-Tonnerre had said, "The constitution will be or we shall no longer be," but now Lafayette was more confident: "The constitution will be even if we shall no longer be."

[4] Lafayette to [Mme de Simiane], July 13 *Mémoires,* II, 314.

[5] This is the phrase used by Lafayette, *ibid.*

Its confidence renewed, the Assembly voted at once and unanimously, not only to hold the ministers responsible for the present emergency and its outcome but also to make all the king's civil and military agents answerable for any acts contrary to the rights of the nation and the decrees of the Assembly. Then it went on to express its confidence in Necker, to ask again for the withdrawal of the troops and the establishment of a citizens' guard, to reassure the states' debtors by repudiating any thought of bankruptcy, to reassert the inviolability of deputies, and to reaffirm its oath to separate only after it had finished the constitution—measures intended to restore public confidence but certain to aggravate the conflict between court and Assembly. It ordered these decrees sent to the king and published.[6]

Rumors of impending arrests had already been spreading alarm among the deputies. During the night, it was said, the king's troops would take possession of the Hôtel des Menus Plaisirs and dissolve the Assembly.[7] Fearing thus to be dispossessed, the deputies determined to remain in uninterrupted session in the hall of the nation's representatives, perhaps the safest place for men who, like Lafayette, had reason to believe themselves proscribed. Moreover, the Assembly was resolved to proceed unremittingly with its work. A continuous session, however, would require that a presiding officer sit continuously in the chair, and since the Archbishop of Vienne, though resolute, was old, he obviously needed a deputy. So, for the only time in its career the National Assembly chose a vice-president. It balloted by *bureaux*, and Lafayette was elected (by 589 votes out of 711).[8] Prolonged applause greeted the announcement of this logical choice of a young, prominent, and daring leader for a post of danger, and he acknowledged the honor with a hastily prepared speech: "Gentlemen, on another occasion I would have reminded you of my inadequacy and the peculiar situation in which I find myself [being still bound by the Riom instructions], but the cir-

[6] Bailly, I, 340; *Mémoires*, II, 254; *Point du jour*, July 14, p. 188; *Courrier de Provence*, July 9–14, pp. 425–26; A.F. Bertrand de Moleville, *Histoire*, I, 314; *Journal de Duquesnoy*, I, 197–98; and Lafayette to [Mme de Simiane], [July 13], *Mémoires*, II, 314–15.

[7] Etienne Dumont, *Souvenirs sur Mirabeau et sur les deux premières assemblées législatives*, ed. J. Benetruy (Paris, 1951), pp. 112–13, and Bailly, I, 342.

[8] *AP*, VIII, 230. Cf. Robespierre, *Le Défenseur de la constitution* (ed. Laurent), p. 171 n.

cumstances are such that my chief sentiment is to accept with enthusiasm the honor which you have done me and under our venerable president to carry out its functions with zeal, as my chief
duty is never to separate myself from your efforts to maintain
peace and confirm public liberty."[9]

As the Assembly applauded, the old president retired, and the
young vice-president took the chair. In a letter written at 9 P.M.
Lafayette claimed that "there is a great deal of unity in the Assembly,"[10] and its firmness bore him out. When he put the question
whether they ought not to adjourn, the great majority insisted that
they must not separate, although formal debate was suspended at
11:30 P.M. Over a hundred deputies remained in the Salle des
Menus Plaisirs all night long, some stretched out on floors and
benches, some sleeping upright in their seats, others pacing the
hall.[11] While reports came in of midnight inquiries at their homes
about the whereabouts of several deputies, other reports, stating
that Paris was quiet and well guarded by its citizen militia, encouraged their vice-president to believe that perhaps the crisis had
passed and the deputies could go home to bed. Nevertheless, after a
sleepless night stretched out on a bench, he wrote to Mme de
Simiane at six in the morning: "There is nothing more singular
than the situation in which we find ourselves. The day will be
interesting. . . . We must maneuver in regard to the ministers and
work without let-up for the public good. . . . The national party and
the ministerial party are going to become quite distinctly separate
now."[12]

At 9 o'clock in the morning of July 14,[13] the National Assembly,

[9] The original draft of the speech (with corrections) in Lafayette's hand is in AN, C 28,
liasse 224. The version in *Mémoires*, II, 254–55 is only slightly different. See also *Journal
de Paris*, July 16, p. 887, and J.-P. Rabaut, *Précis historique de Révolution française, Assemblée constituante* (Paris, 1809), Bk. I, p. x.

[10] Lafayette to [Mme de Simiane], [July 13], *Mémoires*, II, 315.

[11] Bailly and Duveyrier, I, 238–50; Duveyrier, pp. 36–44; Ernest d' Hauterive (ed.),
Journal d'émigration du comte d'Espinchal (Paris, 1912) (hereafter cited as Hauterive),
pp. 12–13; *Gazette de Leide, supplément*, July 28; *AP*, VIII, 230; and Lafayette to [Mme
de Simiane?], July 14, *Mémoires*, II, 316.

[12] *Mémoires*, II, 316.

[13] If Lafayette was present, he took no part in the morning session: see *AP*, VIII,
230–32. Some historians (see Chassin, III, 551 n.) believe that Lafayette was in Paris on

the Archbishop of Vienne once more presiding, resumed its deliberations. It tried to revert to its regular order of business, and in due
course Lafayette's declaration of rights came up again. The debate
centered on the relation of a declaration of rights to the constitution. Should it be a preamble laying down precepts to which the
nascent governmental structure must conform or was it a set of instructions for the newly established regime, to be stated only at the
end of the Assembly's labors? Unable to agree, the Assembly decided merely that the constitution should at some point contain a
declaration of rights, and it proceeded to select a new committee to
draft the constitution. The committee was to have eight members
and eight alternates, and Lafayette was chosen eleventh (third of
the alternates) to sit on this committee.[14] Then came the president's
report on his second interview with the king, which had taken
place only that morning, before the opening of the Assembly. All
that the president had to report was that the king had consented to
examine the Assembly's resolutions of the night before.

The day proved to be more "interesting" than Lafayette could
have anticipated, for Paris erupted. Still frantic from the fear of
"brigands" and military within the city gates and of "aristocrats"
and royal mercenaries without, the inhabitants of the city went
from place to place looking for arms. As the day advanced, disorder
intensified. Only at the forbidding towers of the Bastille did the
self-appointed defenders of the city encounter stiff resistance, and
siege of the ancient fortress, long a hated political prison, began by
mid-afternoon. Crowds swarmed into the Hôtel de Ville, demanding that the forces of the Marquis de La Salle, in command of the

---

July 14. This belief is based on a pass dated July 14 and signed by La Salle and Lafayette.
But this pass, though issued by La Salle on July 14, obviously was countersigned by
Lafayette at some later time. The story of a conspiracy of Lafayette and Bailly with the Duc
d'Orléans on July 14 (Grace D. Elliott, *Journal of My Life during the French Revolution*
[London, 1859], pp. 31–32, and Ernest Daudet [ed.], *Mémoires du Cte Valentin Esterhazy*
[Paris, 1905], p. 222) is unlikely, although Bernard Faÿ, *Louis XVI, ou la fin d'un monde*
(Paris, 1955), pp. 316, 319, believes it. On the other hand, future Jacobins were to claim
that Lafayette had engineered the plot for his own advantage: see Robespierre, *Défenseur
de la constitution* (ed. Laurent), pp. 174–77, and Louis Bigard, *Le comte Réal, ancien
Jacobin* (Versailles, 1937), p. 190. See also n. 61 below.

[14] Bailly, I, 359.

incipient citizen guard, join in the attack and hurling threats at the Permanent Committee when it hesitated to lay siege to the Bastille. The committee hastily dispatched two of its members to Versailles to report the "terrible state" of things to the National Assembly.[15] Before they could arrive at their destination, however, the situation had changed. Some of the French Guards went to the aid of the besiegers of the Bastille with artillery, and its garrison surrendered. Soon the heads of its commander and of the provost of the merchants, chief municipal official of the crumbling old regime of Paris, were being paraded on pikes along streets filled with rejoicing people (since those who were shocked or doubtful prudently remained indoors). Before nightfall the capture of the Bastille had begun to symbolize the triumph of liberty over tyranny. Bells rang, guns boomed, and the bourgeois militia marched in the streets.

News of armed revolt and mounting turmoil reached the National Assembly from 6 o'clock onward—news all the more foreboding because it was already stale and incomplete. For a third time the Assembly decided to send its president at the head of a deputation to convey the latest tidings to the king and to ask once more for the withdrawal of the menacing forces. Lafayette again took the chair in the president's absence, and he urged the Assembly to attend to its regular business calmly and courageously; not only the dignity of the Assembly but also its duty required it not to interrupt its work.[16]

Lafayette was still presiding over the Assembly when two emissaries of the Paris Electors arrived. They urged "the promptest action possible to spare the city of Paris from the horrors of civil war." Lafayette replied—"with noble and touching sorrow"[17]— that the Assembly had worked day and night to prevent "these public misfortunes" and that at that very moment a deputation was engaged in petitioning the king to remove the troops whose presence had precipitated revolt. Before the Assembly could inform

---

[15] Bailly and Duveyrier, I, 342–44.

[16] *AP*, VIII, 233. Cf. *Point du jour*, July 16, pp. 201–3; *Gazette de Leide, supplément*, July 28; and J.-J. Brethé (ed.), *Journal inédit de Jallet, curé de Chérigné, député du clergé de Poitou aux États-généraux de 1789* (Fontenay–Le Comte, 1871), pp. 135–36.

[17] *Mémoire du comte de Lally-Tollendal*, p. 41.

the king of the Electors' request, the Archbishop of Vienne and the deputation returned. The king, they reported, now somewhat more compliant, had given them a written statement, which they proceeded to read. It indicated His Majesty's intention to summon his Paris officials to Versailles and concert measures with them for the restoration of order; he had already ordered his military officers in Paris to "second the zeal of good citizens" by taking command of the bourgeois guard and to withdraw his troops stationed in the Champ de Mars. Did this mean that Louis intended to get control of the citizen guard or that he was beginning to falter? Another deputation this time headed by the Archbishop of Paris, went off to the Château at 10:30 P.M, but it returned in half an hour to report that since Louis, though deeply moved by the suffering of Paris, refused to believe that his troops were its cause, he had nothing to add. The Assembly then decided to send still another deputation in the morning.[18]

Since it was already late, the Archbishop of Vienne once more retired, and Lafayette once more took his place. So it fell upon him, along with Lally-Tollendal as secretary, to sign a written version of the Assembly's answer to the Electors of Paris. Telling of the Assembly's fruitless efforts to get the king to withdraw "the extraordinarily mustered troops," they promised an even more vigorous resumption of those efforts in the morning "until they have achieved the success which it has reason to expect both from the justice of its complaint and from the heart of the king when strange influences do not arrest his action."[19] Lafayette independently warned the departing Electors to beware of putting the king's generals in charge of Paris's citizen guard.[20] And so the Electors departed, to return with small consolation to a city which in their absence had gone much farther toward successful revolt than when they had left it; and the National Assembly "in a state of uncertainty and grief"[21]

---

[18] *AP*, VIII, 233–34; *Gazette de Leide, supplément,* July 28; *Point du jour,* July 16, pp. 201–3; and *Mémoires du marquis de Ferrières,* ed. Berville and Barrière (Paris, 1822), I, 88–91.

[19] *AP*, VIII, 234; *Gazette de Leide, supplément,* July 28; Bailly and Duveyrier, I, 401–5; and Duveyrier, pp. 152–59.

[20] Bailly and Duveyrier, I, 404–5, and Duveyrier, p. 154.

[21] *Point du jour,* July 16, p. 203.

prepared for another all-night vigil, troubled by thoughts of jail and civil carnage.

This time there was to be, however, no restless sleeping on benches. Late at night the electrifying news arrived that the Bastille had fallen to the people—to the defenders of the Assembly's cause —and its commander massacred. What to do now? Send another deputation to notify the king at once? Debate went on until 2 A.M., when the Assembly, deciding to wait until morning, adjourned discussion. The vice-president announced, however, that the Assembly remained in session, ready to resume debate at any instant. But one of the king's gentlemen in the Assembly, La Rochefoucauld's cousin, the Duc de Liancourt, grandmaster of the royal wardrobe, convinced that if only His Majesty realized the truth, he would cease to be hoodwinked by the more reactionary members of his retinue, went of his own accord to see the king. Liancourt persuaded Louis that he had to deal not with a local revolt but with a national revolution and that further resistance would lead only to widening disaster. At last the monarch was persuaded, and he called a meeting of his inner circle, which decided, over the Comte d'Artois' protest, that the king should himself go to the National Assembly and announce the withdrawal of the resented soldiery.[22]

Meanwhile the National Assembly had resumed its session. Its first order of business on the morning of July 15 was to name a new deputation to carry its requests to the king. This time the Assembly decided to put Lafayette at the head of the deputation, instructing him to express directly to His Majesty its "grief and anxiety." But before he and his colleagues could leave, Liancourt announced that His Majesty had decided to come himself to the Assembly. The announcement brought forth a joyous expression of confidence in the king's personal good will whenever he was not misled.[23]

At 11 o'clock the king came, accompanied by his two brothers.

---

[22] Pierre Caron, "La Tentative de contre-révolution de juin-juillet 1789," *Revue d'histoire moderne et contemporaine*, VIII (1906–7), 672. Jallet (in Brethé [ed.], *Journal*, p. 138) says that Lafayette perhaps went with Liancourt, but there is no good reason to think so.

[23] *AP*, VIII, 234; minutes of the National Assembly, AN, C 28, liasse 222; and *Mémoires*, II, 256.

Lafayette's deputation, now converted into a reception committee, met them in the foyer and escorted them into the Salle des Menus Plaisirs. By prearrangement there was no applause. Standing (as was not the royal custom) and addressing his hearers for the first time formally as "the National Assembly," Louis asked for their help in restoring order in Paris. Assuring them of their own personal safety, he announced that he had ordered the removal of troops from the neighborhood of Paris and Versailles, and he asked them to let Paris know of his decision. The deputies then broke their silence with applause. Graciously thanking His Majesty for the removal of the troops, the Archbishop of Vienne renewed his colleagues' entreaty that he reconsider the recent changes in his ministry and that he re-establish "free and direct communication" between king and Assembly. Louis granted the request for direct communication but avoided any commitment regarding his ministry.

A jubilant, triumphant Assembly escorted the king back to the palace, joined on the way by a growing, cheering throng. The demonstration lasted until the king, his queen, and his children showed themselves on the Château balcony. On its return to its meeting place, the Assembly instructed the deputation designated two days earlier now to bear the news of the king's good intentions to Paris and, it was hoped, restore order. By 2 o'clock that afternoon a train of forty carriages carrying scores of deputies started out. As vice-president Lafayette rode in the first carriage.

Throngs greeted the deputies all along the way, the applause growing louder and longer the nearer they drew to the city.[24] New bourgeois guardsmen and old soldiers lined the streets on both sides from the city gate to the Hôtel de Ville as joyful people of all ranks watched and cheered from street and window. At the Place de Louis XV (now Place de la Concorde) the deputies left their carriages and proceeded on foot to the Palace of the Tuileries. There a deputation of the Electors greeted them, and together they

---

[24] *AP*, VIII, 236–37; Bailly, II, 48; *Point du jour*, July 16, pp. 203–12; *Journal de Duquesnoy*, I, 211–12; *Gazette de Leide, supplément*, July 28; and *Mémoires*, II, 255–56. *AP*, VIII, 237, gives the number of deputies who went to Paris as 88, but over 100 are actually listed, *ibid.*, p. 238.

marched to the Hôtel de Ville, Lafayette at their head. In the Place de Grève (now Place de l'Hôtel de Ville), persons of all ranks, from knights of St. Louis and bankers to day-laborers, crowded together to catch a glimpse of the procession, cheering for the "nation" and the "king" and the "constitution" and yelling, "Bring back Necker!" With Lafayette still leading, the deputies went to the Grande Salle, the meeting place of the Assembly of Electors in the Hôtel de Ville. There amid rounds of applause Lafayette, Bailly, the Archbishop of Paris, and other prominent figures among the National Assembly's deputation took seats beside the Permanent Committee's desk, located near the mantel on which stood the Houdon bust of Lafayette.[25]

The presiding officer of the Permanent Committee of the Electors was M.-L.-E. Moreau de Saint-Méry. Bringing the meeting to order, he first called upon Lafayette as leader of the deputation from the National Assembly. Congratulating the Electors and the citizens of Paris on the liberty they had won by their courage, Lafayette solemnly affirmed Louis XVI's surrender: "The king was deceived, but he is so no longer," and now the deputies hoped to take back to His Majesty the assurance of peace and order "which his heart needs." The speaker's every sentence was greeted with applause. Then he read the king's statement to the National Assembly, and when he was done, cries of "Vive le roi!" more hearty than before arose amid those of "Vive la nation!" Other speakers followed. One of them, the Archbishop of Paris, invited all present to join him at the Cathedral of Notre Dame to give praise to the Lord for the happy turn of events. Finally, Moreau de Saint-Méry formally thanked the deputies for their help in making that day the most memorable in the thirteen centuries of France's history.[26]

The deputation prepared to leave, but the meeting did not end there, for an impromptu though not unpremeditated act gave added significance to the day. Though chief of the bourgeois militia, La

---

[25] Bailly and Duveyrier, I, 440–50; Duveyrier, pp. 185–87; *Journal de Duquesnoy*, I, 211–13; Ferrières (ed. Berville and Barrière), I, 97; *Point du jour*, July 16, pp. 203–12; *Gazette de Leide, supplément*, July 28; and Bailly, II, 48.

[26] Bailly and Duveyrier, I, 450–53; *Point du jour*, July 16, p. 210; *Gazette de Leide, supplément*, July 28; La Rochefoucauld, *Mémoires*, III, 19; and *Mémoires*, II, 256.

Salle was not generally known or widely popular, and a demand had arisen in various quarters that Lafayette be named in his stead. A prime mover behind that demand was the writer Brissot de Warville, a friend of Lafayette.[27] Very early that morning (July 15), as the Grande Salle filled with Electors and others bringing in accounts of greater and greater disturbance, they had heard outspoken complaints about La Salle's shortcomings and a corresponding demand for a stronger leader. Moreau de Saint-Méry had himself crystallized that demand by pointing to Lafayette's bust, and his suggestion had found ready and unanimous response among his colleagues. And so, as the National Assembly's deputation now prepared to leave the Grand Salle, someone asked Lafayette if he would take command of the Paris militia. Before Lafayette could reply, an unknown spectator shouted: "Make Lafayette commandant general!" and immediately the audience took up the cry.[28]

Lafayette was taken by surprise.[29] Though some of his well-wishers had carefully prepared the scene, he had not himself pulled any wires, as he was soon accused of having done.[30] Nor did he need to do so. He was obviously the most popular man among those in the revolutionary party qualified to command an army,[31] and he was, by a fairly wide consensus, the logical choice for the post, with or without wire-pulling. None of the other revolutionaries, not even the partisans of Orléans, had any reason yet to feel unhappy about the choice. The cry, "Make Lafayette commandant general!" might have come from any of a number of throats for any of a

[27] Clermont-Tonnerre to Lafayette, July 16, Charles Du Bus, *Stanislas de Clermont-Tonnerre et l'échec de la révolution monarchique (1757–1793)* (Paris, 1931), pp. 107–8. Cf. A. Mathiez, "Brissot électeur de Lafayette," *Annales révolutionnaires*, XIV (1922), 419–22. On Brissot's previous relations with Lafayette, see Gottschalk, *Between*, pp. 247, 370, 384–85, 388, 417. Mounier apparently considered the choice of Lafayette cut and dried. In his report to the National Assembly he said succinctly: "The Marquis de Lafayette was informed that he had been named general of the Paris militia" (*AP*, VIII, 239).

[28] Bailly and Duveyrier, I, 200, 259–61, 281–87, 422, 459–60; Duveyrier, pp. 52–54, 68–72, 170; *Mémoires*, II, 259–61; Lafayette to [Mme de Simiane], July 16, *ibid.*, p. 317; and *Journal de Duquesnoy*, I, 211–14.

[29] *Mémoires*, II, 259.

[30] Daudet, p. 222; Espinchal, "Lafayette jugé," *Revue retrospective*, XX (1894), 297–98; Robespierre, *Défenseur de la constitution* (ed. Laurent), pp. 174–77; and Bigard, p. 190.

[31] See above, p. 91. Cf. Eugene Welvert (ed.), *Mémoires de Théodore de Lameth* (Paris, 1913), p. 111; Bouillé, *Souvenirs et fragments*, I, 138 n.; and Rabaut, p. 190.

number of different reasons. Whoever voiced it, it quickly became so insistent that when Lafayette rose to speak, cheers drowned out his words. To show his readiness to do the bidding of the sovereign people, he drew his sword, raised it high, and then lowered it in a salute they all understood:[32] he surrendered to their will. Now also a civil head for the revolutionary government of Paris seemed needed, and a new clamor arose. This time it was to choose Bailly "mayor of Paris" (a new title with a more popular connotation than "prevost of the merchants"), and again the candidate graciously bowed to the wishes of the sovereign people.

The selection of two of its members for top municipal posts put additional responsibility upon the National Assembly's delegation. Obviously it was desirable that some of the more popular deputies should stay behind to lend their prestige to the restoration of order in Paris while the rest returned to Versailles to report on what had been done. Lafayette and the other deputies asked that the Electors designate some of their number to accompany the returning deputies and some others to confer with those who would stay behind; thus deputies and Electors would join forces to bring stability to the recent municipal innovations. The Electors appointed the two groups, and nine deputies decided to stay in Paris—Bailly and Lafayette in the dual capacity of national deputy and local official and the seven others (Latour-Maubourg, Clermont-Tonnerre, Target, La Rochefoucauld, and Duport among them)[33] as—to use a phrase which was later to become common—"deputies on mission."

At length the meeting at the Hôtel de Ville broke up to go to the Cathedral of Notre Dame, as the archbishop had suggested. When Lafayette emerged from the Hôtel de Ville, hundreds of men crowded around him, pressed his hand, and embraced him, and amiably smiling and thanking them, he embraced them in return. Slowly he made his way through the crowd which again and again broke into shouts of "Vive Lafayette!" He got to the cathedral

[32] Bailly and Duveyrier, I, 459–60; *Journal de Duquesnoy*, I, 213–14; Jacques Godechot (ed.), "Mémoires d'Etienne-Louis-Hector Dejoly, dernier garde des sceaux de Louis XVI," *AHRF*, XVIII, (1946), 307; *Gazette de Leide, supplément*, July 28; and *Journal de Paris*, July 16, pp. 889–90.

[33] Bailly and Duveyrier, I, 461–62, and II, 3; Duveyrier, pp. 198; and *Point du jour*, July 16, p. 212.

only when the *Te Deum* was nearly over.[34] The sacred precincts prompted the suggestion that Lafayette should then and there take his oath of office, once the services were over. To the members of the Permanent Committee of the Electors who asked him to do so, he replied that he was ready but could accept only provisionally, for as a member of the National Assembly he must have its approval. The committee being satisfied with this reply, Lafayette took his oath of office in the Cathedral of Notre Dame, swearing to "defend with his life the precious liberty entrusted to his care."[35]

As arranged, after the *Te Deum* a special committee of Electors and deputies met at the Archevêché (the archbishop's palace), next to the cathedral. Its immediate problem was to give some semblance of regularity to Lafayette's appointment as commander-in-chief of the Paris guard. This precaution was not merely a matter of legal scruple; it was also simple foresight against the time when, in an emergency, the commander's authority might be questioned because of his having been selected merely by unauthorized Electors and popular acclamation without approval of either king or National Assembly.

The special committee's first step was to decide the status of La Salle. Until then he had been in command of the guard and had not yet either formally resigned or been dismissed. Although suddenly and unceremoniously superseded, he quickly removed embarrassment by modestly announcing his pleasure in transferring his command to "hands as pure" as Lafayette's and by accepting service as second in command.[36] Lafayette's relationship to the National Assembly was not so quickly arranged because of the distance between Paris and Versailles. The functions of a man who was at the same time a deputy, an officer of the National Assembly, a major general in the king's service, and commander of the nascent citizens' army obviously required some clarification. The Electors at the Archevêché agreed that sanction of his new responsibility by a duly constituted authority was desirable, but they did not want

---

[34] Bailly and Duveyrier, I, 461–62, and II, 3, and Duveyrier, pp. 197–98.

[35] *Journal de Duquesnoy*, I, 214, and Duveyrier, p. 196.

[36] Bailly and Duveyrier, I, 462, and II, 17–18.

him to return to Versailles to get it; in their estimation the welfare of Paris demanded that he should not be absent for a minute.[37] He therefore left it to the returning deputies to explain his absence to the Assembly and to indicate that he awaited its orders before definitely accepting the municipal office with which his fellow citizens had honored him.[38] The meeting broke up about an hour before midnight.

While most of the National Assembly's deputation prepared to return to Versailles, Lafayette, Latour-Maubourg, and a few others went with La Salle and some Electors to the Hôtel de Ville. They found Bailly and other Electors already engaged in the Grande Salle on the numerous unsolved problems of city administration. This group had set aside military and police matters for Lafayette to handle. Also the decision of what to do about the Bastille seemed to fall within his jurisdiction. Only seven prisoners had so far been "rescued" from the Bastille, and as that prison was supposed to contain miserable dungeons packed with horror, the suspicion grew that other prisoners were still immured in secret, unopened cells. Lafayette and his fellow deputies went into a smaller conference room to discuss this matter with the Permanent Committee. They decided to have a systematic search of the old fortress made immediately and sent out instructions to that effect. It was now nearly 2 A.M. So, postponing other matters and giving a few orders to the guards, Lafayette left, promising to return at seven.[39] He had had little sleep since July 13, almost three days previous, and less than five hours was the most he dared to look for now.

July 15 had turned out to be a day of glory for Lafayette. A friendly observer, referring to him as "the conqueror of the Bastille" (although he had been miles away when the Bastille surrendered), noted how everyone sought to contribute to his glory. "Never," the observer added, "have I seen a man more embarrassed by his triumph."[40]

---

[37] Lafayette to [Mme de Simiane], July 16, *Mémoires*, II, 317.

[38] *AP*, VIII, 238.

[39] Bailly and Duveyrier, I, 466, 473-75.

[40] [Louis-Antoine de Carracioli], *La capitale délivrée par elle-même* [Paris, 1789], p. 11.

Despite his good intentions, Lafayette reached the Hôtel de Ville again only around 9 A.M. on the sixteenth. He had started out in time to keep his 7 o'clock appointment, but on the way he encountered an immense crowd, and when he asked what was the matter, he was told: "Nothing, only an abbé they are going to hang." Moving to the center of the mob he found a few armed men trying to save a monk from lynching. The mob's leaders said their prey was a traitor named Roy, but he stoutly maintained that he was a patriot named Cordier. Lafayette was able, perhaps by a ruse,[41] to persuade the angry people to have their captive's case examined inside the Hôtel de Ville.

Before he could enter the city hall, however, Lafayette and La Salle, who had joined him, were obliged to give their attention to another threat of lynching. Led by a young lawyer named Georges-Jacques Danton, who had assumed the rank of captain in the bourgeois guard of the District of the Cordeliers, some zealous fusiliers had brought up in a fiacre a prisoner whom they accused of being "the second governor of the Bastille." Like the recently assassinated first governor, they explained, he had refused to let the people enter the prison gates, and they proposed to treat him like the first. It proved true that their victim was the new governor of the Bastille. La Salle recognized him as an Elector named Soulès whom the revolutionary city authorities had put in charge of the fortress on the night of its capture, and if he had refused to let the people in, he was doing only what he considered to be his duty. At stake in this episode was not merely a life endangered by a false accusation but also the readiness of the new city government to stand up for its agents. Lafayette walked up to Soulès, took him by the hand, and informing the crowd in the square who their prospective victim was, declared that if the authority of the city's government was not respected, he must himself resign. Soulès was saved, and La Salle returned his sword

---

[41] *Mémoires*, II, 264, n. 1, says that by chance his nine-year-old son, George Washington Lafayette, came up at that time in the company of his tutor, and Lafayette introduced him with studied formality to the crowd, who were so pleased that they momentarily forgot Cordier, whom Lafayette's aides were thereupon able to spirit away. But neither the account of the episode to the Electors (Bailly and Duveyrier, II, 45–48) nor Cordier's *Exposé*, quoted in Chassin, III, 132–33, mentions the child.

to him on the steps of the Hôtel de Ville, but the episode could hardly have endeared the commandant general to Captain Danton.

Shortly afterward inside the Hôtel de Ville the other prospective victim was exonerated. The Electors identified the suspect monk as indeed what he had said he was—a patriot named Cordier. The very people who had just sought to stretch his neck now were eager to embrace him, and Lafayette, giving him a certificate testifying to his good citizenship, sent him home with an armed escort.[42] Lafayette or his aides had to intervene several other times that day to rescue perhaps not always innocent men and women.[43]

These near-lynchings were only the beginning, for the calm brought by the visit of the Assembly's delegates on the previous afternoon quickly vanished. Agitated crowds were setting themselves up as judges, juries, and executioners, overwhelming, when not abetted by, recently enrolled militiamen. Wearing in their hats the red and blue cockade (the improvised insignia of the bourgeois guard in the colors of the city of Paris), groups of the new militia roamed about, apparently at will, wherever their officers or the promise of action led them. Obviously some semblance of systematic direction and responsibility had to be brought into this energetic and allegedly patriotic activity. When the deputies who had chosen to remain in Paris arrived at the Hôtel de Ville, they joined Lafayette and the Permanent Committee in the Governor's Room, and together they took steps to bring the populace under control. They decided that each district's company of militia would have its own staff, which would be charged with policing a specified area but would be directly responsible to the city hall. They also drew up a set of regulations designed to hold the vagrant and the homeless in check, restore normal business and order, and keep traffic moving freely. Copies of these regula-

[42] Bailly and Duveyrier, II, 45–48, 147–48. On Danton's association with the Soulès episode see Chassin, III, 581, n. 1 and Alphonse Aulard, "Danton au District des Cordeliers et à la Commune de Paris," *Révolution française, XXIV* (1893), 116.

[43] *Mémoires,* II, 264–65 and nn., and Lafayette to [Mme de Simiane], July 16, *ibid.,* p. 317.

tions were sent to the district authorities, and the next day they were posted in all the streets.[44]

The joint committee of deputies and Electors now turned its attention to the Bastille, which was a continuous source of alarm and conflict. The Assembly of Electors had earlier that morning voted in favor of solving that problem by razing the old prison. The deputies of the National Assembly at first concurred, but then their authority was questioned, and it was agreed that they did not have the right to issue orders inside the city. As both a deputy and a city official Lafayette presented a special case, but it was argued that as commander of the bourgeois guard he had only military authority, and everyone present agreed on the principle that the military should be subordinate to the civil branch of government. In fact, the minutes expressly recorded that Lafayette was "subordinate to the civil power." And so he could not authorize the razing of the Bastille. Finally, the Permanent Committee alone did so but assigned him the duty of carrying out its purpose. Electors were sent with trumpeters to all corners of the city to proclaim in Lafayette's name that the work of demolition would begin at once, and he then signed an order instructing the stonemason Pierre-François Palloy to begin tearing the building down.[45]

A wordy discussion about who might sign an order for the demolition of an ancient fortress was the sort of debate that might be expected in a situation where a revolutionary body sought to proceed in as traditionally legal a fashion as possible. Nevertheless, the outcome did violence to an old tradition and helped to create a new one. Even as the demolition of the Bastille, carefully contracted with a professional housewrecker, betokened the end of generations of French absolutism, Lafayette's and his colleagues' scruples set a precedent for the subordination of the new military to the new civil power.

[44] Bailly and Duveyrier, II, 3; *Recueil des arrêtés, délibérations et autres actes divers émanés tant des comités de l'Hôtel de Ville de Paris que de l'Assemblée des Electeurs depuis le lundi 13 juillet 1789* [Paris, 1789], pp. 26–28.

[45] Bibliothèque de la Ville de Paris (hereafter cited as BVP), FG, Ms. 38, fols. 81–92, and Bailly and Duveyrier, II, 5–6.

The joint committee then took up other urgent matters. To handle the ever present problem of food shortage in the city, it set up a Committee on Subsistence with authority to call on the commander of the bourgeois militia for convoys of food shipments if necessary.[46] To amplify the regulations hurriedly drafted for the Paris Guard on July 13, Lafayette suggested that representatives of the districts of Paris be asked to cooperate with him. Consequently, the Permanent Committee agreed to recommend to the Electors that each district immediately send one representative to a body that should help him work out further details of the militia's organization, pay, and discipline, and he was authorized to send a circular to the sixty district assemblies asking them to cooperate accordingly.[47] Feeling their duty done, the deputies from Versailles then took leave of the Permanent Committee. Lafayette accompanied them to the Grande Salle, where they expressed to the Assembly of the Electors their satisfaction with the steps which the joint committee had taken to restore tranquility, and the Electors in their turn expressed their appreciation of what the deputies had done.[48]

When his colleagues of the National Assembly were gone, Lafayette returned to the Governor's Room. The hostile attitude of the commander of the royal troops stationed in the suburb of St. Denis, the interference of the crowd with the housewreckers already at work on the Bastille, and the need of a convoy for flour coming into the city occupied some of his time, but it went chiefly to hearing accusations against persons (mostly military officers and noblemen) brought in by his militia. Two officers of the king's army were arrested as suspect characters by a district patrol, but Lafayette released them on their parole. A Comte de Saint-Marc was arrested while loitering around the Bastille, and Lafayette, although he considered the accused's motives patriotic and exonerated him, detained him in the Hôtel de Ville to protect

[46] Bailly and Duveyrier, II, 6–9, 56.

[47] *Ibid.*, I, 466, and II, 9–10; Bailly, II, 51; *Procès-verbal de la formation et des opérations du Comité militaire de la ville de Paris* (hereafter cited as *Procès-verbal du Comité militaire*) (Paris, 1790), Part I, pp. 1–4; and *Journal de Paris*, July 21, pp. 905–6.

[48] Bailly and Duveyrier, II, 28.

him from other suspicious patrols. The Comte de Boisgelin, a Breton nobleman who had a reputation for opposing the popular cause, was haled before Lafayette as an enemy of the country but made good his exit while attention was fixed upon a hapless officer of the bourgeois militia who had been dragged in. This was M. de La Barthe, whom angry accusers charged with promising to pay for the arrest of aristocrats and then failing to keep his promise. His dishonorable behavior had led to his arrest in the Palais Royal and had induced Lafayette to have him brought to the Hôtel de Ville for examination by the Permanent Committee.[49] Lafayette, unlike the man's furious captors, thought the promise a worse offense than the failure to keep it and required the culprit to resign.[50]

All these acts were the work of a man chosen to a previously nonexistent office by popular acclaim in a moment of revolutionary fervor. They were legally backed only by the authority of an Assembly of Electors that owed its own existence to decrees for another purpose by a king whose intentions were neither unambiguous nor dependable. Nevertheless, there was now room for hope that the king would be either amenable or powerless. He had formally sanctioned the National Assembly, and if the National Assembly in turn sanctioned the acts of the revolutionary government of Paris, that was all the sanction it wanted and perhaps all it needed.

By that time the National Assembly had enthusiastically received the reports of several of the deputies who had returned from Paris. The restoration of order and Lafayette's deference in asking for the Assembly's approval of his new post were greeted with applause. Mounier in a particularly laudatory speech described Lafayette in words that in various versions were soon to become

---

[49] *Testament de mort de l'ancien commandant de la milice parisienne ou lettre de M. Bertrand, citoyen de Paris . . . du 20 septembre 1789* [Paris, 1789], p. 2–3; *Mémoires*, II, 259; and *La circulaire des districts; dénonciation forcée des apôtres du despotisme . . .* [Paris, 1789], p. 22.

[50] For the story of these rescues see Bailly and Duveyrier, II, 56–60, 69, 71–74; *Journal de Paris*, August 10, p. 1002; Chassin, III, 559–68; *Le Grenadier patriote, ou le despotisme détruit en France . . .* (Paris, [1789]), pp. 36–37; Alexandre Tuetey, *Répertoire général des sources manuscrites de l'histoire de Paris pendant la Révolution française* (Paris, 1890–1914), I, 49, No. 464, and 348, No. 3137.

common—"a hero whose name is dear to liberty in the two worlds."[51] The Assembly, tactfully avoiding brave new titles like "commandant general" and "mayor," decided to ask Louis XVI to accept Lafayette as "colonel-general" of the militia of Paris and Bailly as "prevost of the merchants." Other welcome bulletins told the Assembly that two of the king's recently appointed ministers had resigned and that precise orders had gone to the royal troops to retire from the neighborhood of Paris and Versailles within two days. As secretary of the National Assembly Clermont-Tonnerre sent Lafayette a letter telling him about these concessions.[52] Being addressed to Lafayette or, if he were absent, to "the Permanent Committee of the Hôtel de Ville," this letter was tantamount to recognition by the National Assembly of the capital's new regime. When Lafayette reported these developments to the Assembly of the Electors, they ordered the news to be published in order to assure the people once more of the king's good will.[53]

Certain now of royal sanction, the Assembly of Electors was ready to take another step to establish control of the turbulent city. Since the outbreak of revolutionary disorder on the thirteenth, royal soldiers, singly or in groups, and private, semi-military units had been clamoring to enter the new militia. The Electors now empowered Lafayette to administer an oath by which such volunteers would become part of the Paris militia without thereby being relieved of their allegiance to the king. The formula was "to be faithful to the nation, the king, and the commune of Paris." As if to emphasize that popular sovereignty was replacing royal sovereignty, "nation," which, as Lafayette used the word, meant the whole people of France regardless of status, was carefully placed first. Although "king" took priority over "commune of Paris" the reference to the new government of Paris as the commune—"the commonwealth"—emphasized its new autonomy and its derivation from popular sovereignty.

[51] *AP*, VIII, 239.

[52] *Journal de Paris*, July 18, p. 895; *Courrier de Versailles à Paris*, July 17, pp. 165–71; *Point du jour*, July 17, pp. 214, 216–17; Du Bus, pp. 107–8; Bailly and Duveyrier, II, 44–45; *AP*, VIII, 244; and Tuetey, I, 64, No. 627.

[53] Bailly and Duveyrier, II, 44–45.

If Lafayette was not the author of this formula, it certainly was one of which he could readily approve. In the presence of the Assembly of Electors, he administered the new oath of allegiance to the deputies of several military groups that had thronged to the Hôtel de Ville seeking to enter the new service. They came from the French Guards, the Swiss Guards, the Mounted Night Watch (Guet à Cheval), the Gendarmerie, the Marshalcy of the Île de France, and other royal units stationed in and around the city and from paramilitary units such as the Basoche (guild of law clerks) of the Palais de Justice and of the Châtelet and as the Company of the Arquebus.[54]

Every such oath administered to a royal army or police unit meant not only added strength for the new citizen militia but further crumbling of the military and the police of the old regime. With the adherence of professional soldiers who in some instances were not even regular residents of Paris the "bourgeois guard" had ceased to be strictly a voluntary militia of Paris citizens. Moreover, the French Guards, already distinguished by their display of patriotic fervor, had to be brought under some new discipline, having repudiated the old, if they were to be defenders of order rather than disseminators of disorder. More important still, the other cities of the realm were likely to follow the example of Paris and, upon establishing communes, to confide their internal defense to a corps of armed citizens.

With these considerations in mind Lafayette now asked the Assembly of Electors for formal approval of the measures already taken to bring system and discipline into the organization of the Paris bourgeois guard. As had several of his hearers before him,[55] he envisaged a nationwide organization of disciplined and armed citizens ever ready both to defend the rights of the people and to maintain order wherever right or order might be threatened. The general title which appealed to him as most suitable for these citizen soldiers, "armed for the defense of the national constitution," was "the National Guard"—the guard of all the people of France without distinction. Each separate commune then would

---

[54] *Ibid.*, pp. 48–49, and Bailly, II, 48.

[55] Bailly and Duveyrier, I, 107, 130–74, 195–200; Bailly, II, 50; and *Mémoires*, II, 257–58, and IV, 93.

merely have to add its name to the general title in order to designate its part of the whole; for Paris, the full name would be "the National Guard of Paris." Such a Paris National Guard would be "legal and possible," he submitted, only if the details of its organization were elaborated in concert with him by a committee of all the districts representing "the general will of the commune." The Assembly of Electors after a brief deliberation accepted the proposed title and committee.[56]

This decision marked another step forward to revolution. It had taken the Estates General from May 5 to June 17 to call itself the National Assembly, and that name had won a grudging royal sanction only on July 15. The "bourgeois militia" had come into existence without royal sanction. It had now received the name not of *royal* or *bourgeois* but of *national*—and that within three days of its birth. And the word *national*, in addition to connoting the geographical solidarity of the people of France and their common stake in their country's welfare regardless of estate or status, had by this time come also to imply a loyalty higher than that owed to a king, a loyalty of which the king was only a part and a symbol. Of this step toward revolution subordinating king to nation Lafayette, though not alone, was the most conspicuous leader. Even among those hitherto generally sympathetic some were soon to think that he was going too far,[57] while others regretted that he did not go far enough.[58]

The good news from Versailles and the obvious efforts of the new city authorities to restrain popular emotions had the desired effect. The Comte de Montlosier, on his way from Versailles to Riom to get new instructions from his bailiwick (an errand which Lafayette had just recently thought he too might run), had occasion to notice the temper of Paris. Feeling it wise to have a passport signed by the new military authority, he called upon Lafayette at

[56] Bailly and Duveyrier, II, 49–51, and *Mémoires*, II, 263–64.

[57] See Jacques Necker, *Oeuvres complètes*, ed. Baron de Staël (Paris, 1821), IV, 23, and J.-J. Mounier, *Recherches sur les causes qui ont empeché les françois de devenir libres . . .* (Geneva, 1792), II, 31–32.

[58] Robespierre, *Défenseur de la constitution* (ed. Laurent), p. 176; Gerard de Rarecourt, *Adresse aux soixante districts de Paris, sur la necessité d'exclure les gentilshommes du corps de la milice bourgeoise* [Paris, 1789]; and Bigard, p. 190. See also *Mémoires*, II, 272.

the Hôtel de Ville. Lafayette granted the passport readily and on his side asked his visitor to represent to their constituents his desire to have his own mandate changed. The passport obtained, Montlosier walked down the stairs arm in arm with his cordial host. As they passed the door of the Hôtel de Ville, they found the Place de Grève filled with militiamen, noisy, disorderly, and off guard. At the sight of Lafayette, they scurried back to their posts and saluted. "They give me honors rather than obedience," Lafayette remarked. "I may seem to be their chief but I am far from being their master."[59]

Still, the new chief took a justifiable pride in his control of this extraordinary force. "The people," he wrote to Mme de Simiane, "in the delirium of its enthusiasm can be mollified only be me. . . . A word from me disperses them." But he was too realistic to think that his power would last if they became doubtful of the king's good will: "This drunk and furious people will not listen to me always."[60] Meanwhile, they respected only the papers that Lafayette signed, and he signed and countersigned a number that day— several of them confirmations of passports, receipts, orders, and commissions previously issued by La Salle.[61]

As the day (July 16) wore on, the tension inside Paris once more became forboding. The crowd around the city hall, which earlier had numbered, according to Lafayette's estimate, 40,000 and had dispersed at his request, had grown to 80,000 by the same estimate (probably exaggerated) toward the end of the day.[62] The thousands milling in the Place de Grève were beginning to murmur: We are deceived again. Why don't the troops in and around Paris actually withdraw? Ought not the king himself to come to Paris? Lafayette wondered whether he should not personally go to Versailles to ask for the troops' withdrawal, but he did not dare to leave Paris: "If I leave for more than four hours, we are lost." When he described to his trusted friend this trying dilemma, he suspected that not all the popular agitation was genuine and spontaneous:

[59] Montlosier, I, 213–17.

[60] Lafayette to [Mme de Simiane], July 16, *Mémoires*, II, 317.

[61] *Ibid.*; Archives de la Seine (Paris), D4 AZ, No. 812, p. 5; and see above, n. 13.

[62] Lafayette to [Mme de Simiane], July 16, *Mémoires*, II, 317.

"I reign . . . over a people driven to fury by abominable cabals. On the other hand, they have been subjected to a thousand infamies of which they have reason to complain. Right now they are setting up a terrible outcry. If I put in an appearance they will quiet down, but others will come up."[63] Along with other city officials he remained on the alert. About eleven o'clock at night some of the Assembly of Electors went home, but Moreau de Saint-Méry and other Electors, along with Lafayette and the Permanent Committee, stayed all night, ready for emergencies.[64]

Another day of crisis was averted by the king's willingness to make further concessions. As a member of the National Assembly's deputation to Paris and as one having access to the royal chambers, La Rochefoucauld had told Louis XVI of the election of Bailly and Lafayette,[65] and His Majesty had decided to recall Necker, go personally to Paris, and make his peace with his disaffected subjects. Several persons and eventually the National Assembly heard of these courageous decisions that evening in Versailles, and Lafayette learned of them in the early hours of July 17. Probably a more complete statement of the king's intentions reached him by personal letter sent with the king's knowledge by La Rochefoucauld.[66] Apparently this private advice came about the same time that official word was received—1 A.M. on July 17.[67]

Lafayette had so far overlooked his obligation as a court noble and a general to keep his king informed of his movements, but he now saw fit to make amends. He sent off a letter to Louis, explaining that things had happened with such urgency and unexpectedness as to leave no time "to bring to His Majesty's feet the explanation of all that I have seen, thought, and considered necessary to risk." Even now that the king was expected "in the capital," the pressure upon him in (as Lafayette put it) His Majesty's service permitted him time only to express his regret at being unable

[63] *Ibid.* See also Bailly and Duveyrier, II, 52.

[64] Bailly and Duveyrier, II, 75.

[65] *Mémoires,* II, 262.

[66] See Lafayette to Louis XVI, [July 17], Jean-L.-G. Soulavie, *Mémoires historiques et politiques du règne de Louis XVI* (Paris, 1801), VI, 385–86.

[67] Bailly and Duveyrier, II, 77–78.

to present his report in person. "What the Duc de la Rochefou-
cald [*sic*] writes me, Sire, seems to me to be an order not to leave
this city or a permit to await Your Majesty here." He described his
situation as one "which astonishes me more than anyone [else] in
the world, to which I would owe an inexpressible happiness if
Your Majesty deigns to read my heart and finds there the sentiments of gratitude and devotion that are eternally engraved
thereon."[68] The tone of this letter was perhaps more deferential
than even eighteenth-century protocol required, but the situation
called for more than tact alone; it called also for a becoming
generosity, since an absolute king was about to swallow his pride
in the presence of his rebellious subjects, of whom Lafayette was
an acclaimed leader. Even in this letter, however, Lafayette spoke
of his zeal as due to "my country and my king"—a precedence
that must have sounded somewhat novel to His Majesty. Another
act that demonstrated an unusual degree of thoughtfulness for so
tired and harassed a man as Lafayette must have been at that moment was his sending a courier to Necker's daughter, Mme de
Staël, to inform her of her father's recall.[69]

The king decided that it would be inappropriate for his bodyguard and escort from Versailles to accompany him inside the
Paris city limits.[70] This gesture of respect for the city's autonomy
placed an added responsibility upon the new citizens' guard.
Besides preserving order in a hungry and resentful city, it now had
to provide for a potential target of that resentment an escort splen-
did enough to give the occasion the dignity it deserved and strong
enough to guarantee the monarch's safety. Lafayette passed another night without much sleep. He assigned posts to the companies under his command and sent aides to each district with
orders for its patrol. He would himself meet the king at Point
du Jour, just outside of Paris, with his staff and a few hundred
selected men. La Salle with three hundred well-equipped guards

[68] Soulavie, VI, 385–86.

[69] [Baillard?] Huber to William Eden, [July 17], *Journals and correspondence of
William Lord Auckland* (London, 1861–62) (hereafter cited as Auckland), II, 336–37.

[70] Bailly and Duveyrier, II, 82. That it was Lafayette who required the bodyguard to
halt at the city barrier (unknown to Comte de Raincourt, July 24, R. Garmy, "Glanes,"
AHRF, XXVI [1954], 171–73) seems an aristocratic imputation.

would escort Mayor Bailly and the other city officials to the Place de la Conférence, where they would receive the king.[71] Things soon began to click in a fashion that was to win the reluctant praise of some who had come to scoff at the citizen soldiery and was to bring a proud satisfaction to its admirers.[72]

The king did not reach Point du Jour until about 3 P.M., but preparations to receive him had been going on for ten or twelve hours. Lafayette, with nine of his aides (of whom La Colombe and Jean Baptiste de Gouvion had served with him in America) and a detachment of mounted guards, reached Point du Jour that morning. The commander was dressed in the ordinary attire of a French bourgeois except for a sword and a red and blue cockade in a panached hat.[73]

Though the king's personal appearance was "simple if not humble," his arrival was not without the traditional regal pomp. He rode with four of his gentlemen in a large, plain coach drawn by eight horses,[74] escorted by a picket of his bodyguard, a detachment of the Versailles militia, and numerous carriages bringing a hundred deputies appointed by the National Assembly to accompany him. About three hundred other deputies had of their own accord come in ahead of them.[75] Taking care to reassure His Majesty in "a few respectful words,"[76] Lafayette took over. The procession started from Point de Jour with some mounted men leading the way, Lafayette riding behind them with naked sword in hand, followed by the king's coach, flanked by two rows of

[71] Bailly and Duveyrier, II, 78–81.

[72] *Gazette de Leide*, July 24 and 28; Mège, *Gaultier*, II, 183 n.; Mazzei, *Memorie*, II, 32–33; Espinchal, "Lafayette jugé," *Revue retrospective*, XX (1894), 298–99; *Du règne de Louis XVI, histoire des évènemens remarquables . . . pendant . . . juillet & aout . . .* (Paris, 1789), pp. 37–46; Eastlake, pp. 88–91; Morris diary, July 20, Davenport (ed.), I, 156; Morris to Washington, July 31, *ibid.*, p. 171; [Comte F.-L. d'Escherny], *Correspondance d'un habitant de Paris . . . jusqu'au 4 avril 1791* (Paris, 1791), pp. 100–115; Bailly, II, 57–69; *AP*, VIII, 246–47; Duveyrier, pp. 234–53; and *Révolutions de Paris*, No. 1, July 12–17, pp. 31–36. The statement that Lafayette and others were on the Versailles road at 2 A.M. (*Mémoires du général Bon Thiébault*, ed. Fernand Calmette [Paris, 1893], I, 228–30) is contradicted by better evidence.

[73] Bailly and Duveyrier, II, 82, 89.

[74] Eastlake, p. 80.

[75] Bailly and Duveyrier, II, 81–84.

[76] *Mémoires*, II, 265.

National Assembly deputies on foot.[77] At the Place de la Conférence, Bailly presented Louis with the keys of the city and pointedly, but appropriately and with patent good will, stated: "These are the same [keys] that were presented to Henry IV; he had conquered his people, now it is his people who have conquered their king. . . . This is the most beautiful day of the monarchy; it is the occasion of an eternal alliance of monarch and people."[78] Then the procession moved forward, spectators filling the streets or looking on from roof tops and appropriately adorned windows.

All the way the road was lined on both sides with French Guards (by Lafayette's order under their sergeants, for their officers were not dependably sympathetic), citizen guards (even some clerics among them),[79] and volunteer and regular military units, "armed with guns, pistols, swords, pikes, pruning hooks, scythes, and whatever they could lay hold of."[80] French Guards, parading several artillery pieces, kept the Place de Louis XV clear. About a hundred thousand men, by several contemporary estimates, scrupulously carried out Lafayette's commands that day.[81] The procession was orderly even after the women of the Halles joined it, dressed in white (which was their traditional garb for gala events) with blue and red ribbons and carrying flowers and laurel.[82] The sound of trumpets and occasional cannon shots mingled with prolonged cheers—for the nation, the king, the deputies, the Electors, or some popular figures like Bailly and Lafayette. At times Lafayette felt called upon to signal for more quiet and solemnity, giving some bystanders the impression that

[77] Escherny, p. 100; Huber to Eden, July [17], Auckland, II, 337; Bailly, II, 69; *Journal de Paris*, July 19, p. 900; Duveyrier, p. 237; and *Révolutions de Paris*, No. 1, July 12–17, p. 33.

[78] Bailly and Duveyrier, II, 85–86.

[79] *Mémoires*, II, 266 n., and III, 280, and Jefferson to Paine and to Richard Price, July 17, and to Madison, July 22, Boyd, XV, 279–80, 300.

[80] Jefferson to Madison, July 22, Boyd, XV, 300.

[81] *Mémoires*, II, 266, n. 1; *Gazette de Leide*, July 24; Espinchal, "Lafayette jugé," *Revue retrospective*, XX (1894), 298–99; *Journal de Paris*, July 19, pp. 899–900; *AP*, VIII, 246; Bailly, II, 62–64; and Bailly and Duveyrier, II, 89–91.

[82] Deux Amis de la Liberté, *Histoire de la Révolution de France* (Paris, 1792–97), II, 44–45; Escherny, pp. 101–10; and Eastlake, p. 88.

he wished to repress the public display of good will toward the monarch.[83] It was past four o'clock when the king reached the Hôtel de Ville.

Many of the personages who had thus traversed the streets of Paris were the same as those who in May had paraded in Versailles when the Estates General began its meetings, but on that occasion the king had been resplendent both as person and as symbol. Now some of his splendor had passed to others, not least to the heroic mounted figure who with drawn sword ushered the king's coach to the Hôtel de Ville appropriated by a revolutionary commune.[84]

Before Louis entered the Hôtel de Ville with the civilian officials of the city and the deputies of the National Assembly, Bailly asked him to accept a cockade of the city's colors—"the distinctive mark of Frenchmen." The king graciously did so, putting it in his hat.[85] Lafayette stayed behind with the military in the Place de Grève to preserve order. Inside, the king went to a throne which had been prepared in the Grande Salle, now packed tight with onlookers. After a series of ceremonies and speeches, he rose and in a low, scarcely audible voice made a short statement expressing his satisfaction with the new arrangements for Paris and with the selection of Bailly as "mayor" and Lafayette as "commandant general." Bailly repeated the royal sentiments so that all could hear, and a loud cheer burst from the audience: "Vive le roi!"[86] Wishing to show himself to the people in the square outside, Louis then made his way to a balcony, and the sight of their ruler wearing a red and blue cockade "roused . . . transports that it is impossible to describe."[87]

All this time Lafayette had remained in the city hall square

---

[83] Bailly and Duveyrier, II, 91–92; Mazzei, *Memorie*, II, 32–33; *Gazette de Leide*, July 28; and Morris diary, July 17 and 20, Davenport (ed.), I, 152–53, 156. See also below, "Bibliographical Notes," pp. 130–31.

[84] In addition to the sources already cited see *Point du jour*, July 19, pp. 223–26; *Journal de Paris*, July 18, pp. 897–98, and July 20, p. 903; Ferrières (ed. Berville and Barrière), I, 150–52; and *Journal de Duquesnoy*, I, 226–29.

[85] Bailly and Duveyrier, II, 92–93.

[86] Bailly, II, 57–58; Bailly and Duveyrier, II, 102–3; Escherny, pp. 110–12; Mazzei, *Memorie*, II, 32–33; *Gazette de Leide*, July 28; and *Mémoires*, II, 266 and n.

[87] Bailly and Duveyrier, II, 103–5.

supervising measures for the preservation of order. Shortly after Louis returned to the Grande Salle, the new commandant general entered the Hôtel de Ville to escort him to his carriage.[88] Several of the bourgeois guardsmen and their commander stood by. "M. de la Fayette," the king said, "I have been looking for you to tell you that I confirm your nomination to the post of commandant general of the Paris Guard."[89] Louis seemed to think that decisions were still his to make.

Lafayette and his guards accompanied the king back to Point de Jour, where Louis' Versailles escort waited. The National Guard of Paris and its *ad hoc* auxiliaries stood with arms reversed all along the route, in the traditional sign of peace, while cries of "Vive le roi!" and "Vivent le roi et la nation!" rent the air.[90] Leaving the king at Point du Jour, Lafayette returned to the city hall. The celebration continued all that day throughout the city, but despite his "horrible fatigue,"[91] despite his well-wishers' anxiety that his strenuous labors might cause his collapse,[92] he had still other serious business to attend to. The Military Committee was supposed to meet that evening for the first time to help him draw up the regulations of the National Guard of Paris. But others were not so assiduous or compulsive as he; only a handful of representatives, from the more fully organized districts, showed up, and the meeting had to be postponed.[93]

If the enforced rest gave him time to take stock, Lafayette must have been greatly pleased with what had happened. Much certainly remained to be done in actuality, but in principle the Revolution appeared over and well won. The stirring events which had occurred in dizzying succession between July 8 and July 17 seemed to him "a national insurrection"—the one, as he judged a decade later, that was "the last which was needed and the last which I

---

[88] *Ibid.*, p. 105.

[89] *Ibid.*, pp. 105–6; Bailly, II, 68–69; and *Mémoires*, II, 266 and n. 1.

[90] Escherny, pp. 112–15; *Mémoires*, II, 266; Bailly, II, 69; *Journal de Paris*, July 18, p. 898; and Duveyrier, p. 253.

[91] Lafayette to [Mme de Simiane?], July 18, *Mémoires*, II, 318.

[92] *Mémoirs of Mazzei*, trans. Marraro, pp. 320–21.

[93] Bailly and Duveyrier, II, 108–9, and *Procès-verbal du Comité militaire*, Part I, pp. 1–2.

wanted."[94] It apparently assured the kind of regime he sought—a constitutional monarchy in which the king subordinated his will to the will of his people, who followed leaders who meant to base law on the rights of man. That Lafayette was now perhaps the most conspicuous and commanding of those leaders, having thrown king and Orléans, Necker and Bailly, into the shadows, did not escape him even if he tried not to appear too boastful about it.[95] In after years, when a new king, successor to Louis XVI, was to try to undo this revolution and the ones that were to follow, Lafayette was still to feel that the events of July 1789 were the expression of the true will of the French people: "Our electors of '89 were children. The tocsin of July 14 made men of them."[96] And by July 17 the tocsin of July 14 had become a tintinnabulation of rejoicing.

BIBLIOGRAPHICAL NOTES

Wherever the *Mémoires* print a letter of a tender and confidential nature without indicating the addressee, we are usually inclined to infer that she was Mme de Simiane. That is because the letters to other ladies are generally easily discerned as such; those to Mme de Lafayette are usually headed with her name by the editors and contain the salutation "mon cher coeur," and those to Mme de Tessé are likewise usually headed with her name and contain the salutation "ma chère cousine." In a few instances letters whose addressee is not indicated in the *Mémoires* seem less obviously to be for Mme de Simiane than in others. In citing these we have named the addressee when we could, or have said that he or she is unknown, or have indicated (by brackets and question mark) that she was probably but not certainly Mme de Simiane. André Maurois in *Adrienne ou la vie de Madame de La Fayette* (Paris, 1960; English trans., New York, 1961) has been less cautious than we in that regard. Two sets of copies of letters said to be addressed to Mme de Simiane are now in the Lafayette Archives, Cornell University Library, and they are probably the copies which the editors of the *Mémoires* used. See also below, Appendix I.

The *Souvenirs de la princesse de Tarente* (Nantes, 1897) p. 2, makes it appear that Lafayette required that the king be greeted with "the most profound silence" on his parade in Paris on July 17. Mazzei's *Memorie* (II, 32–33), Morris' diary (I, 156), and Bailly and Duveyrier (II, 91–92) also

[94] Lafayette to M. d'Hennings, January 15, 1799, *Mémoires*, III, 227.

[95] Lafayette to [Mme de Simiane?], July 18, *ibid.*, II, 318; Morris diary, July 20, Davenport (ed.), I, 156; and Morris to Washington, July 31, *ibid.*, p. 171.

[96] Lafayette to "mon cher compagnon de 89," [1814], Collection of S. W. Jackson, Yale University Library.

either state or imply that Lafayette required silence, but they clearly mean only on occasion, not throughout the parade. Besides, as several eyewitness accounts testify (and the Duchesse de Tarente does not appear to have been an eyewitness), the spectators were not often silent.

The early volumes of the *Archives parlementaires* are generally regarded as having been prepared with insufficient attention to scholarly completeness. Hence we have rarely used them without confirmation in other contemporary accounts. Among these one of the most reliable, partly because of its long career as a respected newspaper before the Revolution, was the *Journal de Paris* (founded in 1777). Lafayette himself was one of its subscribers, and a run of it (October 23 to December 30, 1789) in the Lafayette College Library, Easton, Pennsylvania, the gift of S. W. Jackson, is said to have been of Lafayette's personal copies.

E. B. Smith, "Jean-Sylvain Bailly, Astronomer, Mystic, Revolutionary, 1736–1793," *Transactions of the American Philosophical Society*, n.s., XLIV (1954), 512, argues unconvincingly that since Orléans and Mirabeau viewed the appointment of Bailly and Lafayette on July 15 with favor, they perhaps engineered it.

The most recently published eyewitness account of the events covered in this chapter is Daniel Ligou (ed.), "La Suite des papiers de Poncet-Delpech, *AHRF*, XXXVIII (1966), 561–76.

CHAPTER VII

Two Lynchings and a Resignation

TO OVERTHROW a government already close to collapse like that which had ruled Paris until July 13 was one thing. To build an elective regime that would endure was quite another. If Lafayette's experience with the American Revolution had not already taught him that destruction is easier than construction, he was soon to learn.

Two tasks seemed foremost in the days immediately following the king's acceptance of Paris' revolution. The first was to keep a still panicky, effervescent, resentful, and triumphant people from taking justice into its own hands. The second was to give some semblance of regularity and authority to the newly improvised institutions which because of the very spontaneity of their creation lacked system, coordination, and regulations. These tasks were not Lafayette's alone, but almost everyone who shared them counted upon his leadership, and he was to find that either was harder than the one he had performed when, to use a phrase attributed to him, he "had marched his Sovereign about the Streets as he pleased."[1] It made the two tasks no easier that both had to be tackled simultaneously, that order had to be maintained by an authority which had yet to be put in order.

Demands for decisions and actions came pouring into the Hôtel de Ville from all quarters in the week following the king's surrender. Whether addressed to the Electors, the mayor, or some other agency of the new commune, they were likely, especially if they dealt with police matters, to come sooner or later to La-

[1] Morris diary, July 20, Davenport (ed.), I, 156. Cf. Morris to Washington, July 31, *ibid.*, p. 171.

fayette's attention. Several of these demands arose from the brief insurrection which had just torn Paris asunder.

What, for one thing, was to be done with captured properties? When the captors had some kind of official status, the answer to that question was relatively simple. For example, the king's troops, upon evacuating the Champ de Mars, had moved so hastily that they had left their baggage behind; the National Guard of Paris had taken possession of it as a prize of war, but the original owners now reclaimed it. Lafayette decided that in this case private property should be restored but that the Guard might retain military equipment.[2]

Not all the prizes of war, however, were made by the National Guard. Private persons had seized arms at the Hôtel des Invalides and other military establishments in the course of the recent outbursts. Some of these arms, it was feared, had fallen into the hands of those whom more fortunate citizens, sometimes indiscriminately, called "brigands." Doubtless a certain number of the less fortunate who styled themselves "patriots" were little better than dangerous criminals, but many of them were only unemployed and homeless—vagrants or vagabonds perhaps but as yet law-abiding. Some of them pretended to be or with some reason thought of themselves as being volunteer militiamen. In any case, whatever arms they appropriated meant both a further loss to the city's already depleted supply and an aggravation of the police problem which the miserable as a potentially lawless element always present. Attempting to forestall both dangers, the Assembly of Electors and Lafayette instructed the National Guard to disarm all Parisians not enrolled in their district battalions and to confiscate the weapons of those who might seek to keep their arms by leaving Paris.[3]

Disarming the many workingmen of Paris who, though not formally enrolled in the National Guard, had acquired weapons

[2] Bailly and Duveyrier, II, 163–64, and *Lettre intéressante de M. de La Fayette suivie de la septième et huitième lettres d'un commerçant à un cultivateur sur les municipalités* (n.p., [1790?]).

[3] Bailly and Duveyrier, II, 124–25, and Bailly, II, 74.

as the spoils of war proved to be no simple undertaking. Besides fighting in the patriotic cause, they had given up several days' wages in the turmoil ending with capture of the Bastille. To make the return to their unheroic routine more palatable to these conquerors of a symbol of tyranny, the Electors decided that unenrolled workers now should be paid to hand in their arms. Following an example already set by the Paris deputies in the National Assembly and by other public-spirited men, the Electors urged those who could do so to contribute to a fund for that and certain other charitable purposes. Among those ready to contribute in this fashion were several theatrical companies of Paris, which, anxious to reopen their doors closed by the week's disorders, offered to devote the proceeds of their premier performances "to the profit of the poor." The Electors accepted the theaters' offer, but apprehending that audiences at benefit performances for a patriotic cause might be moved to renew rioting, they enjoined Lafayette to take special police precautions.[4]

The injunction was not an idle one, for the opening of the theaters met with opposition in some quarters. Until Necker should resume his place in the king's ministry, some people, believing that the "aristocrats" were still in control at Versailles, had determined that the theaters should not open. Their threatening attitude induced the theater managers to postpone their openings and to ask for additional protection. Lafayette undertook to provide the necessary police force, and the theaters gave their benefit performances on July 21 without incident.[5]

The hydra of disorder, however, produced new heads whenever old ones were lopped off. Attracted by reports of secret stores of arms, indignant crowds threatened to storm several likely hiding places, and the Electors had to take measures to defend them. They deputed some of their number to restore order, empowering their deputies or the local authorities to make their own official search for arms, and Lafayette dispatched a contingent to escort and reinforce them.[6] A tax-collector imprudent enough to try to

---

[4] Bailly and Duveyrier, II, 152–58, 193–95.

[5] *Ibid.*, pp. 229–30.

[6] *Ibid.*, p. 214; Tuetey, I, 17, No. 146; and *Recueil des arrêtés*, p. 40.

do his duty at a city tollgate was nearly mobbed, and Lafayette had to send a company of Guards to protect him and his post.[7] When wagons on the highways and barges on the rivers brought food to the hungry city, he had to provide military convoys. On the twenty-first he was able to inform the Electors that great supplies of breadstuffs were ready at Rouen for shipment to the city, and upon an encouraging report of the Committee on Subsistence, the Electors temporarily lowered the price of bread.[8]

The destruction of the Bastille, where crowds gathered to watch hundreds of masons pulling the venerable fortress apart stone by stone, presented special complications. Any who ventured too near were in danger from falling stones and debris, and the prison's treasure and records were in danger of purloining by souvenir-hunters. The Electors called upon the nearby districts to take the necessary precautions, and Lafayette posted guards. When, however, La Salle put up warning signs, the nearby districts protested against their "imperious tone."[9] To those who fretted that prisoners might still be buried alive in the Bastille's dungeons, the Electors gave assurance that a rigorous search had been made on Lafayette's own orders.[10]

While thus occupied with the repeated menace of disorder, Lafayette had to deal with ubiquitous seekers of favor and patronage. Some aristocrats, embittered or frightened by the recent violence, wanted passports enabling them to leave Paris unmolested. The first wave of the emigrations that were to take enemies or victims of the Revolution from France to foreign countries, there to await the end of what they fondly hoped was a passing hysteria in their country and to grow impatient and vindictive as they waited, had begun, the Comte d'Artois being one of the first to go. Almost no one was concerned that they should not go, but some were anxious that their flight should not bring in its wake

[7] Bailly and Duveyrier, II, 218.

[8] *Ibid.,* pp. 244–46, 259, 285, 420–21; Tuetey, I, 349, No. 3153; Duveyrier, p. 317; and Chassin, III 589.

[9] Bailly and Duveyrier, II, 218–19. See also *ibid.,* pp. 217–72, 278–80; Tuetey, I, 55, No. 538; and Chassin, III, 584–85.

[10] Bailly and Duveyrier, II, 113–14.

the economic hardships which an excessive flight of capital might precipitate. Accordingly, detachments of bourgeois militia sought to prevent the exportation of largish sums of money.[11] Lafayette himself, however, gave out passports fairly liberally to those who applied to him, apparently satisfied to make émigrés of men who, if they stayed home, might become foes of the Revolution. On the other hand, zealous patriots importuned him for commissions in the National Guard.[12] Yet he was not always able to get the men he wanted as staff officers. Perhaps his greatest disappointment in that regard was that a former aide, the Chevalier de Moré de Pontgibaud, proved to be one of the few French officers who, though he had fought in the American Revolution, refused to serve the cause of revolution in France.[13]

At least two Americans were among those who sought favors. Jefferson, having long had the intention of leaving France, thought it prudent to secure a municipal passport endorsed by Lafayette as well as one already requested from the royal authorities.[14] And Morris added to Lafayette's difficulties because of his own and some friends' curiosity about the Bastille. He recognized that Lafayette was "as busy as a Man can be"—so busy that he could not find time even to answer Washington's last letter,[15] imparting his "adoptive father's" reluctance to become president of the United States.[16] Morris after "much Difficulty" found Lafayette, "exhausted by a Variety of Attentions," at the Hôtel de Ville, but he persisted, and although the Electors had decided to

[11] Gaultier to his constituents, July 25, Mège, *Gaultier*, II, 200–201.

[12] For an example of the passport seekers see Lafayette to [Mme de Simiane], July 18, *Mémoires*, II, 319. For examples of office-seekers see Sigismond Lacroix, *Actes de la Commune de Paris pendant la Révolution* (Paris, 1894–98), 2d ser., IV, 366–67, and VI, 427, and Lafayette to Destaimond, December 1811, quoted in Librairie Damascene Morgand's autograph catalogue of March 1956, No. 9.

[13] Geoffroy de Grandmaison and Comte de Pontgibaud (eds.), *Mémoires du comte de Moré (1758–1837)* (Paris, 1898), pp. 132–33. See also Marquis de Maleissye, *Mémoires d'un officier aux Gardes français (1789–1793)*, ed. M.-G. Roberti (Paris, 1897), pp. 94–95; Espinchal, *Journal*, p. 234; and Mathieu Dumas, *Memoirs of His Own Time* . . . (Philadelphia, 1839), I, 98, 101–103.

[14] See the facsimiles in Boyd, XV, facing p. 424, and *ibid.*, pp. xxxiv–xxxv.

[15] Morris to Washington, July 31, Davenport (ed.), I, 171.

[16] January 29, Fitzpatrick, XXX, 184–87.

discourage visitors to the doomed prison, on a visit to Lafayette's home he got a pass to the infamous prison.[17] About this time a less prominent American merchant in Paris, James Swan, published a series of letters to Lafayette detailing the reasons for the slackening of Franco-American trade, with a dedication to the addressee and a preface that spoke glowingly of the marquis' heroic efforts in America and Europe,[18] but Swan's Franco-American propaganda apparently occasioned Lafayette no additional labor.

To attend to the police work which had to be done, the new commandant general drew heavily upon the two volunteer companies of Basoches and upon the crack royal regiment of the French Guard. The Basoches comprised about three thousand employees of the law offices associated with the courts of the Palais de Justice and the Châtelet, usually aspirant notaries and attorneys themselves. Having long had a paramilitary organization of their own—mostly for social purposes—they were relatively well trained and free from district control.[19] The French Guard had done and still stood ready to do valiant service, but Lafayette was uncertain about his right to use it or the wisdom of encouraging its further indiscipline. As public heroes fully armed and uniformed, the French Guards had become willy-nilly the centers of excitement, sometimes of fantastic rumors regarding "aristocratic" plots against them.

Assigned to the king's service in both Versailles and Paris, the French Guard was regularly divided into two parts, four companies, relieved on a fixed schedule, being always on duty at the Château of Versailles. Immediately after his return from Paris Louis called this schedule to Lafayette's attention, since the next exchange of posts was due soon. Possibly because the Paris battalions seemed to him to have turned too revolutionary, the king preferred that they stay in Paris and asked Lafayette to keep them

---

[17] Morris diary, July 20, Davenport (ed.), I, 156. See also *ibid.*, pp. 157–58, and above, p. 135 and n. 9.

[18] *Causes qui se sont opposées aux progrès du commerce entre la France et les Etats-unis . . .*, July 22, 1789.

[19] See F. Foiret, *Une Corporation parisienne pendant la Révolution (les notaires)* (Paris, 1912), pp. 38–40.

there.[20] On the day after Louis' visit to Paris the matter came before the Assembly of Electors because a group of French Guards, distrusting their aristocratic officers, petitioned the Electors for permission to stay in Paris. Asked if they wished to serve under Lafayette, the Guards' deputies answered with a decided affirmative. Lafayette inquired whether the Versailles contingent would be willing to remain at its post for a while, and they answered that his orders "would be sacred to the whole regiment."[21] Accordingly, he received permission from the Electors to send an aide to ask the Versailles companies to stay where they were while the Paris companies continued in Paris. The aide was instructed to suggest that the Versailles contingent should not use Lafayette's name, if it were not necessary, in order to keep up appearances and shield the king's dignity. "You see," Lafayette reassured his uneasy confidante, "that the power I wield has made me respectful and moderate."[22]

The king's hold upon some of his own soldiers appeared to hinge upon Lafayette's cooperation, thereby rendering the problem of military reorganization all the more delicate. Morris, invited to dinner at Lafayette's house on July 20, discussed the French Guard with his host, his hostess, La Rochefoucauld, and some others.[23] Adrienne now lived in constant dread. As she afterward told her children, she never saw her husband leave home any more without wondering whether she had said goodbye to him for the last time. Yet, as a devoted helpmate she entertained his guests and espoused his views, too proud to let anyone guess her fears or her doubts.[24] Perhaps independently (though similar views were current) Morris had conceived the idea that the French Guard should be made into a city guard receiving special pay and recruiting its ranks only from superior soldiers, and before he left the Lafayettes, he thought he had persuaded

<hr />

[20] July 18, *AP*, LV, 520 and 541–42. See also Lafayette to [Mme de Simiane?], July 18, 1789, *Mémoires*, II, 318.

[21] Bailly and Duveyrier, II, 164–65. See also *ibid.*, pp 150–51.

[22] Lafayette to [Mme de Simiane?], July 18, *Mémoires*, II, 318.

[23] Morris diary, July 20, Davenport (ed.), I, 156.

[24] Virginie de Lasteyrie, *La Vie de Madame de Lafayette* (Paris, 1869), pp. 213–16.

his host.[25] At any rate, the next day Lafayette sent word to the National Assembly that the French Guard wished to serve in the Paris National Guard.[26]

The French Guard provided a conspicuous example of the general unrest that infected the armed forces of the country. The revolutionary contagion had spread rapidly among the king's troops, and large numbers of soldiers joined the vagabonds, unemployed, and curious who flocked to the city. They hoped not only to escape the injustices of an army in which high rank was usually reserved for the high-born and hardship for the common soldier but also to serve the shining cause of the Revolution. One group came in from Meaux, half famished and angry. Informed that these men might make trouble, Lafayette ordered that they be fed and then went to see them. When someone referred to them in his hearing as "deserters," Lafayette retorted: "Softly, Gentlemen. 'Deserters?' They will gladly join the Paris militia."[27] In general, he promised such "deserters" that if their conduct warranted it and the king consented, he would let them volunteer for the National Guard.[28]

In keeping with his new conciliatory policy, Louis XVI combined expediency with graciousness in settling the status of the royal troops that sought to join the National Guard.[29] He gave Lafayette formal permission to deal in either of two ways with those soldiers who up to that time (July 21) had already left their regiments. The commandant general might incorporate in the National Guard those who wished to be transferred or he might provide notes explaining the absence of any who preferred to return to the royal standards; the latter, Louis promised, would be

[25] Morris diary, July 20, Davenport (ed.), I, 156. Cf. *Lettre à Monsieur le Marquis de la Fayette sur la formation d'un régiment à Paris,* signed D* B***N, Paris, July 20, 1789.

[26] *Point du jour,* July 22, p. 248.

[27] *Révolutions de Paris,* No. 2, July 19–25, pp. 12–13; [L. P. de Bérenger], *Mémoires historiques, et pièces authentiques sur M. de La Fayette . . .* (Paris, [1790]), p. 262; and *Mémoires,* II, 271.

[28] Bailly and Duveyrier, II, 163.

[29] Bailly's *Mémoires* (II, 104) implies that Lafayette spoke directly to the king on this matter, but there is no evidence that the two men met again after July 17 until after the matter was disposed of.

reinstated without punishment. The king was especially conciliatory regarding the French Guards who were stationed in Paris, not only permitting them to join the National Guard but also agreeing to maintain them at his own expense until the city was ready to provide for them. He retained in his own service, however, the four companies of the French Guard stationed in Versailles. When Lafayette read the king's letter to the Electors (July 22), they ordered it printed and circulated.[30] It was a welcome concession indeed, for with one stroke it reduced the royal forces at the same time that it provided the city with a number of trained men.

Even with the Basoches, the French Guards in Paris, and volunteers from both the royal forces and other private military units the number of men at Lafayette's disposal was insufficient for the police of a city of over half a million. Obviously, the city itself had to provide some additional means of meeting the constant demands for police action. But to get volunteers to submit to regulations and discipline was going to be hard, and it would probably be harder to get the sixty districts of Paris either to act in coordination or to accept direction from the commune. Each of the district assemblies was obviously jealous of its authority. If his prestige still held up, Lafayette confessed, it was "despite the efforts of ill-intentioned men who seek to get rid of me in every district." He recognized that his stature as commander-in-chief required a militia that would serve regularly, rain or shine, night and day, humdrum and emergency, and hence that it was dependent upon the full acceptance of the city government by the Paris population as well as by the king.[31]

The commandant general put this problem before the Assembly of Electors upon the earliest opportunity after Louis' visit to Paris. On the morning of July 18, while admitting that his nomination to his post by acclamation of the Electors was flattering, he proposed that his fellow citizens be asked to vote in a formal, city-wide ballot not only upon his own election but also upon the future

[30] Bailly and Duveyrier, II, 295–96; *Copie de la lettre du roi à M. le marquis de La Fayette, Versailles, le 21 juillet 1789;* and *Mémoires,* II, 271.

[31] Lafayette to [Mme de Simiane?], July 18, *Mémoires,* II, 318.

organization of the municipal government as a whole. Bailly, desiring confirmation of his own position as well, seconded his colleague's plea. The Assembly of Electors readily agreed to procure a reconfirmation of their emergency appointments by a formal referendum. They therefore asked the sixty districts of Paris to assemble for the purpose of electing a mayor and a commandant general, and applying the principle of "consent of the governed" to their own government of Paris, they called for the election of new district representatives to consider the problem of municipal organization.[32]

Lafayette sent a circular on the subject to the district assemblies. Believing, he said, that authority must emanate from the people, he preferred, since the emergency was over, that his "fellow citizens choose a chief by regular means," although he would continue to act as such until the people formally selected a commander, "reserving the honor in any event to serve as the most faithful of their soldiers." He also urged the districts to hasten their choice of the representatives who were to cooperate with him in the organization of the National Guard, so that they might meet the next morning at the city hall to begin work. He took advantage of the circular, furthermore, to inaugurate some regularity in the National Guard's service by urging each district to send daily for the orders of the day.[33]

Lafayette recognized that the burden of organizing the Guard was bound to be his: "I have no doubt of the choice in view of the kindnesses which have been piled upon me." Nor, despite "horrible fatigue," "the ill-intentioned," and the paucity of collaborators, did he want any other outcome.[34] When Morris suggested that he ought to reach out and take responsibility beyond the limits of Paris, Lafayette responded that he already had all the power he wanted and would like as soon as possible to return to

[32] Bailly and Duveyrier, II, 115–17, 121–24; Bailly, II, 72; Ethis de Corny to the districts, July 18, *Recueil des arrêtés*, pp. 23–30; and Lacroix, I, xiii–xv. (Unless otherwise indicated, references to Lacroix are to the 1st ser.)

[33] *Journal de Paris*, July 20, pp. 906, and *Mémoires*, II, 270. A copy of the circular signed by Lafayette is in the Lafayette College Library, Easton, Pa.

[34] Lafayette to [Mme de Simiane?], July 18, 1789, *Mémoires*, II, 318.

private life. Morris was unconvinced of Lafayette's sincerity, for, in his opinion, Lafayette was a "Lover of Freedom from Ambition, of which there are two Kinds, the one born of Pride, the other of Vanity and his partakes most of the latter."[35] Yet perhaps Morris again was too cynical; perhaps once more Lafayette, with Washington's recently avowed reluctance to be president in mind, was patterning his role upon that of his revered model.

The first Sunday after the capture of the Bastille (July 19) seemed to herald the devoutly wished new era. The streets and gardens were filled with peaceful and orderly folk, and when Lafayette arrived at the Hôtel de Ville, he learned that the night had been "perfectly quiet."[36] In the Governor's Room he found enough representatives of the city's districts to enable him to hold the first meeting of the body that was to become the Paris Military Committee. When the verification of their credentials was completed, forty-six fully accredited representatives formally inaugurated that body, the first committee of the city government directly chosen by the consent of the governed.[37] The day soon brought its sufficiency of evils—disputes among districts, angry crowds at the Bastille, and threats of hunger riots. Yet before Lafayette left for his night's rest, sometime after midnight, he had the satisfaction of knowing that thirteen districts of the city had already formally confirmed his election as commander-in-chief.[38]

The first matter to engage the commander's attention on Monday morning was the systematic organization of the National Guard battalion in each separate district. In a haphazard way almost any volunteer had been accepted so far. Obviously, specific qualifications ought to be required in order to keep vagabonds and migrants off the lists of eligibles. The Electors, on Lafayette's request, ruled that all ablebodied taxpayers must enroll in their district Guard, charging the commandant general to secure from the tax officials and deliver to each district a list of its taxpayers.[39]

---

[35] Morris diary, July 20, Davenport (ed.), I, 156.

[36] Bailly and Duveyrier, II, 172.

[37] *Ibid.*, pp. 206–10, and *Procès-verbal du Comité militaire*, Part I, pp. 2–5.

[38] Bailly and Duveyrier, II, 203–5, and Tuetey, I, 74–76, Nos. 707–25.

[39] Bailly and Duveyrier, II, 213–14.

If the commander-in-chief reflected that by requiring his National Guardsmen to be taxpayers he was automatically excluding not merely the transient and the homeless but also the resident poor and thus assuring that his militia would be a middle-class body, he does not seem to have objected. In the eyes of the eighteenth-century liberal, aristocrats and poor were both suspect—aristocrats because their interests were too deeply rooted in obsolete institutions, the poor because they had too shallow roots in the common weal. Nor, indeed, could the poor afford to take time from their work for unpaid militia service. That morning, too, the organization of the Military Committee moved forward. It created a subcommittee to draw up regulations for the Guard, and it chose the committee's secretary, Lafayette acting ex officio as its presiding officer.[40]

That day (July 20) a series of unpleasant incidents broke the relative calm that had prevailed since the king's visit. Tax riots, arrests, commotion at the Bastille, protests against the opening of the theaters, demands for the convoy of food all clamored for attention. Perhaps even more distressing, because it interfered with the organization of the National Guard, was the continuing display of jealousy among district authorities over the Hôtel de Ville's growing power. Who, the district authorities wanted to know, was to send for orders of the day—the commander of the district's Guard or the president of the district? Lafayette, despite his scruples concerning the subordination of the military to the civil authority apparently did not consider it good military practice to put any civil intermediaries between himself and his district commanders; it would suffice that he as their general would take his orders from the commune. On his recommendation the Electors decided to make the district commanders responsible for receiving the commandant's orders of the day;[41] and Lafayette indicated to those concerned that, to be valid,[42] orders emanating from his command would thenceforth have to be signed by him and countersigned by one of his aides.

[40] *Recueil des arrêtés*, pp. 34–36, and *Procès-verbal du Comité militaire*, Part I, pp. 5–7.

[41] Bailly and Duveyrier, II, 215–17.

[42] Tuetey, II, 386, No. 3627, and *Journal de Paris*, July 24, p. 920.

By nightfall of July 20 several additional districts had approved Lafayette as commander-in-chief.[43] On the whole, the situation seemed well in hand, and Lafayette sent an informal, hasty, but encouraging report of his manifold, complex labors to the National Assembly through the Duc de Liancourt, who was its new president. Tranquility seemed restored; the theaters were going to open; traffic was moving better; Guard contingents had gone out to help police neighboring towns; the organization of the Paris Guard seemed well under way; unauthorized persons were being disarmed; if only other cities followed the example of Paris, the heavy, continued demand on his troops for service outside Paris would be reduced. The convoying of food supplies, he owned, was his hardest problem—"to which I shall devote myself with the greatest zeal."[44] When Liancourt read this letter to the Assembly later that day, it was greeted with applause and placed in the Assembly's archives.[45]

The next day several more districts of Paris confirmed Lafayette as commandant general.[46] Not content merely with its unanimous vote, the District of Petit Saint-Antoine addressed to him as "liberator of the new world, hero of mankind, defender of its imprescriptible rights" an open letter which spoke of liberty, equality, and fraternity (still an unfamiliar trinity) as if they were inextricably bound together and destined to move ever onward: "We shall henceforth breathe only fraternity, harmony, equality.... You will be at our head, guaranty of this liberty. Who better than you has learned its value, recognized equality, loved his brothers?"[47]

Not to be outdone by Petit Saint-Antoine, about a hundred and fifty residents of the District of Sainte Elisabeth paraded to the city hall to the sound of fifes and drums. There, standing in the square

[43] Bailly and Duveyrier, II, 242–44.

[44] Lafayette to Liancourt, July 20, *Mémoires*, II, 319–20.

[45] *Point du jour*, July 22, p. 248; *Procès-verbal de l'Assemblée nationale*, No. 28, pp. 11–12; and *AP*, VIII, 255 (July 20). The original letter is in AN, C 28, plaq. 224, pièce 38.

[46] Lacroix, I, xiv, and Bailly and Duveyrier, II, 251–52, 272–73.

[47] *Adresse à M. de La Fayette, général de la milice parisienne, par l'Assemblée générale du District du Petit Saint-Antoine, du 21 juillet 1789.*

in military order, they waited until Lafayette joined them. Then one of their Electors addressed them: Lafayette is "the hero of America . . . who as a young man sped to foreign countries to learn the art, then unknown in Europe, of at last breaking the chains of despotism"; he "crosses the seas and New Yorck [*sic*] is free"; he "returns to Europe and France breaks her chains; it seems that to achieve the most astonishing revolutions in the world the two hemispheres waited for him to be either author or witness"; now he can count on the "submission and faithfulness" of the bourgeois militia, "the attachment and respect" of his electors, and the "undying devotion" of all patriotic citizens. When Bailly joined them, he received a similarly flowery address. And both men replied "in the most obliging terms with the greatest affability."[48]

All was not peace and brotherhood for long. That day, exactly a week after he had taken command of the bourgeois militia, Lafayette for the first time undertook to inspect the National Guard posts in some of the districts.[49] Before he could leave the Hôtel de Ville, however, an unruly crowd gathered in the Place de Grève. They had captured the Prince de Lambesc, who had incurred the hatred of Parisians by giving the order to his troop to charge the people gathered in the Tuileries Gardens on July 12. As he was apparently trying to flee Paris disguised in his servant's coat, he was arrested and brought to the Place de Grève. Lafayette succeeded only with difficulty in extricating him from physical harm.[50]

Worse could now be expected. Two days earlier the Paris Electors had learned that Berthier de Sauvigny, royal intendant of Paris, whom some held responsible for the bread shortage, had

[48] AN, C 134, dossier 11, pièces 3 and 4. These are the manuscript copies sent to Lafayette on July 23, but the address was also printed and published. See also Charles Braibant (ed.) *La Fayette: exposition organisée par les Archives nationales . . . pour la célébration du bi-centenaire de la naissance de La Fayette* (Paris, 1957) (hereafter cited as Braibant [ed.], *Exposition*), p. 86, No. 245.

[49] Bailly and Duveyrier, p. 331.

[50] Lafayette to the Duc de [Liancourt], July 22, Archives de la Seine, 4 AZ 16. See also Braibant (ed.), *Exposition*, p. 86, No. 246. The *Gazette de Leide*, August 4, and the *London Chronicle*, August 8–11, pp, 142–43, mistakenly say that the arrested man was M. de Lambert, who as a Ministry of War official had initiated military punishment with the flat of a sword.

been arrested at Compiègne and that town's authorities, afraid that he might be lynched, wished to place him in a Paris prison. The Paris Electors agreed to have him brought to Paris under a sort of protective arrest, and Lafayette had thereupon sent a strong contingent to bring him in.[51]

Later another "aristocrat" had been arrested in the vicinity of Paris. He was Joseph-François Foulon, a financier whose chief crime was that he had taken the portfolio of finances in the ministry which with such dramatic consequences had recently replaced Necker, but he was also alleged to have said that if the people did not have bread, they could eat hay. This man had been transferred from authority to authority until he was brought to the Paris city hall for custody early on the morning of July 22. It was entirely coincidental that Berthier was Foulon's son-in-law.

When the Electors met later that morning, they anticipated trouble. Recognizing that some new legal machinery was needed, they petitioned the National Assembly to constitute a tribunal to try persons denounced "by public clamor," making Lafayette responsible meanwhile for the protection of those thus placed in jeopardy. They ordered Foulon transferred as a prisoner to the Abbaye Saint-Germain secretly and after nightfall, and they sent orders to the officers escorting Berthier from Compiègne to deliver him similarly. Later that morning they asked Lafayette to take no measures in the neighborhood of the Hôtel de Ville which would give the impression that important prisoners were nearby. Although Lafayette seems to have agreed with Bailly that Foulon should have been sent to the Abbaye under heavy escort at once and that subterfuge was not the best means to assure the two men's safety, before he left on his tour of inspection he did as he was instructed.[52]

The expectation of unrest in the districts induced Lafayette to undertake his tour of inspection. It was probably on this occasion that he was invited to attend a crowded meeting of the District of the Cordeliers, at which the militant young lawyer Danton presided. Among the audience were a number of French Guards.

---

[51] Bailly and Duveyrier, II, 329–30.

[52] *Ibid.*, pp. 286–90, 296–97, and Bailly, II, 102, 106–7.

After the applause at the commandant general's entrance died
down, Danton announced that the district had just agreed to request that the French Guard be re-established as before but under
the command of the Duc d'Orléans, and "we have no doubt of the
approval of the commandant general of such a patriotic proposal."
Taken by surprise, Lafayette temporized, for he was suspicious of
any step that was associated with the aggrandizement of the Duc
d'Orléans, and gradually he persuaded the assembly to drop its
proposal.[53]

Other than this awkward moment the tour of inspection gave
Lafayette no reason to apprehend further trouble.[54] Before returning to the city hall, he apparently stopped en route to report the
day's activities to the National Assembly. Despite "the disorder in
which I am obliged to write," he deferentially explained, "the
honor of accounting to the National Assembly is too important"
to forgo. He intimated that there was no cause for alarm, however,
since in actuality nothing more serious than the attempt upon
Lambesc had occurred, nor had he found any excitement in other
parts of the city. But there was a report of a rabble gathering at the
Halles, which he intended to look into after he had taken some
necessary precautions at the Place de Grève. There he expected to
quiet the people's fear that their enemies would get off scot free
by proposing a preliminary hearing—"a kind of inquiry by jurors
which will decide whether the accused should be brought to trial."
He also detailed the steps he had taken to provide food for the
hungry city.[55]

Satisfaction was cut short, however, by a messenger sent posthaste from the Hôtel de Ville. The expected crisis was brewing.
By late morning the hubbub in the Place de Grève had grown
loud enough to disturb the Electors' conferences. By two o'clock
a huge mob was crying for Foulon's head. At that point the
Electors sent a messenger to find Lafayette and bring him back

<hr />

[53] *Mémoires*, II, 272, and IV, 139. See also Alphonse Aulard, *La Société des Jacobins*
(Paris, 1889–97), VI, 47, *La Gazette nationale ou le Moniteur* (hereafter cited as *Moniteur*),
20 Germinal An II (April 9, 1794), p. 819; and "Mélanges," *Revue historique*, I (1876),
506.

[54] Lafayette to the Duc de [Liancourt], July 22, *loc.cit.*

[55] *Ibid.*

to the city hall at full speed.[56] The situation at the Hôtel de Ville had become desperate. If the commanding officer at the city hall ordered up new troops, as he afterward told Bailly he had, for one reason or another they had not come.[57]

Despite Lafayette's confidence in his ability to master the impending crisis, he did not get to the Halles that day. He barely reached the Hôtel de Ville before disaster struck. To assuage the mob's fear that the prisoner had escaped, the Electors had had Foulon brought to a window, but when the populace saw him, they grew only more vengeful. They swept past the guard into the building, up the stairs, and into the Grande Salle, determined to pounce upon their prey. Hoping to temporize until Lafayette could come, the Electors consented to try the unfortunate man then and there. They chose judges and a prosecutor from their own number, and Lafayette, though still absent, was named one of the judges. Since the prosecutor moved too deliberately for them, the mob grew suspicious and threatening. Yielding to the clamor, the Electors had Foulon brought in.[58]

At this point Lafayette arrived. As he crossed the room to take his seat next to President Moreau de Saint-Méry and to address them, the mob calmed down. "I am known to all of you," he began. "You have made me your general, and that choice, which honors me, imposes upon me the duty of speaking to you with the freedom and frankness that are the basis of my character. You want to destroy this man without a trial. That is an injustice that dishonors you, that would brand me, that would brand all the efforts I have made in favor of liberty, should I be so weak as to permit it." He proposed to carry out the decree of the Assembly of Electors, and hence he wished the accused to be imprisoned until he could be duly tried. "I want the law to be respected, the law without which there is no liberty, the law without whose aid I would have contributed nothing to the revolution in the New World and without which I could make no contribution to the

---

[56] Bailly and Duveyrier, II, 300, and Duveyrier, p. 331.

[57] Bailly, II, 105-7. The commanding officer said (if Bailly was not mistaken) that Lafayette countermanded the order. If so, the countermand probably was given earlier in the day, before Lafayette went off, in accordance with the instructions to avoid concentrations of troops in the Place de Grève. Cf. *Mémoires*, II, 274-75, n. 1.

[58] Bailly and Duveyrier, II, 304-11.

revolution now in progress." He was defending not Foulon, whom, he said, he had already censured on several occasions, but the majesty of the law. The more guilty the accused seemed, the more necessary that legal forms be observed, in order that his punishment be the more impressive and that his testimony reveal his accomplices. "So I am going to order that he be taken to the prison of the Abbaye Saint-Germain."[59]

Two men from the crowd went to the president's desk to second Lafayette's efforts. But not everyone in the Grande Salle had heard the commandant's words, and the two were not permitted to speak. Foulon himself then made a personal appeal for mercy and justice, but it was lost in the fury of the multitude. Agitation spread to the square outside, fomented, Lafayette thought, by some well-dressed men among the crowd.[60] Since he was in mufti, the agitators believed or pretended to believe that it was not the commandant general who was addressing them.[61] Several times more he spoke, each time bringing a lull in the excitement. But newcomers kept coming in, filling the stairways and the corridors, screaming and jostling, packing the room, crowding toward the president's desk, knocking over the chair on which Foulon sat. "Take him to prison," Lafayette ordered at last as loudly as he could,[62] and he tried a final appeal to reason. Vigorous applause greeted this appeal, and it looked for a moment as if the forces of law might finally prevail. But someone noticed that Foulon himself had joined in the applause. "Look," a voice shrieked, "they're in cahoots!"[63] That shriek sealed Foulon's fate. Uncontrollable, the mob tore him away from the Electors who tried to protect him. Frustrated, mortified, exhausted, Lafayette no longer found the physical strength even to make himself heard. The mob dragged their victim to the square outside and hanged him to a lamppost.[64]

The prisoner Berthier was at that moment being brought

---

[59] Ibid., and Mémoires, II, 275–76.

[60] Bailly and Duveyrier, II, 313–14, and Mémoires, II, 276–77.

[61] Mémoires, II, 279.

[62] Bailly and Duveyrier, II, 314–15, and Mémoires, II, 277–78.

[63] Mémoires, II, 278.

[64] Ibid; Bailly and Duveyrier, II, 315; Duveyrier, pp. 338–41; and Journal de Paris, July 25, pp. 923–24.

toward the Hôtel de Ville, having been protected from public fury so far only by his National Guard escort. Hoping to save him from a fate like his father-in-law's, Lafayette had called up extra guards to police the Place de Grève and the Hôtel de Ville, some of them merely armed civilians with fixed bayonets. The precaution, though wise, proved ineffective. Even a more thoroughly organized and practiced militia than the National Guard of Paris then was could hardly have restrained the inexorable crowd. At 8:45 in the evening a sudden crescendo of excitement in the Place de Grève announced a new crisis—Berthier had arrived. Having retired to their suites in the Hôtel de Ville, Lafayette and Bailly hastened to the Grande Salle to join the Electors, who ordered Berthier to be brought before them immediately. Thereupon Lafayette instructed a small detachment to take a post inside the Grande Salle to protect the prisoner, and Berthier was brought in under heavy guard. As Bailly questioned the unhappy man, the mob in the Place de Grève grew increasingly boisterous. Finally, breaking through the guard, it poured into the Grande Salle, pushing guard and prisoner against the mayor's desk. Having obtained the consent of the Electors, Bailly ordered the accused taken to prison, but on the way someone shot Berthier.[65] Hardly had a frightened man come running into the Grande Salle shrieking the horrible news than in strode a man in a dragoon's uniform carrying a bloody, palpitating object in his hand. "Here is Berthier's heart," he cried. Horror-stricken, the Electors did nothing but urge the man to leave—which he did, accompanied by a triumphant throng. Then it was announced that someone was bringing in Berthier's head, whereupon Lafayette and Moreau de Saint-Méry sent word that the Assembly was extremely busy and the head must not be brought in. In that at least they were obeyed.[66]

Despite the still reverberating encomiums of the districts of

[65] *Mémoires,* II, 278–79, and Bailly and Duveyrier, II, 320–25.

[66] Above we have followed Bailly and Duveyier, II, 318–25, but corroborative accounts are given (with variations) in (among others) Bailly, II, 120–23; *Révolutions de Paris,* No. 2, July 18–25, pp. 21–25; *Courrier de Versailles à Paris,* July 24, pp. 286–87; Duveyrier, p. 348; *Journal de Paris,* January 26, 1790 (suppl.), p. ii; and *Lettres à Monsieur le Comte de B**** (Paris, 1789–90), V, 491.

Petit Saint-Antoine and Sainte Elisabeth, despite his own confidence in his ability to control the populace, Lafayette had failed to preserve law and order. His position, as even a less sensitive person must have realized, had become untenable. In the space of a few hours two men had been lynched almost before his eyes in the area where he was responsible for the preservation of life and liberty. Bourbon absolutism seemed to have given way only to lynch law. This was not the revolution he had envisaged, and perhaps he could be more useful to his country if he returned to his post in the National Assembly. The next morning, July 23, he went to see Bailly and offered his resignation. Bailly refused to accept it. He believed (as Lafayette did)[67] that the lynchings had been instigated by conspirators who, to sully the Revolution, had pushed the people on to atrocity, that Lafayette and himself were the only ones who, having the confidence of the people, could counter this cabal, and that if they withdrew, the tranquility of Paris, and hence the course of the Revolution, would be jeopardized. Lafayette did not deny all this but insisted that his position differed from Bailly's, for a commander whose authority had been flouted must give way to a better man. When Bailly asked him to name a man in whom the people had more confidence, he could not.[68]

Thus constrained, Lafayette changed his line of argument. The people must be taught to obey, he said. If the law were not supreme, if the magistrates were not obeyed, the welfare of the people would be jeopardized, and no one would be willing to take the command of the popular forces. That point must be brought home to the people most forcefully, and he knew no better way to do so than by resigning. Even if they refused to accept his resignation, he must offer it. Bailly thereupon consented to run the risk and agreed that Lafayette submit a formal resignation.[69] Apparently neither man expected or perhaps intended the resig-

---

[67] See *Mémoires*, II, 277, 279, 280, 320, 321.

[68] Bailly, II, 124–125, 129–32.

[69] *Ibid.* Since Lafayette commented upon Bailly's *Mémoires* on occasion but did not comment on Bailly's account of this interview, it may be assumed that he considered it essentially correct.

nation to be accepted, but both meant to underscore their displeasure with recent events by a vivid gesture.

The letters that Lafayette now prepared were designed to be sermons on civic obedience as much as letters of resignation. They were obviously so couched as to reach the minds and hearts of the better elements of the population. One was addressed to Bailly. In circumstances like those then facing France, Lafayette stated, the people's confidence in their military commander must be complete if he were to be useful; his very devotion to the popular interest rendered him incapable of buying their favor by an injustice; since the people in two instances had violated not only the regular processes of justice but also "their solemn obligations . . . to the National Assembly and the king," he must believe that he had lost "the confidence that they had promised"; and so, he concluded, "I must . . . leave a post where I can no longer be useful."[70]

The second letter was a circular to the districts. Enclosing this letter of resignation, it said that Lafayette's resignation had been dictated by his "conscience and . . . sense of fitness." Gratitude for the districts' kindness to him and zeal for their interests, he assured them, "would have inspired my devotion to the duties which you have assigned me, had I not lost the power to execute them adequately." He begged the districts to give renewed attention to the preservation of order within their jurisdictions and to lose no time in making a fresh choice, setting him free.[71] Thus Paris was called upon to elect a new commander-in-chief of its volunteer militia although it had not yet finished the formal balloting for the old one. That very day the fifty-sixth and fifty-seventh of the districts to confirm Lafayette's acclamation as commandant general of the National Guard sent in their approval[72] (leaving only three districts still to be heard from).

When Bailly sent Lafayette's letter of resignation to the Assembly of Electors, they were dumbfounded. As one man they rose and followed their president, Moreau de Saint-Méry, to call on the leader who was abandoning them. They found him still

---

[70] Bailly and Duveyrier, II, 346–47, and Bailly, II, 129.

[71] Bailly and Duveyrier, II, 348–49, and *Mémoires,* II, 281.

[72] Lacroix, I, xvi.

conferring with Bailly in the meeting room of the Committee on Subsistence. He must not resign, they pleaded; Paris would be unsafe without him. But he persisted. Since he lacked public confidence, he replied, he could no longer answer for the safety of the city, but because their distress had touched him, he consented to meet with them later that day to consider some joint action for the public welfare, which would always be his chief concern.[73] Upon return to their meeting place the Electors approved a letter which Bailly proposed to send to the districts asking them to elect two representatives each to meet with him in order to draft some form of regular government for the city. Bailly's letter carried (possibly by error rather than intent) the name of Lafayette as one who would also act in concert with these representatives.[74] Somehow Lafayette appeared to be the indispensable man.

When Lafayette's letters of resignation reached the districts, amazed and unhappy presidents called hasty meetings. A number of districts sent deputations that very afternoon to urge him to reconsider. The Basoche of the Châtelet and the men in one of the local barracks joined in the appeal.[75]

As he had promised, Lafayette met with the Assembly of Electors that evening. He told them that the friendly concern of these deputations moved him deeply and increased his regrets at leaving. Yet it could not be taken as an expression of the general will, which alone would justify his retaining authority. The Assembly, protesting that the general will had already acclaimed him, offered to give him all the power he needed to re-establish respect for the law. Yet he would not consent to reconsider his resignation and started to leave the hall. The Electors crowded around him. One of them, the venerable priest of the Church of Saint Etienne du Mont, fell on his knees and begged him to continue to work with them. Lafayette raised him gently, embraced him, and allowed himself to be led back to his seat.

[73] Bailly and Duveyrier, II, 347–50; Bailly, II, 132; and *Mémoires*, II, 281–82.

[74] Bailly and Duveyrier, II, 350–52; Bailly, II, 143–44, 152–53; Duveyrier, pp. 363–66; Lacroix, I, 407; and *Recueil des arrêtés*, pp. 47–50. Cf. H. E. Bourne, "Improvising a Government in Paris in July 1789," *AHR*, X (1905), 302–3 and n.

[75] Bailly and Duveyrier, II, 361, 363, and Tuetey, I, 82–84.

New district deputations had meanwhile arrived. The spokesman of each went to the presiding officer's desk and read a resolution entreating the commander-in-chief not to desert them. Before the meetings ended, deputations from about forty districts[76] had praised his virtues and implored him to stay. They came from every quarter of the city except the Halles. The Electors then proposed a solemn oath, which they and the district representatives should take, pledging rigorous obedience to the orders that "the prudence and patriotism of M. le Marquis de la Fayette would indicate to him for the public safety." The district representatives promptly took this oath in turn, as Electors and spectators applauded. Lafayette was moved to tears, his emotion mixed with fear that the "consternation" of his supporters, if not assuaged, might lead to disorder during the night. After the last oath was taken, he rose and, without hiding his feelings, told the assembly that such signal proof of esteem and devotion called for every sacrifice; he was ready to give his life to the commune.

Although the commandant general had not explicitly withdrawn his resignation, instantly the atmosphere in the Grande Salle changed. Anxiety became rejoicing. "Vive la Nation!" "Vive la liberté!" "Vive Lafayette!" re-echoed through the room. Electors, gathered around their hero, "embraced him and mingled their tears with his." The Assembly then decided to draw up a resolution solemnizing their readiness to follow his leadership. It declared that, in keeping with the unanimous wishes of the capital's citizens and with their own confidence in Lafayette's virtues, talents, and patriotism, they once more acclaimed him to be general of the National Guard of Paris and promised, in their own name and in that of their armed brethren of the districts and other military corps of the city, "submission and obedience to all his orders" to the end that his zeal, seconded by all patriotic citizens, might bring to perfection the great work of public liberty. The Electors' secretary wrote out the resolution; every man in the room but Lafayette went to the desk and signed it; and as the

---

[76] The reason for doubt upon the number of deputations is that the lists given in Bailly and Duveyrier (II, 361, 363) do not correspond with the data in Tuetey (I, 82–84). Bailly and Duveyrier give the district of Filles Saint Thomas twice (p. 361), and only twenty-five deputations seem to be on both lists. If all deputations mentioned by either source are counted, the total would be over forty.

others applauded, the Electors escorted the man of the hour to his meeting in the room of the Military Committee, there to resume the meticulous planning of the National Guard's future.[77]

Doubtless most of this display of loyalty was genuine and spontaneous. The better citizens of Paris, as probably is true of better citizens everywhere after riots and lynchings, must have felt ashamed and indignant that due process of law had been disdained, and the district authorities must have felt impelled to dissociate themselves from the lawless elements that had perpetrated atrocities and to rally around the man who, despite his temporary failure, still embodied the best chance of avoiding perhaps worse atrocities in the future. Nevertheless, Lafayette had played his hand skillfully. By doing the correct and possibly the only honorable thing, by resigning outright and unconditionally, he had given a histrionic emphasis to his regard for the legal forms and had rallied the respectable parts of the population behind him. He was now stronger than ever—reassured, reacclaimed. Things had turned out so well for him that several unfriendly writers inferred that he must have plotted every step,[78] forgetting that chance sometimes achieves better results than planning and that even the cleverest plotter can succeed only if his plots have backing and circumstances make them feasible. Lafayette was not the only one seeking to be a leader in those days. If he had outstripped the others so far, for once at least it seems to have been because patriotic motives prevailed. Letters of appeal and of thanks continued to come in from the districts and from various military units of the city that evening and all of the next day.[79] One of them was pre-

---

[77] The above account is based chiefly on Bailly and Duveyrier, II, 361–66, but see also *Mémoires*, II, 281–83; Duveyrier, p. 363; Bailly, II, 134–35; Tuetey, I, 82–84; and [Bérenger], pp. 255–56 and n. For Lafayette's fear that "consternation" might lead to disorder see below, p. 156 and n. 82. For the meeting of the Military Committee, see *Procès-verbal du Comité militaire*, Part I, pp. 7–8.

[78] Beaulieu, II, 11–12; Bertrand de Moleville and Montlosier as cited in *Mémoires*, II, 276 n., 278 n., and in Louis-Philippe de Ségur, *Décade historique*, Vol. V of *Oeuvres complètes*, ed. P. Tardieu (Paris, 1824–30), II, 13 and n.; Clermont-Gallerande, I, 151 and n.; and Mss du Comte d'Espinchal, Bibliothèque de Clermont-Ferrand, E. I. 27, Ms. 306, T. VI, p. 242.

[79] Tuetey, I, 84, Nos. 806, 810, 812–14; *Le Général La Fayette: catalogue des livres, autographes et souvenirs composant la collection de M. Blancheteau . . .* (Paris, 1934) (hereafter cited as Blancheteau catalogue), pp. 43–44, No. 139; and Bailly and Duveyrier, II, 377–78, 471, and III, 230–31.

sented by "the founder of modern chemistry," the farmer-general Antoine-Laurent Lavoisier.[80]

The ensuing respite gave the newly reacclaimed commander an opportunity to re-examine his position. In the course of July 24 he reported more or less formally to Liancourt, who was a personal friend as well as president of the National Assembly, that Paris was calm. "The infernal cabal" which hounded him now appeared to him to be "instigated by foreigners"—which made him feel better, "for nothing is so cruel as to be tormented by one's fellow citizens." But "the touching scenes" occasioned by his resignation, he hoped, would stand him in good stead.[81] To a more intimate friend he was more confidential: "Yesterday I had to hold out the hope that I would stay on for the sake of preserving order during the night." Nor could he "abandon citizens who put their complete trust" in him. Yet his difficulties, he suspected, were likely to redouble if he stayed on as commandant, for some conspirators were obviously ready to undermine him with "outrageous calumnies." And how long would the people, "led by an invisible hand," retain their confidence in him? If he remained, he might be "in the terrible position of witnessing evil without remedying it."[82]

Perhaps the commandant general was still seriously considering resignation. But even if his "resignation" was meant to be something more than a carefully prepared rebuke to a population that had forgotten its civic responsibilities, he would have had to be made of sterner stuff to resist the appeals which now were directed to him from every quarter. The maneuver, in so far as it was a maneuver, was well timed. On the morning of the next day, July 25, one hundred and twenty delegates, elected by the districts of Paris in accordance with the Electors' recent instructions, assembled. This was the assembly that was to help provide a municipal constitution for Paris. Bailly opened its session by thanking

---

[80] Bailly and Duveyrier, II, 377; Lucien Scheler and W. A. Smeaton (eds.), *Lavoisier et la Révolution française* (Paris, [1961]), II, 67–68, 181–83; and Maurois, *Adrienne* (Paris), p. 204.

[81] Lafayette to Liancourt, July 24, *Mémoires*, II, 321. This is obviously the letter referred to in *Procès-verbal de l'Assemblée nationale*, No. 32, p. 9, and *AP*, VIII, 278 (July 25).

[82] Lafayette to [Mme de Simiane], July 24, *Mémoires*, II, 320.

the districts for his election as mayor and pledged to "this first body really representing the commune" to perform his duties faithfully.

As the only other elective official of the city, Lafayette was obviously called upon to speak next. Would he now act as commandant pro tempore, waiting for his successor to be named, or would he consider himself the regular and permanent commandant? Explaining once more his reasons for having offered his resignation (including this time, along with the disregard for law and order, the delay of the districts in creating a central body), he nevertheless expressed his satisfaction with the "sentiments of concord" and with the readiness to accept discipline which all the districts were now displaying. He was at last satisfied that "scenes of horror would not recur." Hence he felt moved to repeat his pledge "to devote his whole life to the service of the brave and generous people of Paris"; and so he swore "faithfully to fulfill the duties of commandant general, to act within the limits that would be placed upon the office, and never to forget that the military was subordinate to the civil power." For their part the delegates gave renewed pledges of confidence. In the names of their respective districts and of the citizens of Paris as a whole they all pledged obedience to orders dictated by the public welfare and emanating with proper authority from the commander-in-chief, to the end that the general will might be joined to his and the glory of the nation placed upon a firm, unchanging foundation.[83] Bailly, apprehending that this pledge might subordinate the districts, a civil authority, to a military officer, now suggested that he and Lafayette bind themselves to each other by an oath of mutual esteem. So, to the manifest satisfaction of the assembly, the two men embraced in token of their readiness as "its two chiefs . . . to serve the public interest."[84]

Convinced at last that the city had not lost the affection and the services of its beloved commander, the district representatives

---

[83] Lacroix, I, 2–12, 16. Cf. Bailly, *Mémoires*, II, 145.

[84] Bailly, *Mémoires*, II, 145–46; *Mémoires*, II, 283–85; Scheler and Smeaton, II, 72; and *Procès-verbal des séances de l'Assemblée des Représentans de la Commune de Paris* (Paris, [1789]), pp. 12–15.

could now turn to their work of organizing a new government for Paris. A week of horror, perhaps also of intrigue, thus came to a close. Lafayette might easily have been pleased with the outcome, for he could flatter himself that he had strengthened his hand. His threat to withdraw had brought a clear-cut demonstration in favor of lawful processes and properly constituted authority. If it was a great personal triumph, it was also a triumph for order. But order was not enough; it could be only a means. A means to what end?

BIBLIOGRAPHICAL NOTES

The catalogue of the exposition at the Archives Nationales commemorating the bicentenary of Lafayette's birth in 1957, prepared under the auspices of Director General Charles Braibant, quotes liberally from a number of not easily accessible documents. Much the same can be said of the Blancheteau catalogue drawn up for the centenary of Lafayette's death. The Blancheteau collection is now in the Cornell University Library.

The letters of Bailli de Virieu, the minister of Parma in France, to his government have been edited by Vicomte de Grouchy and Antoine Guillois under the title of *La Révolution française racontée par un diplomate étranger* (Paris, 1903). They give a well-informed but usually second-hand account of the events of July 1789 (as well as of other events).

The minutes of the Assembly of Electors were edited by Duveyrier with the assistance of Bailly and the other Electors in a way that will be described in a future volume. Because they were the composite work of several eye-witnesses, they have a high degree of credibility, but they are likely to err in the direction of enthusiasm for the Revolution.

CHAPTER VIII

Armed Citizens into National Guard

AT ITS inaugural meeting the new assembly of delegates
from the districts of Paris immediately assumed a share of
the responsibility for running Paris. Once assured of the
continued service of the mayor and the commandant general,
it appointed its own members to each of the Electors' standing
committees and at the same time appointed a committee of six-
teen, one from each quarter of Paris, to draft a plan for the city's
government. At a later session that day it decided to call itself "the
Assembly of the Representatives of the Commune of Paris," implying that the Electors were not representatives and thus indicating its own intention at the right time to displace them.[1]

Lafayette lost no time in informing the municipal body that
his Military Committee was studying the reorganization of the
city's militia. Although he did not think he should formally
submit a plan for the military until the civil organization was completed, he nevertheless imparted some general views on the subject. In accordance with the principle that the military be subordinate to the civil authority, he asked the municipality to designate
all the officers of the Paris National Guard (except, of course,
the commanding general, who held office by popular election).
The Assembly of Representatives expressed warm appreciation of
his readiness to subordinate the military to the civil authority, but
convinced that military efficiency required mutual confidence in
the top echelons, it requested him to nominate those he wanted on
his staff.[2] An impressive number of persons came to Lafayette

[1] Lacroix, I, 10–11 (July 25).

[2] *Ibid.*, pp. 10–13, and *Procès-verbal des séances de l'Assemblée de Représentans*, pp.
12–15, 21.

seeking officers' commissions as well as safe conducts, certificates of service in the Paris Guard, or other documents,[3] and such documents became sufficiently valuable to induce the municipality's provisional committee of police to issue a warning against counterfeiters.[4]

Lafayette's subordination of the military to the civil arm should have allayed suspicion that he was scheming to make himself a military dictator. Nevertheless, some observers remained apprehensive. The *Journal de Paris*, the oldest daily of France, reporting the inaugural session of the Representatives on July 25 in an all too succinct account, described the assurances given to Bailly and Lafayette as a pledge to obey those two officials "in everything that they would command for the public service."[5] The District of the Cordeliers, where Danton was the prominent figure, interpreted this journalistic report to mean that the Representatives had promised unconditional obedience, and it sent a deputation to the Hôtel de Ville to protest against such a sweeping submission to the will of any man. The matter was easily settled by the Representatives' decision to publish a more correct version of the pledge.[6] In addition, Lafayette disarmed his critics by denying all imputations that he intended to established a military dictatorship. In a letter (July 29) to the presidents of the sixty districts, he urged them to submit their problems to their civil officials—the mayor and the Representatives—not to him. While the plans for the organization of the military branch of the city government, he pointed out, were further advanced than those for the civil branch, both would delimit the powers of the military, and meanwhile the danger of

[3] For example, see Morris diary, July 27–29, Davenport (ed.), I, 163–65; Mège, *Gaultier*, II, 200–201; Lafayette to Bailly, August 5, BN, Fr. 11697, p. 3; Bailly and Duveyrier, II, 471; Lafayette to M. Serieys, July 31, Huntington Library, HM 20682; André Girodie, *Exposition du centenaire de Lafayette 1757–1834. Catalogue* (Musée de l'Orangerie, 1934), item 141; Librairie Henri Sauffroy, catalogue No. 70 (July 1933), item 18995; certificate dated August 4, Indiana University, Ball Collection; BVP, Collection Liésville, carton marked "Révolution française divers," Série 21; and Armand Brette, *Recueil de documents relatifs à la convocation des Etats généraux de 1789* (Paris, 1844–1915), II, 596.

[4] *Révolutions de Paris*, No. 4, August 2–8, pp. 42–43.

[5] July 27, p. 937.

[6] Lacroix, I, 16, 26–27, 32–33, 36, and *Suite des procès-verbaux des séances de l'Assemblée de Représentans de la Commune de Paris* (Paris, 1789), pp. 7, 13–14.

confounding the two must be avoided. As for himself, "to see to the safety of the capital and to good order among its armed citizens, to execute the decrees of your representatives, to live with the intent to obey you, and to die, if need be, to defend you—these are the only duties, the only rights of the one whom you have deigned to name commandant general."[7]

One of the first problems to receive attention from the newly inaugurated municipality was the indiscriminate bearing of arms. On the very day of their formal inauguration (July 25), the mayor and the commandant general issued a joint announcement to manufacturers, dealers, and owners requiring them to turn their muskets over to the district military committees—for compensation, if surrendered within three days, otherwise to be confiscated outright. This announcement went to the district authorities with a letter from Lafayette explaining that its major intent was to disarm persons without regular domicile; those who brought in their arms might be permitted to retain weapons for their own defense, and a careful inventory of the rest was to be made. In this way the districts would easily be able to locate the weapons left in safe hands and to keep them out of unsafe ones.[8] The commandant general also took measures to apprehend and to disarm the unauthorized patrols that continued to roam the streets.[9]

Deputations from other cities came to the Hôtel de Ville looking for advice on the organization of their militia, and nearby towns which had not yet organized their own guards or, if they had, found them inadequate asked to be protected by the Paris Guard.[10] Demands for muskets poured in from neighboring communities as well as from the Paris districts, but shipments of firearms out of town were held up until Lafayette could determine that they were intended for a legitimate purpose.[11] He distributed

[7] *Journal de Paris*, August 1, p. 957, and *Mémoires*, II, 283. A contemporary copy (perhaps one of the originals) is in Indiana University, Ball Collection.

[8] July 26, *Recueil des arrêtés*, pp. 60–61, and *Révolutions de Paris*, No. 5, August 9–15, pp. 2–3.

[9] Bailly and Duveyrier, II, 399–400.

[10] *Ibid.*, pp. 401, 425–28, 448–49, 454–55, 500; Tuetey, I, 89, No. 855; and Lacroix, I, 101. Cf. Mège, *Gaultier*, I, 233, and II, 222–23.

[11] Bailly and Duveyrier, II, 411.

what arms he had, depleting his own reserves, and sent regrets that he had no more, while the Military Committee commissioned all of Paris' gunsmiths and armorers to work at full capacity.[12] In their anxiety to be well armed some district battalions stripped nearby public edifices and private châteaux of their cannon, parading them as "spoils from the aristocrats" and installing them at strategic points in their districts amid the blare of bands and the plaudits of onlookers.[13] If Lafayette disapproved of this kind of lawlessness, he made no record of his disapproval. One prudent or patriotic lady presented him personally with nine small cannon from her château as a gift to the city.[14]

Extraordinary measures like these to arm the forces of law and order seemed barely to match the continual threat of lawlessness. An always potential source of danger was the incendiary portion of the press. At some point the kind of liberty of the press which ought to be preserved seemed to pass into the kind of license which ought to be suppressed. The Assembly of Electors, believing that at least anonymously printed matter might be kept from circulation, ordered the National Guard to arrest all vendors of newspapers, broadsides, pamphlets, and other publications which did not carry the printer's name.[15] So another category of suspects was added to those of the brigand, the agitator, the illegally armed, the "undomiciled," the disorderly, the criminal, and other offenders, real or potential, whom the National Guard already had to hold in check.[16]

The danger of new outbursts was exacerbated by the continuing threat of famine. Despite cheerful assurances from Paris' own magistrates, despite agreements with other cities and their promises to speed up food deliveries, the bread shortage remained deplorable.[17] Even with the best intentions promises were hard to

---

[12] *Du règne de Louis XVI*, pp. 99–91; Lacroix I, 98–99; and *Révolutions de Paris*, No. 5, August 9–15, pp. 2–3.

[13] *Révolutions de Paris*, No. 4, August 2–8, pp. 16–17, 30. Cf. Tuetey, II, 389, No. 3660.

[14] *Journal de Paris*, August 4, p. 971.

[15] Bailly and Duveyrier, II, 367–69.

[16] *Ibid.*, pp. 396–97.   [17] *Ibid.*, pp. 367–69, 383, 396–97, 417–21.

keep, because the other cities had their own shortages of food as well as of guards. They had to reduce shipments to a minimum and to ship what they could under convoys all too inadequate to ward off hungry inhabitants and brigands along the way.[18] On July 31 the Assembly of Representatives, having consulted with Lafayette, instructed him to take up the matter with the royal ministers.[19]

Meanwhile the likelihood of bread riots mounted. Distress in the Faubourg Saint Antoine had been little assuaged by a distribution of 45,000 livres raised by the theaters and other subscribers, and the citizens of nearby Saint Denis, after lynching one of its officials accused of causing food scarcity, forced the town authorities to lower the price of bread. The Assembly of Representatives, fearing a similar outbreak in Paris, posted a proclamation in Paris and Saint Denis declaring that to sell bread at less than the Paris price was impossible, and Lafayette had to send three hundred guardsmen with seventeen cannon to Saint Denis in order to make its meaning clear.[20] When the city of Provins arrested the agents of the Paris Committee on Subsistence and impounded the provisions which they had gathered, the Representatives appealed (in one of the earliest calls for national solidarity, for the solidarity of Frenchmen rather than of Man in general) to "the sentiments of union and fraternity . . . which should be common to all Frenchmen as children of the same *patrie*." The Representatives ordered Lafayette to support the deputies dispatched to Provins with their patriotic appeal, whereupon he reinforced their rhetoric with four hundred guardsmen and two pieces of artillery.[21] The food

---

[18] *Ibid.,* p. 493; Tuetey, I, 352, No. 3178; Committee on Subsistence of Meulan to that of Paris, July 26, 1789, *Bulletin trimestriel, année 1907* of the Commission de recherche et de publication des documents relatifs à la vie économique de la Révolution (Paris, 1907), p. 39; G. Lefèbvre, "Mélanges: documents sur La Grande Peur . . .," *AHRF,* X (1933), 172–73.

[19] Lacroix, I, 61–62 (July 31).

[20] *Ibid.,* p. 88 (August 4), and IV, 623; Bailly, II, 202, 206; and *Du règne de Louis XVI,* p. 98.

[21] Lacroix, I, 91–92 (August 4); Bailly, II, 207–9; *Courrier de Provence,* August 5, p. 108; and *Recueil des arrêtés,* pp. 78–79.

shortage induced Saint Priest, now minister of the king's household, to assign five hundred royal soldiers to convoy duty, asking Lafayette where to post them so as to be most helpful to the Paris militia.[22]

Restlessness was engendered by still another specter to haunt the people of France that summer. As the other cities, following the Parisian example, hastened to reorganize their governments on an elective basis, the country areas suffered an astonishing mass hysteria which moved from province to province and came to be known as the Great Fear. Panic fed upon mixed apprehensions— that the aristocrats were plotting to prevent reform, that foreigners would take advantage of French instability to invade France, that brigands would ravage the countryside in search of food and plunder, that the peasantry, beguiled by hopes of betterment, had been forgotten by their betters. Sometimes encouraged or instigated by the example and the leaders of neighboring cities, mobs of rural inhabitants attacked the châteaux of their districts, destroying the records of their seignorial obligations and, if opposed, those who tried to guard them. The Great Fear reflected and at the same time was reflected by the same kind of uneasiness as threatened to undermine the tranquility of Paris.

Lafayette's announcement to the National Assembly that unrest in Paris was attributable to the instigation of foreigners lent currency to the consoling thought that the mischief was not entirely the fault of Parisians. The British ambassador, not at all consoled by the imputation against his government, formally denied it in a note to the French minister of foreign affairs, who sent it to the National Assembly with the comment that his own investigations supported the ambassador's statement. The president of the National Assembly forwarded both notes to the Paris Electors, who had them printed and circulated in the hope of calming Parisian fears.[23] In general, foreign diplomats and other foreigners in Paris were not hostile to what had happened that July but, rather, were

[22] August 4, A. Dufresne and F. Evrard, *Les Subsistances dans le district de Versailles* (Rennes, 1921), I, 30–31, and Tuetey, I, 353, No. 3182.

[23] Bailly and Duveyrier, II, 459–64, and *AP*, VIII, 287–88 (July 27), 342 (August 4).

favorably impressed by the rapidity with which Lafayette's militia had begun to function and by its ability to preserve order.[24] If, however, foreigners were not responsible for Paris' troubles, all the more reason for holding French aristocrats responsible.

Rumor had it that certain court aristocrats were gathering forces in the provinces and preparing to attack the capital, and so fear of a *complot des étrangers* quickly gave way to, when indeed it was not reinforced by, that of a *complot des aristocrates*. The National Guard, already overtaxed, undertook to withstand a possible assault of aristocrats.[25] More immediate, though potentially less dangerous for the moment, was a more subtle aristocratic "plot" to which Morris lent credence. Morris made it his business to get around, and one of his numerous acquaintances was Bishop Talleyrand, who shared with him a common interest in the Comtesse de Flahaut, who probably was Morris' source of information about goings-on at the court of Versailles. Morris now was fearful that Louis XVI, unhappy about his humiliating and perhaps hazardous position, was considering leaving France and going to Spain. The result might be a kingless state, anarchy, and civil war.

Morris went three times to see Lafayette about this menacing turn of affairs. The first time the marquis was not at home, but Morris saw him the next morning, before he left for the Hôtel de Ville, and suggested that "some consolation" be given the king. Being bound by a pledge of secrecy, Morris did not answer Lafayette's questions directly, and having to leave, the commandant general asked him back for dinner that afternoon. Morris was no more explicit about his source of information at dinner than before, but he did suggest that an association be formed to protect the king and that those who insulted the royal personage be declared public enemies. He also urged that the National Assembly

[24] Jules Flammermont (ed.), *Relations inédites de la prise de la Bastille par le duc de Dorset . . . et le comte de Mercy-Argenteau . . .* (Paris, 1885), pp. 31–32, 120 n.; A. de Nesselrode (ed.), *Lettres et papiers du Chancelier Comte de Nesselrode, 1760–1850* (Paris, [1904]), I, 114; and Massimo Kovalevsky (ed.), *I Dispacci degli ambasciatori veneti* (Turin, 1895), I, 48–49.

[25] Bailly and Duveyrier, II, 425–28.

end its work as soon as possible, drawing up a constitution which should not be "too democratical."[26]

Events soon seemed to indicate that while the king probably was wavering about the course to pursue, Morris had perhaps been misled. For the court again gave evidence of readiness to cooperate with the leaders of the Revolution. One of the underlying causes of tension in Paris had been a suspicion that the aristocrats at Versailles were deliberately keeping Necker out of reach. But Necker returned to Versailles on the very day Morris spoke to Lafayette.[27] That news, broadcast through the city by order of the Electors, brought a feeling of relief. As soon as he reasonably could (July 30), Necker came to Paris, accompanied by his wife, his daughter, some deputies of the National Assembly, Saint Priest, and other friends and relatives.

Once more, citizens, city officials, and the Paris National Guard turned out to greet a celebrity. Lafayette, probably too busy to change his plans on short notice, did not go with the escort which he sent to the city gate, but Adrienne joined the ladies in the party which greeted the city's guest and accompanied him to the Hôtel de Ville. There Lafayette presented him with a revolutionary cockade.[28] Then Necker and some of his party, attended by the mayor and the commandant general, entered the Governor's Room, where the Representatives were assembled. Bailly made a speech of welcome, and Necker replied. Aware that his presence that day put the finishing touch upon the defeat of the court's recent counterrevolutionary effort, he begged the Paris authorities to give every care to the restoration of order, prosperity, and normal legal practices. He lamented especially that the Baron de Besenval, one of his countrymen (Necker was Swiss by birth), had been arrested outside of Paris on his way to Switzerland; Besenval was considered an enemy of the people because he had been commander of the royal troops in the Paris region during the

[26] Morris diary, July 27–28, Davenport (ed.), I, 164–65. See also Morris to Washington, July 31, 1789, *ibid.*, pp. 170–71.

[27] Bailly and Duveyrier, II, 475 (July 28).

[28] *Courrier de Versailles à Paris*, July 31, p. 50.

recent Bastille crisis. The Representatives ordered that Necker's wish for his countryman's release be granted.

The whole assemblage then went to the Grande Salle, where the Electors had foregathered. After more speeches, they decided to commemorate the day by decreeing a general amnesty; the only ones to be considered enemies of the nation thereafter would be those whose excesses troubed the public peace again.[29] Now a close friend of Lafayette, Moreau de Saint-Méry, as one of the two presidents of the Electors, marked the occasion with a gallant flourish. He presented Mme de Lafayette with a gift from her husband's colleagues in the city government—"the colors of liberty," a red and blue cockade.[30] So "that young hero whom a brilliant destiny seems to summon to the revolutions of empires and the triumph of liberty" shared Necker's spotlight.[31] When Necker was ready to leave, Bailly and Lafayette conducted him to his carriage, and the women of the market decorated it with branches of olive and laurel. The National Guard escorted the ministerial party back to the city gate.[32] Although Lafayette wanted his friend Moreau to take a high post in the National Guard, somewhere in the course of the day's formalities he had found the opportunity to present to Necker his friend's preference to be named royal interdant of his native Martinique. (When that appointment actually came through later, however, unsettled conditions in that island colony helped Lafayette to induce Moreau to remain in Paris.)[33]

Necker's triumph once more made the Revolution seem victorious. That night the people danced and sang in the squares, houses were illuminated—Lafayette's among the rest—and market women strolled the streets chanting couplets in praise of the king,

[29] Bailly and Duveyrier, II, 502, 506–7, 523; Bailly, II, 171–75; and Lacroix, I, 44–52.

[30] Bailly and Duveyrier, II, 507.

[31] *Journal de Paris,* July 31, p. 953.

[32] *Courier national,* June 23, suppl. p. 2, and *Entrée triomphante de M. Necker à l'Hôtel de Ville* . . . [Paris, 1789].

[33] A.-L. Elicona, *Un Colonial sous la Révolution en France et en Amérique: Moreau de Saint-Méry* (Paris, 1934), pp. 69–70.

the dauphin, and Necker.[34] That night, too, another event seemed to betoken the end of an epoch. Without ceasing to exist entirely, the Assembly of Electors, the body which had so far guided the Revolution in Paris, merged into the Assembly of Representatives, which it had called into being. Commandant General Lafayette now considered himself formally responsible to both the mayor and the Assembly of Representatives. It was plain for everyone to see, however, that real power rested with the National Guard or, if sufficiently roused, the fighting public, and Lafayette was chief of the one and a principal idol of the other.

Within the next two weeks, Louis XVI reorganized his ministry. Necker, Montmorin, and Saint Priest, friends of Lafayette and of the Revolution, were reappointed, and two of the new ministers were chosen from among the liberals of the National Assembly itself. One of these was Archbishop Champion de Cicé of Bordeaux, who became keeper of the seals, and the other was the Comte de Latour du Pin, likewise a personal friend of Lafayette, who became minister of war. In reporting these appointments to the National Assembly, the king stressed his desire to ensure the "most constant and amiable harmony."[35] Lafayette had reason to feel pleased. With a royal ministry made up almost entirely of his own friends, with words like "amnesty" and "harmony" in the air, he might well have concluded that perhaps Morris had overestimated the need for some "consolation" to a king said to be contemplating flight.

Any illusion, however, that disaffection had ceased proved ephemeral. Many were dissatisfied with what had been done because it was either too little or too much, and in the still effervescent state of public opinion they cast their private views and their public actions on the side of continued political agitation even at the risk of disorder. Perhaps, if Lafayette's suspicions were correct (and it was his business as well as his interest to keep well informed on such matters), agitators slipped silver coins into the pockets of those who gathered to listen to their harangues, even forging his signature to spurious orders forbidding millers to

[34] Lacroix, 2d ser., IV, 204, and *Du règne de Louis XVI*, pp. 86–87.

[35] *AP*, VIII, 341.

grind flour for the capital.[36] His lifelong hatred of the British induced him to believe, despite the British ambassador's denial, that foreign agents, particularly British agents, jealous of the power that freedom would bring to France, were engaged in machinations "to make liberty appear contemptible."[37] His distrust of aristocrats and Orléanists led him into the same kind of error as his enemies committed in describing his activities; he ascribed to conspiracy the course of events of which he disapproved, while at the same time discounting conspiracy as a factor in creating the Great Fear, which he ascribed instead to an expression of the "electric effect of a generous impulse for which the [National] Assembly, the caiptal and its chiefs had openly given the signal."[38]

Doubtless there were agitators, perhaps in conspiratorial groups, at work in both the capital and the provinces of France. But they were working at cross purposes, and they probably canceled each other out—except in one regard: they all added to the current unsettlement, greatly enhancing the probability of disorder. The very day after Lafayette withdrew his proffered resignation and repledged himself to the city's service, he was called from his Sunday rest (July 26) by a courier bringing an urgent message from the Hôtel de Ville: the city hall was in peril! Some "ill-intentioned persons" had spread the canard that vast quantities of silver lay hidden in the Hôtel de Ville, and it was feared that a crowd would gather in the Place de Grève, each seeking a share. Hastening to the spot, Lafayette called up "an imposing military force," but no mob appeared.[39] Whether he had been the victim of a false alarm or his show of strength had scotched a riot, he dared not relax his vigil.

The next day another unpleasant episode indicated how precarious was the plight of those who had incurred the wrath of "patriots." The Maréchal de Castries, an old acquaintance of Lafayette and a former minister, was known to be unfriendly to the Revolution. Even though he had taken the precaution to acquire a

[36] *Mémoires*, II, 287.

[37] *Ibid.*, III, 233–34.

[38] *Ibid.*, II, 285–86.

[39] Bailly and Duveyrier, II, 438–39.

passport, he was arrested on trying to leave Paris. Learning of his arrest, the Electors offered him a special permit if he preferred to leave the city or an escort of Electors if he preferred to return. In addition, Lafayette ordered all Guardsmen to take every step to afford proper respect for the passports issued by the Hôtel de Ville and, in particular, to carry out the wishes of the Electors regarding Castries.[40] A few days earlier Castries would probably have fared badly, but lynching seemed for the moment to have passed out of style.

The very next day, however, the Besenval affair reached a new climax, with a new threat of "popular justice." Hardly had his compatriot Necker successfully requested Besenval's release than one of the more radical districts of Paris, the Oratoire, questioning the legality of the amnesty, sent its own agents to rearrest him, and protests against his release came in from other districts as well. That night (July 30) the Assembly of Representatives, thus challenged, decided to rescind Besenval's amnesty, obviously intending to put him under a sort of protective custody and forestall a lynching. When they learned that Besenval had been rearrested at Brie-Comte-Robert, they ordered Lafayette to send a hundred men to keep him safe though a prisoner there.[41]

Subsequently, acting upon an appeal from the Paris municipality, the National Assembly decided that Besenval, as an agent of the "perfidious" ministry which it had declared responsible for the catastrophe of July 13–14, should be held for trial by a tribunal which the National Assembly would itself appoint. The purpose of this decision was to place the prisoner "under the protection of the law" and guard him from becoming a victim of popular fury.[42] This subtlety, however, did not diminish the public's demand for Besenval's head; on the contrary, the demand was aggravated by recurrent reports of a plot to help him break out of prison. In consequence, Lafayette sent two officers to Brie-Comte-Robert

---

[40] *Ibid.*, pp. 456–58, and Tuetey, I, 88, No. 848.

[41] Lacroix, I, 53–55 (July 30), 62–63 (July 31); Bailly and Duveyrier, II, 534–36; Bailly, II, 181–83; and *Mémoires du Baron de Besenval,* ed. Fr. Barrière (Paris, 1882), II, 372–73.

[42] Lacroix, I, 67–68, and *AP*, VIII, 308–14.

to take the necessary precautions against such an eventuality. On their return he took them to the Assembly of Representatives to report the steps they had taken for Besenval's security, and the Assembly ordered their report posted in the hope of quieting public apprehension that the accused might yet cheat justice. To make certain that no one would free the prisoner on forged orders, Lafayette received permission to require Besenval's guards to respect only such instructions as bore, in addition to the signatures of the mayor and the commandant general, those of the two presidents and one secretary of the Representatives and were besides sealed with the arms of both the city and Lafayette.[43] Thus, out of deference to the more vociferous elements of public opinion Besenval was not amnestied, but at least "popular justice" gave way to legal police measures. (Besenval eventually was released without incident.)[44]

Under Lafayette's chairmanship the Military Committee had meanwhile kept steadily at work upon a plan for the organization of the Paris National Guard. Several on the committee were army officers, and it profited from the advice of other experienced soldiers—among them Gouvion, who at first substituted for Lafayette when he was absent, and Comte Mathieu Dumas, who had been a member of the recently dissolved royal Council of War and whom Lafayette now considered the committee's spokesman (*rapporteur*).[45] Both of these men could apply their experience as officers in the American War of Independence to the formation of the new citizen army, and Lafayette was later to say of his own part in the enterprise: "My observations in America and in several parts of Europe had been directed toward that end."[46] In addition, he consulted another veteran of the American war, Alexandre de Lameth, and still other members of the National Assembly—Joseph Barnave, La Rochefoucauld, and Duport among them.

[43] Lacroix, I, 74–75 (August 1), 171–75 (August 11); *Révolutions de Paris*, No. 5, August 9–15, pp. 26–27; and *Du règne de Louis XVI*, p. 116.

[44] Besenval was released in January 1790.

[45] *Mémoires*, II, 266, and IV, 93–94. A list of the members of the committee is given in Appendix V of Lacroix, VII, 639–44.

[46] *Mémoires*, III, 227.

They all met together at least once at his house to discuss such problems as the best use of the French Guard.[47]

The Military Committee met daily in long double sessions, and Lafayette sat with it almost every day for some time. But since he had many other things to do and Gouvion also eventually had to give most of his attention to staff work, the committee chose the Marquis de Chabert to act as vice-chairman, and Lafayette's aide Pierre-Auguste de Lajard sometimes served as liaison between the committee and the commandant general. Its minutes amply testify that Lafayette was kept fully informed of its progress, which he regularly prompted and superintended.

Until the committee's plan could be completed and approved, Lafayette had to put up with a makeshift organization of the National Guard. He moved troops from one district which was well provided to another which was less so, and he employed the French Guard, the Basoche, and other volunteer units freely. One of the first things that the Military Committee wanted to know was how many able-bodied men Paris actually could provide, so as to fix the number of companies, the length of service, the need for paid professionals, and similar problems; and so Lafayette had to circularize the districts to ask for their most precise data on available effectives.[48]

Ten days of hard work brought the Military Committee's draft to the stage where its first sections were ready for consideration by the civil authority. Obviously wishing to lend the occasion as much gravity as possible, on July 31 Lafayette sent two aides to request permission to bring the Military Committee to the Representatives' meeting in the Governor's Room. Permission granted, the commandant general's aides and the committee filed in, and Lafayette followed a little later. When all were finally seated, he presented the first three titles of the committee's draft proposal, with explanatory remarks where he thought they were needed. He made clear that neither he nor the committee considered their

[47] Dumas, I, 101–3; *Mémoires de T. Lameth* (ed. Welvert), pp. 110–11; and A. Lameth, I, 71.

[48] Lafayette to Messieurs, July 25, E. Girard and Georges Andrieux, *Autographes* (catalogue of sale of November 22–23, 1937), item 131; Lafayette to the District of Saint Joseph, July 25, Tuetey, II, 79, No. 740; and Lafayette to Messieurs, August 5, Columbia University Library, De Witt Clinton Collection.

proposal final; experience would doubtless suggest the desirability of some changes.[49]

The proposed "Regulations" (*Règlement*) of the Paris National Guard was considerably detailed. Title I began by suppressing all troops previously employed as guards or police or for other service in Paris. Then it proceeded to organize the "Infanterie Nationale Parisienne." Conforming to the realities rather than to patriotic, egalitarian aspirations, it counted principally upon paid professional soldiers to perform regular duty and do the hard work. Volunteers were to assist in policing the districts and to provide mass strength in case of emergency or parade; they were to be subject to call but to pay their own expenses. Each of the sixty districts of the city was to provide one "center" company of paid troops, barracked within the district, and four companies of "non-paid" (i.e., volunteer) troops, residing locally. These five companies, each numbering one hundred men, were to constitute a district's battalion. All regularly domiciled citizens aged twenty to fifty, but no transients (*non domiciliés*) and no workers and artisans, "who ought to be left to their work," and no domestics, were to be registered and subject to call. A district which could not provide the required number might draw on the nearest district with a surplus. Ten battalions would compose a division, each battalion and division being assigned a number by lot. There would thus be six divisions for the whole city. Each division was to have a company of grenadiers (i.e., an elite unit), which was to be the center company of the battalion designated by lot to be its first battalion. Including officers, whose ranks and number were specified, the infantry of the entire city was expected to reach 31,058 (a more realistic figure than the 48,000 that had been called for by the Electors before the capture of the Bastille). In addition, a troop of cavalry and a park of artillery were envisaged for the future. All officers and men were to swear allegiance to the municipality.[50]

Title II dealt principally with the selection of officers. The com-

---

[49] *Procès-verbal du Comité militaire*, Part I, pp. 26–27 (July 31); Lacroix, I, 64 (July 31); and *Mémoires*, II, 266.

[50] *Règlement* [sic] *pour la formation, organization, solde, police et administration de l'Infanterie nationale parisienne* (Paris, 1789) (hereafter cited as *Règlement*), pp. 1–8.

mandant general was to be elected in the same manner as the mayor of the city. Staff officers, whether of headquarters or of the divisions, were to be chosen by the municipality on nomination by the general; division chiefs by representatives selected for that purpose by the ten districts concerned; battalion commanders by their district; paid company captains by vote of their district; paid company lieutenants by seniority from the most deserving of the non-commissioned officers; and "non-paid" company officers by their districts. When vacancies were to be filled, all officers of the paid companies were to be eligible for a paid post, and all officers of the non-paid companies for posts within their battalions. In the advancement of non-commissioned officers seniority, merit, and literacy were to be taken into account. Thus the elective principle was tempered by a respect for service and competence. Commissions were to be signed by the mayor as civil authority as well as by the commandant general. Remuneration was left for future decision.[51]

Title III prescribed the uniform, flags, and equipment of the Guard. The soldier's uniform was to include a royal blue coat with white lapels and facings, scarlet collar, white lining, scarlet edging, and yellow buttons, a white vest, white breeches, black leggings in winter and white in summer, and a uniform hat trimmed with black braid. Every man, private or officer, was to wear a cockade in his hat, and here the *Règlement* introduced an innovation: the cockade was to be not blue and red but white with a blue and red border. (How this modification of the revolutionary cockade came about we shall presently see.) Officers' uniforms were to be the same as the men's but distinguished from theirs by such things as epaulets, trimmings, cords, swords, and feathers, different ranks of officers wearing various distinguishing appurtenances. For example, the feather that the commandant general was to wear in his hat was to be white with red and blue borders, whereas division chiefs and some other high officers were to wear white feathers and aides-de-camp red ones. The paid troops were issued their uniforms and equipment gratis, with provision for periodic repairs and replacements, but non-paid officers and men

[51] *Ibid.*, pp. 8–11.

were required to provide their own effects.[52] In short, a poor man could hardly afford to be a volunteer member of the National Guard.

When the reading of the three lengthy titles of the *Règlement* ended, Lafayette indicated that, not expecting approval on the first reading of his complicated report, he was prepared to have the document printed for further study. Some Representatives, uncertain whether the Assembly had the power to approve the *Règlement*, feared that the districts would protest if it did so. After considerable debate the Assembly authorized Lafayette, as soon as he had enough copies printed, to send one to each representative, who would thereupon go to his district and request approval— after which the Assembly would re-examine the document.[53] Once more the issue of district autonomy as opposed to central control was raised, to the advantage of the districts. Lafayette had to wait, even if emergencies and crises might not, for district approval.

When the report was printed and distributed, a fourth title had been added, with the indication that, although approved by the Military Committee, unlike the first three titles the fourth had not been approved for printing by the Assembly of Representatives. Title IV dealt with such matters as lodging of the paid (center) companies, military discipline and etiquette, accounting methods, parade and police duties, and the responsibilities of men and officers.[54] A fifth title, to deal with enlistments, pay, and records, was promised.[55] Article 17 of Title IV anticipated a method of training of recruits which was to become more famous in the Revolutionary and Napoleonic armies as the *amalgame:* "The men of a company will be divided into as many squads as there are corporals so that the new soldiers will be mixed with the old."[56]

---

[52] *Ibid.,* pp. 11–18.

[53] *Ibid.,* pp. 18–19; Lacroix, I, 64 (July 31); and *Procès-verbal du Comité militaire,* Part I, pp. 27 (July 31), 29–30 (August 2).

[54] *Règlement,* pp. 25–42.

[55] *Ibid.,* p. 25. The Military Committee, in fact, continued beyond Title V to Title VII: see *Procès-verbal du Comité militaire,* Part I, p. 54 (August 12).

[56] *Règlement,* p. 34.

The change required by Title III in the cockade of the National Guard, simple though it was, had a lasting symbolic effect. The single uniform article all the guardsmen had worn up to that time was the red and blue cockade. It so happened that while red and blue were the colors of Paris, they were also those of the Orléans family. To make certain that no one would misunderstand where the Guard's loyalty lay, Lafayette decided to add to these colors that of the reigning family—the Bourbon white. In consequence, the Military Committee had agreed, and hence the Regulations required, that the Guards' hat be decorated with "a cockade of white demity piped with blue and red."[57] Thence arose the tricolor—blue, white, and red—colors prominent also in the proposed uniform of the National Guard. Lafayette recognized when he instituted the new cockade that he was introducing something momentous, and he made a little speech which, as he afterward remembered it, foretold the brilliant future of the tricolor and of the citizen army: "I place before you a cockade which will go around the world, and an institution, civil and military at the same time, which is bound to triumph over the old tactics of Europe and which will reduce arbitrary governments to the alternative of being conquered unless they imitate it." He proudly recalled that speech on several later occasions.[58]

On August 2 the commandant general provided the Representatives with printed copies of the *Règlement,* and the Assembly referred them to the districts. In some districts the plan provoked heated discussion, but the reports which came to the city hall were generally favorable.[59]

[57] *Ibid.,* p. 12. See also *Procès-verbal du Comité militaire,* Part I, pp. 18 (July 27), 29 (August 2), and *Mémoires,* II, 266–67, n.2.

[58] *Mémoires,* II, 267. The version of this speech *ibid.,* III, 281, is shorter by the omission of the words *qui doit triompher des vieilles tactiques de l'Europe, et,* but otherwise it is almost verbatim the same. The longer version in Vol. II was recollected later, about 1829 (see *ibid.,* p. 262); that of Vol. III about 1815 (see *ibid.,* p. 271). Perhaps the freshness of the memory of the Revolutionary and Napoleonic "liberations" accounts for the omission in 1815; a reference to the same speech (*ibid.,* II, 228) seems to corroborate such a supposition. The editors of Bailly's *Mémoires* quote (II, 194 n.), with only a slight change of wording, the longer version. See also below, Appendix III.

[59] Lacroix, I, 79 (August 2); *Procès-verbal du Comité militaire,* Part I, p. 30 (August 2); BN, Fr. 6687: [S.P. Hardy], *Mes loisirs, ou journal des événemens . . .,* VIII, 418; and *Patriote français,* August 5, p. 3.

The atmosphere was still charged with recriminations over the Besenval affair when a new furor exploded—this time with the Marquis de La Salle, second in command of the National Guard, as its target. He had never been popular, and of late complaints against him had become outspoken. Now he was the innocent victim of a misunderstanding. In the continuing quest for gunpowder a supply had been ordered from the powder works at Essonne, down the Seine River, and to make room for it, a large quantity of low-grade powder used for blasting outside Paris was to be removed from the Paris Arsenal. This powder was known as the *poudre de traite* because it was a common article of commerce in the slave trade (*traite*). During one of Lafayette's numerous absences La Salle had signed the order to remove the inferior powder.

On August 5 the *poudre de traite* was being loaded on a boat which was to take it away when some chance bystanders became suspicious. Hastening to the Hôtel de Ville about six o'clock in the afternoon, they reported to Bailly and Lafayette that someone was making off with the city's gunpowder supply. Neither of the two officials knew the facts, but since they were aware that counterfeit orders were not uncommon, they too became suspicious. So they sent a detachment of the Guard to hold the boat until morning.[60] The detachment placed under arrest the four National Guardsmen whom the commandant of the local district (Saint Louis de la Culture), satisfied with La Salle's order, had sent to watch over the boat.

The next morning the commandant of the District of Saint Louis de la Culture demanded the release of his men, and the Representatives quickly recognized that another public eruption was in the making. Word had already got around that men claiming to be National Guardsmen had been caught in the act of taking from the Arsenal a boatload of *poudre de traitre* ("traitor's powder") on an order signed only by La Salle, and strident voices once more rent the air of the Place de Grève. When La Salle later reported for duty, he learned even before he got out of his fiacre that he was in

[60] Lacroix, I, 106–9; *Révolutions de Paris,* No. 4, August 2–8, pp. 28–29; *Courrier de Versailles à Paris,* August 8, pp. 177, 182; and Bailly, II, 222–24.

danger, and he hastily withdrew.[61] The Assembly of Representatives ordered the boatload of powder returned to the Arsenal at once and decreed that thereafter no war materials were to leave the city except on the express order of the mayor and the commandant general. This order was immediately proclaimed in the Place de Grève.[62]

That afternoon Lafayette went to the District of Saint Louis de la Culture to clarify the misunderstanding created by the seemingly unauthorized orders of La Salle. Thence he proceeded to the District of Saint-Etienne-du-Mont to see the first casualty in his militia—a guardsman who had been seriously injured by the carelessness of a comrade. With his habitual generosity he assumed personal responsibility for the wounded man's care, sent him to the hospital, and promised him a pension.[63]

After Lafayette's departure from the District of Saint Louis de la Culture, La Salle's plight grew worse. Zealous patriots from other districts arrived at the Arsenal and, seizing Lavoisier, who was one of its directors, and another director, took them to the city hall for trial. Before the commandant general could return to the Hôtel de Ville, the directors of the Arsenal succeeded in explaining that the powder they had tried to move out had small value for Paris even as industrial powder and that they had been authorized by La Salle to move it. Immediately the wrath of the spectators turned against La Salle. Several Representatives tried to assure them that there had been no plot, only a misunderstanding, and the Assembly passed a resolution to that effect, which they ordered publicized in the Place de Grève at once.

When Lafayette at last reached the Hôtel de Ville, the Representatives were still in the Grande Salle with a roomful of angry people demanding that someone be punished. It looked as if another lynching was about to take place. Before entering the Grande Salle, Lafayette sent orders to the districts to send up de-

[61] Mémoires, II, 288.

[62] Lacroix, I, 109; Bailly, II, 223–24; and Courrier de Versailles à Paris, August 15, p. 299.

[63] Hardy, pp. 423, 429; Patriote français, August 7, p. 2; and Scheler and Smeaton, II, 118–20.

tachments at once to occupy the Place de Grève and the nearby streets. No matter how hard his messengers drove their horses, however, he would need time, since it could be expected to take hours for the districts to assemble enough Guardsmen to be truly helpful. His cue was obviously to play for time.

Hardly had Lafayette entered the Grande Salle and been informed of what had happened in his absence when a huge, angry crowd burst in. The proclamation that there had been no plot seemed only to have enraged the people out on the square, and pushing their way through the doors, they thronged up the stairs and into the meeting hall.[64] What is it you want? Lafayette asked the vindictive citizens. "La Salle," they shouted back. Why? Someone answered: Because he had tried to betray them and had forged Lafayette's name to an order. Lafayette explained that La Salle had not forged his name but had acted only as his deputy, and he recounted events down to the Assembly's proclamation, which he then asked to have read once more. But the clamor only rose higher.

Another approach seemed needed. Why not, Lafayette asked, allow the accused to defend himself? The mob approved of that, and Lafayette dispatched a contingent to La Salle's home to put him under arrest. Which prison should he be sent to while awaiting trial, Lafayette now inquired. The crowd answered that they wanted him brought immediately to the Hôtel de Ville for trial. That would not do, Lafayette replied, for no man should be tried except by a court of law. Moreover, La Salle deserved special consideration, for he had held a position of trust and had rendered devoted service. Some were persuaded, but others (Bailly described them as "agitators")[65] persisted, and as newcomers crowded into the hall, the tumult revived. Someone accused Lafayette of shielding the traitor, hiding him all the while in the city hall, and to demonstrate how false that suspicion was the commandant general ordered a detachment of Guardsmen to make a search, taking

[64] Lacroix, I, 109–16; *Du règne de Louis XVI*, pp. 103–4; Bailly, II, 224–26, 227–29; *Révolutions de Paris*, No. 4, August 2–8, pp. 29–30; and *Patriote français*, August 10, pp. 3–4.

[65] Bailly, II, 229.

some civilians with them, and he posted heavy units at all the exits so that La Salle, if he were there, should not escape.[66] Actually Lafayette was still playing for time. As he argued and tried to demonstrate the hollowness of the mob's suspicions, the districts had been sending up their detachments. As more and more guardsmen arrived and joined those already at the city hall, they formed a continuously growing square, spreading out in all directions from the entrance of the city hall, forcing the crowd to make room for them. Slowly they pushed the demonstrators out of the square and into the adjoining streets.[67] When the contingent that had gone searching for La Salle inside the Hôtel de Ville returned to the Grande Salle to report that they had not been able to find him, it was about eleven o'clock.

By that time the Place de Grève was under the complete control of the National Guard. That was apparently the cue which the commandant general had been waiting for. He addressed the overflowing crowd again and said in effect: "It is very late; you are tired, and so am I. The Place de Grève is now free of disorder; let's all go home."[68] When some of the more persistent of his hearers rushed to see whether he was telling the truth, they saw only orderly files of Guardsmen in the square. Realizing that they had been outmaneuvered, they again quieted down. Several speakers, Lafayette among them, then urged respect for justice and humanity, and slowly the numbers in the Grande Salle dwindled.[69]

By 3 A.M. the detachment sent to La Salle's home to find him

[66] Lacroix, I, 113–16, 118. See also *Du règne de Louis XVI*, pp. 104–5; *Courrier de Versailles à Paris*, August 8, p. 183; and Eugène de Mirecourt, *Avant, pendant et après la Terreur, echos des gazettes françaises independantes, publiées à l'étranger de 1718 à 1794* (Paris, 1865), II, 261–63.

[67] *Mémoires*, II, 288–89, and Bailly, II, 227.

[68] Bailly, II, 228, n.1, and H. Monin (ed.), *Mémoires sur la Bastille: Linguet, Dusaulx* (Paris, 1889), pp. 263–64.

[69] In general, except as otherwise indicated, the account of the La Salle episode has been based on Lacroix and the *Mémoires* of Lafayette, Dusaulx, and Bailly (who, however, was away in Versailles on business until past midnight). Some details in several other accounts—e.g., *Révolutions de Paris* (No. 4, August 2–8, pp. 28–30); *Du règne de Louis XVI* (pp. 103–6); *Deux Amis de la Liberté* (II, 297–98), and the so-called *Mémoires de Condorcet* (II, 70)—have been disregarded on the grounds that they probably were not based upon first-hand observation.

returned without him; he had apparently gone off to his country home. Sending out an order to search for him there, the Assembly adjourned. In the morning small, unrelenting groups headed once more for the Hôtel de Ville to find La Salle, but they were stopped by the National Guard, and murmurings against him in the Palais Royal were rendered harmless by a vigilant district patrol.

Another lynching had been averted by a combination of ruse, reason, cajolery, and, most essential, force. But how long would the combination work? In its minutes of the meeting that had so nearly ended tragically for La Salle the Assembly of Representatives inserted a "résumé" pleading with a people that "had won its liberty" not to deliver itself up to "whatever rumor anyone pleases to spread in order to arm citizen against citizen"; and Lafayette, learning of the possibility of a lynching of a Parisian in Rouen wrote to the authorities there to urge "as man, as Frenchman, and as a citizen honored by the confidence of Parisians" that the accused be judged "in a regular and lawful manner" and not be exposed to "those irregular forms of judgment which without being of any public advantage serve only to make justice and humanity groan."[70] Nevertheless, on August 8 Lafayette, Bailly, and other leading members of the municipality had to spend ill-spared hours cross-examining a drunken man's obviously fantastic story about the Prince de Conti, a prince of the blood, who, the man said, was ready to surrender in order to exculpate himself from charges made against him; the city's officials felt constrained to waste their precious time in that way because they did not dare to let it be said that they were shielding Conti.[71]

In the days which followed, the Representatives took fresh measures to prevent a recurrence of disorder. They authorized the commandant general and the district commanders to prevent "seditious gatherings" (which were not, however, to be confused

[70] "Résumé" in Lacroix, I, 116 (August 6), and Lafayette to Messieurs, August 8, Bibliothèque de Rouen.

[71] On the continued excitement regarding La Salle see *Révolutions de Paris*, No. 4, August 2–8, p. 40; Bailly, II, 299–33; and *Du règne de Louis XVI*, p. 106. On the story about Conti see Lacroix, I, 138–43 (August 9), and Bailly, II, 240–41.

with "assemblies of peaceable citizens").[72] Subsequently, they put control over military supplies as well in Lafayette's hands; he was instructed to place a strong guard at the Arsenal, permitting no munitions to leave without his written order, and even quarrymen were required to get authorization from him (among others) to remove mere blasting powder from the city. But as new supplies of gunpowder arrived, these stringent orders were relaxed, and the demands of the districts and neighboring towns were satisfied. Cartridges were likewise scarce; on August 12, when Lafayette asked the Arsenal for a supply, he found that the districts had already taken all there were. The Assembly thereupon instructed the Arsenal to let the districts have no more except on requisition signed by Bailly and Lafayette.[73]

Meanwhile, the districts had been considering the four titles of the *Règlement* which had been submitted to them. By August 8, forty-three had approved them without reservations, and so the Assembly instructed Lafayette to put the adopted titles into operation. He had meanwhile had his own new uniform made, and on August 9 he put it on for the first time. With its breeches, vest, and facings of white, its coat of royal blue with a red collar it resembled the uniform of the Light Infantry he had commanded during the American war, and it was not greatly dissimilar from that of the French Guard.[74]

Some of the provisions of the Regulations quickly proved impracticable, for a few districts were unable to find four hundred qualified men to form the non-paid companies. Hence they favored enrolling "undomiciled" young men, and Lafayette upon the request of the Military Committee took this problem to the Assembly of Representatives. The Representatives considered amending the Regulations so as to permit any resident of the city to serve if engaged in commerce, finance, shopkeeping (*la pratique*), or the arts and if vouched for by his nearest relative or

---

[72] Lacroix, I, 124 (August 7). See also *Révolutions de Paris,* No. 5, August 9–15, pp. 1, 5, and Bailly, II, 231–32.

[73] Lacroix, I, 120–29, 131, 138, 185–87, 218–19; *Révolutions de Paris,* No. 5, August 9–15, p. 11, and No. 7, August 23–29, p. 21; and Bailly, II, 229, 261.

[74] Lacroix, I, 124–25 (August 7), 126–28, 134–35 (August 8), and Bailly, II, 242.

a domiciled citizen, and they submitted such an amendment to the districts. Most districts, however, took no action, while "undomiciled" young men, particularly members of the Basoche, became impatient.[75]

What to do with the French Guard and the Basoche, his principal standbys in the days before the *Règlement*, now became one of Lafayette's main perplexities. That of the French Guard was favorably solved, but not before some trying experiences. The Duc de Châtelet, their commander, having found them hard to handle after some of them had taken the popular side in the capture of the Bastille, had resigned his command. Without their commanding officer they had become still less docile, and some of them had gone so far as to claim the duke's horses and carriage as war loot. Embarrassing though this situation was in itself for one who wished at the same time to court the French Guard and to preserve a respect for law and order, it was made worse by Châtelet's claim that the carriage was not his but his niece's, and his niece was no other than Adélaïde de Simiane. When the matter came to the attention of the Hôtel de Ville, Bailly thought that the French Guards might sell the carriage and pocket the proceeds, but Lafayette insisted that it must be returned to its owner, and the question had to be put before the highest authority in the city, at that time still the Assembly of Electors. Before the Electors could render a decision, however, the French Guard as a regiment sent a letter thanking them and Lafayette for their good will, affirming its devotion to the revolutionary cause, and giving up its claim. Relieved and impressed, the Electors ordered the letter printed as an example of unselfish patriotism.[76]

The French Guards, however, whether patriotic or merely discreet in this instance, were still without a colonel and were sometimes encouraged to depart from pre-revolution standards of discipline by their non-commissioned officers. Since they did not

---

[75] Lacroix, I, 146–47 (August 10), 191-92 (August 12), 252–54 (August 17); *Procès-verbal du Comité militaire*, Part I, pp. 39–40 (August 8); and *Révolutions de Paris*, No. 5, August 9–15, p. 35, and No. 6, August 16–22, pp. 9–11.

[76] Bailly and Duveyrier, II, 375–77, 408–9; Duveyrier, pp. 369–70; and Bailly, II, 137–38.

know what was going to happen to them, the more aristocratic officers and the men were acting at cross purposes. Some of these officers would have preferred to disband the rebellious unit, but the men, wishing to retain their solidarity as a corps, sent a deputation to Lafayette to protest. Since the king had given him permission to incorporate the French Guard companies in Paris into the National Guard, Lafayette did not want them to disintegrate entirely before some such incorporation could be arranged. Accompanied by his aides, he rode out to meet them one Sunday afternoon (July 26), and amid admiring spectators he addressed them as a superior officer and a friend. He informed them of the king's willingness that they become National Guardsmen, but he gave permission to leave to those who preferred to do so. The Guards cheered, and for the nonce no one left.[77]

The companies of the French Guard in Versailles shortly created a new crisis. They had long wanted to join their comrades in Paris, and now they did so, leaving their officers behind and taking their equipment with them.[78] The French Guards now hoped to be incorporated as a single, complete, unchanged unit into the National Guard without giving up their old regimental identity, their ancient blue flag with its gold crown and fleurs-de-lis, their honored uniform, their non-commissioned officers, and their tradition of glory. Besides, while some of them had been maintained by the Paris districts in which they were quartered, others had received no pay since July 12—i.e., since they had participated in the outbreak which had brought about the capture of the Bastille. The darlings of Paris, they sometimes took their grievances to their district meetings and received a sympathetic hearing.[79] That was why Lafayette and others feared that they might be suborned by "patriots" with ulterior motives; the

[77] Hardy, VIII, 405–6; *Mémoires*, II, 271–72; *Du règne de Louis XVI*, p. 80; and *Courrier de Versailles à Paris*, July 27, p. 328.

[78] Bailly, II, 192–93; Bailly and Duveyrier, II, 500–501; Comte de Saint Priest, *Mémoires*, ed. Baron de Barante (Paris, 1929), I, 244–45; and Mège, *Gaultier*, II, 218.

[79] Dumas, p. 102; Lacroix, I, 90, 93–94 (August 4), 99–100 (August 5); and *Révolutions de Paris*, No. 4, August 2–8, pp. 11–16.

Duc d'Orléans was believed to have had large sums of money distributed among them.[80]

Not daring to take any risk that the French Guards might slip through his fingers, Lafayette reopened the question of their future with the king. He explained that the municipality of Paris contemplated enrolling them in the Paris forces but that their officers were giving them permanent discharges with the evident intention of preventing their incorporation. Such deliberate disorganization, he apprehended, together with the resulting frustration of the Parisians' pride in the French Guard, would make it impossible to re-establish public confidence, and he would not be answerable for the consequences. He sent off two aides with this letter to Versailles, reporting to the Representatives what he had done.[81] While awaiting a reply, he asked the Sieur de Mathan, one of the lieutenant colonels of the Guard, to come to see him and found him willing to cooperate. They agreed that while unconditional discharges would be given to those who wished them, Lafayette should have a chance to prevail upon the French Guards to enlist in his force.[82]

The Paris commandant general lost no time in beginning his campaign. On August 3 he addressed a bulletin to the French Guards and had it posted all over Paris. He had always told them, it said, that he wanted "to keep only soldiers of good will"; others might apply for discharge immediately; the *Règlement* of the National Guard would soon be ready for them to examine, and he would welcome those who wished to join the National Guard under those regulations. He also announced his intention to visit each battalion of the French Guard during the course of the next two days.[83]

Lafayette's bulletin was necessarily concise and businesslike; no

[80] *Mémoires*, II, 272, and Clermont-Gallerande, I, 117.

[81] August 2, 1789, Charavay catalogue No. 492, item 75; *AHRF*, II (1925), 102; Lacroix, I, 79 (August 2), 90–91 (August 4).

[82] Lacroix, I, 81 (August 4), and Hardy, VIII, 420.

[83] Hardy, VIII, 420; *Révolutions de Paris*, No. 4, August 2–8, p. 13; and *Courrier de Versailles à Paris*, August 5, pp. 128–30.

more had been authorized. Nevertheless, he undertook to persuade the Assembly of Representatives to court the French Guards by an appeal to their pride. Various steps which he took toward that end were first discussed in the Military Committee and then submitted to the Assembly of Representatives. He proposed granting, in addition to the discharge which the former regimental commander might give, a "National Certificate" to every non-commissioned officer and soldier of the regiment "who had served in the Revolution." He also proposed that regimental properties, funds, and effects be placed under city seal until they could be sold and the proceeds distributed equitably to every French Guardsman, whether or not he joined the National Guard. The Assembly accepted these proposals. To discourage individual Guardsmen from selling their now obsolete uniforms to unauthorized persons, the Assembly forbade old-clothes dealers to resell uniforms and requested Guardsman not to dispose of theirs without first stripping off the braid and insignia.[84]

Armed with this demonstration of the municipality's good intentions and gratitude, Lafayette went to visit the French Guards in their several barracks. He spoke to them frankly about the arrears in their pay and their desire to retain their old uniform in their new service, and he gave them what satisfaction he could. In fact, he went to his own bankers and asked for an advance to the city of 1,200,000 livres to pay the French Guard—which the bankers gave on no other security than his word.[85] Again with the approval of the Military Committee, on August 5 he took up the matter of pay and uniform with the Assembly of Representatives, asking that every French Guardsman whose pay was in arrears receive 20 sous (more than double their previous pay) for every day after July 12, those who had received less from their districts being reimbursed the difference by the Hôtel de Ville. He also requested that the French Guards, though they would be required when incorporated in the National Guard to wear the same uniform as other National Guardsmen, be authorized to display a

---

[84] *Procès-verbal du Comité militaire*, Part I, pp. 33–34 (August 3); Lacroix, I, 87–88, 90–91 (August 4); and *Révolutions de Paris*, No. 4, August 2–8, pp. 14–16.

[85] Dumas, I, 102–3. Cf. *AP*, XXXI, 91.

distinctive decoration recognizing "the glory that they had won and the gratitude that was due them."

The Representatives applauded Lafayette's request as a way of reconciling special treatment for the French Guards with the sense of equality which they wanted to prevail in the National Guard, and it accorded him his requests.[86] He and Bailly soon began to sign and distribute to the French Guards the authorized "Certificats nationaux."[87] Furthermore, since the French Guard had more than 120 sergeants, although only that number of lieutenants would be required by the Regulations for the 60 paid companies of the National Guard, he arranged, with the consent of the Military Committee and the Representatives that the senior sergeants would be promoted to lieutenant, the rest being brevetted as second lieutenants (*sous-lieutenants*) and assigned as drill masters to the unpaid companies until the paid companies needed them as lieutenants. He also endorsed the French Guards' request for enlistments of indefinite duration in the paid companies with the right to resign upon six months' notice—a suggestion which the Assembly of Representatives submitted to the districts for consideration.[88]

The French Guards were duly appreciative of Lafayette's efforts. In a public *Lettre des Gardes-françoises à Monsieur le marquis de La Fayette* they thanked him for his kindness: "Of all the favors that a generous nation bestows upon us . . . unquestionably the greatest is that of having somehow associated us with the glory and destiny of the citizen-hero who has helped so effectively to establish in two worlds the empire of reason and liberty and to avenge the overlong assaults of barbarity and error upon the dignity of man."[89]

[86] Lacroix, I, 99–100 (August 5); *Révolutions de Paris*, No. 4, August 2–8, p. 26; *Procès-verbal du Comité militaire*, Part I, pp. 33–34 (August 4), 36 (August 6), 36–37 (August 7); and Paul Olivier, *Iconographie metallique du général Lafayette* . . . (Baltimore, 1933), p. 1.

[87] See BVP, Collection Liésville, Révolution française, divers, Série 21, and Yale University, Jackson Collection, for examples of this *certificat national*.

[88] Lacroix, I, 129–31 (August 8), and *Procès-verbal du Comité militaire*, Part I, pp. 19–20 (July 27), 33–34 (August 4), 36–37 (August 6 and 7), and 40–42 (August 8).

[89] [*Ca.* August 10, 1789]. André Monglond, *La France révolutionnaire et imperiale. Annales de bibliographie méthodique et description des livres illustrés*, I (Grenoble 1930), col. 219, lists also a *Discours prononcé à M. le marquis de La Fayette, au Comité des Représentants du régiment des Gardes françaises . . . le 12 août 1789*.

They had good reason to feel satisfied. When the *Règlement* finally went into effect, they remained distinguishable and particularly honored within the National Guard, of which they formed the continuously active force and the nucleus. From their ranks were to come some of the most devoted and distinguished officers of the wars of the French Revolution and Napoleon.

The corps of the Basoche did not meet with parallel treatment. They were neither professional soldiers nor equally popular, and their initial appeal to the Assembly of Representatives and the Military Committee for some kind of recognition of "their zeal and their services" led only to words of praise and a decision to leave the matter to the National Assembly.[90] When some of the Basoche tried to enroll as individuals in the district battalions, they found they were welcome in some but not in all. When they again brought their troubles to the Assembly of Representatives, it again expressed appreciation of their patriotism and deferred to the districts.[91] When a group of "undomiciled" young men then asked permission of the Military Committee to form a volunteer military corps outside of but cooperating with the National Guard, Lafayette, pointing out the "inconveniences" of their plan, urged the Assembly of Representatives to ask once more that the districts give friendly consideration to the claims of these deserving young men—which the Assembly did. The next day he was able to tell the Assembly that the young men were satisfied to wait for the districts to act.[92] The Basoche was destined, however, to get no special consideration and to pass into limbo with the eventual reorganization of the law courts. But it continued to hang on as a corps serving Lafayette and the commune meanwhile, many of its members joining the National Guard as individuals.

On August 10 the National Assembly at Versailles at length put the finishing touch on the whole theoretical structure of the National Guard. It empowered municipalities to call on the na-

---

[90] Lacroix, I, 89–90 (August 4). See also *Procès-verbal du Comité militaire*, Part I, pp. 60–63 (August 16), 70–72 (August 19), 83–85 (August 24).

[91] Lacroix, I, 191–92, 199–200 (August 12).

[92] *Ibid.*, pp. 252–53 (August 17), 265 (August 18), and *Procès-verbal du Comité militaire*, Part I, pp. 60–65 (August 16).

tional militia, as well as the constabulary and the troops of the line, to preserve order and to aid in disarming vagrants and unemployed (*sans aveu, sans métier ni profession, et sans domicile constant*). The National Assembly also by formal decree prescribed the oath of the new military: they were to swear in the presence of their commanders to maintain the peace, defend their fellow citizens, and oppose disorder, and they were to pledge to be faithful to "the nation, the king, and the law" (a revolutionary ranking of loyalties).[93] The National Guard thus became an arm of the nation, the sovereign people, owing only secondary allegiance to the king and expressly subordinate to the civil authority. This was the kind of National Guard that Lafayette had wanted, and it was, more than any other man's, his creation.

On August 12, as authorized by the Regulations Lafayette nominated his staff. He designated Gouvion for chief of staff with the rank of major general, and Lajard, La Colombe, and Jacques Souet d'Ermigny for lesser staff ranks. Of Gouvion he remarked, with a touch of the hyperbole characteristic of letters of recommendation: "He lived in America all during the Revolution; he rendered the greatest services to the cause of liberty under the orders of General Washington, whose special friend he is."[94] For his part Gouvion modestly thought Lafayette's confidence in him might be difficult to justify and so he offered to serve without pay for a trial period not to exceed three months.[95] For staff secretary Lafayette nominated his secretary during the American war, Joseph-Léonard Poirey. Of these five men only Lajard (who had been recommended by Dumas) and Ermigny had not served in the American army during the War of the American Revolution. On the following day the Representatives approved these nominations unanimously and ordered the approved names posted, together with Lafayette's letter of nomination. On the grounds that a commissary-general would have control of the funds, Lafayette had considered it unethical to nominate one, but the Assembly of

---

[93] *AP*, VIII, 378 (August 10), and Mège, *Gaultier*, II, 244-45.

[94] Lacroix, I, 189.

[95] Gouvion to the Assembly of Representatives, August 13, BVP, Charavay VIII, FG ms. 39, fol. 200.

Representatives, "in order to reconcile the regard it owes M. de La Fayette with the duty which the public interest places upon it," asked him nevertheless for four nominations from which they would make a choice.[96]

Although many difficulties had yet to be encountered, a permanent organization of the National Guard seemed at last well under way. In later years Lafayette and others were to recognize that his extensive experience as a major general in the American army, along with his so far limited experience as *maréchal de camp* (equivalent to major general) in the French army, and as an observer of Frederick the Great's Prussian army, had enabled him to lay the foundation of "the nation in arms." For the present, however, his principal (though not exclusive) concern was to provide Paris with a good police force rather than to provide the nation with an army that would carry the tricolor around the world. What he wanted most of all was a tranquil atmosphere in which the National Assembly might proceed with the task of drawing up a constitution.

BIBLIOGRAPHICAL NOTES

Bailly's *Mémoires* were written in diary form. While they obviously were composed after the events with which they deal and sometimes with the aid of others' testimony, they exhibit a genuine effort to be just and accurate. Volume III is not by Bailly but by an unknown continuator.

Lacroix (I, 69–71) contains an excellent note on the organization of the Military Committee.

The *Journal de Paris* and the *Patriote français* (ed. Brissot de Warville) were at this time particularly friendly to Lafayette. The *Journal de Paris* as the oldest daily of France had a sort of semiofficial status in reporting the meetings of the National Assembly, and Brissot as a member of the Assembly of Representatives had a special advantage in reporting municipal affairs.

Olivier's *Iconographie,* while incomplete, is the best available study of the numismatics relating to Lafayette.

[96] Lacroix, I, 202 (August 13). See also Bailly, II, 261–63; *Révolutions de Paris,* No. 5, August 9–15, pp. 36–37; Dumas, I, 101–4; and Bailly and Duveyrier, II, 240, 330–41.

CHAPTER IX

"*Nation, King, Law, and Commune*"

IN THE France of August 1789 "the hero of two worlds" seemed a fitting answer to the never-ending quest, rarely more earnest than in times of revolution, for a charismatic leader. To be sure, in several regards he was no more distinguished than some other possible choices. Bailly held a higher office than he in the new government of the capital; Necker, Mirabeau, and the Duc d'Orléans had been no less conspicuous in advocating reform; the Duc d'Orléans, besides, was the only Patriot celebrity with royal blood in his veins. Lafayette could counterbalance these distinctions, however, by unique advantages. He already had an army at his command, and in addition he was rapidly becoming the most popular man in France, the king alone a possible rival. Songs, poems, addresses were written to, for, or about him. He was a frequent subject of paintings and engravings, occasionally caricatural but generally laudatory. Babies were given his name at baptism. Books and plays, sometimes explicitly dedicated to him, mentioned him or were popularly thought to allude to him. The newspapers gave copious reports of his activities.[1]

The city's dignitaries yielded to none in conferring honors upon

[1] Hardy, VIII, 440 (August 17) reports Lafayette's presence at a baptism. On the bibliography and iconography of Lafayette see below, Appendix II, and Braibant (ed.), *Exposition*, p. 81, item 219. Examples of theatrical pieces dealing with him were *Les sauvages civilisés. . . . Opéra national, présenté à l'Académie Royale de Musique* (published July 31, 1789), *Le Triomphe du patriotisme, comédie nationale* (which may be of a later date, however), *Le Retour de Camille à Rome* by Joseph Aude (advertised in the *Journal de Paris*, August 14, p. 1022). The last piece was a one-act play in verse, performed for the first time at the Théâtre de Monsieur on August 14. In the character of Camille, "the benefactor of his country and often persecuted," the repeatedly applauding public saw "a more modern liberator, far more worthy of its homage" (*Journal de Paris*, August 16, pp. 1033–34). Cf. M. A. Carlson, *The Theatre of the French Revolution* (Ithaca, N.Y., [1955]), p. 20.

the commandant general. When the Representatives adopted their rules of order, they made Lafayette an honorary member of their Assembly and of all its committees, with the right to express his opinions.[2] When the Military Committee approved its minutes for publication, it incorporated an expression of appreciation for his "genius" in organizing the National Guard and for his personal influence in keeping order.[3] The first public act of a newly created Council of the French Guards was to draw up a resolution of thanks to the city fathers, in which it also petitioned the commandant general to continue "his paternal goodness" (Lafayette was not yet thirty-three years old), assuring him of its "fullest confidence" in "his talents, bravery and partiotism."[4] If some of this praise was extravagant, it was nevertheless largely deserved, and in any case it betokened a deep-felt gratitude.

Provinces and districts joined the capital in pronouncing testimonials of confidence and gratitude.[5] A deputation from Rouen having come to express their city's good wishes to the new Paris authorities, complimented Lafayette (among others), referring to him as "a general who in the springtime of his life is a hero"—whereupon all eyes turned to the young general, and the Grande Salle filled with "a thousand cheers of joy and appreciation." He acknowledged the cheers with only a brief, modest speech, but M. Delavigne, one of the Electors' two presiding officers, followed with a long one in praise of "the hero-citizen who, after having laid the foundations of American liberty, returned, strong in his virtues, his principles, and his experience, to assure forever the liberty of the capital."[6] Some of the Paris districts went out of their way to show Lafayette honor, but Saint André des Arts was perhaps more demonstrative than the others. Having invited the commandant general to visit them, the district officials presented him (August 5) with a gold medal decorated with religious, historical,

---

[2] Lacroix, I, 329 (August 24).

[3] *Procès-verbal du Comité militaire*, Part I, p. 3.

[4] Lacroix, I, 160 (August 10), and *Révolutions de Paris*, No. 5, August 9–15, pp. 15–16.

[5] Bailly and Duveyrier, II, 414, and III, 230–31, 239, 242, 279, 286, 332–34; *Journal de Paris*, August 4, p. 971; and *Révolutions de Paris*, No. 4, August 2–8, p. 14.

[6] Bailly and Duveyrier, II, 444–51. See also Tuetey, I, 305, No. 2706.

and revolutionary symbols. Thanking the district for the pleasure and honor they were giving him and putting the medal on over the coat of his uniform, he departed, amid universal applause.[7]

Nor were all such demonstrations of confidence, gratitude, and affection merely official. Sometimes young women dressed in ceremonial white and escorted by the National Guard of their district came to the Hôtel de Ville to honor Bailly and Lafayette. Groups on a similar errand might be made up of tradeswomen with a designated spokesman and a prepared address, of laundresses bearing flowers and brioches, or of hungry mothers pleading for cheaper bread for themselves and their families.[8] On one such occasion the workers engaged in demolishing the Bastille, having found some Frondeurs' cannonballs in the fortress walls, presented them to the general with appropriate sentiments.[9]

The Lafayette family shared in the glory of its paterfamilias. The press mentioned Mme de Lafayette's presence at civic ceremonies—as when she and her elder daughter, Anastasie, took up a collection for the poor in a parish church or prayed for the repose of the souls of patriots or witnessed the blessing of a battalion's colors.[10] The District of the Sorbonne even sought to compliment the father through the son, whom, though only ten years old, it chose as a second lieutenant of one of its companies. When Lafayette, thanking the district for the compliment, indicated that George was too young for a commission but would be honored to serve as a simple fusilier, the district persisted, and the easily persuaded father yielded with a *belle parole:* "Gentlemen, my son is no longer mine; he belongs to you and to our country."[11]

[7] Hardy, VIII, 423, and *Journal de Paris,* August 6, p. 981.

[8] Jeanne Bouvier, *Les Femmes pendant la Révolution* (Paris, 1931), pp. 91–92 and n.; *Du règne de Louis XVI,* pp. 111–12, 131; Bailly, II, 245; and *Révolutions de Paris,* No. 5, August 9–15, p. 10, and No. 7, August 22–29, p. 14.

[9] *Journal de Paris,* August 26, p. 1073.

[10] *Ibid.,* August 21, p. 1052, and August 30, p. 1089, and *Révolutions de Paris,* No. 5, August 9–15, p. 6.

[11] *Révolutions de Paris,* No. 5, August 9–15, p. 35; [Bérenger], p. 262; and B.-J.-B. Buchez and P.-C. Roux, *Histoire parlementaire de la Révolution française ou journal des assemblées nationales depuis 1789 jusqu'en 1815* (Paris, 1834–38), II, 267. M. Serieys, *La Révolution de France, ou la liberté. Poème nationale* (Paris, 1790), p. 194, n. 13, apparently borrowed a description of this episode from the *Révolutions de Paris.*

Such displays of appreciation and patriotism did not suffice, however, to banish crime, unemployment, hunger, and unrest, and so vigilance could not be safely relaxed. Patrols of the National Guard picked up suspects on all kinds of charges, whether or not legally considered crimes—such as intent to incite riot, insulting French Guards, selling anonymous pamphlets, or threatening violence against Lafayette. Every now and then district assemblies sent to the Hôtel de Ville for police reinforcements, and in some emergencies the commandant general himself felt called upon to take a hand, if only to reason with a disturber and "make clear the harm that any cabal would do to the public and to himself."[12] In this way, the city's penchant for feverish activity was usually kept under control, and the Assembly of Representatives, while continuously on the alert, no longer sat in continual dread of a mob's surging through the Place de Grève and into its meeting room.

Despite the improved effectiveness of the city's new army, equipping it adequately remained a vexing problem, since rifles and powder seemed to disappear about as rapidly as they could be passed out. Paradoxically, one reason for their disappearance was the very attempt of the National Assembly at Versailles to assuage the violent outbursts in the provinces—the so-called Great Fear—arising from the peasants' resentment of their servile status. On August 4-11 the National Assembly went part way toward satisfying the peasant demands, abolishing a number of the special privileges of clergy, nobles, provinces, and towns. In the belief that by its destruction of seignorial and local privileges the National Assembly had opened up the royal game preserves, Parisians swarmed into the hunter's paradise at Montesson to shoot for food and for sport. Lafayette, lamenting the reckless slaughter of game, the waste of hard-won powder and shot, and the probable increase of disorder, requested and received from the Assembly of Representatives permission to keep people from leaving the city to

[12] Lafayette to Messieurs, August 11, Archives de la Seine, D⁴ AZ, no. 61. See also Lacroix, I, 124, 126, 137, 175, 265; Bailly, II, 231–32; *Révolutions de Paris,* No. 5, August 9–15, pp. 1, 5, 24; Tuetey, I, 94, Nos. 896, 898–900, and pp. 96–97, Nos. 911, 913, 915, 916, 918–19, 921.

go hunting. [13] But his vigilance as a sort of game warden, while it diminished the rate of depletion of military supplies, did nothing to increase them. Appeals to Saint Priest and Latour du Pin had a better outcome; they produced a promise of 6,000 guns of the latest model with bayonets attached, and Saint Priest himself came to Paris to work out a plan for their safe delivery. [14]

The National Guard's shortage of arms was all the more appalling because fear of counterrevolutionary plots would not down. Reports of secret communications between émigrés or others abroad and their families or servants at home were never too fantastic to be incredible, and they led the city authorities to ask Lafayette to take special precautions against foreigners. One such report constrained Lafayette to send fifty men to the Polignac château near Paris to confiscate the family papers—which it did, despite some armed resistance, only to find the papers to be utterly harmless. [15] But not all the potential sources of disorder proved equally innocuous.

Outside the north gates of the city lay the community of Montmartre. There the previous spring the royal government had opened *ateliers*, or "workshops," for the unemployed; and perhaps as many as 17,000 job-hunters, doubtless some shiftless and criminal among the deserving unfortunates, had poured in from the city and the provinces. In ordinary years such a concourse of unemployed would have broken up by August, lured to the country by the prospect of work in the harvest, but this was no ordinary year, and political agitation augmented the dissatisfaction of the unemployed with the inadequacy of the day-by-day distribution of food and jobs. The new Paris government, with little enough money for its own needs, had inherited responsibility for the Montmartre workshops, and it sought to reduce the already pitiful wages passed out to the workers by not paying them for fete days. The resulting distress among the unemployed caused the Representa-

---

[13] Lacroix, I, 148 (August 10), 257–58 (August 17); *Journal de Paris*, August 12, p. 1009; *Du règne de Louis XIV*, pp. 110–11; *Révolutions de Paris*, No. 5, August 9–15, pp. 7–8; and Bailly, II, 244.

[14] Lacroix, I, 254–56 and 262 (August 17) and 306–7 (August 22); *Révolutions de Paris*, No. 6, August 16–22, p. 12; Bailly, II, 274; and *Patriote français*, August 25, p. 3.

[15] Lacroix, I, 162–65 (August 10), 207 (August 13) and Bailly, II, 250.

tives to reconsider, but they persevered in their economy program to the extent of ordering that no new workers be employed. That order, together with reports of a lack of bread, fanned the honest workers' fears and played into the hands of agitators.[16]

Both charity and the dread of riot called for action. On August 15 Lafayette rode out to Montmartre, accompanied by a small detachment of National Guards. If the *Révolutions de Paris*[17] counted correctly, 6,000 worried, bedraggled, emaciated men met him— not with sticks and stones but with bouquets of flowers. He spoke to those unfortunates kindly, and they listened respectfully. The municipality, he promised, would continue to pay their wages (20 sous a day) for yet a few days, but it simply did not have funds for more, and they must go back home. If they did not go, he would have to send soldiers to keep them in order.[18] One of Lafayette's guardsmen, impressed by the picture of the uniformed marquis reasoning with the poor, commemorated the occasion in a labored though well-meant poem.[19]

Upon his return to the Hôtel de Ville, Lafayette delivered the opinion that Montmartre would probably remain tranquil for the time being.[20] Yet the dread persisted in the metropolis that this "truly savage horde,"[21] many of whom were suspected of being "secret agents of despotism,"[22] would erupt into violence at any moment. Two days after Lafayette's touching encounter with the destitute, the Assembly of Representatives ordered that the workshops be closed within the week—i.e., as of August 23—and that the workers meanwhile leave for home, granting each of those

[16] Lacroix, I, 168 (August 11), 177–78 and 192–93 (August 12), 204–5, 208, and 212–13 (August 13), 225 (August 15), and Bailly, II, 257–58, 265.

[17] No. 6, August 16–22, pp. 5–6.

[18] *Ibid.; Du règne de Louis XVI*, p. 125; and letter dated August 30, 1789, BVP, Collection Liésville, Rev. papiers divers, 1789–Juin 1791.

[19] "Impromptu à M. le Marquis de la Fayette, visitant les ateliers de Montmartre le 15 août 1789, par un soldat de la Compagnie de Saint-Même," *Journal de Paris*, August 20, p. 1049. Cf. *L'Observateur*, No. 5, [August 21?], p. 28.

[20] Lacroix, I, 226 (August 15), and Bailly, II, 272.

[21] *Patriote français*, August 19, p. 4. See also *ibid.*, August 20, p. 4.

[22] *Courrier de Versailles à Paris*, August 20, pp. 269–70.

who did not live in Paris a passport and 20 sous on the day of departure plus 3 sous per league for travel expenses.[23]

Once more (August 20) Lafayette went to Montmartre to speak to the unemployed, again accompanied only by a small contingent of the National Guard. This time, too, thousands came out to greet him in a friendly mood. He urged them to go home peacefully: they would have more to eat in the provinces, their passports would protect them on their way, and the city and they would be better off if they went. The crowd listened, apparently with approval. When the speaker promised to come to see them again before their workshops broke up, and to come alone, without a guard, his listeners applauded. Some cried out, "We will be your guard."[24]

Lafayette did not keep his promise, however. Although the Montmartre workers stayed on beyond the date fixed for their departure, getting no more satisfaction than before and becoming more and more militant,[25] he did not go back, chiefly because Montmartre was not the only quarter where violence menaced. The Faubourg Saint Antoine was also malcontent. Despite 48,000 livres already distributed among the "heroes of the Bastille," complaint had not diminished. On the day of his first visit to the Montmartre ateliers (August 15), Lafayette had been required to send an armed contingent to Saint Antoine;[26] and he went there with his men. He found a truly distressing situation. Some wounded "heroes" had been left entirely without medical attention, and some widows and orphans had received not a sou from the municipality's bounty. The poor had begun to wonder what good the great Revolution had done for them, and they were ripe for the

---

[23] Lacroix, I, 259–61, 263 (August 17); Tuetey, *Répertoire,* I, 95, No. 905; and A. Tuetey (ed.), *L'assistance publique à Paris pendant la Révolution* (Paris, 1895–97), II, 98. (Hereafter "Tuetey" not followed by an abbreviated title will refer to the *Répertoire.*)

[24] Hardy, VIII, 442 (August 20), and Nuñez to Floridablanca, August 30, Albert Mousset (ed.), *Un témoin ignoré de la Révolution, le comte de Fernan Nuñez, ambassadeur d'Espagne à Paris (1787–1791)* (Paris, 1923), p. 71. Cf. *Démarches patriotiques de M. de La Fayette à l'égard des ouvriers de Montmartre [24 août 1789]* (Paris, 1789).

[25] See below, pp. 214 and 230–31.

[26] Lacroix, I, 225.

first provocation that would stir them to new revolt. Lafayette promised to try to get them medical care, food, and clothing, and he put their case before the Assembly of Representatives that evening. Immediately physicians among the Assembly offered their services free to the sick and wounded, the founder of a charity school agreed to find places for two orphans, the Assembly appointed a committee to consider new contributions to the faubourg's needy, and when the newspapers carried the story of Lafayette's visit to Saint Antoine and his speech to the Representatives, other philanthropic men made donations to the cause.[27] The young general's solicitude for the poor raised him in at least one journalist's estimation "higher . . . than his military talents."[28]

Charity, however, solves few problems permanently, and Saint Antoine soon had fresh cause for dissatisfaction. The inequalities in the old system of taxes were so palpable that few, least of all the poor, wished to retain them. Yet the Representatives, always in need of money, felt that the old taxes must be kept until a better system was devised, and so it had reconfirmed the existing *octrois* on goods entering the city, ordering Lafayette to provide police assistance whenever needed by those who collected them. On August 16 a protest against such payments induced the Assembly to reissue that order, but armed men, "determined to meet force with force," prepared to resist the re-establishment of the customs barriers in the faubourg.[29] This time the Representatives, no longer helpless against public pressure, did not swerve; they authorized Lafayette to take "the necessary precautions for the safety of the city"[30] and, running the risk of bloodshed, ordered troops into the faubourg. But no pitched battle occurred, for Gouvion prevailed upon the Representatives to hold up the execution of their order. The next day, Lafayette again went to Saint Antoine with mem-

---

[27] *Ibid.*, pp. 228–29; Caron de Beaumarchais to Lafayette, September 2, E. S. Kite, *Beaumarchais and the War of American Independence* (Boston, [1918]), II, 247; and *Révolutions de Paris*, No. 6, August 16–22, p. 6. *Du règne de Louis XVI*, p. 110, speaks of a visit to the Faubourg St. Antoine on August 9 but apparently means that of August 15.

[28] *Révolutions de Paris*, No. 6, August 16–22, p. 6. See also Malone, p. 226.

[29] Lacroix, I, 228, 289, 290 (August 20). See also *ibid.*, pp. 170–71 (August 11), 234–35 (August 16).

[30] *Ibid.*, p. 289 (August 20).

bers of his staff. This time he passed out some money, and once more his personal popularity and generosity prevented conflict. Upon his return he was able to report to the Representatives that order was re-established.[31] "Since he was beloved," Bailly recorded, "he calmed things down."[32] But how long could a big city's needy, unsettled by revolution and frustrated in their expectations, be constrained by the charm and liberality of a single general?

Crowded though many of the commandant general's hours were with damping threats of insurrection, his chief objective during these August days was the perfecting of a regular police system for Paris. Balloting for company and battalion officers created keen excitement in the districts, especially in those where the elections were contested.[33] In a few cases the choice of actors brought a protest to the Military Committee in favor of maintaining the traditional exclusion of "comedians" from posts of civic honor. The Military Committee with Lafayette's concurrence ruled that "every citizen was eligible to be chosen an officer" but that until the National Assembly might legislate on the point, no officer might remain an actor.[34] While most of these electoral incidents passed without violence, in some instances Lafayette felt obliged to take strenuous measures, and a few arrests took place.[35]

After the district companies and battalions were formed, the divisions had to be created. In an effort to forestall disputes over precedence among districts and divisions the *Règlement* had provided that the district in which the six district battalions of each division were to assemble and the order of march when two or more divisions assembled should be determined by the drawing of lots, and that drawing took place on August 12, in the presence of the Representatives and the Military Committee, joined together in

[31] *Ibid.*, pp. 290 (August 20), 300–301 (August 21); Tuetey, I, 95, No. 903; Bailly, II, 287–88; and F.-V. Fournel, *Le patriote Palloy et l'exploitation de la Bastille* . . . (Paris, 1892), p. 17.

[32] Bailly, II, 288. Cf. *Mémoires*, II, 287, and Scheler and Smeaton, II, 164–66.

[33] Lacroix, I, 252 (August 7), 264 and 266 (August 18), 279 (August 19), 287 and 291 (August 20), 305–6 and 332 (August 24), and *Patriote français*, August 18, p. 1.

[34] *Procès-verbal du Comité militaire*, Part I, p. 68, and *Mémoires*, II, 290.

[35] Lacroix, I, 137 (August 9), 209–10 and 213 (August 13); Bailly, II, 265–66; *Révolutions de Paris*, No. 5, August 9–15, pp. 31–33; and *Du règne de Louis XVI*, pp. 117–18.

the Grande Salle to emphasize the solemnity of the occasion.[36] Subsequently, as each of the six divisional chiefs was named by the electors designated for that purpose in the *Règlement*, the commandant general presented him to the Representatives, and the new officer thereupon took his oath of loyalty. Among them were illustrious nobles and rich bourgeois, former high civil officials and royal officers.[37] Bailly was frankly astonished that men of such stature were ready to serve in such capacities: "Nothing less than the Revolution was needed to produce such metamorphoses!"[38] In fact, a leading "patriot" journal criticized the districts because they still thought of themselves as honored if they got nobles to agree to act as their military chiefs.[39] Lafayette, himself to the manor born, was not impressed by titles, but neither did he think that a title should disqualify the holder for office. On one occasion when a nobleman, seeking special consideration, made mention of his exalted birth, Lafayette responded: "Monsieur, that is no obstacle."[40] If the election of officers of the National Guard went off smoothly on the whole and with astonishingly imposing results, the credit belonged chiefly to the Military Committee, which had not only tried to anticipate complications but had also diligently supervised almost every step; and the Military Committee rarely made a decision without consulting the commandant general and getting his approval.

Lafayette considered it good policy to be seen frequently and to be associated directly with his men and their uniform, and opportunities to do so were numerous. Although the municipal authorities of Paris were revolutionary in their politics, they were still good Catholics, and a new political enterprise like a citizen guard, they felt, ought to start out wth the church's blessing. The parish priests were glad to cooperate. Hence arose the practice, as soon as

[36] *Procès-verbal du Comité militaire*, Part I, pp. 13 (July 26), 52–54 (August 12), and Lacroix, I, 180–83, 193–95 (August 12).

[37] Lacroix, I, 259 and 262–63 (August 17), 265 and 270 (August 18), 273 and 280 (August 19), 318 and 324 (August 23), 362 and 370 (August 27). See also *Procès-verbal du Comité militaire*, Part I, pp. 55, 58.

[38] Bailly, II, 274.

[39] *Révolutions de Paris*, No. 7, August 22–28, pp. 29–30.

[40] *Mémoires*, II, 291.

a district had designed and acquired its battalion standard, of having it blessed at the parish church. Lafayette attended several of these ceremonies, sometimes accompanied by his wife.[41] On other occasions he went out to address newly formed battalions or to visit points of interest, escorted by some of his officers. Wherever he went, he created a flurry of attention.[42]

A special opportunity for the display of esprit de corps presented itself when on August 10 the National Assembly finally provided a uniform organization for all the National Guard of the realm. The new law required that each unit of the country's new forces take an oath of loyalty in a ceremony to be marked by "the most august solemnity," in which the men were to swear never to abandon their colors, to be loyal to the nation, the king, and the law, and to observe the rules of military discipline, the officers swearing in addition never to employ the men under their command against fellow citizens except upon an order issued by civil officials and read before the assembled troops.[43] On August 20 Lafayette asked the Assembly of Representatives to arrange such a ceremony for the Paris Guard officers already elected and to fix the exact wording of the prescribed oath. The Representatives decided to retain only the phrases which called for loyalty to "the nation, the king, and the law" but to add a pledge of loyalty to "the commune of Paris,"[44] presumably on the assumption that the rest was thereby rendered tautologous. Within an hour the officers were ready, and the Assembly went down the Place de Grève to witness the oath-taking. The square was crowded with spectators. The mayor officiated, standing on the steps of the Hôtel de Ville, with the Representatives massed behind him and the officers lined up below. The new officers swore to be faithful to "the nation, the king, the law, and the commune."[45]

<hr>

[41] *Révolutions de Paris*, No. 5, August 9–15, p. 6; [Bérenger], pp. 275–76; *L'Observateur*, August 23, p. 43; and *Journal de Paris*, August 21, p. 1052.

[42] *Du règne de Louis XVI*, p. 110; Scheler and Smeaton, II, 132; *Les Comédiens commandans . . . à Messieurs les parisiens à Paris* (Paris, 1789), p. 9; and Fournel, p. 17.

[43] *AP*, VIII, 378, and Lacroix, I, 224.

[44] Lacroix, I, 284, 294 (August 20).

[45] *Ibid.*, p. 286; Bailly, II, 283; and *Patriote français*, August 22, p. 2.

By the end of the month most of the subsequently elected officers of the unpaid companies were ready to take the prescribed
oath. On August 30, escorted by 2,000 of their men in uniform,
they too marched to the Place de Grève. Unfortunately, the mayor
had not been properly notified, and until he could be found they
had to wait in a hard rain which soaked the officers' bright new
attire. When the discomfited, apologetic Bailly finally arrived,
the president of the Representatives administered the oath, while
mayor, Assembly, Military Committee, commandant general, and
National Guard staff, together with soldier and civilian spectators,
looked on. Drawing their swords and saluting in token of submission to the civil authority, several hundred men pledged "to be
loyal to the nation, the king, the law, and the commune of Paris."[46]

The newly installed officers of the incipient army and their men
required an astonishing number of things, and the Military Committee had to attend to many details, major and minor. It had to
select an ensign for the Paris National Guard, to approve model
uniforms, to obtain bids for tailoring the approved uniform in
quantity, and to get funds for outfitting the paid troops. A model
sword also had to be designed. Although some of the committee
thought the best model would be Lafayette's own sword, they left
the ultimate decision to him, and he suggested one whose hilt
would be decorated with a liberty cap, thus making this revolutionary symbol, already familiar in America, even more familiar
in France.[47]

Housing for the paid company in each district proved a particularly thorny problem. Districts sometimes were reluctant to
incur the necessary expense, and proprietors were sometimes unwilling to allow suitable buildings to be converted into barracks.
A special joint committee was appointed from among the Assembly of Representatives and the Military Committee to resolve
this difficulty, but valuable days passed without a complete solu-

---

[46] Lacroix, I, 386 and 390 (August 29), 396 (August 30); Bailly, II, 322–23; *Révolutions de Paris*, No. 6, August 16–22, p. 24, and No. 8, August 29–September 5, pp. 8–9;
and *Procès-verbal du Comité militaire*, Part I, p. 107.

[47] *Procès-verbal du Comité militaire*, Part I, pp. 35, 43–45, 55–56, 65–66, 72–74;
Bailly, II, 241–42, 296–97; Lacroix, I, 136–37 (August 9), 236 and 245–46 (August 16),
264 and 265 (August 18), 227 (August 19), 318 and 323 (August 23); *Révolutions de
Paris*, No. 7, August 22–28, pp. 5–6; and *Mémoires*, II, 290 n.

tion. When Lafayette and the Military Committee summoned the division and the battalion commanders to report on housing and other pressing complications, they gave a gravely unsatisfactory report. So he went to the Assembly of Representatives and personally pressed for immediate action. They authorized the joint committee to lease houses at municipal expense for National Guard units not yet provided for and to buy the furnishings of the former French Guard's barracks (already sequestered by the city) for distribution among the district barracks. As a result, on August 22 Lafayette was able to order, with a reasonable expectation of compliance, that within two days all barracks be ready for occupancy.[48]

Recruiting a largely volunteer army *de novo* proved no simple matter when volunteers had to provide their own "effects."[49] Some districts lagged behind in finding enough men willing or able to buy the required equipment. To speed up the complement of the unpaid companies—4 companies of 100 men each in each of 60 districts—and to avoid having unequipped or unequally equipped units, the commandant general asked the Assembly of Representatives to find 50 livres per man—1,2000,000 livres in all—to provide the unpaid soldiers with weapons and equipment (other than uniforms, for the volunteer was still expected to furnish his own uniform). The immensity of this sum staggered Bailly, but reasoning that he was faced with an emergency, that "the safety of Paris, the National Assembly, the King, the constitution and liberty" depended upon an effective citizens' guard he recommended the appropriation, and the Representatives authorized the purchase of the desired equipment at municipal expense.[50] Thus subsidized, the lagging districts were enabled to fill their quotas from among volunteers now required to be only prosperous enough to provide their own uniforms.

A subcommittee of the Military Committee worked meanwhile

[48] *Procès-verbal du Comité militaire*, Part I, pp. 55–56, 69–70, 72–74, 79–80; Lacroix, I, 202 (August 13), 283–84 (August 20), 299 (August 21); and Marcel Fosseyeux, "L'Hôtel-Dieu de Paris sous la Révolution, 1789–1802," *La Révolution française*, LXVI (1914), 44.

[49] *Règlement*, Title III, Articles 8, pp. 17–18.

[50] Bailly, II, 296, and Lacroix, I, 208 (August 13), 308–9 (August 22), 318 and 323 (August 23).

on the creation of the cavalry unit which the *Règlement* envisaged, and ultimately it recommended that the National Guard cavalry comprise 600 men to be paid, uniformed, and equipped by the commune, though each man was to provide and maintain his own horse out of an allowance for that purpose. The cavalry was to be recruited from former mounted constabulary units like those that formed the cavalry in the Guet de Paris (city watch) and the Garde Municipale de Paris and from royal soldiers who had "contributed to the restoration of liberty" between July 12 and 22. Lafayette himself wanted 100 horses stabled close to the Hôtel de Ville so as to have mounted men on the spot for messenger and other service. The Representatives approved this plan and sent it for confirmation to the districts.[51] There (as we shall see) it rested for a long time, undecided. Meanwhile, Lafayette was charged with coming to some sort of agreement with the Garde Municipale looking toward cooperation until its mounted men might become part of the National Guard.[52]

The relationship of the new citizens' army to other units of the old army and police likewise long remained a source of vexing complications. Sometimes, misunderstanding that the king had sanctioned the transfer of only such of his military as had applied before July 22, soldiers meaning to serve in the National Guard continued to stream into Paris. There they added to the food shortage and to the excitement fomented by the French Guard, the Swiss Guard, the Guet de Paris, the Garde Municipale, and other uniformed units which expected to form the paid troops of the people's army.

Of these units the French Guard continued to be the most favored. After the Representatives had authorized for them a distinctive decoration, the French Guards with a tact that matched their gallantry, assured the Military Committee that, attaching no importance to the intrinsic value of the decoration, they were pleased merely to have the honor it conferred. Nonetheless, some

---

[51] *Procès-verbal du Comité militaire*, Part I, pp. 11, 18–19, 42–43, 45–46, 48–51, 57–60, and Lacroix, I, 238–40 and 248–49 (August 16).

[52] *Procès-verbal du Comité militaire*, Part I, pp. 70, 97, and Lacroix, I, 238–40 and 248–49 (August 16). See also below, pp. 390 and 419, n. 30.

districts (and some French Guards) wanted something more honorific, or at least more costly, than the copper gilt medal which the Military Committee at first had had in mind. So Lafayette took up the matter with the Council of the French Guard, and eventually all concerned agreed to a gold medal. While it was being prepared, the French Guardsman was given the right to wear a tricolor ribbon in its place.[53] Despite this display of mutual readiness of city officials and French Guards to cooperate, not until August 29 could Lafayette indicate to the Representatives that the king would formally consent to the disbanding of the French Guard in order that its members might become National Guardsmen,[54] and hence, only on September 1 did the Assembly of Representatives accept the final suggestion of the Military Committee for the medal. It was to have engraved on one side a broken chain with the legend "Liberty won, July 14, 1789," and on the other a device, proposed by Lafayette himself, showing an unsheathed sword surmounted by a crown of oak and laurel with the inscription (adapted from Lucan's *Pharsalia*): "Ignorantne datos ne quisquam serviat enses?" ("Don't they know that swords have been bestowed in order that no one be enslaved?").[55]

Meanwhile, the French Guards had been distributed among the city's districts to form the nucleus of the "center" companies, those made up of paid National Guardsmen. Being only one regiment strong, they comprised fewer than the 6,000 men needed for that purpose, and to fill the vacancies Lafayette's staff had given priority to former Swiss Guards who, though relatively well-paid foreign mercenaries, had applied before July 22. There were still

[53] *Procès-verbal du Comité militaire*, Part I, pp. 36–38, 57–58; Lacroix 121–22 (August 7), 287–88 (August 20), 330 (August 24); Bailly, II, 231; *Révolutions de Paris*, No. 4, August 2–9, p. 38; and *Du règne de Louis XVI*, p. 113.

[54] *Ordonnance du roi portant réforme du régiment des Gardes-françoises, le 31 août 1789* (Paris, 1789), and Lacroix, I, 386 (August 29).

[55] The Loeb Classical Library edition of Lucan, trans. J. D. Duff (London, 1928) reads: *Ignorantque datos, ne quisquam serviat, enses* (p. 216) and renders it, "And men are ignorant that the purpose of the sword is to save every man from slavery" (p. 217), but Lafayette, who had suggested the verse, twice cited it as above (*Mémoires*, II, 290, and III, 209 n.). See also *Procès-verbal du Comité militaire*, Part I, pp. 57–58, 110–11; Lacroix, I, 434–35 and 445 (September 1); Olivier, pp. 1–2; and *Chronique de Paris*, September 14, p. 88.

other vacancies, however, and the clamor among the other applicants for them appeared as despicable to the enemies of the Revolution as laudable to its friends.[56]

That clamor soon became a cause of bloodshed. Early in August
a group of militia from the *banlieue* came to present their flags to
the Paris commandant general, and in so doing they set a precedent. Acting on this precedent, the French Guards brought their
old regimental standards to the city hall and with a ceremonial
flourish presented them to their new commander. The former
Swiss Guardsmen who had joined the Paris militia wanted to
follow suit, but since their old regiment, until recently commanded
by the still imprisoned Besenval, had not disbanded, they did not
own its standards, and when they sent a detachment to their old
barracks at Chaillot to get them, the regimental officers would not
give them up. In the ensuing confusion an officer of the constabulary (*maréchaussée*) was shot and killed. Only Lafayette's prompt
dispatch of some National Guardsmen to the scene prevented a
bloody fight. To calm both sides he provided a funeral with full
military honors for the unfortunate police officer and, making a
special visit to the Swiss Guards under his command, arranged for
their taking their oath in a special ceremony. That was done on
August 15, in the presence of the mayor and (because he was
himself that day at Montmartre) Lafayette's representatives.[57]

Regimental rivalries and friction did not end there. The number of soldiers who, having left their regiments, had come to the
capital to join the paid units of the National Guard now numbered
in the hundreds, and more were known to be on the way.[58] They
put not the municipality alone but the country as a whole in a
grave predicament. On the one hand, they added a new leaven to
the fermentation in Paris, reflecting at the same time the general

[56] See, e.g., Mirecourt, II, 260; *Révolutions de Paris*, No. 5, August 9–15, p. 25; and
Comte de Fersen to his father, August 15, R.-M. de Klinchowstrom, *Le Comte de Fersen
et la cour de France* (Paris, 1877), I, xlix.

[57] Lacroix, I, 149–56 and 166–67 (August 10), 226 (August 15); Bailly, II, 245–49,
272; *Du règne de Louis XVI*, pp. 111–12; *Patriote français*, August 21, p. 4; *Révolutions
de Paris*, No. 5, August 9–15, pp. 17, 38, and No. 6, August 16–22, pp. 18–19, 27; *Journal
de Paris*, August 23, pp. 1060–61, and September 16, pp. 1176–77; and Mirecourt, II, 278.

[58] *Révolutions de Paris*, No. 6, August 16–22, pp. 221–23, and *AP*, VIII, 433.

collapse of morale in the royal army; there even was reason to believe that some of the more vociferous "soldiers" were in fact troublemakers in disguise. On the other hand, a number of them were doubtless acting out of patriotic motives, fearing to be used as royal troops to quell citizens whom they might wish instead to help.

A way out of the dilemma was presented when the king on August 14 reconfirmed his willingness, already explicitly stated on July 21, to take back deserters (and no questions asked) if they returned by October 1.[59] The Swiss Guard, for example, was thus divided into three parts—those who remained under their regimental colors, those who, having volunteered before the king's intention had first been made public (July 22), had been duly mustered into the National Guard of Paris, and those who had volunteered too late. In answer to a request from the Swiss for clarification of their position, the Assembly of Representatives, persuaded that some soldiers had sought to join the National Guard because its new loyalty oath freed them from the dread of having to shoot down patriotic citizens, agreed to ask the officers of the Swiss Guard for honorable discharges for those who had desired to enroll without knowing of the king's previously announced deadline. At the same time it required all Swiss Guardsmen in Paris not already actually enrolled in the National Guard to return to their regiment and ordered Lafayette to enforce this policy.[60] When he consulted the Military Committee, it proposed a way out of the difficulty: the Paris Assembly of Representatives should arrange for soldiers not properly discharged from the royal service to return to their posts with 3 sous per league to help them on their way; the king's ministers should make known to the army as a whole that no more royal soldiers would be accepted in the Paris National Guard, although those who had intended to volunteer in good faith but in ignorance of the king's wishes would receive not only a travel allowance for their return to their regiments but also full amnesty; and those who had left the royal

[59] *Mémoires*, II, 271; *AP*, VIII, 433, 437–38; *Journal de Paris*, August 20, p. 1049; and *Révolutions de Paris*, No. 6, August 16–22, p. 33.

[60] Lacroix, I, 217–18 and 223–24 (August 14).

service after July 22 and did not return to it should be considered deserters.[61]

Feeling between the frustrated would-be National Guardsmen and the former French and Swiss Guards who were now certain of their places in the paid companies had meanwhile grown bitter. Some of the migrant soldiers sought to create suspicion regarding the loyalty of the French Guards. To offset these innuendos and at the same time to express their gratitude for the special consideration they had received, a deputation of the Council of the French Guards went on August 18 to the Hôtel de Ville to affirm their comrades' devotion to the city's welfare. They presented their declaration to Gouvion, for Lafayette was not there to receive them; he was out quelling a riot involving their comrades. Fighting had erupted between the French and Swiss Guards on one side and the aspirant guardsmen on the other, and the commandant general, having thrown a cordon around the melée, had rushed to the scene. Once more he was able to restore order.[62]

Lafayette must have felt more than ever that he was sitting on the edge of a volcano, for, as if fighting among soldiers along with the current dissatisfaction in the Montmartre ateliers and the Faubourg Saint Antoine were not sufficient evil unto the day, the journeymen tailors demonstrated against their masters at the Louvre, and the journeymen wigmakers (*perruquiers*) created an uproar in the Champs-Élysées. The prevalent political instability had not been good for business, and the luxury trades were especially hard hit, since civic turbulence made their good customers among the aristocracy stay indoors if indeed they did not flee abroad. Moreover, the putative abolition of privileges on the night of August 4–5 encouraged journeymen to protest against the privileged gilds and gild restrictions, which regulated, among other things, their wages and their status within their crafts.

Journeymen tailors were among the first to complain: wages had not kept pace with rising costs, and second-hand dealers were competing with tailors by making new clothes. Expecting soon to be engaged in filling the demand for uniforms for the National

---

[61] *Procès-verbal du Comité militaire*, Part I, pp. 66–68 (August 17).

[62] Lacroix, I, 266–67 and 268 (August 18); Bailly, II, 275; and *Révolutions de Paris*, No. 6, August 16–22, pp. 12–18.

Guard, the journeymen tailors wanted these conditions corrected, and they called a meeting to air their grievances. The meeting soon got out of hand. On the same day (August 18) that he kept Guardsmen and would-be Guardsmen from slitting each others' throats, Lafayette had to send reinforcements to the District of Saint Leu to aid the commander, who was losing control of a demonstration in the Place du Louvre.[63] Through the intervention of Bailly and Lafayette, representatives of masters and journeymen consulted together, with the result that the master tailors agreed to raise wages to 40 sous a day.[64]

The journeyman wigmakers also found that the Revolution had frightened away many of their best customers, and on the same day they brought their complaints to the city hall. Although they were noisy rather than dangerous, Bailly and Lafayette succeeded in quieting them only after considerable difficulty. Here too the two men acted together as peacemakers, arranging for a conference with the master *perruquiers* and ultimately securing some of the benefits the journeymen wanted.[65]

This successful handling of labor disputes cast Lafayette in a new role. Some days later, when the master shoemakers reported to the Assembly of Representatives the imminence of an "insurrection" among their workers (for strikes were illegal and hence were in employers' minds rebellion), the Assembly merely confirmed its earlier stand against illegal assembly and referred the matter to the commandant general's "wisdom."[66] And when a group of domestics, aggrieved that they were not eligible for the National Guard and threatened with unemployment as more and more aristocrats emigrated, sent a deputation to the Hôtel de Ville to protest, they were calmed down by the tactful words of several officials, of whom the commandant general was one.[67] Lafayette had thus become not merely a policeman handling workers' dem-

---

[63] Bailly, II, 288, and Lacroix, I, 265 (August 18).

[64] Lacroix I, 268 and 270 (August 18); Bailly, II, 276–77; *Du règne de Louis XVI,* pp. 129–30; *Courrier de Versailles à Paris,* August 21, pp. 384–85; and *Révolutions de Paris,* No. 6, August 16–22, pp. 15–16, 27.

[65] Bailly, II, 277; Mirecourt, II, 295; *Révolutions de Paris,* No. 6, August 16–22, p. 27; and *Courrier de Versailles à Paris,* August 21, pp. 383–84.

[66] Lacroix, I, 416 (August 31).

[67] Hardy, VIII, 455, and Lacroix, I, 381 (August 28).

onstrations as potential threats to order but in addition a sort of labor mediator.

Confronted by this almost uninterrupted chain of trying incidents, which made all the more manifest that a well-disciplined police force was indispensable, the commandant general put the problem of the migrant soldiers squarely before the Representatives. Decisive action was no longer avoidable, for on August 19 a report came that 250 new "volunteers" were on their way to Paris. The Representatives sent two of their number to stop this invasion and, acting upon the recommendations of the Military Committee, posted notices and announced in the press that migrant soldiers would no longer be mustered into the Paris National Guard. In order to give that warning the widest possible publicity, the Representatives sent similar announcements to the minister of war and to the other municipalities of the realm, and then authorized the commandant general to use all the force necessary to maintain order inside the city and to keep other "deserters" out.[68] A member of the Military Committee favored forming a new corps to include all the "deserters," but Lafayette and the committee rejected this suggestion as a violation of the king's published intention. Instead, the committee reconfirmed its purpose to enroll in the center companies first French Guards, then eligible Swiss Guards, and then such other soldiers as had arrived in Paris before July 22; all other royal troops were to be provided with passports and travel allowances and to leave Paris within twenty-four hours.[69]

The newcomers were in fact stopped outside the city gates, and on August 23 the Representatives who had been delegated to send them back were able to state that they had accomplished their mission.[70] This strict adherence to the king's orders meant more than that the National Guard would not raid the regular army; it meant also that its paid ranks, though still undermanned, would not be filled with self-selected strays, that it would contain only men who were picked for some particular reason from a larger number of applicants.

[68] Lacroix, I, 273–74 (August 19), and *Journal de Paris,* August 25, pp. 1068–69.

[69] *Procès-verbal du Comité militaire,* Part I, pp. 74–76.

[70] Lacroix, I, 296–97 (August 21), 317 (August 23).

A month after the day (July 22) now settled as the last permissible date of "desertion" the Paris National Guard seemed to be well on the way toward effective organization. On August 23 Lafayette arranged for the division chiefs who had not yet taken their service oath to do so, and he commanded the former French and Swiss Guards to move into their several district barracks the following day.[71] On that day (August 24) Paris saw a fully uniformed and equipped district battalion for the first time. It was the battalion of the District of Saint André des Arts, which in new blue, white, and red uniforms marched as a unit to its parish church to have its new standards blessed.[72] Lafayette was not present, but even without him the numerous spectators had good cause to be proud of their army. Along with the National Assembly it was the only body officially to have the word *National* (i.e., representative of the whole people) in its name. In this popular national revolutionary force theoretically (if not financially) open to all legally qualified citizens regardless of birth, the Paris Guard was the major unit, and it could now cooperate with lesser sister units all over the country.

For a moment Lafayette was free to pause and take stock— which he did in a letter to Adélaïde de Simiane. She was, it would appear, naturally distressed by her ambivalent position as a lady at court and as the confidante of a conspicuous revolutionary figure. At Versailles the National Assembly had recently embarked upon a hot debate over the lawmaking process to be provided in the forthcoming constitution,[73] and she put to him some leading questions on that subject. In reply, he candidly avowed his preference for a liberal constitution, one which he proposed to support even if the king were to reject it. He spoke with the confidence and self-satisfaction of a man whose ends were clear-cut and honorable and who was conscious of commanding the means toward those ends: "Do not consider what I *can* do, I shall make no use of it. Do not consider what I *have* done, I want no compensation. Consider the public welfare, the well-being and the liberty of my country, and, believe me, I shall decline no burden, no danger, provided

---

[71] *Procès-verbal du Comité militaire*, Part I, pp. 79–80, and Lacroix, I, 318.

[72] Bailly, II, 299, and *Révolutions de Paris*, No. 7, August 22–28, p. 14.

[73] See below, Chap. X.

that the moment calm is restored, I shall again become a private citizen. For I am ambitious for only one further step: that is to arrive at zero."[74] (Washington, as Lafayette well knew, had recently spoken in that vein when he was urged—by Lafayette, among others—to take up the responsibility of leading the United States through its new constitutional crisis.)[75] His own circumstances, Lafayette admitted to Adélaïde, were "rather extraordinary": "I am in the midst of a great adventure, and I take pleasure in the thought that I shall finish it without having had even an ambitious gesture to reproach myself with, and after having put everything to rights, I shall withdraw with a quarter of the fortune I had upon entering the world." For the present, however, "all hell is conspiring against us"; the food situation was particularly bad, and he could use his friend's "angelic prayers." Yet he wanted her to feel reassured: "I believe that we'll pull the kingdom through."[76]

The letter also informed Adélaïde that he would soon come to Versailles. The proposed visit was on no simple errand. It was related to an annual ceremonial, which was intended this time to be both a demonstration of the Paris National Guards' effectiveness as an instrument of the people and a token of the Paris municipality's submission to the constitutional monarch. August 25 was St. Louis day, hence the fete day of King Louis XVI. The city's population showed an unmistakable desire to celebrate the first such fete since the Revolution in a way that would indicate loyalty at the same time to the king and to the new regime, and the Assembly of Representatives had accordingly decided that that day would be most appropriate for the mayor, accompanied by some of his colleagues, to go to Versailles and take his oath of office in the king's presence.[77] Lafayette would, of course, have to provide an escort.

[74] Lafayette to [Mme de Simiane], [August 24], *Mémoires*, II, 321–22. (The italics are ours, added for the sake of clarity.) The manuscript copy of this letter in the Cornell University, Lafayette Archives, Box 2, varies slightly from this published version.

[75] Washington to Lafayette, January 29, Fitzpatrick, XXX, 185–86. Cf. Lafayette to Washington, May 25, 1788, Gottschalk (ed.), *Letters of Lafayette*, p. 207.

[76] See above, n. 74.

[77] Lacroix, I, 272 (August 19), 318–19 (August 23); Bailly, II, 279; *Du règne de Louis XVI*, p. 131; and *Révolutions de Paris*, No. 7, August 22–28, p. 14.

In the fervid, suspicious atmosphere which prevailed in both Paris and Versailles the contemplated absence of the metropolis' chief magistrates with part of its police force immediately raised the specter of conspiracy. Distress over unemployment and the scarcity of bread was unabated; moreover, Louis had of late shown reluctance to accept the constitutional changes proposed by the National Assembly;[78] and so, despite his continuing popularity, not all of Paris could be counted upon to be respectful and forebearing. Reports persisted that swarms of Parisians, some intending to carry arms, were planning to move upon Versailles on St. Louis day. The risk of some untoward incident was made all the more probable by the desire of every one of the city's National Guard units to take part in the fete, thus not merely depriving Paris of police protection but possibly adding to patriotic excesses in Versailles. For their part, the king's ministers shuddered at the prospect of a descent on Versailles of a large body of armed Parisians.[79] Was Lafayette going to attempt a coup d'état? Actually, he had no such intention. That was probably why he had assured Mme de Simiane (who would presumably inform others) that he had no ambition except to restore order and then become a private citizen again.[80]

The circumstances attendant upon King Louis' fete day thus imposed a double obligation upon Lafayette. It behooved him to go to Versailles with enough of the National Guard to preserve order and to make a show worthy of its prestige and the dignity of the occasion and yet without lending credibility to the lurking suspicion of a military coup. And he was also obliged to leave enough of a force behind in Paris to foil an insurrection if one were attempted, whether by counterrevolutionaries or by anti-aristocrats.

After consulting with the Military Committee, his division commanders, and the Assembly of Representatives, Lafayette made plans to meet these obligations. He designated to go with him to Versailles a group of Guardsmen representative of every rank from fusilier to division chief, forbidding all other Guards-

---

[78] Bailly, II, 299, and see below, Chap. X.

[79] Bailly, II, 297–98; Lafayette to [Mme de Simiane], [August 24], *Mémoires*, II, 322; and *ibid.*, pp. 291–92.

[80] See above, n. 74.

men to leave Paris. He doubled the number of men on duty in all the guardhouses and at the city gates, and at the gates leading to Montmartre he also placed cannon loaded with grapeshot, since the ateliers were not yet closed and a breakthrough of the unemployed was still to be feared. The infantry contingent was ordered to leave Paris at 4 A.M. and wait outside Versailles for the rest of the procession. The cavalry would escort the mayor and the deputation of Representatives from Point du Jour. All together the military escort would number only a few hundred. To relay messages from Paris, aides would be stationed at three separate intervals along the road, and in Versailles a horse was to be kept saddled ready to carry Lafayette posthaste back to Paris at the first notice of trouble there.[81] Although he believed the royal ministers would be "very pleased" with his plans, he privately acknowledged that it would be "a pretty difficult *tour de force*" to keep armed citizens from going to Versailles.[82]

Everything went off well, however. Early in the morning, Lafayette rode with the designated cavalry escort through the western gate to Point du Jour. The guards seemed on their toes at the assigned posts, and everything appeared in order. When Bailly and the deputation of the Representatives arrived at Point du Jour, Lafayette entered the mayor's carriage, and the cavalcade continued toward Versailles. The National Guard of every town on the way was drawn up to salute them. The Paris infantry joined them at the appointed place, where they found also some of the National Guard of Versailles and some of the Paris marketwomen, whom the king customarily received on his fete day. With the marketwomen leading the way, the Versailles Guard following them, and the carriages of the Paris deputation flanked by its escort closing the line of march, they paraded, about 1,200 strong, through the streets of Versailles to the Château. Hundreds of onlookers lined the pavement and crammed windows and balconies. Shouts of

---

[81] *Procès-verbal du Comité militaire*, Part I, pp. 77–79, 83; Lacroix, I, 321–23 (August 23); Bailly, II, 297–98, 299–300; and *Révolutions de Paris*, No. 7, August 22–26, pp. 5, 16–18. Lafayette (*Mémoires*, II, 322) estimated that the entire number of Parisians would be 175, but the official report to the Assembly of Representatives (Lacroix, I, 340) indicated that the number of Paris Guards alone who waited at Versailles was 300.

[82] Lafayette to [Mme de Simiane], [August 24], *Mémoires*, II, 322.

"Vive Bailly!" "Vive Lafayette!" "Vive la Commune de Paris!" burst forth on all sides. Women and girls strewed flowers along the way. Bailly believed that never in living memory had Versailles given such an ovation to any but a king.[83]

Arrived at the Château, the Paris magistrates were conducted into the king's presence. Louis, his brother the Comte de Provence, and several officials of his court received them with much ceremony. Bailly solemnly took the prescribed oath before the king and then gave him a bouquet prepared by the women of the Paris market and wrapped in gauze on which was inscribed in gilt letters "Homage to Louis XVI, the best of kings." That done, the mayor presented his colleagues, and after the commandant general was presented, he in turn presented the officers selected as delegates of the Paris National Guard. It was all somewhat unprecedented, for normally a presentation at court was a much more formal and complex ritual, but the king received them all affably, stating that he was pleased with what they had already done and that he "counted on their zeal to restore order and public tranquility in the capital." Those who had been thus presented then went to other parts of the palace to pay their respects to the queen (who did not seem pleased), the dauphin, other members of the royal family, and the more popular ministers.[84]

Lafayette perhaps meant to keep in the background, since the ceremonies were essentially a civil matter,[85] but certain episodes occurred that thrust him into the limelight. With Saint Priest acting as host, but as the guests of the king, the Paris civil deputation and senior Guard officers dined in the royal apartments. Before that repast was over, Lafayette and four Representatives went, upon invitation of the Versailles National Guard, to another

[83] The above account is derived principally from the official report in Lacroix, I, 339–42 (August 25). Bailly (II, 300–306) borrows largely from the same source. See also *Révolutions de Paris*, No. 7, August 22–28, pp. 16–18, and Mirecourt, II, 306.

[84] Lacroix, I, 341–42 (August 25). See also Bailly, II, 302; Marquise de La Tour de Pin, *Journal d'une femme de cinquante ans, 1778-1815*, ed. Aymor de Liederkerke-Beaufort (Paris, 1913), I, 207–9; and *Gazette de France*, September 1, p. 348. The Marquise de La Tour de Pin (pp. 208-9) implies that the queen considered it highly improper for Lafayette to have presented his staff to her (presumably because some of them at least had not previously been formally admitted to court). Cf. *Mémoires*, III, 208.

[85] *Mémoires*, II, 291–92.

room, where other officers along with the men of both the Versailles and the Paris National Guard were dining. It happened that the Versailles National Guard had no commander at the moment. The Prince de Poix, Adrienne's cousin and Lafayette's close friend, had been its commandant, but after the French Guards left Versailles, he had resigned to devote himself to his duties as an officer in the King's Bodyguard. This dinner of the National Guard of the two cities was perhaps the first occasion on which two units of the new citizens' army met together—in a "federation," as Frenchmen were soon to learn to call a joint meeting of National Guard units. Good comradeship and fraternal hospitality were capped when the idea cropped up, quickly received with acclamation, that the Versailles Guard name Lafayette as its commander.[86]

Had Lafayette really intended to be a man on horseback, little more would have been wanting than to be commandant at one and at the same time in the city of the king's residence and in the king's capital. But he declined the honor in a little speech—the only one he permitted himself to make that day.[87] The responsibilities of deputy to the National Assembly and of commandant general of the Paris Guard were burdensome enough, and, as he had imparted to Mme de Simiane, he wanted only to contribute what he could to the Revolution and then "approach zero."[88] Ambition should be made of sterner (or at least more competitive) stuff.

Lafayette now returned to Saint Priest's dinner. He told of the good spirit he had found among the two National Guard units, and his listeners applauded. When the time came for after-dinner toasts, Bailly raised his glass in turn to the health of the king, of various members of the royal family, and several "patriot" ministers, and Saint Priest responded with the health of Bailly and of Lafayette, but, as Bailly noted, no one offered to toast the nation or the commune.[89]

---

[86] Bailly, II, 302. See also Lacroix, I, 342.

[87] *Mémoires,* II, 292. See also Bailly, II, 303.

[88] See above, n. 74.

[89] Bailly, II, 302–3.

The Paris troops had asked their general to arrange for them, too, to present a bouquet to the king, and Louis had acquiesced. When the proper time came, the Guards stacked their arms, and with their civil officials at their head, marched into the innermost, marble-paved courtyard of the Château, the Cour de Marbre, where the king, watching from a balcony, received them. Some of the court, their concern over Lafayette's ambitions in no wise assuaged, seemed to him unduly alarmed as he and his men, with the Representatives' deputation at their head, filed past. But nothing untoward occurred. The Paris Guards shouted "Vive Louis XVI!" and he graciously accepted their flowers and their cheers. When they had marched out of the court and picked up their arms again, they went with the civilian delegates to make the rounds of the ministers' homes and were received with all signs of "the happy accord which ought henceforth to prevail between the king's ministers and the nation."[90] Somewhere in the course of the day Lafayette seems to have elicited from several Patriot colleagues in the National Assembly a promise to come to Paris and consider with him how to avoid a rupture among them over the more thorny constitutional issues of the day.[91]

On the way back to Paris, enthusiasm and good will were again manifest everywhere. Spectators cheered as the Versailles National Guard saw the Paris delegation and its escort out of town. None of the aides posted along the route had received any disturbing messages from Paris. The mayor and his party reached the Place de Grève at eight o'clock that evening without further incident.[92]

Well might Lafayette have congratulated himself. Not only had his Guard been formally acknowledged by the king in permitting its representatives to be presented at court but also in both Paris and Versailles it had met the demands of the occasion with dignity and aplomb. So far the Paris National Guard had been able without ambivalence to live up to its oath of loyalty to nation, king, law, and commune. If there were inconsistencies inherent in these loyalties, a choice among them did not yet seem imperative.

[90] Lacroix, I, 342. See also *Mémoires,* II, 292, and Bailly, II, 303.

[91] See below, pp. 227–28 and n. 18.

[92] Lacroix, I, 343, and Bailly, II, 303.

BIBLIOGRAPHICAL NOTES

Marcel Rouff, "Le peuple ouvrier de Paris aux journées du 30 juin et du 30 août in 1789," *La Révolution française*, LXXIII (1912), 497–502, says that the workers of Montmartre blamed Lafayette for their misery. We have found no evidence for this.

The account of the Montmartre episodes by E. V. Tarle, "Rabochyi Klass vo Frantsii v epokhu revoliutsii" (The Working Class in France during the Revolution) in *Zapiski Istoriko-Philologicheskago Faculteta Imp. Peterburgskago Universiteta* (*Notes of the Department of History and Philology of the St. Petersburg Imperial University*), XCI (1909), 65–66, seems to be based principally on *Du règne de Louis XVI*.

In addition to the sources cited above for the events of August 25, see the *Journal général de l'Europe, supplément*, September 6, p. 57; *Journal des Etats généraux*, III, 110; Mège, *Gaultier*, II, 259; and *Mémoires du Comte de Paroy: souvenirs d'un défenseur de la famille royale pendant la Révolution (1789–1797)*, ed. Etienne Charavay (Paris, 1895), pp. 93–95. Mirecourt (II, 305) says the National Guard of Paris presented Louis XVI on that occasion with one of its uniforms with diamond-studded epaulets, but we have found no other testimony to confirm his statement.

George Rudé, *The Crowd in the French Revolution* (Oxford, 1959), p. 64, is mistaken in stating that the workers of Montmartre did not receive Lafayette's address well.

The Journal général de l'Europe, September 3, p. 9, reports that Lafayette made a threatening speech at the Saint Martin barracks on August 22, but we have found no confirmation of such a speech, and it seems to us out of character.

CHAPTER X

Strong Legislature or Strong King?

THE GOOD WILL displayed at Versailles on St. Louis day showed that since July 17, when the king had come to Paris and approved of the city's revolution, he was generally regarded, and perhaps regarded himself, as a friend of constitutional reform. To be sure, he was unwilling to accept the National Assembly's decrees of early August, intended to eliminate the most striking inequalities and privileges in the political and economic structure of France, but in those very decrees he was called "the Restorer of Liberty." His hesitation was attributed to the evil influence of his friends and relations rather than to his own inner promptings. To all but a few Frenchmen he himself was still *le roi bien aimé*. If Paris had at times been disorderly since the day it had "captured its king," the disorders were only indirectly antimonarchical in origin or purpose. They were spontaneous or, at worst, crudely planned bread riots, labor conflicts, demonstrations of the unemployed, or lynchings of hated men rather than premeditated and international manifestations of political principles. Although they prominently reflected a passion for the new "liberty" and although a self-appointed leader here or a chance instigator there might have had definite political designs, the rank and file had only mixed, and generally ill-formed, political programs in mind. If they were moved by slogans, sometimes incompatible one with another, those slogans were rarely aimed at the throne.

In August and early September, however, the debates in the National Assembly at Versailles rapidly made the Parisian much more intensely interested in the application of abstract political principles to a going monarchical structure. Discussions of the relative share of king and people in legislation became no less keen in Paris journals, district assemblies, cafés, and parks than on the floor of the National Assembly. To the dread prospect of famine, unemployment, and faction now was added a reason for unrest derived from conflicts over political theory, and the already harrowed days of the commandant general of the Paris National Guard were further harrowed.

The National Assembly's Committee on the Constitution, named on July 14, had kept steadily at work since then. Because Lafayette, though one of that committee's alternate members, had to stay close to Paris nearly all the time, he had taken no direct part in its deliberations. Nevertheless, his proposed declaration of rights of July 11 was in the forefront of its early discussions.

Opposition to a declaration of rights had developed quickly. It came not only from members of the National Assembly who wished to obstruct reform and revolution but also from some friends of reform who were genuinely distressed by the sometimes homicidal violence which had spread from Paris to the other cities of the realm and accompanied the Great Fear in the rural districts. As these men saw life and property being destroyed along with privilege in the name of "liberty," they wondered whether it might not be wise first to distribute the separate powers and fix the concrete "responsibilities" of government before promising general, abstract "rights" to citizens.

On July 27 Mounier as spokesman of the Committee on the Constitution presented its draft of a declaration of rights.[1] The committee had adapted articles from various proposals which had been submitted for its consideration—by Lafayette, Mounier, Target, Sieyès, and others. In place of Lafayette's pithy statement, consisting (in the printed version) of nine paragraphs and fewer than three hundred words, the new proposal contained twenty-three sometimes longer articles. The committee, explicitly acknowledging its indebtedness to Lafayette,[2] had included in its draft all but a few of his ideas.[3] It omitted his requirement that taxes be levied only by free consent and his final article permitting

---

[1] *AP*, VIII, 285–86, and *Courrier de Versailles à Paris*, July 31, p. 57.

[2] *AP*, VIII, 282.

[3] *Ibid.*, pp. 285–86.

periodic re-examination of the consititution, and it also recommended that a provision like his for the responsibility of government agents, since it belonged more appropriately in a statement of "Principles of the French Government," should be subsequently considered. Yet in some of its phrasings the committee's draft followed Lafayette's, and in others the intent had been retained though the phrasing was more elaborate.

The tenor of the committee's compilation differed from Lafayette's chiefly in its emphasis upon duty and law. The committee's draft began not with an enumeration of men's rights but with a statement that men have duties as well as rights: while the object of government is to insure general happiness and while to be happy the individual needs to have free exercise of his faculties, yet, since others have the same need, each has a duty to respect the rights of others. Although the committee accepted all of Lafayette's list of natural rights, it did so in a sentence which seemed to tone down their significance, mentioning them only by way of example: "Government . . . ought above all to guarantee the imprescriptible rights which belong to all men, such as personal liberty, property, security, care of honor and life, the free communication of their thoughts, and resistance to oppression." And the committee's project tended more than Lafayette's to stress the role of law: rights should be protected, duties indicated, and evil punished by laws, but no laws were binding on the individual unless freely consented to by him or his representatives, "and it is in that sense that law is the expression of the general will."[4]

Far from the ringing "manifesto and ultimatum" of liberty which Lafayette had intended his terse sentences to be,[5] in the committee's hands the declaration had become a more wordy and sober warning by fearful men of the threat to law and order. Yet many of the bold phrases were still there, and for the more resolute Patriots all that was needed was to restore their vigor and glow. On the other hand, for other deputies even the committee's proposal was much too bold. Hence, the National Assembly did not accept it but appointed a special Committee of Five to

[4] *Ibid.*, pp. 289–90.

[5] *Mémoires*, III, 227.

study all the proposals for a declaration of rights so far submitted and to make an acceptable compendium out of them.[6]

The Committee of Five, Mirabeau reporting, made its recommendations a few days later (August 17). Its draft, too, differed from Lafayette's not only by its greater length but also by its stress upon the necessity of obedience. The difference was attributable in part perhaps to Mirabeau's greater cynicism regarding human nature but certainly likewise to the differences in the political circumstances between July (before the fall of the Bastille) and August (after the shock of the Great Fear). When Lafayette submitted his declaration of rights, the greatest danger to the success of the Revolution had seemed to be the threat of a royal coup; when the Committee of Five reported, the greatest danger seemed to be the popular unrest in capital and provinces.

For the same reasons as had prevailed against Mounier's draft, few in the National Assembly received Mirabeau's report with enthusiasm, and the Assembly referred it to its thirty *bureaux* for further study. Discussions in the *bureaux* brought no greater agreement, and finally it was agreed that one of the dozen or so drafts already available should be selected as basic and be debated article by article, each article to be rejected, revised, or accepted in turn. Several prominent members of the Assembly recommended Lafayette's draft for that purpose, but others preferred some other,[7] and when a vote was taken (August 19), the Sixth Bureau's draft received 605 votes and one by Sieyès 245, while Lafayette's ran a bad third with only 45.[8]

The draft of the Sixth Bureau,[9] like all the others, was longer than Lafayette's, and it differed from his in at least two other important regards. Written largely by an archbishop, Champion

[6] *AP*, VIII, 399.

[7] *Ibid.*, pp. 222, 260–61, 285–86, 288–89, 289–90, 306–7, 325–26, 400–403, 406–7, 422–24, 428–31, 431–32, 438–39, 468–70.

[8] *Ibid.* pp. 438–40, 455, 457–58; *Courrier de Versailles à Paris*, August 19 and 21–23, pp. 364, 389, 400–401, 417 n.; Duquesnoy, I, 300–301; *Point du jour*, August 20, pp. 169, 171–72; and *Courrier de Provence*, August 18–19, p. 226. A draft by Mounier personally—not the one he had presented on behalf of the Committee on the Constitution but one based largely on Lafayette's (see Mounier as quoted in *AP*, IX, 563, and Egret, pp. 115–16, 135)—ran fourth with 4 votes.

[9] *AP*, VIII, 431–32.

de Cicé, now keeper of the seals, it contained a reference to the religious inspiration of human rights ("the presence of the Supreme Legislator of the Universe"), and it mentioned society's obligation not merely to guarantee to the citizen the enjoyment of his rights but also to require of him the performance of his duties and hence to maintain religion and morality. The emphasis upon religion and duty in the preceding discussions had obviously struck a responsive chord among the deputies.

The next week (August 20–26) was devoted chiefly to article-by-article deliberation of the Sixth Bureau's text. A preamble was adopted which placed the rights of man and of the citizen "in the presence and under the auspices of the Supreme Being," but then departure from the bureau's text began. Its first six articles were, after a lengthy debate, discarded in favor of a single paragraph of two sentences, which became Article I of the final Declaration of the Rights of Man and of the Citizen of 1789. The first of these two sentences read: "Men are born and remain free and equal in rights"—a statement which, though longer than Lafayette's and implying legal as well as natural freedom and equality, was, as several of its advocates pointed out,[10] much like his sentence "Nature has made men free and equal." The second was taken almost verbatim from Lafayette's declaration: "Social distinctions may be based only upon the general utility." Article II of the Declaration did not literally repeat Lafayette's words, but in listing "the natural and imprescriptible rights of man" as "liberty, property, security, and resistance to oppression" it used some phrases which he had used (while omitting others—at least here—for he had spelled out "liberty" and "security" at greater length). Article III came almost verbatim from his draft: "The principle of all sovereignty rests imprescriptibly in the nation. No body and no individual may exercise authority which does not emanate expressly from the nation." Article IV, defining liberty, contained a sentence which closely resembled his: "The exercise of the natural

[10] *Ibid.*, p. 463; Mounier, "Exposé," quoted *ibid.*, IX, 565; Mège, *Gaultier*, II, 248; La Rochefoucauld, *Mémoires*, III, 468; and *Courrier de Versailles à Paris*, August 22, p. 401. See also Gilbert Chinard "La Déclaration des droits de l'homme et la Déclaration d' inde-pendance, d'après un document peu connu," *Cahiers d'histoire de la Révolution française*, No. 1 (1947), p. 71.

rights of each man has for its only limits those that secure to the other members of society the enjoyment of the same rights."

Still following the order of Lafayette's draft, the Assembly next took up the right of the citizen to participate in making the laws which bound him. The next two articles, while not copying Lafayette's words exactly, nevertheless fell in with his ideas. They stated, for example: "No one may be constrained to do what it [the law] does not prescribe [Art. V]. . . . All citizens have the right to take part personally or through their representatives in its formation [Art. VI]." The next three articles (VII, VIII, and IX) dealt with the legal rights of the individual—such as freedom from arbitrary arrest, presumption of innocence until guilt is proven, and freedom from torture—with a particularity which Lafayette's proposition on legal right did not have. But Article VIII, almost in exact repetition of a paragraph of his, stated: "No one may be punished except by virtue of a law established and promulgated prior to his offense and legally put into force."

Up to Article IX, then, Lafayette's proposed declaration seems clearly to have been the Assembly's principal model. Although the Assembly borrowed from the Sixth Bureau's, Sieyès', Mounier's, and others' drafts a few words or sentences, thereby making the paragraphs of its final Declaration of Rights longer and more numerous, practically every one of Lafayette's first five paragraphs had been embodied in the longer version, in approximately the same order and often, indeed, with nearly the same words.

The next eight articles of the Assembly's Declaration likewise were indebted to him, though considerably less so. Two of them (X and XI) dealt with freedom of thought, which Lafayette had briefly dismissed by a mere listing of freedom both of opinion and of communication among the natural rights. The Assembly gave to each of these two freedoms a separate article, expressly granting in addition in Article X liberty of opinion "even in religion," of which Lafayette had studiously avoided making special mention. Article XII was based upon the Sixth Bureau's draft; it dealt with the subordination of the armed forces to the general welfare—an idea which Lafayette, though he had implied it in his initial draft, requiring that the army's allegiance to its royal commander be limited by the need "to guarantee public liberty," had omitted from his published version but of which, as his recent public behavior and expressed opinions amply demonstrated, he approved. The next two articles of the Assembly's Declaration dealt with taxes, Article XIII providing that they should be apportioned among all citizens according to their means and Article XIV that every citizen have the right directly or through his representatives to determine their assessment and purpose. Since Lafayette's eighth paragraph had said similarly that "subsidies" should be "freely consented to and proportionately distributed," the Assembly's articles were different from his only in length, not in spirit. The Assembly's Article XV was devoted entirely to specifying the responsibility of government agents, which Lafayette had mentioned in his sixth paragraph. Article XVI stated that without the guarantee of rights and the separation of powers a society could not be said to have a constitution, and Lafayette, implying the same, had been explicit at some length upon the separation of powers. Article XVII was devoted entirely to underlining the sacredness of property, an emphasis which Lafayette (perhaps at Jefferson's suggestion) had not employed.

In sum, as Lafayette claimed about forty years later, the Declaration of the Rights of Man and the Citizen of 1789 was based more upon his project than upon any one other,[11] and the greater part of his was incorporated in it.[12] The first nine of the Declaration's articles (more than half) were largely derived from his first five paragraphs. Its next eight were largely in keeping with his next three. Only his last paragraph, the one which contemplated amendment of the constitution by a special convention, was entirely omitted. The National Assembly debated a motion in favor of such a convention, employing some of Lafayette's phraseology,[13] but in the end did not adopt it. Nevertheless, something like it was to reappear, complicated by provisions for an elaborate procedure, as Title VII of the Constitution of 1791 when finally completed.

[11] *Mémoires*, II, 303.

[12] *Ibid.*, IV, 44 n., 188 and n. For the possible influence of Jefferson on Lafayette's draft, see above, pp. 81–90.

[13] *AP*, VIII, 489, and *Patriote français*, August 28, p. 2.

Certainly no name occurred oftener in the Assembly's intermittent debates on the Declaration of Rights (from July 11 to August 26) than Lafayette's, although, unlike the authors of the other drafts, he was not present to uphold his.[14]

The Declaration of Rights, without solving the eternal problem of right, made the immediate problem of power more complex. Louis' refusal to accept the August decrees intended to abolish seignorial and local privileges, had already led committees, caucuses of the National Assembly, other politically minded persons, and the now numerous journals to debate the place of the king in making a constitution which was bound to hedge his absolutism. The already warm debate now grew hotter when Louis refused to approve the Declaration of Rights without qualification. Even before this fresh rebuff of revolutionary reform the Patriots in the National Assembly had begun to disagree about the king's role in legislation. One group, of whom Mounier was the most conspicuous, felt that the royal right of veto was, as he supposed it was in England, absolute. This "Anglophile" position, however, was earnestly repudiated by another group, of which Duport and Alexandre de Lameth were the outstanding figures. They preferred that the king have either no veto at all or one like that in the American system, whereby the executive might exercise a veto which the legislature might override. Disagreement on this issue threatened to split the Patriots between advocates of the "absolute veto" and advocates of the "suspensive veto."

The threat to Patriot solidarity worried Lafayette. It seemed particularly unfortunate in view of the readiness of aristocrats and Orléanists to take advantage of every sign of discord—the aristocrats because they would undo the Revolution, the Orléanists ("factious people," as he styled them) because they would undermine Louis in the hope of shoring up their own man's pretensions

---

[14] The *Chronique de Paris* (August 31, 1791, pp. 29–30) named the principal author of each article of the Declaration of Rights. It assigned only Articles XII–XVI to the Sixth Bureau. Articles I–IX were assigned to Mounier, Lameth, Talleyrand, Target, and Duport (all of whom were avowedly indebted to Lafayette). Article X is attributed to the Comte de Castellane and Article XVI to Duport. The debates in *AP* corroborate this distribution of credits.

to the throne.[15] The prospect of serious dissension thus loomed large in Versailles at the very juncture that as commandant general he was getting things under control in Paris.

For some time before Louis XVI's nameday (August 25) Lafayette had tried to get the Patriots to hang together in the debate over the constitution, already so embittered that armed conflict seemed possible, and he had held one or two meetings[16] with Mounier and others at his own home in an effort to reconcile the clashing Patriot leaders. Just before he started out for Versailles that day, he had declared to Mme de Simiane; "If the king were to reject the constitution, I would oppose him. If he accepts it, I shall defend him. . . . The day on which he surrendered to me as a prisoner [meaning July 17] made me more devoted to his service than if he had promised me half his kingdom. But we have to have a constitution in the end, and we are going ahead with it."[17]

Having apparently already shared his anxieties with Jefferson, Lafayette counted upon the American minister's prestige to help prevent the collapse of his hopes for a viable constitution. When he got back to Paris from Versailles on King Louis' fete day, he wrote to his American confederate, entreating him "for Liberty's sake" to break every other engagement and let him and seven other deputies come to dinner on the twenty-sixth. An agreement among these eight colleagues, he pointed out, was "the only means to prevent a total dissolution [of the National Assembly]," and "if they don't agree in a few days, we shall Have no Great Majority in a favor [*sic*] of Any plan, and it must end in a [civil] war Because the discontented party [among the Patriots]

---

[15] Lafayette to Jefferson, [August 25], Boyd, XV, 354. See also Jefferson to Jay, August 27, *ibid.*, p. 359, and September 19, *ibid.*, pp. 458, 460, and Jefferson to Madison, August 28, *ibid.*, p. 366. Jefferson used stronger language than did Lafayette about "the faction," but he probably got his information largely, if not entirely, from Lafayette and reflected his views.

[16] Mounier says two (*Exposé de ma conduite dans l'Assemblée nationale; et motifs de mon retour en Dauphine* [Paris, 1789], p. 41) and Lafayette, writing long after, said one (*Mémoires*, IV, 200–201).

[17] [August 24], *Mémoires*, II, 321–22. We have followed the contemporary copy of this letter in the Lafayette Archives, Cornell University Library, Box 2 which reads: "*Mais il nous faut enfin* [not *aussi*] *une constitution.*"

will unite either with Aristocratic or factious people." He apologized for this impromptu imposition on Jefferson's hospitality:
"these gentlemen" wanted to learn Jefferson's views, but his own
house was "alwais [*sic*] full," and the dinner was "of an immediate and Great importance." He hoped that a meeting at Jefferson's
would "find some Means for a Suspensive Veto so strong as [he
apparently meant *and*] so Complicated as to Give the king a due
influence."[18]

Despite his scruples about intervening in the domestic affairs
of the country to which he was an accredited diplomat—scruples
which had previously constrained him to decline an invitation to
meet with the Committee on the Constitution[19]—Jefferson, given
such short notice, had small choice but to receive Lafayette and his
friends. And so on the afternoon of August 26, some of the most
distinguished deputies of the National Assembly foregathered at
his home. They were Lafayette, Mounier, Duport, Alexandre de
Lameth, Barnave, Latour-Maubourg, the Marquis de Blacons, and
and the Comte d'Agoult.[20] Dinner began at four o'clock, and as
soon as the cloth was removed ("with wine set on the table, after
the American manner"),[21] Lafayette got to the business in hand.
He was sorry to see the Patriots divided, he began, and he hoped
that their differences could be reconciled. As for himself, he intended to support neither side in the evening's discussion, not
merely because his duty as commandant general imposed neutrality upon him but also because he was prepared to sacrifice his
own convictions for the sake of a united front against the enemies
of the Revolution. Whatever the gentlemen present would decide,
he promised, as head of the National Guard, to try to enforce.[22]

---

[18] Boyd, XV, 354 (slightly revised above on the basis of LC, Jefferson Papers, p. 8686).

[19] Champion de Cicé to Jefferson, July 20, Boyd, XV, 291, and Jefferson to Champion de Cicé, July 22, *ibid.,* p. 298.

[20] *Ibid.,* p. 355. H. E. Bourne, "American Constitutional Precedents in the French National Assembly," *AHR,* VII (1903), 480–81, mistakenly puts this meeting on August 27 and includes Malouet.

[21] Jefferson's autobiography, quoted in Boyd, XV, 355.

[22] *Ibid.*

The meeting, thus begun, went on without interruption until ten o'clock. Jefferson, concerned that he had acted improperly in permitting his home to be used for a council on France's domestic controversies, took no part, but he was "a silent witness to a coolness and candor of argument unusual in the conflicts of political opinion; to a logical reasoning, and chaste eloquence, disfigured by no gaudy tinsel of rhetoric or declamation, and truly worthy of being placed in parallel with the finest dialogue of antiquity."[23] The obstacles to agreement proved stubborn, for Mounier, convinced that France needed a strong monarchy and elite leadership, would yield on neither an absolute royal veto nor an upper house in the legislature,[24] while Duport and Lameth, advocating government by representatives of the nation, of the people as a whole, were equally adamant on limiting the veto power and eliminating an upper house. Most of the company seemed to favor the Duport-Lameth position, Lafayette himself insisting only that if there were to be an upper house, it must be chosen not by hereditary or royal prerogative but (as in the American system) by some sort of election.[25] Yet, when, after about six hours of conference, the meeting broke up, the prevailing spirit was sufficiently friendly to induce Jefferson to assume that unanimity had been achieved in favor of a suspensive veto and a unicameral legislature.[26] Mounier was, however, shortly to make clear that he had not changed his mind.

As a consequence of Mounier's intransigence Lafayette's attempt at compromise seemed doomed to failure, with a resulting rift in Patriot leadership. Still hoping to avoid that outcome, and considering the veto question less crucial than his colleagues did, he continued to strive for solidarity. The debates over the veto, however, had already begun to churn up a public furor, making the commandant general unwilling to leave Paris, but he kept in touch with his colleagues chiefly through a spirited correspondence with

[23] *Ibid.* See also Jefferson to Jay, September 23, *ibid.,* p. 459.

[24] Mounier, "Exposé," *AP,* IX, 566.

[25] *Mémoires,* III, 202–3. (Lafayette here mistakenly places the meeting in September.)

[26] Jefferson's autobiography, quoted in Boyd, XV, 355. See also Jefferson to Jay, September 23, Boyd, XV, 458–59.

Latour-Maubourg,[27] pleading for a compromise. Duport and Lameth at first seemed more ready than Mounier to heed his pleas, possibly because they overestimated the strength of Mounier's backing. They offered to accept a bicameral legislature (provided the upper house were elective) and a suspensive royal veto (provided the king would have no power to dissolve the legislature, which might act "permanently"—that is, would assemble each year without royal summons, the king having no power to convoke or dissolve it). In return they asked for a provision allowing periodic amendments of the constitution.[28] Except for the "permanent" legislature, these were all concessions which Lafayette too favored,[29] but Mounier remained inflexible. He did not even reply to a letter from Lafayette protesting continued respect and affection despite differences of opinion, and his stubborn silence worried Lafayette.[30]

On August 28, as spokesman for the National Assembly's Committee on the Constitution Mounier presented an unyielding report which stipulated that "no act of legislation may be considered law unless . . . sanctioned by the monarch."[31] An inflamed debate ensued that day and the next, and while in Versailles partisanship flared, uneasiness spread in Paris. Political conflict was but one of the grounds for the rise of Paris' temper. Unemployment and high prices caused grumbling again in the Montmartre "workshops" and in the Halles, and Lafayette once more had to divide his energies between politics and police duty.

The unemployed in the charity ateliers of Montmartre had stayed on beyond the date fixed for their departure (August 23), growing more and more malcontent. On August 29, Lafayette learned that riot threatened among them. Having no guardsmen

---

[27] As previously indicated (see above p. 20), the originals of a number of Lafayette's letters to Latour-Maubourg are still to be found in AN, F [7] 4767. The published versions are often inexact, but, except where the differences are important, they will be cited from the printed versions.

[28] Ferrières, I, 222.

[29] Lafayette to unknown, September 6, Mémoires, II, 322–23. See also ibid., pp. 299–300, and III, 202–3 and 229–32.

[30] Lafayette to Latour-Maubourg, [September 1], Mortimer-Ternaux, I, 435–36.

[31] AP, VIII, 504.

to spare, he requested a favored private unit, known more or less justifiably as "the Conquerors of the Bastille," to go to Montmartre and keep order. They succeeded in doing so, but the Assembly of Representatives lost all forbearance and now peremptorily obliged the receivers of dole to move out. In a fairly systematic way passports and allowances were distributed, the workers were forced to leave for their Paris districts or their provincial homes, and the Montmartre ateliers were soon deserted.[32] A combination of force and persuasion (in this instance fortified by a little cash) had averted bloodshed.

About the same time food riots wrought havoc in the Halles of Paris. On two successive days (August 28 and 29) the Garde Municipale de Paris proved unable to preserve order, but with the help of the National Guard peace was restored. Thereupon the Assembly of Representatives charged Lafayette to keep a National Guard contingent in the Halles regularly.[33] The affiliation of the Garde de Paris with the National Guard, though still under debate, thus grew closer, providing Lafayette informally with a mounted contingent in the event of need.

And none too soon, for Lafayette now had to attend to a still more critical emergency. On August 30 the garden of the Duc d'Orléans' Palais Royal was, as usual on Sundays, packed with people. The district patrols made crowds in the open move on, but the Café de Foy and other cafés facing the garden became forums for haranguing orators, who again raised the bugbear of an aristocratic plot. A coalition of clericals and nobles in the National Assembly, excited speakers declared, was conspiring with some misguided commoners to give to the king the power to veto the Revolution itself. Reports even circulated that Mirabeau was being threatened by assassins, that he had actually been wounded. Patriots were urged to rush to his defense; or they must go to Versailles and bring the king and the dauphin to Paris, where they would no longer be exposed to the evil influence of palace cliques. The meeting in the Café de Foy sent a deputation to the city hall to vent

[32] *Patriote français*, September 4, p. 2, and Lacroix, I, 399 (August 30), 411–12.

[33] Lacroix, I, 380 (August 28), and *Révolutions de Paris*, No. 8, August 29–September 6, p. 6.

their concern, but it soon returned, only to report that it had received no satisfaction. The meeting then decided that one of their number, the Marquis de Saint Huruge, should that very day lead a force to Versailles.[34]

Saint Huruge and his party (generally said to have numbered 1,500) were already on their way when the Assembly of Representatives learned what was afoot. They sent for Lafayette immediately and authorized him to stop Saint Huruge's advance.[35] The general called out all the mounted men he could muster, ordered them to several strategic points to head off the self-appointed patriots, and instructed district commanders "to let no armed bands pass under any pretext whatsoever."[36] The Representatives dispatched a warning also to Saint Priest as minister of the king's household to prepare for trouble.

The warning proved premature. Saint Huruge was overtaken by Lafayette's mounted men and turned back without resistance.[37] Smaller groups reached Versailles and made a commotion but did no serious damage. Saint Huruge and his band sent off some threatening letters to selected deputies (probably including Mounier), and then he went with another group to present a protest to the Paris Representatives. The Representatives, however, having decided that it was improper to receive deputations of private citizens, had adjourned, and he had to content himself with interviewing only Bailly and Lafayette. Bailly rebuked him for inciting riot and attempting to intimidate deputies; if he wanted to show his patriotism, why had he not tried instead to pacify his people? Saint Huruge, all defiance vanished, became apologetic. Then Lafayette employed what Bailly called "a pretty adroit stratagem." If Saint Huruge really wanted to keep the peace,

---

[34] *Révolutions de Paris*, No. 8, August 29–September 6, pp. 7–12, and No. 11, September 19–26, p. 38; *Patriote français*, September 1, pp. 1–3, and September 3, pp. 1–2; *Courrier français*, September 1, pp. 1–2; *Journal général de l'Europe*, September 8, pp. 56–57, and September 10, pp. 68–69; and *Gazette de Leide, supplément*, September 11.

[35] Lacroix, I, 400 (August 30), 412, and Ferrières, I, 149.

[36] Lafayette to the commandant of the District of Saint Philippe du Roule, August 30, Indiana University, Ball Collection. See also Bailly, II, 333.

[37] Lacroix, I, 412, 414, and *AP*, VIII, 512.

as he now claimed, why didn't he join the National Guard?[38] The next day Saint Huruge appeared in a sergeant's uniform among the district patrols preserving order in the Palais Royal.[39]

Despite this farcical denouement the episode had been alarming, and the alarm did not fade away. When the Assembly of Representatives renewed its session on August 30, it stayed at the city hall for hours, receiving reports and preparing for an emergency. Only by two o'clock in the morning of August 31 was Lafayette able to announce that all was quiet in the Palais Royal. The Representatives then sent a second letter to Saint Priest telling him that "the precautions taken by M. the Commandant have been successful; all is calm." At three they broke up and went home.[40]

If those who were wrought up by political discontents or victimized by poverty, hunger, rising prices, and unemployment resented the National Guard as defenders of the status quo, others were resentful because they were not permitted to join it. Among the aspirant National Guardsmen, the Basoches continued to create a special problem. Their petition to be allowed to survive as a corps, whether inside or outside the Paris National Guard, had been referred by the commune to the National Assembly, which had more urgent matters to attend to. As the young men, especially the Basoches of the Châtelet, became impatient for a decision, Lafayette and his Military Committee asked the Assembly of Representatives to render them some honor public enough to compensate somewhat for the neglect they were suffering.

The Assembly approved, and an appropriate ceremony took place on August 31. Decked in their scarlet and silver uniforms, about 600 men of the Basoche of the Châtelet followed their standard bearers into the Grande Salle of the Hôtel de Ville. The commander of the battalion, thanking the city officials and especially "the illustrious general," to whom he reconfirmed his con-

---

[38] Bailly, II, 334. See also Lacroix, I, 401 (August 30), 412–14, and *AP*, VIII, 512–13.

[39] Bailly, II, 333–34; Nuñez to Floridablanca, September 3, 1789, Mousset, p. 75; and *Mémoire . . . du marquis de Saint-Huruge, sergent dans les Gardes nationales-parisiennes au District de Saint Roch . . .* (Paris, 1789) (hereafter cited as Saint Huruge), p. 7.

[40] *AP*, VIII, 512, and Lacroix, I, 401–2 (August 30), 414.

freres' "perfect submission," indicated its willingness to disband
if the authorities so decided. The president of the Assembly and
Lafayette in turn praised the battalion for its glorious service and
its willing submission to authority—sentiments which elicited
loud and prolonged applause. But nothing otherwise resulted beyond a promise that the Assembly would try to reach a decision as
soon as it could, and within a few days some of the provincial
members of the Basoche decided to return home, the Representatives having provided them with special passports testifying to their
faithful service.[41]

On September 1 some members of the National Assembly,
having learned of Saint Huruge's attempts to march upon Versailles, expressed their indignation, thereby precipitating still another bitter exchange between supporters of the absolute veto,
presumably Saint Huruge's intended target, and their opponents.
Outraged, Clermont-Tonnerre moved that "the mayor of the city
of Paris and the commandant of the national militia of Paris be
invited to come to take their seats [as deputies] to declare if they
can answer for the tranquility of Paris; and in case they cannot, the
National Assembly, in order to insure the liberty of its deliberations, should move to another place." This motion intimated not
merely a lack of confidence in the ability of the Paris commune
to preserve order but some doubt about the wisdom of even remaining within the neighborhood of Paris. Whether or not it
passed, it could easily be interpreted as a rebuke of the city's inhabitants and officials, no less shameful because Clermont-Tonnerre
was himself a deputy from Paris. But since Paris was at least momentarily tranquil, the Assembly passed to "the order of the day"
—that is, to its regular agenda—and once more resumed the debate
upon the royal sanction.[42] Those who recollected that Clermont-
Tonnerre and Lafayette had but recently had only words of
admiration for each other must have observed that the rift among

[41] *Procès-verbal du Comité militaire*, Part I, pp. 70–72, 95–97; Lacroix, I, 220 (August
14), 362–63 and 372–75 (August 27), 416–21 (August 31), 438 and 447 (September 1);
Foiret, pp. 36–37; and *Patriote français*, August 31, p. 3.

[42] *AP*, VIII, 512–14.

the Patriots which Lafayette had dreaded seemed to have opened and to be rapidly widening.

A wiser leader than Saint Huruge now appeared in the Palais Royal Garden. He was Elisée Loustalot, of the *Révolutions de Paris*, a journal which so far had been consistently friendly to Lafayette. Loustalot was thoroughly opposed to the absolute veto, but he also opposed intimidation of deputies. The proper way to proceed, he thought, would be for the National Assembly to suspend debate on the veto until the Assembly of Representatives, having called meetings of the city's districts for the purpose of sounding out public opinion, could instruct the Paris deputies to the National Assembly accordingly. His listeners at the Palais Royal agreed and dispatched him with a deputation to the city hall to present a proposal along those lines. The Assembly had already adjourned its early session when they arrived, but they were able to speak to Lafayette. Since they were a peaceful mission engaged in a lawful enterprise, he asked them to return for the later session.[43] When the Assembly reconvened, on his advice and despite its recent ruling not to deal with deputations from private groups it received Loustalot and his colleagues, who proposed sounding out public opinion not in Paris alone but in the provinces as well. The Representatives debated the proposal but only in the end to express their displeasure that pressure should be applied by a self-appointed group "gathered in a garden, where, all classes of citizens finding themselves assembled, the factious would often have the harmful privilege of imposing upon them."[44]

Lafayette agreed that in expecting deputies in the National Assembly to be pliant agents of a possibly misled public opinion rather than independent judges of the issues before them, Loustalot had pushed the idea of popular sovereignty too far. Nevertheless, he saw reason to fear that Loustalot's idea might find an importunate following at the Palais Royal; hence, if the Assembly of Representatives did nothing, it might lose its leadership, justifying Cler-

---

[43] *Révolutions de Paris*, No. 8, August 29–September 6, pp. 13–18, 21, and No. 11, September 19–26, pp. 38–39.

[44] Lacroix, I, 423–25 (August 31), 429, and Bailly, II, 334–38.

mont-Tonnerre's insinuation that the city's magistrates were powerless to preserve order. The next morning the commandant general proposed that the Representatives take a clear-cut public stand in favor of the National Assembly's freedom of judgment; by thus informing the National Assembly of their respect for its decrees they could effectively "eliminate all notion that Paris sought to influence its deliberations by demonstrations or petitions." And since by this time agitation over the veto power had spread well beyond Paris, a resolution expressing such a neutral stand would serve also to "give the provinces an example of submission to the National Assembly."[45]

To adopt a resolution of neutrality in the National Assembly's debates would have been tantamount to publicly rebuking a widely esteemed journalist (Loustalot), and the Representatives at first seemed no more willing to incur that risk than they had been the day before to act favorably on Loustalot's petition. Exerting all his personal influence, however, Lafayette persisted, pointing out that the stakes were not merely the National Assembly's freedom of deliberation but also the commune's reputation for maintaining public order. Gradually the Assembly of Representatives rallied to his point of view, and it finally decided to give to the apprehensive national deputies the reassurance which he recommended. It adopted a resolution which denounced "seditious movements," renewed its pledge of "sincere devotion" to the king, and indignantly repudiated the doubts cast upon its ability to guarantee tranquility in Paris. Declaring that the Assembly of Representatives "stands unalterably by its decrees against assemblages and motions at the Palais Royal" and that "nothing can induce it hereafter to relax its most effective measures for repressing disorders which might deprive France of the fruits of its most auspicious Revolution and dishonor the reputation of Frenchmen," the resolution instructed Lafayette to use all the commune's forces to arrest and hold for trial any disturbers of the peace. Copies of this resolution were sent forthwith to each of the districts, and every member of the district assemblies was asked to sign a copy of it "in order

[45] Lafayette to Latour-Maubourg, [September 1], Mortimer-Ternaux, I, 434.

that it might serve as an authentic disavowal of all excesses and disorders for which the city of Paris would forever have to blush if true citizens could be suspected of having had a hand in them."[46]

Lafayette's proposal thus converted Loustalot's suggestion to defer to public opinion on the veto question into a referendum favoring repression of disorderly interference with parliamentary judgment. That afternoon, as if to confirm Lafayette's foreboding that if they did not lead they might have to follow, the Representatives were called upon to give ear to a deputation petitioning that the Representatives ask the National Assembly to suspend its deliberations until the nation's deputies could consult their constituents on the veto. Immediately the Representatives renewed their debate on what Paris' attitude should be. In the end (sometime about 1 A.M.)[47] on the insistence of Lafayette, Bailly, and others, the Representatives decided, by way of answer, to give to the deputation a copy of its earlier resolution.[48]

In the course of the day Lafayette had found time to write to Maubourg from the Hôtel de Ville, intending through him to conciliate Mounier and to placate the malaise of the National Assembly. As he wrote, the Paris Representatives had once more got around to a committee report on the food crisis, and the never-ending wrangle disgusted him: "We are in the hands of people who understand nothing, and . . . after having done so much to establish order in Paris, we are perhaps going to perish through the inefficiency of all these committees." At the same time he took pride in informing Maubourg (and the National Assembly) that his policy of preventing interference with parliamentary freedom would prevail, although "if I were not the author of the proposal and if I were not staying here to get it passed, it could well get hung up." He intended to see the matter through, even if it displeased the districts and the "frondeurs."[49] (He was to discover that the districts did not respond readily.)[50]

[46] Lacroix, I, 435–37 (September 1). See also *ibid.,* pp. 445–47, and Bailly, II, 341–44.

[47] Lafayette to Latour-Maubourg, [September 2], Mortimer-Ternaux, I, 438

[48] Lacroix, I, 438, 447–48, and Bailly, II, 345.

[49] Mortimer-Ternaux, I, 434.   [50] Bailly, II, 344.

Lafayette went on to give Maubourg (and hence Mounier) his views—the first statements of them to survive—on the burning constitutional issues of the day. On that of the veto he proposed an arrangement which he considered a compromise between absolute veto and no veto. The royal veto, he wrote, ought not to be absolute, yet it ought to bind two successive legislatures; thus, even if ultimately overridden, it might stand for an appreciable interval; and if the legislature had a two-year term, as he advocated, that interval might be as long as four years or more. A less lasting veto than that would, he feared, weaken the royal prestige too much.

On the structure of the legislature Lafayette also proposed a compromise. He shared Mounier's preference for two houses, but his concept of the upper house, bearing conspicuous marks of his American experience, was, if not unique, certainly unusual. In keeping with his earlier views, he wanted no hereditary house of lords but, instead, a "Senate" to be chosen for a six-year term by none-too-large provincial assemblies. It too, however, would have only a suspensive veto on the legislation of the lower representative body.

Since the National Assembly had begun to consider the reform of local government, Lafayette expressed to Maubourg a definite opinion on that subject as well. He wanted the number of provinces considerably increased, thus making them too small to constitute autonomous federative states and hence keeping them dependent upon the central authority. Reverting to the idea of the constitutional convention, he also advocated that a vote of three-quarters of the provincial assemblies be required for convoking one; he wanted such convocations to be possible without being frequent.

Lafayette intended these suggestions to enable Maubourg to conciliate Mounier. Even if, as now seemed probable, Mounier failed to win an absolute veto and might therefore feel defeated and alienated, "his interest, talents, and virtue" were still needed for "public service." As for himself, Lafayette made no secret of his desire, even at the sacrifice of his own preferences, to prevent the splintering he so much feared of the Patriot group: "Get the most votes you can for the opinions that sway people in order to have a big majority for the views which rouse passion."[51] The political strength of the Patriots obviously was more important to him than the philosophical merit of the issues which might rend them asunder.

Agitation in Paris over the veto question did not diminish because the city government had adopted an official policy of respect for the National Assembly's freedom of debate. The Palais Royal still boiled with indignation over the veto, and five neighboring districts felt called upon to dispatch patrols there. The patrols made arrests (including Saint Huruge) and enforced a curfew—high-handed actions, but taken with the commune's approval, and always, Lafayette claimed, "with courtesy and respect for the liberty of decent citizens," though also "with a combination of considerable forces."[52] When the Assembly of Representatives sent a packet of copies of its resolution on parliamentary freedom to Versailles, it assured the National Assembly that "the disorders of the Palais Royal ended yesterday, [and] we dare to promise that they will not recur."[53] Lafayette nevertheless deemed it wise to keep several hundred men on guard at the bridge across the Seine at Sèvres, with orders to prevent a hostile movement against Versailles. They did not fully restore confidence, however, for the friends of the absolute veto saw (or pretended to see) in the presence of so many troops evidence that the danger remained grave.[54]

[51] Mortimer-Ternaux, I, 435–36. See also *Mémoires*, IV, 187. These views in favor of an upper house render unlikely the anecdote (Sabatier, II, 114–15, and A. Rivarol, *Mémoires*, ed. M. Berville [Paris, 1824], p. 217) that Lafayette boasted to a departing Englishman that the British House of Lords would have disappeared by the time he got home. The anecdote seems to be based upon a conversation which Lafayette and Montlosier perhaps had had earlier (Montlosier, I, 214), but Montlosier's account probably misrepresents Lafayette's views even for that time. It is true, however, that Lafayette did not admire the House of Lords; see below, n. 78.

[52] Lafayette to Latour-Maubourg, [September 3], Mortimer-Ternaux, I, 433. The original (AN, F 7 4767) gives the date of this letter as "ce 3." See also Lacroix, I, 449–50 (September 2).

[53] Lacroix, I, 450.

[54] *Patriote français*, September 3, p. 3; Marquis de Vergennes to M. de Bellejeant, September 3, Pierre de Vaissière (ed.), *Lettres d' "aristocrates," la Révolution racontée par des correspondances privées 1789–1794* (Paris, 1907), p. 91; Nuñez to Floridablanca, September 5, Mousset, p. 73; *La voix du peuple, ou les anecdotes politiques du Bonhomme Richard* No. 1, [*ca.* September 1], p. 6; Saint Huruge, p. 8; *Chronique de Paris*, September 3, p. 43; *Courrier de Versailles à Paris*, September 4, p. 64; and *Mémoires*, IV, 148.

The commandant general again thought he detected in the continued agitation the hand of conspirators and *factieux*. To bring the protracted crisis to a close as soon as possible, he tried a direct appeal to Mounier.[55] As a member of the National Assembly Lafayette perhaps had a duty to express his opinion openly on national issues, but he preferred as a city official to act publicly in keeping with the policy of neutrality which he had persuaded the commune to adopt—at least to seem to be impartially preserving order and the freedom of expression of the National Assembly without publicly committing himself. But he did not hesitate to express a partisan opinion privately, and so he personally appealed to Mounier for compromise. Intrigues at Paris might lead to violence, he argued, if the majority of the deputies failed to unite and give the country a constitution soon,[56] and (as Mounier understood his argument) in the event of violence he (Mounier) would have to share the responsibility "for the blood that was going to flow."[57]

If, as was reasonable to suppose, Mounier kept in touch with the court, this letter could also have been expected to bear upon the king's calculations. At any rate, Lafayette heard of a rumor rapidly spreading in Versailles to the effect that he was *requiring* the king's ministers to accept the suspensive veto.[58] What he really wanted, however, as he indicated to Maubourg, was to forestall a scheme, which he attributed to the Duc d'Orléans' partisans, to take advantage of the prolonged tension and reorganize the national militia, giving Orléans major control of it. While he felt confident that (despite Clermont-Tonnerre's rebuke) his own popularity would defeat Orléanist purposes and win a victory for himself if the National Assembly fell in with such a scheme, he was opposed to any reorganization which "puts a big armed force in other hands

[55] Lafayette to Maubourg, [September 1] and [September 3], Mortimer-Ternaux, I, 435–36, 433, respectively. (Mortimer-Ternaux did not puzzle out the chronological order of these letters, and he gives them in the wrong order.)

[56] So far as we know, the letter to Mounier is not extant. It is quoted above as cited in Lafayette to Maubourg, [September 2], *ibid.*, p. 437. See also below, n. 58.

[57] These words are from Mounier's paraphrase of Lafayette's letter, September 1, as cited in Mounier, *Exposé*, p. 50, and *AP*, IX, 568. Cf. Egret, p. 141.

[58] Lafayette to Maubourg, [September 2], Mortimer-Ternaux, I, 437.

than those of the king and would make me more king than he."[59] He did not want power; he wanted a strong but constitutional monarchy.

The very next day Lafayette continued his efforts to mend the rift in Patriot ranks with another letter to Latour-Maubourg. This time he further elucidated his ideas on the kind of constitution France should have. He wanted, first of all, a bicameral legislature, frankly modeled upon the American example. Ten years of experience with a single chamber under their loose Articles of Confederation, he pointed out, had taught the Americans the desirability of two chambers. The French upper house, or Senate, ought to be composed of men of greater distinction than those in the lower house, the Chamber of Representatives, and elected for a longer term (six years or life). The legislative process that Lafayette desired differed, however, from the American precedent: the lower house was to have the exclusive right to initiate legislation; a bill would be in print eight days before debate began in the lower house; it would be read three times, over a period of fifteen days, and voted upon after the third reading; if passed two separate times, it should then go to the Senate, which might exercise a veto of at least one year's duration.

The king's veto, Lafayette held, should likewise be only suspensive. A suspensive veto, he assumed, would be acceptable not only to those who opposed the absolute veto but to the king as well, since it preserved the royal authority. "Do not permit the royal prerogative to be diminished more than necessary," he urged, "especially in reference to army and foreign affairs"[60] (two areas where, along with the veto power and ecclesiastical organization, Louis was to prove to be most sensitive). He repeated his preference for a royal veto which would be binding on two successive legislatures but (as he now conceived it) might be overridden by a two-thirds vote in the Chamber of Representatives of the

---

[59] [September 1], *ibid.,* p. 435. For the initiation at this time of a proposal to make Lafayette the commander-in-chief of all the National Guard of the realm see below, pp. 262–65.

[60] Lafayette to Maubourg, [September 2], Mortimer-Ternaux, I, 436.

third legislature. Or, if the king regarded a pending law as unconstitutional, he might call a special convention, consisting of others than members of the regular legislature, to examine it and change the constitution or sustain his veto. This sort of suspensive veto, Lafayette maintained, "without harm to the principle of the will of the people, makes it possible to give the king something much stronger than the absolute veto, which he will never use"[61] (presumably because it would be impolitic to do so).

On the question of local administration Lafayette, as in his earlier letter to Maubourg, advocated a large number of small provincial assemblies and, hence, of provinces directly responsible to the central authority, with Paris having the rank of a province rather than of a municipality. It probably did not escape him that such a system of local administration would provide another channel of royal influence in legislation, for if, as his previous letter had advocated, the provincial assemblies were to choose the Senate and if the provincial assemblies were to be subordinate to the executive, the king would be likely to dominate the Senate.

Lafayette took no pains to conceal his hope that the legislative structure he proposed, because it was designed to delay precipitate action through deliberation by two houses and the king, would appeal to the court, Mounier, and their Anglophile supporters. He confessed to Maubourg, however, that he had so far had no success. That he had received no reply from Mounier to his overtures left him disappointed but not oversensitive; he was more indignant over the charge that he had required certain ministers to support a suspensive veto: "I have required nothing. I have asked nothing." He admitted, however, "that it was hard to watch the quarrels of the nation's representatives leading to anarchy and civil war," and he counseled "that instead of everyone insisting stubbornly upon his own system based upon variations which are nothing less than geometric, we need to agree peaceably upon a plan which would unite a big majority and give us a constitution very soon."[62] He obviously thought of his own plan as being based upon the historical experience of another country rather than upon pure

[61] *Ibid.*, p. 437.
[62] *Ibid.*

geometric rationalism, apparently forgetting that Mounier (though perhaps with less understanding of Britain than Lafayette had of the United States) probably was thinking the same thing of his.

In Lafayette's opinion, as he confided to Maubourg, the importance of the veto had been exaggerated. What was truly important was the threat of disunity in the face of "a plot about which I have no doubt." The utmost he could himself do publicly was to show impartiality in the dispute (and he urged that the National Assembly give the resolution of neutrality which he had pushed through the Paris commune full endorsement and wide publicity), but in his private correspondence he did not hesitate to disclose his desire for a compromise between those who favored the royal veto and those who opposed it. He hoped that Mounier might be persuaded by the spread of opposition to the absolute veto outside of Paris as well as within, and toward that end he asked Maubourg to inform Mounier of a threatening letter he had received from Metz, which Maubourg was to show also to any who might be "able to oppose the hostile municipality."[63] Thus Lafayette brought his personal influence to bear on Mounier (probably also on Duport),[64] even to the point of transmitting threats. Small wonder that in an atmosphere filled with recriminations the Anglophiles accused him of intimidation, even if he considered his purpose to be only to call attention to the explosive temper of public opinion and to the misguided intentions of "the factious."

On September 2 the National Assembly, its apprehensions allayed indirectly by Lafayette and officially by the Assembly of Representatives, voiced its "satisfaction and confidence" in the capital's "zeal to maintain order,"[65] and Mounier, finally responding to Lafayette's overtures, showed a disposition to talk things over.[66] The next day, in a third letter in as many days, Lafayette

---

[63] *Ibid.*, p. 346. Lafayette did not indicate the contents of the letter from Metz, and it is not clear whom or what it threatened.

[64] In AN, F [7] 4767, there is a line written on a separate sheet of paper, undated, permitting Maubourg to show "this note" to Duport if he thinks it "useful" to do so. It seems to have accompanied one of Lafayette's letters to Maubourg in early September.

[65] *AP*, VIII, 513, 543, 547–48; *Courrier français*, September 3, p. 4; and *Patriote français*, September 8, p. 3.

[66] Lafayette to Maubourg, [September 2], Mortimer-Ternaux, I, 438.

requested Latour-Maubourg to "find occasion to say in the Assembly that I have established better order in the Palais Royal than has existed there for a year." He made obvious that he felt himself master in the restive city. While he was "always surrounded by conspiracies" which were "always ready to explode" and could not be expected to head off the initial steps of a plot, once it became known he was "ready to answer to the Assembly and his friends for its suppression." If he could find proof against a leader, "whoever he is, I will rid you of him quickly." Yet, he insisted, he did not like the "dictatorial role" in which recent commotions had placed him, and he wished it to end as soon as possible. That wish was all the more reason why he wanted a sober discussion of his ideas for a constitution, which, he believed, would put a close to the hot-headed debates in the National Assembly, reunite the country, mire "the factious" down, and in so doing, make his own services expendable.

If Mounier was angry with him, Lafayette confided, he was sorry, for he admired and liked Mounier. Yet "he has made me impatient, I admit, because I fear whatever may prevent unity and lead to trouble." And he urged Maubourg to "pledge our friends of both groups, for the country's sake, to talk with moderation and to get the constitution finally anchored."[67]

While Lafayette spoke thus frankly to private correspondents, he still made a point of limiting himself on public and semi-public occasions to urging strict neutrality, without committing himself to either Anglophiles or Anglophobes. He had been so politic that some of his friends did not know exactly where he stood. One of them, one who apparently knew Mounier also, now asked him his views on the current controversy, and Lafayette, still writing only for off-the-record consumption, answered candidly and at length. He was pleased, he admitted, that he had been publicly so noncommittal that his correspondent did not know what his views were. That he had to be asked proved that he had "carefully preserved the character of impartiality," which "alone is fitting to the force armed for liberty but whose influence ought to be nil

---

[67] *Ibid.*, pp. 432–33. See above, n. 52. We have used the original rather than the printed version of this letter.

upon the opinions of the Assembly." He then set forth his preference for a suspensive veto, which he now described as one which
might "give the king six years to consult the nation or to influence
the representatives." He expected it to win a big majority, "but if
the absolute veto passes, I shall not feel sorry, for there is much to
be said in its favor, and I would have more fear of the opposition
of others than desire to put up any [of my own]." In short, he
believed, "the famous veto is a fairly indifferent dispute." All
parties agreed that the absolute veto would never be used and was
only "a crown jewel," but an "iterative veto" (i.e., one which would
be binding upon several legislatures in succession) would be "more
useful to authority than one of which no use ever was made."

On the issue of a bicameral legislature Lafayette was less flexible.
He wanted "not a hereditary chamber but a Senate elected for six
years or even longer." And he described his ideas of the senators'
qualifications and powers as he had for Latour-Maubourg, requiring of them now, however, a property qualification and assigning to them "certain judicial functions." He believed that senators
could just as well be found "here as in America."

In this letter Lafayette reiterated his predilection for a strong
executive. Numerous provincial assemblies were desirable, he once
more maintained, in order to avoid the old abuse of privileged
provinces and the new danger of "confederated" (i.e., loosely
interrelated) provinces, but they should have "very direct relations
with the executive power, which would assign to them part of its
functions and upon which they ought to be dependent." And the
armed forces of the realm ought under no circumstances to be
independent of the executive. The bourgeois guards' relations to
the executive, he conceded, would be difficult to arrange since they
would be dependent upon the municipalities, "and yet they cannot
be outside the king's influence."

These ideas Lafayette offered to this correspondent as well only
in confidence. "It is proper that I defend the *Congress* without
influencing its deliberations," he said (choosing to overlook for the
moment his private letters to Latour-Maubourg). "I do not want
anything of mine written or even positively said on this question.
The [National] Assembly is perfectly free and ought to be per-

fectly tranquil. We shall accept whatever it will have decreed."
Almost in the next breath, however, he revealed again that his
desire to be publicly neutral came into conflict with his desire
to use his personal influence to keep the Patriots united. Whoever the addressee of this letter was, he or she apparently was
acquainted with Mounier and Lafayette, and so Lafayette hoped
to use him or her as a liaison: "I expect you tomorrow at dinner
at Madame de T***'s [Tessé's] home," he concluded, and "I
would be happy if Mounier would be one of us."[68] In the prevailing
hostile political climate, however, where, as Lafayette recognized,
some of the popular party wanted the two leaders to remain bitter
opponents,[69] the uncompromising Mounier probably did not comply with even this personal, indirect, moderate gambit.

On the day that this letter to their mutual friend was written
(September 6) Lafayette undertook to assure Mounier again that
the National Assembly need have no misgivings about disturbances
in the capital, but Mounier, who had received and was still receiving threatening communications, was not reassured.[70] In Paris
discontent was in fact under only uncertain control. The districts
divided between support of Loustalot's proposal for a popular

[68] Lafayette to [Mme de Simiane?], [September 6.], *Mémoires*, II, 322–24. We consider the probable date of this letter to be September 6 because it was obviously written
before the vote on the legislature (September 10) and is dated "ce Dimanche," the only
likely Sundays being August 31 and September 6. The editor of the *Mémoires* (II, 322 n.)
placed it early in September.

We are indebted to Professor Julian P. Boyd for the help he gave us in deciding that this
letter was probably not to Jefferson. The reasons for thinking that it was addressed to him
seem almost persuasive. Jefferson wrote Lafayette a letter on August 30 which Boyd (XV,
374) has been unable to find, and this letter sounds as if it were a translation of Lafayette's
answer to that one. Moreover, this letter seems to have been addressed to someone who
was familiar with American institutions, who might as a general rule have expected to be
informed of Lafayette's views on current issues, who dined at Mme de Tessé's, and who
apparently knew Mounier. Very few fit this description better than Jefferson.

Nevertheless, in view of the close cooperation between Lafayette and Jefferson and of
the latter's earlier informed guesses regarding the probable outcome of the current constitutional debates (see especially his reports to Jay, August 27, *ibid.*, p. 359, and to
Madison, August 28, *ibid.*, p. 365) and in view of the absence of any record in "Jefferson's
remarkably complete register of correspondence" (Boyd to Gottschalk, May 23, 1966) of
such a letter, it becomes hard to believe that Jefferson formally asked about Lafayette's
views only on August 30 and learned of them only on September 6.

[69] Lafayette to [Latour du Pin], [September 8], *Mémoires*, II, 326, and see below,
p. 250. On Mounier's attitude see Egret, pp. 142–56.

[70] Mounier, "Exposé," *AP*, IX, 569, and Egret, pp. 142–43.

referendum on the veto question and the Representatives' resolution of strict neutrality. Deputations came to the Hôtel de Ville, some to express disapproval; other cities took part in the controversy; and all added to the ferment in the capital.[71] There was reason to fear new outbursts in the Palais Royal gardens.

Indeed, on the very day on which Lafayette wrote to reassure Mounier word reached him of a new threat to march upon Versailles. He ordered his mounted men to take up posts on the Champs-Élysées and alerted all the patrols near the Palais Royal, but though the men were slow in arriving from their various quarters, the threat never materialized.[72] The next day (September 7) order seemed so completely restored that when La Salle, at length exculpated by the National Assembly and released from the protective custody in which he had been detained by the Assembly of Representatives, came to the Hôtel de Ville to express his thanks and to renew his pledge of loyalty, all remained serene, and no one protested when Lafayette embraced him in the middle of the city hall square.[73]

Obviously troubled by the arrest of several citizens—which he held to be unavoidable if he were to do his duty as a policeman—Lafayette was anxious that prisoners now receive a fair and speedy trial. Since he distrusted the court system of the Old Regime still in force, and was concerned lest his men hestitate to make even justifiable arrests if they shared his distrust, he wanted the Representatives to go on record in favor of a system of justice which would be "nearer to the principles of natural law." He had previously broached the subject more than once, but Bailly had urged him to let sleeping dogs lie—not because it was not a pressing matter but because a period of disorder, license, and threats such as the current time was inopportune for the reform of court procedure and would probably result only in the delay of justice. The recent police severity, however, persuaded Lafayette to hesitate no longer,

---

[71] Lacroix, I, 452–53 (September 2), 459–60, 466–67 (September 3), 471 (September 4), 534–35 (September 10), 540–41.

[72] *Procès-verbal du Comité militaire,* Part I, p. 125.

[73] Lacroix, I, 460–61, 490, 497–98, and Lafayette to [Latour du Pin], [September 8], *Mémoires,* II, 326.

and on September 8 he persisted, despite Bailly's doubts. In the morning session of the Representatives, apropos of the need to leave the National Assembly free and to give a good example to the provinces by preserving order he mentioned the desirability of reform of criminal procedure. All he elicited, however, was a renewed compliment on "his characteristic wisdom, moderation and discretion," and he returned to the subject in the evening session. In the end the Representatives agreed to petition the National Assembly "to decree or to request of the king" that an accused be granted counsel, get a public trial, receive notice of the charges against him, have access to the evidence, and be sentenced to corporal punishment only by a two-thirds vote of the magistrates who tried him—reforms which, the petition asserted, "the nation unanimously asks and the king's justice and goodness have already prepared and promised." The petition went off forthwith to Versailles, and on September 10 the National Assembly began to act sympathetically upon it. It appointed a committee, which a month later (October 9) produced the first of a series of projects for the reform of French criminal procedure. Lafayette, who was engaged in founding a good citizen-police force, thus also played a role as leader in the effort to combine a just court procedure with strict police power. Yet, as Bailly had anticipated, one of the first results of this effort was a confusion which slowed the wheels of justice for a time.[74]

The unalloyed partisanship in Paris over the veto meanwhile alarmed the court of Versailles, which was uncertain of Lafayette's willingness or ability to contain the Paris populace. Rumors continued, not unexpectedly, to reach Lafayette of the displeasure of the ministers, who placed a large part of the responsibility for the opposition to the absolute veto upon his shoulders and Duport's. Much more disturbing was a report that Louis, apprehending defeat, proposed to leave Versailles with his retinue and go to

[74] Lacroix, I, 507–8, 510–11. Lacroix does not give the details of Lafayette's speech in the morning session, but Lafayette did in his letter to [Latour du Pin], [September 8], *Mémoires*, II, 324–25. See also *Mémoires*, II, 294–96. Lacroix (pp. 515–17) provides convincing evidence of Lafayette's direct connection with French legal reform. See also *AP*, VIII, 608 (September 10), 641 (September 14), and IX, 392–96 (October 9). On Bailly's attitude see his *Mémoires*, II, 360–62. See also below, pp. 299–300, 319–21.

some distant and more friendly city like Metz. The spectacle of the king's deserting the National Assembly and thereby announcing to the world his disapproval of what was going on in Versailles and Paris, no matter how unattractive to Lafayette personally, was more unattractive to him as a police officer. Parisians might well be expected to rise in fear and protest if their king ran away from the Revolution, with resulting demonstrations which would split the country into camps more irreconcilable than ever.

Apparently with the intention of sounding out whether Lafayette and his friend Maubourg might be won over to the king's side Minister Latour du Pin communicated to him some of the forebodings rampant in Versailles, indicating the court's displeasure with him and criticizing Duport's anti-veto, anti-aristocratic program.[75] This maneuver gave Lafayette a welcome opportunity to respond in a lengthy, frank letter, appealing directly to the king's minister, who was also a personal friend, to prevent the blunder of flight. If the government, he admonished, was not pleased with his efforts, "there will be trouble." He outlined what he had so far done to restrain "the factious," to secure "complete submission" to whatever decision the National Assembly might reach on the veto, and to discourage the alienation, the "federative" spirit, in the provinces. He had been so successful, he claimed, that although the provinces still were troublesome, Paris held forth the promise of "tranquility, impartiality, and obedience"; calm now appeared so certain that he could withdraw his troops, leaving only sentry posts at the bridges across the Seine on the roads to Versailles; and in view of the Paris commune's declaration of loyal neutrality, neither party to the dispute would now be justified in claiming to have been overridden by intrigue or by fear of the Palais Royal.

Lafayette then ridiculed as false the charges made against him personally. Accused of wanting to protect his friends, he was in fact, he retorted, demanding public trials; accused of menacing Versailles, he was in fact withdrawing his troops; accused of trying to influence decisions, he had in fact surrendered "the pleasure

---

[75] The contents of this letter is inferred from Lafayette to [Latour du Pin], [September 8], *Mémoires*, II, 324–27.

and the honor" of participating in the National Assembly's deliberations. If the provinces were ready to fight over the veto—
which it suited his purpose now to describe as one "which could
have left the king the absolute veto [*sic;* meaning, doubtless, an
effective veto] with such a majority that civil war would no longer
need to be feared"—that was not his fault but the fault of those
who refused to consider his compromise plan. He had done what
he "ought to have done as a good Frenchman and a friend of
peace." And "as general of the only army which dares to show
itself" (a claim which could not have been palatable to the royal
minister of war) he repeated (this time with underlining) that
his true objective was *"impartiality," "tranquility."*

He was being attacked, Lafayette reminded the minister, by the
popular side as well as by the court. He had been accused of
"aristocracy," royalism, and coddling of the guilty, and "any other
man but me would have lost popular support a hundred times."[76]
Yet he found it impossible either to prefer civil war to the "iterative
veto" or to believe (as he implied the court did) that men who,
like Mounier, championed the unpopular view took their lives in
their hands if they came to see him if only to invite him to dinner.
He doubted whether since his declaration of rights and his enlistment of the captors of the Bastille he had been acceptable to the
court anyway. And if he did not take overseriously the threats upon
Mounier on the popular side, neither did he approve of the court
party's efforts to defame Duport. The court was mistaken likewise
in thinking that he or Maubourg ("one of the most virtuous men
alive") might break with Duport, for even if the three of them
were not in full agreement, Duport was "a man of exalted principles whose severity [in the Paris Parlement] has ruined many
rich people" and who therefore "may be calumniated with exalta-
tion in these troublous times."

---

[76] *Ibid.,* p. 326. Jeannot (*Jeannot, cousin de Polichinel, aux bons Parisiens* [Paris, 1789],
pp. 6–8) thought Lafayette was in league with aristocrats, as did Robespierre (*Défenseur
de la constitution* [ed. Laurent], No. 6, June 22 or 23, 1792, pp. 176–77). For the fear at
Versailles, see La Marck to Marie Antoinette, December 1790, A. de Bacourt (ed.),
*Correspondance entre le comte de Mirabeau et le comte de la Marck pendant les années
1789, 1790 et 1791* (Paris, 1854), II, 514, and J. M. Augeard, *Mémoires secrets,* ed.
Ebariste Bavoux (Paris, 1866), pp. 194–95.

In a separate note[77] Lafayette took this somewhat belated occasion to congratulate Latour du Pin on having become "head of the king's councils and armies" and promised to cooperate as far as he could: "You will not be unhappy with me," but the king should in turn, he pleaded, take every opportunity to conciliate Paris, without, however, giving the impression of being forced to do so. And the government must deal frankly and honestly with the commune. If the king was contemplating going to Metz, the government must be frank about it: "I shall be as friendly to them as is possible without harming the interests of our precious liberty." And to make sure that what he said would be taken in all seriousness he added in a postscript a brief warning that was at the same time a boast: "I am too strong today to be joking."

In brief, Lafayette spurned the court's effort to separate him from his friends and, in reply, warned that if the court were wise, it would avoid enraging Paris by secret maneuvers. That was strong and bold language to hurl at the minister of a king who still liked to think of himself as only voluntarily surrendering some of his still absolute power, and it could lead to dire consequences if it proved to be false. But it proved true, and it was not heeded.

Despite the bold candor of his private correspondence with deputies and minister, on at least one occasion Lafayette's public reticence led to misunderstanding of his political views. The American painter John Trumbull, preparatory to painting his subsequently famous "Surrender of Cornwallis," had come to France to sketch the faces of Frenchmen like Lafayette who had participated in that event. He was now returning home, and La-

---

[77] *Mémoires*, II, 327. The Lafayette Archives, Cornell University Library, Box 2, contains two sets of copies of a collection of letters said to be to "Mme de S——." This letter is among them, but the last part, beginning "J'ai été charmé d'apprendre que vous étiez à la tête des conseils et des armées du roi," could hardly have been addressed, even in fun, to Mme de Simiane. In these manuscript copies (from which apparently the editors of the *Mémoires* took their text) that last part is separate from the rest (which, however, is made immediately to precede it in the printed version) and is given earlier, after the manuscript version of the letter (of June 25), which ends on page 312 of the printed version. The editors of the *Mémoires* have nevertheless run the two parts together as one letter, presumably because they inferred (and, we think, correctly) that both parts were written about the same time to the same addressee.

fayette invited him to breakfast so that he might say good-bye. The two men had a conversation, which Trumbull understood he was to report to President Washington, bringing news of Lafayette, who had for some time not found the leisure to write to his venerated American friend. Trumbull, however, seems not to have correctly interpreted Lafayette's comments on the French constitution. If his long-delayed recollection of his report to Washington was correct, he gave him the erroneous impression that Lafayette's views corresponded closely to Mounier's (without, however, mentioning Mounier). Certainly at a time when Lafayette was giving Paine and others a much different impression, he could hardly have wanted Washington to think that he regarded the British constitution as "the most perfect model of government which is hitherto known" and that, but for the machinations of the Duc d'Orléans, France could easily have imitated it.[78] Nor, with Jefferson's frequent reports to his government, did Lafayette have to count on Trumbull for communicating his views to the president of the United States. Trumbull's inaccuracy, however, provides another bit of evidence that Lafayette's personal opinions were not common property at the time.

Although Lafayette was in fact too busy to write to Washington with the frequency of former years, yet when he learned, as he along with everyone else had expected, that Washington had been elected the first president of the United States under its new constitution, he found the time to express his delight. His letter of congratulations revealed not only his continued devotion to his "adoptive father" but also his own perplexity over the role of a leader in a revolution. He was all the more pleased with Washington's election, he wrote, "because his paternal friend, with more disinterestedness and moderation than any other, could test in that

---

[78] Theodore Sizer (ed.), *The Autobiography of John Trumbull, Patriot-Artist, 1756–1843* (New Haven, 1953), pp. 153–55, 163. Cf. Jefferson to Jay, September 30, Boyd, XV, 501. Although Trumbull put Lafayette's alleged remarks in quotation marks, their context gives some reason to believe that they were inaccurately recollected at a distant time. Lafayette told Paine that he considered the House of Peers a "Corporation of Aristocracy": see Thomas Paine, *The Rights of Man* (Everyman's Library; New York, 1951), pp. 61–62.

post what degree of executive power was needed for the maintenance of liberty in a republic."[79]

With Lafayette exercising at that juncture a high "degree of executive power" in the reconstruction of the French monarchy, all seemed for the time being well in hand. During the week that followed Clermont-Tonnerre's perhaps deserved but certainly resented rebuke of the Paris government, calm prevailed. "Paris has been more quiet within the last week," a future British prime minister reported, "than at any time since I have been here."[80] And Jefferson believed that "tranquility is pretty well restored in this country."[81] But tranquility was to be short-lived.

Almost as these reassuring words were written, the National Assembly began to vote on the incendiary issues related to the structure of the legislature. By this time the Assembly had come in Lafayette's mind to consist of four groups—"our society," Mounier and his Anglophile supporters, the "aristocrats," and the "faction." The voting soon made clear that the overwhelming majority of the Assembly opposed Mounier's Anglophiles and favored a constitution which would greatly restrict royal prerogative and aristocratic privilege—some because they were genuinely convinced that such restrictions were in the best interest of their country, some doubtless because they were influenced by or fearful of public reaction, and some, as Lafayette always maintained,[82] because, whether aristocrats or *factieux*, for ulterior motives they wanted a bad constitution.

---

[79] *Mémoires*, III, 200. This letter seems never to have been received by Washington (see Washington to Lafayette, October 14, 1789, Fitzpatrick, XXX, 448) and so failed to be included in Gottschalk (ed.), *Letters*. Lafayette's letter of congratulations could hardly have been written before June 1789 (since Washington himself was formally notified of his election only on April 16) and probably not before August 1789. None of the letters of Lafayette to Washington between May 25, 1788, and January 12, 1790, seem to be extant; see Gottschalk (ed.), *Letters*, xx, 345 n.

[80] [R.B.] Jenkinson [later 2d Earl of Liverpool] to [the Duke of Leeds?], September 10, Oscar Browning (ed.), *Dispatches from Paris 1784–1790, Selected and Edited from the Foreign Office Correspondence*, II (London, 1909), 260.

[81] Jefferson to Lucy Paradise, September 10, Boyd, XV, 412.

[82] For example, *Mémoires*, II, 298–300. See also Jefferson to Jay, September 23, Boyd, XV, 458.

On September 9, to begin with, the National Assembly decided that the national legislature would be "permanent," holding regular annual meetings whether or not the king approved. It then took up the crucial question whether the legislative body should comprise one or two houses, and in the furor that followed, the president resigned and walked out. A former president who then took the chair adjourned the session.[83] Hope for a compromise that would reunite the Patriots seemed doomed.

The next day, upon learning what had happened, Lafayette penned an indignant plea to Maubourg to muster all the votes he could in an effort to retract what he called "that torrent of culpable follies which are meant to spoil everything." If the executive authority were further debased, if "the folly of a permanent national Convention" were not reconsidered, if the provinces were not broken up into small administrative units, "France is lost, the Revolution has failed, and those who have put *amour propre* above the commonweal are the most criminal of men."

A chance still remained, however, to repair the evil—by discouraging the tendency of "our society" to vote against Mounier and with "the faction which today drags it along." Hence, "tomorrow let the decent people connected with the faction declare their indignation [over yesterday's actions]; today you make concessions to Mounier." If necessary, Lafayette would himself go to Versailles. "I prefer thirty absolute vetos to yesterday's extravagance," he affirmed at one point, and at another: "I prefer an executive power a little too strong a hundred times more than the plan of federative provinces which will divide France into bits." Mounier and his supporters would be content, he assumed, with a veto which would bind "three or four legislatures" (i.e., as many as eight years), if a well formed Senate were also provided. But he was prepared to grant "whatever they want" in order to avoid civil war or the dissolution of the National Assembly. "The friends of liberty in the two parties are naturally embittered; they must be conciliated by a few concessions; our society must open its heart completely to Mounier, admitting mutual wrongs." To deal with "unworthy plots," good citizens must rally to "a common stan-

[83] *AP*, VIII, 602–5, and Jenkinson to [Leeds?], September 10, Browning, II, 259–60.

dard," and "our society ought to separate itself immediately from the faction which means to wreck everything."[84]

Lafayette's appeal did very little, however, to make the anti-royalist tide recede. That day (September 10), the National Assembly not only did not reconsider its vote of the day before but it even went on to vote (by 490 to 89, with 122 abstaining—out of an initial total membership of about 1,200) in favor of a single chamber. On the next day, after a session which lasted from early morning until late in the afternoon without recess, it voted 673 to 352 (with 11 abstentions) in favor of a suspensive veto binding two successive legislatures and reversible only in the third.[85] Since this was the "iterative" veto which Lafayette had formerly advocated, he could claim a partial victory.

The attempt to placate Mounier, however, had failed. Years later, commenting upon a book which Mounier published to explain his position, Lafayette apostrophized him ruefully: "You were a sincere patriot, but you wanted the absolute veto and the English constitution, and you regarded yourself as the chief of that party. The democrats not supporting you, you sought, in order to get a majority, to recruit aristocrats." Thereby, Lafayette's hindsight enabled him to discern, Mounier had initiated a process which was soon to end with his desertion of "those who remained at their posts to maintain liberty and public order as well as they could."[86] On the other hand, Mounier, despite occasional suspicion of Lafayette's motives, retained his admiration for the man who was thus to accuse him of desertion, saying of his accuser that "his zeal for liberty, his virtues, his talents and his position at the time" gave him a commanding influence.[87]

The split among the Patriots which Lafayette had tried to avert now was plain, but the civil outbreak which he feared did not come immediately. Peace prevailed for yet a few weeks—in part because, although hubbub continued in the Palais Royal, the Na-

---

[84] [September 10], Mortimer-Ternaux, I, 438–39. Cf. *Mémoires*, II, 299.

[85] *AP*, VIII, 607–8, 612.

[86] *Mémoires*, IV, 84, written *ca.* 1800 (see *ibid.*, p. 72, n. 1). Mounier's book was the Paris edition (1792) of *Recherches sur les causes qui ont empeché les Français d'être libres.*

[87] Mounier, *Exposé*, p. 50. For Mounier's suspicion of Lafayette, see below, pp. 346, 353–54.

tional Guard kept the situation well in hand[88] and in part because the symbolic overtones which the phrases *absolute veto* and *suspensive veto* had acquired made the passage of the *suspensive veto* seem a decisive victory for the people and their paternalistic king and a corresponding defeat of the counterrevolutionaries. A contemporary cartoon reflected how hopefully some interpreted what had happened; it showed Necker, with the crown of France in one hand and a liberty cap in the other, standing on a platform supported by Lafayette and Orléans[89]—thus symbolizing the devoutly wished union of (to use Lafayette's terms) the court, "our society," and "the factious." What had in fact happened, however, was that because each of these three groups had been only partly victorious, each felt defeated, while a fourth group had emerged which had carried off a fairly complete victory—the group of Duport and Lameth, now confirmed advocates of parliamentary strength and executive weakness.

BIBLIOGRAPHICAL NOTES

Lacroix (V, 371–75) presents a long note on the Basoche of the Châtelet and of the Palais de Justice.

Egret's *Révolution des Notables* is a study of Mounier's role during this period (as its subtitle, *Mounier et les monarchiens,* would indicate).

Chinard's article "Déclaration des droits de l'homme" in the *Cahiers d'histoire de la Révolution français*, No. 1 (1947), 66–90, deals meticulously with the relative influence of Lafayette's draft upon the final draft of the Declaration of 1789. Roland Mousnier and Ernest Labrousse, *Le XVIIIe siècle, révolution intellectuelle, technique et politique (1715–1815)* ("Histoire générale des civilisations" [Paris, 1953], pp. 377–81), gives a good account of the drafting of the Declaration of Rights but, we think, with too little attention to its resemblance to Lafayette's project.

Bacourt has been severely criticized for inaccurate, even mangled, editing; see Jules Flammermont, "L'Authenticité des *Mémoires de Talleyrand*" and "Encore un texte falsifié par M. de Bacourt," *Révolution française*, XXIII (1892), 385–409, and XXIV (1893), 345–62, respectively. Although the criticism of his editing of the *Correspondance entre Mirabeau et La Marck* has not been so severe as that of some of his other works, we have tried to use it with only the proper safeguards.

We have preferred to quote Jefferson's autobiography (so far) only from Boyd's note (XV, 355), feeling that his version of the relevant portion is probably the most carefully collated even if as yet he has not published the whole of it.

---

[88] *Révolutions de Paris*, No. 9, September 5–12, pp. 34–35.

[89] *Ibid.*, p. 33.

CHAPTER XI

Organizing the National Guard

IN LATE August and early September other matters, though less urgent than the controversy over royal veto and legislative structure, also demanded Lafayette's vigilance. They dealt primarily with local Paris affairs, but so thoroughly had Paris become the hub and mainstay of the Revolution that the public pronouncements of its more articulate districts were likely to determine national opinion and sway the votes of the National Assembly. As Paris went, so France was apt to go, and public opinion in Paris was still disposed to follow Lafayette. If anything, the recent schism in the ranks of the Patriots had strengthened his hand, for his public stand of neutrality had left him unscathed, enabling him to catch up with or to outstrip other popular figures —Louis XVI, Orléans, Mirabeau, Necker, Bailly, and Mounier— in the race for leadership.

Few of the contestants in that race enjoyed both royal approval and the confidence of the representative assemblies, but despite some inevitable rebuke and suspicion,[1] Lafayette remained an object of admiration and trust on all sides. Engravings commemorated his achievements; poems, songs, and sermons extolled him and his family; private individuals, Paris districts, National Guard units, and provincial cities addressed him as leader and patron.[2]

---

[1] [Camille Desmoulins], *Discours de la lanterne aux Parisiens* (Paris, [1789]), pp. 47–48; *Etrennes d'une lettre du Général Washington à M. le marquis de La Fayette,* quoted in Bernard Faÿ, *Revolutionary Spirit in France and America . . .* (New York, 1927), p. 641, n. 63; and *Polichinelle, orateur à l'Assemblée nationale* (Paris, 1789).

[2] E.g., *Journal de Paris,* September 8, p. 1105; *Patriote français,* September 1, p. 3; *Révolution de Paris,* No. 9, September 5–13, p. 28, and No. 11, September 19–25, p. 33; *Ami du peuple,* September 25, p. 131; *Gazette de Leide,* September 15; *Journal des Etats généraux,* September 10, p. 382; *Chronique de Paris,* September 21, p. 115, and September 23, p. 122; *Lettres à Monsieur le comte de B***,* I, 364, 434; *La Voix du peuple,* No. 1, [ca. September 1], p. 72; J.-H. Bancal des Issarts, *Arrêtés proposés au Comité de la Munici-*

Newspapers praised him with such profusion as to rouse suspicion that they were in his pay,[3] and at least one of the most influential journalists of the day—Brissot de Warville of the *Patriote français* —was an old and still devoted friend. The reputation and rewards of other men sometimes unintentionally reflected his glory, paling in comparison with it. When for example, Jean-Antoine Houdon, the greatest sculptor of the day, offered to make a bust of Necker, one of the most popular statesmen of the day, as the defunct Assembly of Electors had voted, Houdon's district recommended him to the Assembly of Representatives as the artist who had made the busts of Washington and Lafayette, and the Representatives accepted the offer because they recognized Houdon's talent "to immortalize great men." In a related letter to the Representatives Houdon himself described Lafayette as "the apostle and defender of liberty in the two worlds."[4]

Lafayette's double role as national deputy and city official added to his opportunities to win acclaim. As either legislator or soldier he was somewhere in the public eye nearly all the time. The opportunity to gain popularity, however, ran neck and neck with the risk of failure. If he accepted the risks along with the opportunities, he did so not without calculation or, in any event, not

---

palité du District des Carmes . . . 3 septembre 1789 (Paris, 1789), p. 1; *Discours de M. [Pierre] Manuel à l'Assemblée générale des districts reunis du Val-de-Grace et de Saint-Jacques, tenue le 30 août 1789* (Paris, 1789), p. 5; *Mercure de France*, September 19, p. 72; and *Courrier de Versailles à Paris*, September 12, pp. 200–201, September 13, pp. 216–17, and September 24, p. 397.

[3] See, for example, L. G. W. Legg, *Select Documents Illustrative of the History of the French Revolution* (Oxford, 1905), I, ix, which states that the *Journal de Paris* was "believed to be under the influence of La Fayette," but although Lafayette subscribed to it, we know of no evidence that its policy was the result of anything other than political conviction. The Marquis de Bouillé, *Mémoires*, ed. Berville and Barrière (Paris, 1821), p. 185, says that Lafayette used funds from the king's civil list to buy writers to his side, but Lafayette denied that (*Mémoires*, IV, 105–6). Lafayette did have secret funds from the Comité des Recherches of the Nationale Assembly (as we expect to show in a subsequent volume) but at a later date than this, and apparently not for the purpose of suborning writers. For numerous examples of apparently spontaneous tribute to Lafayette see Blancheteau, [Bérenger], Girodie, Monglond, and Braibant, as well as André Martin and Gerard Walter, *Catalogue de l'histoire de la Révolution française*, Vol. II (Paris, 1938), and Cornwall Rogers, *The Spirit of Revolution in 1789* (Princeton, 1949). See also below, Appendix II.

[4] Lacroix, I, 497 (September 7), 504–5 (September 8), and *Journal de Paris*, September 18, p. 1184.

without awareness of them, but he accepted both as possible consequences of the conscientious (and sometimes self-righteous) performance of his duty.

As commandant general of the Paris National Guard Lafayette had to act on both urban and militia issues, and the very newness of the elective government raised a multitude of issues which either were unprecedented or had precedents which were considered bad. Prominent among them was finding revenue for the city's numerous needs, usually familiar but sometimes springing full-blown from the Revolution itself. The cost of city government had of late mounted rapidly, while at the same time unsettled political conditions and the resultant disorganization of the old fiscal system interfered with the collection of taxes. Maintenance of the several drilled units which had previously provided the city police had hitherto been a charge upon the royal treasury; now police responsibility fell upon the Paris commune. Economy was imperative, and in consequence the National Guard long remained inadequately armed. The 6,000 rifles and bayonets asked from the royal arsenals in August by the Assembly of Representatives arrived only on September 16, when with becoming fanfare and display of gratitude the National Guard conveyed the weapons to Paris.[5] Royal munificence thus permitted a great saving of an otherwise unavoidable expense. Lafayette suggested (August 27) to the Representatives that they might save an additional sum by petitioning the National Assembly to defray the cost of Besenval's guard at Brie-Comte-Robert, since he was being detained upon its demand. Hard-pressed, the Representatives did so, and the National Assembly acceded (October 14).[6]

Whatever was saved by this sort of begging, the straitened condition of the city treasury reached a danger point when the commune fell behind on wages to its troops. Lafayette and the Military Committee advised the Representatives (August 30) to ask the king to assume responsibility for the payment of the National Guard, which, it was calculated, would be about equal to the sum

[5] Lacroix, I, 254–56 (August 17), 524–25 (September 9), 594 (September 16). For the request of these weapons see above, p. 195.

[6] Lacroix, I, 363–64 (August 27), 464 and 468 (September 3).

formerly required for the city's several police units of the Old Regime. It averaged about 450,000 livres (or $90,000) a month (at a time when a day's labor earned somewhere between 20 and 60 cents). The Representatives went begging again, and again— this time with a significant sum—the royal government bailed out the commune as suggested.[7]

A telling example of the financial distress which arose from the change of the old order to the new was provided when the regimental property of the former French Guard (barrack furniture, hospital supplies, military equipment, etc.) was converted into the property of the Paris National Guard. The *ci-devant* French Guards asked over a million livres for their regiment's property. Lafayette, together with the Military Committee and some officers of the National Guard, spent most of an afternoon examining the inventory of this property, and finally they decided to leave the matter to him alone.[8] The ultimate decision, as Bailly confessed, was reached with a little precipitation, for each of the French Guards, expecting to receive several hundred livres from the exchange, could not be "disobliged"; the French Guard was still "our only really active force."[9] Nor could the city so easily find adequate supplies elsewhere. On September 1, Lafayette recommended the purchase, an *ad hoc* committee of the Representatives approved, and the Assembly authorized the payment of 900,000 livres for the property.[10] The men, not at all displeased, accepted this offer and bestowed the special medal with which the French Guards had been honored upon Bailly, the presidents of the Representatives, and the *ad hoc* committee and (apparently in this connection) sought permission to bestow it also upon the king, the dauphin, and Lafayette.[11]

[7] *Procès-verbal du Comité militaire,* Part I, p. 101 (August 29); Lacroix, I, 395 (August 30), 408–9; and Bailly, II, 325–26. For the high estimate of a day's wages at 3 livres, approximately 60 cents, see Albert Mathiez, "Études critiques sur les journées des 5 et 6 octobre 1789," *Revue historique,* XLVIII (1899), 42–43 (hereafter cited as *RH*).

[8] *Procès-verbal du Comité militaire,* Part I, pp. 93–94 (August 27), and Lacroix, I, 337 (August 25), 345 and 354–55 (August 26), 365–66, 367–70 and 377–78 (August 27).

[9] Bailly, II, 307–8.

[10] Lacroix, I, 435 (September 1).

[11] *Ibid.,* pp. 473 (September 4), 477; Tuetey, II, 459–60, No. 4352; and Bailly, II, 351–52.

The city's depleted treasury was perhaps the principal but certainly not the only reason why the Paris National Guard was not yet totally adequate for its purposes. Another reason was the lapse of military zeal when no crisis needed to be confronted. Even with additional recruits from the Swiss and other royal regiments, former French Guards made up only somewhat more than half the number required for the center companies—about 3,600, whereas the Regulations envisaged 6,000. In a number of districts the unpaid companies, despite strenuous recruiting efforts, were likewise below their quota of 100 men each. In the hope of filling them, the Military Committee recommended applying pressure by establishing district registers of all men liable to gratuitous militia service, stipulating that no citizen would be eligible for any other function, duty, honor, or office in the city until he had registered and had either served or received exemption for good cause. With Lafayette's endorsement this recommendation went to the Representatives, together with another proposing that a fine be imposed on those who failed to serve, contributions for the maintenance of the National Guard being levied upon the exempt and upon widows and spinsters with property. On August 26 the Assembly of Representatives enacted both these recommendations.[12]

A welcome reinforcement of the National Guard came from the *banlieue* ("outskirts") of Paris. Thirty-four nearby communities, having formed three divisions of militia, asked permission for them to wear the uniform of the Paris National Guard, which the Paris commune granted upon the understanding that their buttons be inscribed "Banlieue de Paris."[13] The problem of assimilating the military organizations of these and other communities near the capital without incurring their ill-will or making them dependent upon Paris was aired in the Military Committee, and a few days later the Assembly of Representatives issued a general invitation to all the suburban communities to place their guard units under Lafayette's command, assuring them "of sentiments of fraternity and of all the help they have the right to expect."[14] The *banlieue*

---

[12] *Procès-verbal du Comité militaire*, Part I, pp. 83 (August 22), 86–90 (August 26), and Lacroix, I, 345–48 (August 26).

[13] Lacroix, I, 381 and 384 (August 28).

[14] *Ibid.*, pp. 564–65 and 569–70 (September 13). See also Bailly, II, 376, and *Procès-verbal du Comité militaire*, Part I, p. 142 (September 12).

quickly accepted this arrangement. One of the first to do so was the commune of Belleville, and in the Place de Grève on September 17 Lafayette administered an oath of loyalty to its battalion. On this occasion the oath was modified to read: "We swear to be loyal to the nation, the king, the law, our commune, and the commune of Paris, in accordance with our voluntary affiliation with it."[15]

These affiliations, welcome though they were, increased the multiplying details which competed for the attention of Lafayette and his staff. Routine matters alone consumed extraordinary amounts of time. Certificates of patriotic service had to be drawn up and signed; commissions had to be endorsed and delivered; decorations had to be distributed.[16] The Military Committee advised Lafayette to request the Assembly of Representatives to authorize three new adjutants.[17]

The Duc d'Orléans' friends were not slow to recognize that command of the National Guard of France provided an enormous strategic advantage in the race for leadership. Yet when Lafayette had imparted to Maubourg that any misguided attempt to make Orléans head of the nation's militia would redound to his (Lafayette's) advantage,[18] he had not spoken idly. For he had reason to believe that Paris and the provinces would prefer him to Orléans as generalissimo. The Versailles militia proved to be not the only National Guard unit which sought to make him its commandant.[19] In the midst of the turbulent debates on the royal veto power and

---

[15] Lacroix, I, 605–6 (September 17).

[16] For examples of the numerous documents signed about this time by Lafayette see Anon., "Fournier l'américain, son rôle en juillet 1789," *Revue rétrospective*, XI (1889), 25–26; Blancheteau catalogue, items 149 and 150; Sauffroy catalogue, No. 65 (December 1932), items 16017, and No. 70 (July 1933), item 18996; Parke-Bernet catalogue No. 1064 (1949), item 305; Lacroix, I, 443–44, n. iv; BVP, Collection Charavay, Vol. I, fol. 564 (brevet dated September 1), and Collection Liésville (award of gold medal dated September 4); Yale University Library, Jackson Collection ("certificat national" dated August 11); Musée Carnavalet (Paris), Salle No. 39; Collection of Harrold F. Gillingham (Philadelphia) (brevet dated September 28); American Art Association Galleries Catalogue, sale of November 7–8, 1939, Part II, item 177; White Library, Cornell University Library (commission dated August 13); and Indiana University, Ball Collection (order dated August 30).

[17] *Procès-verbal du Comité militaire*, Part I, pp. 94–95 (August 28).

[18] [September 1], Mortimer-Ternaux, I, 435, and see above, pp. 240–41.

[19] See above, p. 216.

the legislative machinery the Military Committee of Paris received a letter from the military committee of Angers, capital of the province of Anjou, which suggested that a system of communications be established among the country's military committees and that the commandant general of the Paris National Guard be recognized as commander-in-chief of all the National Guard units of the realm. What was more, Angers had already circulated a similar letter to the other cities of France, and soon the National Guard of Rennes and other cities were making a similar request.[20] Orléans was, to be sure, also an obvious candidate for commander-in-chief, and in fact, the National Guard of the city of Orléans did propose him as generalissimo,[21] but letters came every day from the provinces asking for Lafayette in that capacity, and Brissot's *Patriote français* urged him to accept.[22]

The Military Committee of Paris discussed the Angers proposal on August 29. Appreciative of "the just homage . . . rendered by Angers to the virtues and zeal of M. le Commandant-général,"[23] it designated one of its number to draw up a draft of an appropriate reply. On September 5—that is, after Lafayette had already privately expressed his opposition to putting in anyone's hands a force stronger than the king's[24]—the Paris Military Committee considered this draft. Lafayette was present as presiding officer. The draft pledged the Military Committee to give all the help it could to promote the "continuous association" of the whole country toward certain ends—"to maintain its liberty and defend its rights," to keep order, and to collect properly voted taxes. It also praised the "hero, protector of liberty everywhere, who with his well-known valor combines a wisdom of principle and a breadth of enlightenment which are equally rare," and it held up "the organization, order and discipline which this generous commander has estab-

[20] *Procès-verbal du Comité militaire*, Part I, pp. 97–101 (August 29). See also René Toujas, "La Genèse de l'idée de fédération nationale," *AHRF*, XXVII (1955), 215–16, and Albert Macé, "Ouverture des États-généraux de 1789," *Revue de la Révolution*, XV (1889), 2d part, pp. 113–15, 118.

[21] *Patriote français*, September 1, p. 3.

[22] *Ibid*. See also *Procès-verbal du Comité militaire*, Part I, p. 121 (September 5).

[23] *Procès-verbal du Comité militaire*, Part I, pp. 101–2 (August 29).

[24] See above, n. 18.

lished" in the Paris corps as a "fitting model" for the provinces to follow.

On the matter, however, of a reciprocal correspondence among all the units of the National Guard, the draft was so worded as to avoid commitment until the committee heard from other cities. A logical conclusion from its enthusiastic endorsement of Lafayette would have been that "continuous association" after the "fitting model" of Paris might best be achieved by giving supreme command to the wise and valorous "hero" who was the "protector of liberty everywhere." On that point, though, not only did the draft fail to be explicit but instead (and here perhaps the velvet glove of Lafayette is to be detected) it turned away from the inference that the national militia ought to be under the control of a single commander toward a plea that the military always submit to the civil authorities. Accordingly, it held up Paris as a fitting model in that respect as well, inasmuch as that city looked upon the tranquility of the National Assembly's meetings as a logical corollary of the principles of natural right and had confidence in the royal sovereign as the foremost friend of his people and as the restorer of liberty, while the Paris National Guard correctly regarded itself as subordinate to the civil arm of the city. In short, the committee's draft turned a proposal in favor of a supreme military command for Lafayette into a plea for municipal cooperation with National Assembly and king.

Apparently inured by this time to and unabashed by florid encomiums, Lafayette approved the proposed letter to Angers. He then told the committee that in fact, he had received many letters of the same tenor from other cities of the realm and asked for advice in regard to the answer he should give to them as well. He pointed out "with the most sensitive delicacy" that equally good arguments could be made in favor of accepting or of refusing "the honorable proposals which had been made by the national troops of the realm."[25] The committee took the matter up at that evening's session, Lafayette being elsewhere. After a long discussion it decided that it would adopt a resolution only in cooperation with him and in his presence, and so it postponed a decision until he could meet

[25] *Procès-verbal du Comité militaire*, Part I, pp. 121–22 (September 5).

with them again. The draft of the letter to Angers was then read once more, adopted, signed by all the members present, and ordered dispatched.[26]

Certainly this reply to Angers undercut Orléans' chances, if indeed his purpose was, as Lafayette suspected,[27] to acquire a predominant military position. Although it did not answer the widespread demand for a supreme commander, both the demand and Lafayette's refusal to comply with it were to remain unchanged. He apparently had all the force he needed in the Paris National Guard and did not want any more for himself or for any other but the National Assembly and the king.

But regardless of how Lafayette meant to use it, what kind of a force was the Paris National Guard to be? Was it to be a disciplined military body or a loose agglomeration of citizens? No decision had yet been reached, for example, on how long a citizen must serve in the National Guard, whether if good reasons obliged him to find a substitute, he or his district was to find that substitute, whether on changing his residence he must change his battalion, whether a Guardsman might, after completing his service, continue to wear his uniform, whether after serving his term an elected officer returned to the ranks or remained an officer. Preferring not to assume sole responsibility for the answers to questions like these, Lafayette submitted a set of them to the Military Committee. The committee postponed a decision on the length of service, feeling that existing regulations provided a sufficient answer for the present. It decided, however, that a man must find his own substitute among those in his area who had registered but had not yet been called up, that a change of residence required a change of battalion, that completion of service ended the right to wear the uniform unless the wearer re-enlisted, and that an officer whose elective term had expired still owed service, "more honorable and perhaps less burdensome," as a simple soldier.[28]

Despite the committee's persistent efforts to provide an efficient police force, Lafayette had to admit that several shortcomings were all too patent. He had to depend heavily upon a few reliable

---

[26] *Ibid.*, pp. 119–22.   [27] See above, n. 18.

[28] *Procès-verbal du Comité militaire*, Part I, pp. 111–13 (August 31).

companies, thus penalizing the better volunteer units with an increased number of days of service. The roster of several companies fluctuated from day to day, desertions and failure to report for duty were common, and discipline was frequently uncertain.[29]

Moreover, various specialized services were inadequately performed. For one thing, suitably mounted troops were hard to get. Jean Augustin de Rulhière, commander of the Garde de Paris, had been authorized by the Representatives to enroll as a mounted unit any of his own men and other royal cavalrymen who had joined the National Guard during the permissible period, and he was soon able to report that he had eighty-four recruits but insufficient horses. Thereupon the Assembly voted funds to enable him to purchase horses for those who had none,[30] even though that very day it was informed that the treasury of the commune was "already exhausted by many extraordinary expenses."[31]

A special subcommittee of the Military Committee was then put to work upon a set of regulations for the cavalry. Applications for commissions in the proposed mounted force came in rapidly, and Lafayette, having gathered in a dossier the relevant information on each applicant, submitted it to the committee, adding his own recommendation.[32] On September 16 the Military Committee proposed a plan for the organization of the cavalry, worked out step by step with his collaboration, and he accepted it immediately.[33] It provided for one paid troop and one unpaid of 100 horsemen each for each of the six divisions—at an estimated cost of 900,000 livres per year for the paid companies. Lafayette pressed the Assembly of Representatives to put the plan into operation at once, but the Assembly was again on the verge of reorganization,[34]

[29] *Ibid.*, pp. 114–16 (September 2), 117–18 (September 3). See also Tuetey, II, 418, No. 3966.

[30] Lacroix, I, 238–39 and 248–49 (August 16), 433 (September 1), 460 (September 3). See also above, p. 204, n. 51.

[31] Lacroix, I, 464 (September 3).

[32] *Procès-verbal du Comité militaire*, Part I, pp. 48–50 (August 11), 70 (August 19), 90–91 (August 26), 97 (August 28), 125–26 (September 6), 142 (September 12), 155 (September 16).

[33] *Ibid.*, pp. 155 and 156 (September 16) and *Patriote français*, September 22, p. 3.

[34] See below, pp. 282–83, and Lacroix, I, 63 (July 31), 621 (September 18).

and it left the matter to its successor. Under continued pressure from Lafayette and the Military Committee, the new assembly submitted the cavalry regulations to the districts for approval but authorized the enlistment meanwhile of the contemplated 1,200 horsemen.[35]

Ironically, but as might have been expected, the more money the city government tried to raise, the more it was obliged to spend. The *octrois* on goods entering the city was now the municipality's chief source of revenue. On September 17 the outgoing Assembly of Representatives ordered, subject to the approval of the districts, the immediate enlistment of a new paid company of *chasseurs des barrières* for each National Guard division, assigning to them the special duty of enforcing the collection of the *octrois*.[36] Two days later Lafayette and the Military Committee completed a plan for an additional special guard to police the ports, quays, and islands of the Seine. Independently of the collection of taxes, he wanted a small but effective artillery unit too, and the committee, favorably inclined as usual toward his opinion, appointed a subcommittee to report on that matter.[37] They also considered the desirability of a military band.[38]

By the middle of September Lafayette had around 4,800 men in his paid companies, mostly former French and Swiss Guards. The 6,000 flintlock muskets and bayonets provided by the king permitted each of the paid soldiers to be well armed, with a number of rifles left over for some of the unpaid companies.[39] By that

---

[35] Lacroix, II, 7 (September 19), 13 (September 20), and *Procès-verbal du Comité militaire*, Part I, pp. 162–63 (September 19), 172 (September 22).

[36] Thiébault states (I, 233–34) that Lafayette acted surreptitiously in creating the *chasseurs* as well as the grenadiers, but see *Project de formation de six compagnies de chasseurs-nationaux-parisiens . . . affectées specialement à la garde des barrières* (Paris, 1789), presumably sent to all the districts.

[37] *Procès-verbal du Comité militaire*, Part I, pp. 137–38 (September 11), 142 and 143 (September 12).

[38] Lacroix, I, 586 (September 15), 613–18 (September 17) and *Procès-verbal du Comité militaire*, Part I, pp. 157 and 158–59 (September 17), 163–64 and 167 (September 19).

[39] Lacroix, I, 594 (September 16), 607 and 611 (September 17); *Courier national*, September 18, p. 6; and *Procès-verbal du Comité militaire*, Part I, pp. 159–60 (September 18).

time the Paris National Guard seemed to have been molded, step by step, into a systematic police force. The rate of progress nonetheless appeared slow to Lafayette, and he was unhappy about the inefficiency of committees (some of which, however, were his own creation). Yet when he complained to Latour-Maubourg about "the incapacity of all these committees,"[40] his impatience, perhaps a sign of weariness, was not altogether justified; little more than six weeks had gone by since the new city government had been created—almost out of whole cloth.

Still it was all too clear that the *esprit de corps* of the National Guard was not beyond reproach, particularly in the volunteer units. The commandant general complained to the Military Committee: "The ardor of citizens who appear in numbers when they are called upon to act at a time of trouble seems to abate in the performance of their daily routine, the precision of which can alone assure public order and can always successfully forestall any disorders that may be instigated."[41]

In part, the commander-in-chief counted upon the ceremonies attendant upon the oath-takings to promote *esprit de corps*. Not only were these occasions performed with as much dignity and solemnity as he could give them but they also furnished him an opportunity to mingle with his command. Seeking to show "that he was as good a soldier as an excellent general," he deliberately cultivated such personal contacts, resolving disputes among his men, eating at their mess, or demonstrating how a single man, unaided, could load and discharge a cannon.[42] His visits were greeted with artillery salutes or other signs of loyalty and welcome, and on at least one occasion a great dinner was served in his honor.[43] On September 2, after personally administering the oath of loyalty to the center companies of the First and Second Divisions in their own quarters, he reported to the Assembly of Representatives that he was confident his men would serve "with all the

---

[40] Mortimer-Ternaux, I, 434, and see above, p. 237.

[41] *Procès-verbal du Comité militaire*, Part I, p. 127 (September 7).

[42] *Journal général de la cour*, September 24, p. 48.

[43] *Révolutions de Paris*, No. 8, August 29–September 6, p. 31, and *Courrier de Versailles à Paris*, September 5, p. 67.

patriotism which should characterize a truly national corps."[44] These demonstrations of mutual loyalty between commander and men added to the consternation of aristocratic observers, who saw only demagoguery in such a show of democracy.[45]

As frequently happens, however, to those who seek a golden mean, Lafayette was criticized for exactly the opposite reason by those who opposed the critics of an aristocratic stripe. Some egalitarians expressed concern that the citizens of Paris, "all soldiers of the *patrie*," were being undemocratically divided into two classes, one being put into uniform and required to comport themselves like pretorian guards in order to police the other. Yet Lafayette and others knew only too well that all sorts of unpretorian opinions and practices prevailed among his men. Some were wearing uniforms who were not entitled to do so; some who were so entitled did not report for duty when they were supposed to; some who reported for duty spent more time guarding their precious district cannon than patrolling their districts; and some, as soon as they went off duty, joined the agitating or the agitated at the Palais Royal and the Halles.[46] Any one of these infractions might have been a court-martial offense under the Old Regime, but no new military code had yet been drawn up, and so no one knew how a citizens' corps, whether paid or unpaid, should be disciplined in a new regime based upon the natural rights of man.

The Military Committee had been considering the question of discipline for some time, and Lafayette saw fit to call the division and battalion commanders together in order to get their opinions as well. They met with him and the Military Committee on the evening of September 3. He opened the meeting by lamenting the lack of military precision that he had personally witnessed or learned about, and the comments which followed showed that his officers were no less concerned than he. One of the major troubles

---

[44] Lacroix, I, 450 (September 2).

[45] See Clermont-Gallerande, II, 177.

[46] The quoted words are from [Desmoulins], *Discours de la lanterne aux Parisiens*, pp. 47–48, but see also *Courier national*, September 14, p. 7; *Procès-verbal du Comité militaire*, Part I, pp. 117–18 (September 3), 126, 127 and 128 (September 7), 133–34 (September 10), 143–46 (September 12); and *Révolutions de Paris*, No. 9, September 6–13, p. 14.

seemed to lie with the districts' jealous defense of their control over their respective battalions. Without support from the district authorities no regulations could be expected to be accepted or, if accepted, enforced; and the district assemblies were not so amenable to Lafayette's persuasion as other branches of the city government. He expressed the hope, however, that since the districts elected the Military Committee's members and the battalion commanders, he might reach the assemblies through them. He also stressed the unequal distribution of service obligations among the battalions. Insofar as this inequality was due to an unevenness of membership because some districts had not yet met their quotas, neighboring districts could make up for their inadequacy, but that was obviously no way to run an army. His staff, not having dependable statistics of enrollment, was powerless to distribute such burdens equitably. The commandant general requested (he preferred not to order) that each battalion commander give him a report of the actual size of his battalion, and the Military Committee seconded this request.[47]

A particularly glaring instance of insubordination took place on September 3. That day Lafayette went to the District of the Sorbonne to install the battalion's newly chosen officers. Some former French Guards at first protested that at least two of those officers, presumably mere bourgeois, were not worthy to fill their posts, and they threatened to quit the ranks. Only Lafayette's stern insistence upon being obeyed and his demand that those soldiers retire who were not resolved to serve cheerfully restored discipline.[48]

As this episode painfully demonstrated, discipline was still largely a matter of individual choice, but instances of voluntary good will were not lacking. A former French Guard gave an example of respect for the military amenities which won a burst of approval despite its seriocomic nature. Having appropriated an esteemed military decoration, the Cross of St. Louis, from the

---

[47] *Procès-verbal du Comité militaire*, Part I, pp. 85–90 (August 28), 111–13 (August 31), 114 (September 1), 117–18 (September 3).

[48] *London Chronicle*, September 8–10, p. 247, and A. de Lescure (ed.), *Correspondance secrète inédite sur Louis XVI, Marie Antoinette, la cour, et la ville de 1777 à 1792* (Paris, 1886), II, 386.

body of a soldier killed on Bastille Day, he had now been per-suaded that since the king alone could rightly bestow such an honor, he ought to return it. Accompanied by a company of his district militia, he went to the city hall and with much pomp and circumstance requested Lafayette to restore the decoration to the king. The ceremony presented a good opportunity to publicize the benefits of military discipline.[49]

Another came when a militiaman wrote to Lafayette that he had been fined—unjustly, he protested—because he had refused to do guard duty more frequently than the Regulations required. In reply, Lafayette pointed out that, the National Guard being still incomplete, the provision for only periodic guard duty could not yet be safely applied. Nevertheless, he asserted, the fine had not been exacted with his approval: "I never gave such an order against citizens, and my character is well enough known to be above such suspicion." The wronged man was advised to appeal to his district assembly. When the Guardsman published his letter and the commandant general's response by way of justification,[50] Lafayette could hardly have been displeased by this airing of the inadequacy of the present militia for the demands upon it.

Another series of embarrassing episodes arose from the attrac-tiveness of the Guardsman's uniform to the pretentious, the mis-guided, and the ill-intentioned. An especially notorious instance involved a Comte de Saint-Geniès, who, wearing the uniform of a captain of the National Guard, stopped a patrol late one night and upbraided it for insulting one of his friends. When his au-thority was challenged, he claimed to be an aide-de-camp of the commandant general. Suspicious, the patrol's officers took him to the Hôtel de Ville to be recognized, but no one there knew him. Although it was past midnight (September 2–3) they took him to the Rue de Bourbon for Lafayette to look at, and Lafayette ordered him placed under arrest for impersonating an officer.

[49] *Courier national,* September 4, p. 8; Deux Amis de la Liberté, I, 144; Chassin, III, 564, n. 1; *Révolutions de Paris,* No. 8, August 29–September 4, p. 32; and *Discours adressé à M. le marquis de La Fayette par Mlle N . . . lors de la remise à lui faite par Pierre Henry Dubois . . . de la croix de Saint-Louis . . .* (Paris, 1789).

[50] *Lettre de M. du Croisi à Monsieur le marquis de La Fayette et réponse de ce général* (Paris, 1789), and *Patriote français,* September 23, p. 2.

The next morning the Assembly of Representatives ordered him to be publicly stripped of his uniform and detained for trial by the Châtelet.[51]

Despite the districts' jealousy over their prerogatives and despite Lafayette's painstaking attempts to make the military separate from and subordinate to the civil arm, on occasion the separation was tenuous. The districts, their hands full of National Guard problems they could not decide alone, called upon the commandant general for advice. That Guardsmen who failed to report for duty felt free to hire substitutes was no new problem, but in some of the more fortunate districts the shoe was now on the other foot; having enrolled more than 400 voluntary Guardsmen they wanted to know whether they might ask the surplus men to provide money instead of service. Some districts were concerned that worthy and faithful men had not been elected officers; why not honor them by making them substitute officers, to serve only in the absence of the regular ones? And why not allow them, if they had formerly been officers, to retain the insignia and the titles of their former status? The unpaid companies resented the epaulets worn by the paid companies; why not allow them also to wear epaulets? And where were battalion flags to be kept and who was to carry them? When three districts of the city requested permission to sell the property which they had confiscated from the Royal Nassau Regiment on July 14, the civil authority (the Representatives) sent for the military authority (Lafayette) and, following the precedent he had earlier established, ordered the private property of officers returned while permitting the sale of regimental property as spoils of war.[52] When an irate deputy to the National Assembly (a civil body) protested because his Paris district (also a civil body) insisted that he must report for National Guard duty, the Military Committee, itself representative of the districts, called upon the commandant general to advise the district to excuse the deputy and to express

[51] *Courrier de Versailles à Paris,* September 5, pp. 65–67; *Révolutions de Paris,* No. 8, August 29–September 6, pp. 28–29; Lacroix, I, 461 and 468 (September 3); and Tuetey, I, 100, No. 946.

[52] Lacroix, I, 532–34 (September 10). For the precedent see above, p. 183. For the origin of the queries raised by the districts, see below, n. 54.

the committee's regret.[53] A military celebrity could not easily cultivate a position of subordination to the civil authorities if they insisted upon deferring to him in all such matters, large or small.

The debate on these issues went on in the Military Committee, Lafayette frequently taking part, for several days. In the end, it disapproved of permitting unpaid troops to wear epaulets or of issuing brevets to former officers or of creating substitute officers. Lafayette indicated that he was opposed to paid substitutions because they might lead to a mercenary army, and to money payments in place of service because the law made no provision for them, and the Military Committee agreed. The committee, likewise, with Lafayette's approval, decided that battalion colors would be stored in its district barracks and carried by a flag officer of its center company. It also decided that penalties be inflicted for misuse of the uniform and for other minor misdemeanors. When completed, these decisions were sent to the Assembly of Representatives for approval as Title VII of the Regulations.[54]

The committee had meanwhile also completed recommendations for a penal code dealing with military infractions,[55] and Lafayette had submitted it to the Assembly of Representatives. Some Representatives hesitated to adopt it on the grounds that in the past such regulations had emanated from the king and therefore should now come from the National Assembly. Lafayette responded that discipline had grown worse every day since July, destroying morale within the corps and diminishing the citizens' respect for the only armed force capable of preventing anarchy and that, the National Assembly's first obligation being to make a constitution, the National Guard could not wait for disciplinary regulations until that work was over. He won his case, and the Representatives settled down to an article-by-article debate of the

---

[53] *Procès-verbal du Comité militaire*, Part I, pp. 157–58.

[54] *Ibid.*, pp. 114–16 (September 2), 127–28 (September 7), 129–30 (September 8), 138–42 (September 11), 143–46 (September 12), and *Lettre à M. le marquis de La Fayette sur le choix qui a été fait des officiers de la troupe non soldée et sur les épaulettes et dragonnes en or par F[évelat] du District des Petits Pères. Paris, ce 1 septembre 1789.*

[55] *Procès-verbal du Comité militaire*, Part I, p. 126 (September 7). (This code was to become "Titre VIII" of the *Règlement*).

proposed code. They made some changes in the committee's proposals, the most important being in Article 20, providing for courts-martial, which was approved with the stipulation that all judgments of courts-martial had to be confirmed not by the commandant general alone but also by the mayor and the municipality. Then, stating explicitly that the legislative power did not reside in the commune but in the National Assembly, the Representatives accepted the committee's proposal only tentatively. Nevertheless, the code, thus proclaimed to be valid only until the national legislature should act in the matter, remained in force for almost two years (until July 24, 1791), because, as Lafayette had said, the National Assembly had more urgent work to do. Although various other experts had drawn up the original drafts of this provisional code, Lafayette more than any other had assumed responsibility for it. It was the first new code of law to issue from the Revolution.[56]

In the expectation of being thus fortified, Lafayette and the Military Committee had already taken steps to enforce military discipline in the battalions. They authorized a committee named without district approval by one battalion to enforce discipline in that battalion's ranks, provided that it limited such enforcement to the Regulations, and the Military Committee promised eventually to draw up a general set of rules for the internal police of all battalions.[57] When it became known that Lafayette expected Guardsmen who would not cheerfully obey their elected officers to withdraw, the non-coms and fusiliers of the Compagnie de Lamour, former French Guards, pledged explicit obedience to their own officers and to the chief who had worked for liberty in two worlds and asked him to publish their pledge as an example to others. Lafayette went personally to thank the company and again received assurance of unquestioning obedience.[58]

Some others of the old French Guards, however, far from set-

[56] Lacroix, I, 538 (September 10), 543 (September 11), 547–48, and *Courier national,* September 14, p. 6. The National Assembly adopted the code on criminal procedure only on October 9: see above, p. 248 and below, pp. 229–300, 319–21.

[57] *Procès-verbal du Comité militaire,* Part I, p. 179 (September 25).

[58] *Chronique de Paris,* September 21, p. 115; *Révolutions de Paris,* No. 11, September 19–27, p. 33; and *M. le marquis de la Fayette étant venu féliciter la Compagnie Delamour* . . . (Paris, [1789?]), cited by Jackson, p. 95.

ting the best example, were still uncertain where their loyalties lay, and the number of desertions from the center companies was shocking. Deserters not only reduced the ranks of the National Guard but also, since they generally took their uniforms and rifles with them, robbed it of its equipment. Moreover, each desertion meant a cash loss since, in accordance with Regulations, each paid guardsman was to receive 50 livres for the purchase of small articles, and a deserter was unlikely to return any of the 26 livres already advanced against that sum. The commune, always chary of cash outlay, hesitated to pay the remaining 24 livres to each of the almost 5,000 paid Guardsmen already enrolled, since some of them might desert before the year was up. Lafayette tried to meet the claims of the soldiers on the one hand and the fears of the commune on the other by arranging for part-payment before the first year of service ended of the sum still due—one part in January and the other in April. The Military Committee proposed and the Representatives authorized this modification of the Regulations, and Lafayette, explaining to the officers that the change had come about because of "daily defection and abuse," commanded the Guard captains to take every precaution against further desertion. Since deserters from one company sometimes enlisted in another, the Military Committee asked Lafayette to designate an officer to keep a full roster of the paid companies for captains to check against when enrolling new recruits.[59]

Appeals to officers and men, however, did not suffice to end desertions. Lingering royalist sympathies, personal doubts, revolutionary excitability, and widespread suspicion of aristocrats (their officers sometimes among them) reinforced the feeling of some of the French Guards that they had made a bad bargain. Not only were they not paid as well as some of them had expected to be but they also were sometimes badly housed. On several visits to the center companies' barracks[60] Lafayette saw or heard of things he did not like. The barracks were bare and uncomfortable, and at times private landlords and public agencies, their property having

[59] *Procès-verbal du Comité militaire*, Part I, pp. 165–66 (September 20).

[60] *Révolutions de Paris*, No. 8, August 29–September 6, p. 31, and *Procès-verbal du Comité Militaire*, Part I, pp. 117 (September 3).

been converted to military uses against their will,[61] were not co-operative. A spell of cold weather in the middle of September made heating desirable, but when one of the captains bought firewood and asked the Military Committee for reimbursement, the committee replied that it could authorize no such expenditure until the Representatives had ruled in the matter.[62]

In fashioning a revolutionary army which during the very process had to police a city in upheaval, Lafayette did not even have the aid of a complete staff of officers, and he was obliged to select certain non-elective officers at the same time that he was organizing the rank and file. The number of applicants and recommendations from influential persons for the appointive commissions at his disposal was large, and a choice among them was not easy. Tact was needed to avoid offending illustrious applicants or backers of applicants—old friends, ministers, deputies, city officials, and division chiefs among them. When a selection was under consideration, Lafayette proceeded in a manner which by now he had made routine—collecting information upon each applicant in a separate dossier and sending it to the Military Committee, sometimes with a recommendation of his own. Once he considered making an independent appointment but desisted when he found that the committee had already proposed others for the place. In the end he accepted all the nominations of the committee and put them with his approval before the Assembly of Representatives.[63]

Despite Lafayette's compliance, a momentarily awkward situation arose in the naming of the division majors. La Salle came to see him, requesting to be appointed one of them. Lafayette recognized that La Salle was not without friends and influence in the city, and perhaps would have liked, besides, to make some amends for the grievous injustice which La Salle had suffered. Yet he did not wish to interfere with the Military Committee's freedom of choice. So he advised La Salle to make his application directly to

---

[61] Lacroix, I, 429 n. (August 31), 464, 467, and 468 (September 3), 471 and 474 (September 4), 553–54 and 554–56 (September 12), and II, 13–14 (September 20).

[62] *Procès-verbal du Comité militaire,* Part I, pp. 171–72 (September 21).

[63] *Ibid.,* pp. 130–31 (September 8), 132–33 (September 9), 171–72 (September 21), and Lacroix, I, 558–61 (September 13), 586, 587, and 593 (September 15).

the committee. La Salle did so, but he was too late; the Military Committee had already decided on its nominations and would not alter them. The best it would do was to promise La Salle a testimonial of its gratitude and a petition to the commune to compensate him for his services and his losses. Lafayette complied with this decision too.[64]

The recommendations of the committee were ready for the Representatives only on September 12. They comprised the nomination of six division majors and the request that three adjutants be added to the general staff. Since new officers meant increased expenditures for salaries, the Representatives hesitated to add the new adjutants. The Military Committee, however, had recommended also a reduction of salary from 8,000 to 7,000 livres for the division majors, and when Lafayette indicated that the amount so saved might be applied to the pay of the proposed adjutants, the Assembly acceded.[65] In recognition of Lafayette's having deferred to the Military Committee "for the good of the service," the Representatives took care to indicate that in accepting the committee's list they meant to establish no precedent obliging the commandant general to defer to the committee on appointments.[66] Nevertheless, Lafayette continued as before, and the three new adjutants, similarly nominated by the Military Committee, were promptly approved by the Representatives. Except for a commissary general, by mid-September the headquarters staff of the Paris National Guard was at length completed.[67]

Among its numerous tasks the Military Committee had long been engaged in drawing up a table of salaries for National Guard officers. As early as August 3 it had moved to recommend to the Representatives a salary for the commandant general which, in

[64] *Procès-verbal du Comité militaire*, Part I, pp. 135 (September 10), 135–37 (September 11).

[65] *Ibid.*, pp. 130 (September 8), 133 (September 9), 134 and 135 (September 10), 146–47 (September 14), and Lacroix, I, 586 and 587 (September 15), 601–2 (September 16).

[66] Lacroix, I, 587 (September 15).

[67] *Procès-verbal du Comité militaire*, Part I, pp. 156–57 (September 16), and *Almanach royal, année MDCCLXXXX* (Paris, [1791]), p. 428. On the difficulties encountered in choosing a commissary general see Lacroix, I, 227 (August 24), 559–60 (September 13), 613, 614–15, and 618 (September 17).

view of the heavy expense attached to his post, should be no less than 120,000 livres. At the committee's next meeting Lafayette had requested them to rescind that recommendation. For whatever sacrifices the Revolution had required of him, he magnanimously stated, he had already been compensated by the prospective benefits to his country. Members of the committee protested, but in the end they complied with his request.[68]

Nevertheless, as everyone knew, the Revolution was costing the marquis a good deal of hard cash. Although he probably, as a gentleman, left such things to his intendants, he undoubtedly recognized that the Revolution had been costly to him. As his principal intendant, Jacques-Philippe Grattepain-Morizot, was later to estimate, his annual income had dropped from 118,000 livres in 1783 to 108,000 by July 1, 1789, and it was to drop still further. He himself had recently estimated that the Revolution would in the end probably cost him a quarter of his fortune.[69] His "military family" (including at least Gouvion, La Colombe, and Poirey) were living at his house, and having accepted the offer of twenty-five men who had voluntarily sought the privilege of serving as his bodyguard, he was supporting them at his own expense—and, according to Bailly, "well."[70] He had been a liberal contributor to patriotic causes, and as a generous host he kept open house to a numerous company. In addition, he had outfitted himself with expensive uniforms, and his famous white horse—generally, but not always affectionately, known as Jean Leblanc—was alone reputed to have cost him 1,500 louis (nearly $6,000, in days when a good house might have cost less). If these outlays appeared extravagant, Lafayette's friends apologized for them on the ground

[68] *Procès-verbal du Comité militaire*, Part I, pp. 30–32 (August 3).

[69] See above, p. 212, quoting *Mémoires*, II, 322. For Morizot's estimate see Jean de Bernières, "Les Revenus de La Fayette et la Révolution," *Revue bleue*, 3d ser., XIV (1887), 381–82; *Intermédiaire des chercheurs et curieux*, XX (1887), 543; and Mosnier, *Chavaniac-Lafayette*, pp 56, 301. In fact (but chiefly for another reason—because his properties were to be confiscated when he emigrated), the Revolution was to cost Lafayette far more than a quarter of his fortune.

[70] Bailly, II, 349–50. See also *Almanach royal, 1790*, p. 428, and P. W. Clayden, *The Early Life of Samuel Rogers* (London, 1887), p. 134.

that they gave éclat to the National Guard and pleasure to the city's inhabitants.[71]

So the matter of compensation to Lafayette had not ended with his request in August that the matter be dropped. Apparently, during the ensuing month, although the Representatives continually found only insufficient funds for other purposes, they kept their debt to Lafayette in mind. At any rate, on September 2 "upon a proposal made by many members" and without much discussion they voted him a yearly salary of 120,000 livres beginning September 1, and "in order to compensate him for the enormous and unavoidable expenses which circumstances have forced him to incur and which are inseparable from the maintenance of a first-rate establishment," they voted him an additional indemnity for past expenses of 100,000 livres.[72]

Only on the next day (September 3) did the Representatives decide upon compensation for the mayor, and in so doing they made an invidious comparison. While recognizing that the dignity of the mayoral office too required a proper outlay, they estimated the requisite amount as considerably less than that required for a commander who was expected to be constantly available to 30,000 men. Consequently, the Assembly voted a compensation to Bailly amounting to only 50,000 livres, half of the reimbursement voted Lafayette, and seemingly less willing to reach an independent decision in the mayor's case, it referred the matter of his annual salary to the districts.[73] Bailly, while claiming that this "extraordinary and ridiculous" action was designed to punish him for disagreements with the Representatives, admitted that Lafayette's expenses were greater than his (Louis XVI having allowed the former Hôtel de La Police to be converted to the mayor's use as the Hôtel de la Mairie), but he noted that the mayor too had to give

[71] Félix Hézecques, *Recollections of a Page at the Court of Louis XVI*, trans. C. M. Yonge (London, 1873), pp. 307–8, and Thiébault, I, 261 n.

[72] Lacroix, I, 454 and 455–56 (September 2), and Jacques Godard, *Exposé des travaux de l'Assemblée générale des Representans de la Commune de Paris depuis le 25 juillet 1789 jusqu'au mois d'octobre 1790* . . . (Paris, 1790), pp. 50–51.

[73] Lacroix, I, 465 (September 3), 479–80, and Godard, pp. 49–50.

well-attended audiences and that Lafayette made a practice of sending the poor to him.[74]

When a committee appointed for that purpose by the Representatives informed Lafayette of the cash token of his fellow citizens' appreciation, he expressed his gratitude once more for the commune's generosity but observed that the sum was "much too large." Not only, it seemed to him, were the city's other financial obligations more pressing but also a larger sum ought to have been voted for the needs of the mayor, who was the higher officer. It was hard, he added, to determine the cost of the commandant general's office, but if he had found that he needed money, he would not have hesitated to ask for it. At a time, however, when so many citizens were in distress and the city had to incur other expenses, he did not wish to increase them. Besides, though he did not himself put it so crudely, he could afford to be munificent. His private fortune, he indicated, sufficed for the establishment he maintained, particularly since he was now too busy to entertain as much as before. So he begged for a postponement of a decision on the commandant general's pay, suggesting that the sums already voted him be distributed among "those who had suffered most for the country."

This act of beneficence might well have been only an uncalculated example of Lafayette's well-known generosity, but it could hardly have failed to purchase for him some additional popularity. The visiting Representatives were greatly impressed but somewhat embarrassed. The Assembly, they thought, would be insistent, and their oral report of his reluctance to accept a salary and a repayment of expenses might be unconvincing. Would he give them a letter stating his wishes? So Lafayette wrote his remarks out for presentation to the Assembly.[75]

When the Representatives heard the secretary read Lafayette's statement, their response (whether or not he had some sort of ulterior motive) was all that his characteristic appetite for approval could have demanded. His generosity, the Assembly agreed, "added still further to the sentiments of admiration" which "his virtues . . . and his conduct, so full of wisdom and prudence, . . . have won from

[74] Bailly, II, 345–47, 349–50.

[75] Lacroix, I, 500–501 (September 7); Godard, p. 51; and *Mémoires*, II, 292–93.

all citizens."[76] Nevertheless, the Assembly, feeling that distinterestedness had its limits and that patriotic services should not become a charge upon a personal fortune, decided to appropriate a considerable sum to be earmarked for the commandant general's uses. The districts also seemed to think that virtue ought to have more than its own reward, and so a competitive display of generosity prolonged the unusual spectacle of a willing employer pushing compensation upon an employee reluctant to receive it.[77]

A chorus of praise greeted the commandant general's act of self-sacrifice and solicitude. Referring to Lafayette's membership in the society of American Revolutionary War veterans, the Society of the Cincinnati, Loustalot wrote: "So served the virtuous Cincinnatus, whose image our worthy general does not without purpose wear on his breast."[78] And even Jean-Paul Marat, self-constituted "Ami du Peuple" and censor of officialdom, while excoriating the city magistrates for the extravagance of their offer, granted that Lafayette's altruism in refusing it did humanity honor: "What an example for public administrators!"[79] Once more, by adding the *belle parole* to the *beau geste*—conduct which came to him naturally even if he perhaps also appreciated its political value—Lafayette had made a gain in the race for leadership of the Revolution.

Although toward the end of September the Paris citizens' militia was essentially complete on paper, Lafayette still had some trying decisions to make regarding its structure. One of the most trying involved certain groups of volunteers who were eager to serve in his undermanned army but whom he had to discourage. At the very time that some former royal soldiers already enrolled deserted the Paris National Guard, others kept leaving their regiments to join its ranks, only to find that if they had quit the royal service after a certain date, they would be classified as deserters unless they quickly returned. Thus stranded, sometimes penniless, they occa-

[76] Lacroix, I, 500–501 (September 7).

[77] *Mémoires*, II, 328, and Godard, p. 51 n. See also below, n. 79.

[78] *Révolutions de Paris*, No. 9, September 5–13, p. 28.

[79] *Ami du peuple*, September 25, pp. 131–32, and September 29, p. 164. See also, among others, Jean-Paul Marat, *Project de déclaration des droits de l'homme* (Paris, 1789), p. 47 n.; *Courier national*, September 9, p. 6; *Patriote français*, September 8, p. 3; and *La Voix du peuple*, No. 1 [*ca.* September 1], p. 72.

sionally became unruly. Once more Lafayette placed this problem before the Representatives, and he received authority, beginning September 13, to arrest these soldiers and send them back to their royal regiments unless they voluntarily returned before that date—in which case they would get passports and travel allowances.[80]

The fate of the Basoche legions required an even more unpleasant decision. These men were not merely *willing* to serve; they *had* served—with distinction and with expense to themselves. The good of the service nevertheless, Military Committee and commandant general insisted, required a unified force, in which volunteer companies had no place, and the most they would do was to continue to urge the districts to enroll the veterans of the Basoche in the undermanned companies.[81] On September 13 the Assembly of Representatives definitely resolved to maintain privately organized paramilitary units no longer and, reiterating its gratitude to the Basoches, called upon them again to join the district companies as individuals. Likewise authorizing the commandant general to thank the Volunteers of the Bastille for their past services, it relieved them of their self-imposed duty of policing the site of the Bastille.[82] These decisions meant that at last Paris might soon officially have only a single Guard under a single commander.

In fact, for a time in mid-September, after the arrest of Saint Huruge and despite the uproar over the veto, public order remained almost unbroken, leading the Representatives to act as if the municipal revolution were ended. On the assumption that Paris had surmounted the dangers which had hitherto required special precautions, they decreed that passports would no longer be required of persons traveling within the immediate vicinity of Paris and that free traffic inside the city itself (excepting only for military muskets) would be permitted. Further emphasizing that Paris had a new regime, the Assembly of Representatives, having been initially called together merely as a constituent body to draw up a plan of government for Paris, gave way to a new Assembly of

[80] Lacroix, I, 522-23 (September 9), and *Courier national,* September 12, pp. 7-8.

[81] *Procès-verbal du Comité militaire,* Part I, p. 123 (September 6), and Lacroix, I, 521 and 528-29 (September 9), 558 (September 13).

[82] Lacroix, I, 558, 561-62, and 566-69 (September 13).

Representatives. The new body consisted of 300 members (5 per district instead of 3), including nearly all the old 124 Representatives as well as several members of the Military Committee.[83] This assembly (sometimes called the Assembly of Three Hundred) met for the first time on September 19. Though formal legislation by the National Assembly on municipal reorganization still was pending, the government of the city of Paris, including its National Guard, seemed no longer merely a provisional revolutionary contrivance.

BIBLIOGRAPHICAL NOTES

The frequent charges of venality leveled at the press of the French Revolution, largely a mushroom growth nourished by the decay of the royal censorship, make it easy to assume that journalists were bought by one or another faction, but the suspicion is more easily raised than verified. We have followed Eugène Hatin, *Bibliographie historique et critique de la presse périodique française* (Paris, 1866), except where we have corrective evidence, in matters concerning the sometimes fluctuating politics of the numerous journals of the day.

[83] *Ibid.*, pp. 525–26 and 529–30 (September 9), and II, v, 14–15 (September 20), 679–91 (list of members); Godard, p. 15; and *Procès-verbal du Comité militaire*, Part I, p. 172 (September 22).

CHAPTER XII

The National Guard Sanctioned

BY THE END of September Lafayette's staff was practically completed, and the National Guard seemed sufficiently organized to dispense with the services of volunteer auxiliary units. Nevertheless, it did not yet have a full military complement. It still lacked cavalry, artillery, chasseurs, river police, and a band. Cavalry and chasseurs had been formally authorized, and the Military Committee had occupied itself with providing them with regulations and officers,[1] but neither had yet been fully organized. Lafayette had provisionally created an artillery corps too, while awaiting the approval of the civil authorities, but its status remained uncertain pending that approval, and the uncertainty induced some of the cannoneers to quit and enroll in the paid infantry companies.[2] Furthermore, to police the ports, quays, and islands of the Seine, several hundred additional men were needed, but September went by without action by the Representatives on that score either.[3] Meanwhile, trying to acquire for the regular city hall guard and some of the proposed cavalry substantial quarters near the Hôtel de Ville, Lafayette had approved a proposal to take over a nearby orphan asylum, moving the supervising nuns elsewhere.[4] Thus, probably unknowingly and unintentionally, he es-

---

[1] On the cavalry see *Procès-verbal de Comité militaire,* Part I, pp. 155–56 (September 16), 162–63 (September 19), 171 (September 21), 192–93 (September 29), and Part II, pp. 3 (October 1), 4 (October 2). On the chasseurs see *ibid.,* Part I, pp. 157–58 (September 17), 192–93 (September 29), and Part II, p. 3 (October 1).

[2] *Ibid.,* Part I, pp. 155–56 (September 16), 163 (September 19).

[3] *Ibid.,* pp. 50–52 (August 11), 163 (September 19), and Part II, p. 3 (October 1).

[4] *Ibid.,* Part I, pp. 179–82 (September 25), and Lacroix, II, 108 and 114–15 (September 29).

tablished a small-scale precedent for the reorganization of the monastic orders in the near future.

By the end of September, Lafayette, his staff, and his division chiefs were engaged in working out a routine of service.[5] The Military Committee had almost finished drawing up the regulations for the various branches of the Guard, and Lafayette intended them to be united into a single set, which he expected to serve not merely as rules for the Paris Guard but also as a model for those of other cities. That task too was still under consideration.[6] All the same, toward the close of the month a new military manual went on sale, approved by Lafayette and based largely on the *Règlement* as already adopted.[7]

The routine business of the commandant general's office by that time had become a staggering load. The districts, still particularist, sometimes contradicted the commandant general's orders and interfered with his efforts to carry out those of the commune, and he and the Military Committee had to listen patiently to complaints and protests, striving to reconcile the new democratic procedures with the need for military efficiency and discipline. The districts' stubborn defense of their prerogatives required that their approval be secured on even such petty matters as distinctions in the insignia of officers and men, sometimes necessitating the tedious process of sending a circular letter to all of the districts and waiting for replies.[8] Officers still had to be named by the complicated procedure of consensus among commandant general, Military Committee, and commune.[9] Some importunate but influential individuals pushed special candidates of their own. Gouverneur Morris,

---

[5] *Procès-verbal du Comité militaire,* Part I, pp. 173 (September 22), 179 (September 25).

[6] *Ibid.,* pp. 163 (September 19), 189 (September 28).

[7] *Nouveau catechisme militaire approuvé par M. de la Fayette* (Paris, 1789), and *Chronique de Paris,* September 24, p. 126.

[8] *Procès-verbal du Comité militaire,* Part I, pp. 114–16 (September 2), and see below, n. 64.

[9] *Procès-verbal du Comité militaire,* Part I, pp. 156–57 (September 16), 162–63 (September 19), 172 (September 22), 187 (September 26), 192–93 (September 28), and Part II, pp. 3 (October 1), 4 (October 2), and Lacroix, I, 558–61 (September 13), 586–87 (September 15), 613 and 614–15 (September 17), and II, 131 (October 1).

while free in his criticism of the officers Lafayette did accept, was a most persistent wire-puller for a particular friend's protégé— though apparently without success.[10] Across Lafayette's desk, too, came the contributions of National Guard units for distribution to worthy charitable and patriotic funds.[11]

Despite the commune's official discountenancing of volunteer paramilitary organizations and the reluctance of civil and military authorities to incorporate them as unmodified units into the National Guard, the old organizations—the Basoche and the Arquebusiers as well as the students of the College of Surgery, who wished to serve as medical officers—survived.[12] One of the two Basoche legions—that of the Châtelet—finally was satisfied when, with the formal approval of the Representatives and the commandant general, the District of the Enfants Rouges incorporated its members into the district battalion,[13] but the fate of the legion of the Palais de Justice remained unsettled.

Some of these diversified affairs doubtless were too petty to rivet the attention of one of France's leading political figures, but he could not shunt them aside, for a country in revolution turned to him for guidance in things both great and small. Nor could he justly be accused of being unable to depute authority, since he entrusted much of this responsibility to Gouvion and the other members of his "military family." If he attended meetings of the Military Committee with commendable regularity, he was nevertheless often absent or late, because he was busy elsewhere,[14] but sometimes the committee patiently and deliberately postponed decisions on even routine business until he could participate.

One of the most urgent matters that kept Lafayette busy elsewhere was the undiminished disquiet among the people of Paris.

[10] Morris diary, July 27, September 17–18, and October 2, Davenport (ed.), I, 163, 220–23, 238–39.

[11] *Révolutions de Paris*, No. 12, September 26–October 4, pp. 27–28.

[12] Lacroix, II, 102–3 (September 28), 130 (October 1), 144–45 (October 2).

[13] *Ibid.*, II, 146–47 (October 2).

[14] For instances of lateness see *Procès-verbal du Comité militaire, passim*, and for instances of absence, *ibid.*, Part I, pp. 25–26 (July 30 and 31), 103 (August 29), 111 (August 31), 122 (September 5), 177 (September 24), 188 (September 26), 190–91 (September 28–29).

Beneath the apparent tranquility of mid-September there seethed an anxiety born of economic distress, suspicion of plots and counterplots, and the fear of food shortage. Hunger was no stranger to Paris in the eighteenth century, especially toward the end of summer, before the new harvest was in but when that of the previous year was nearly exhausted. A city of about half a million souls dependent upon wagons and barges to bring it food from the neighboring countryside rarely had enough on hand after a bad harvest, such as that of 1788 had been. At such times the price of foodstuffs would go up, leaving the poor, who had neither larders nor money, to face the menace of famine. The city square then was likely to become a forum, where angry voices were raised, sometimes accusing the rich and the powerful of deliberate intent to corner the market and starve the poor. The Halles had of late become a center of discord, and Lafayette's special precautions to police the markets seemed no more than the requisite defense against disorder.

As hunger spread among the miserable, political rivalry and mistrust caused men to blame one another rather than to inquire into the natural, technical, economic, or social conditions which made for food shortages. And so September's optimism, never wholly unmitigated at the Hôtel de Ville, was doomed to a short life. Even in mid-September Jefferson, who only a few days earlier had reported that France seemed tranquil, announced, in the dispatches which were to prove to be his last before leaving France for good, that Paris was "in danger of hourly insurrection for the want of bread" and that the aristocratic cabal was sowing "dissensions in the Assembly and distrust out of it," with the result that "the patience of ... people ... is worn thread-bare" and "civil war is much talked of and expected."[15] Other foreign observers formed a similar dismal impression.[16]

Lafayette, suspicious since the early days of July that Mirabeau

[15] Jefferson to Edward Rutledge, September 18, Boyd, XV, 452, and to Jay, September 23, *ibid.*, pp. 458–59.

[16] Letter of Jenkinson, September 16, Browning, II, 26; Fernan Nuñez to Floridablanca, September 18, Mousset, pp. 81–82; and Morris diary, September 22, Davenport (ed.), I, 226.

and the Orléanists hoped to divert the Revolution to their own purposes, was now preoccupied by the threat of a counter conspiracy. The report would not down that the king or his royalist henchmen were plotting that he leave his palace at Versailles and go to some more friendly point from which he should try to regain mastery of the country. Metz seemed a logical choice. It was a distant border garrison town where the commanding general, the Marquis de Bouillé, was a devoted royal servant and from which it would be easy to communicate with and perhaps get help from the queen's brother, the Holy Roman Emperor Joseph II. Lafayette heard, among other unverified rumors, of a scheme to collect a huge fund to finance the king's flight to Bouillé's headquarters and set up court at Metz. The Spanish ambassador, the Comte de Fernan Nuñez, Jefferson, and perhaps Montmorin also believed that some such plot was under way.[17]

The prospect of the king of France either leading an army, with or without foreign aid, from the eastern frontiers against Paris or fleeing to swell the ranks of the émigrés gathered in foreign cities close to France's borders was particularly unwelcome to an anti-Orléanist monarchist like Lafayette, for the spectacle of Louis XVI either at the head of a counterrevolutionary army or in resentful, if self-imposed, exile might drive into the Orléanist camp many of those who wished neither the Old Regime nor a republic. That was the reason why, in his letter of September 8, Lafayette had asked Minister Latour du Pin to be frank with him: Was it true that the king might go to Metz?[18]

The court, however, was not frank. It was no less suspicious of Lafayette than he was of it. Besides, the king's advisers were divided, and no definite plans had yet been approved. The idea of fleeing to a friendly army in a distant town was only one of several schemes which were being suggested and weighed by someone or other at Versailles. Hence, conflicting rumors, all of doubtful credibility, continued to disturb Lafayette's composure.

---

[17] See below, n. 19, and Fernan-Nuñez to Floridablanca, September 6 and 18, Mousset, pp. 77–82, and Jefferson to Jay, September 23, Boyd, XV, 459–60. Jefferson suggests in his letter that Montmorin also believed it.

[18] [September 8], *Mémoires,* II, 327. See also above, p. 251.

One of his sources of information on what was happening at Versailles was the Comte d'Estaing, fellow officer in the American war, fellow member of the Society of the Cincinnati, and now commandant of the Versailles National Guard. Whether by chance or design, Lafayette and Estaing met as dinner guests on September 13 at the home of Lafayette's banker, T. Jauge (who was also one of his aides-de-camp). The conversation naturally got around to current rumors, and according to Estaing's subsequent report of that conversation, Lafayette told him of the alleged scheme to put the king under Bouillé's protection. Whereupon Estaing, afraid that the servants might overhear the conversation, cautioned his friend to speak softly; a word from Lafayette might mean death for someone. Lafayette replied in a "coldly matter-of-fact" manner that at Metz, as elsewhere, the patriots were the strongest group, and "it is better that one man [perhaps meaning Bouillé] should die for the welfare of all."[19]

Whether or not Estaing's account of the conversation was accurate, he lost no time, as Lafayette perhaps had intended, in acting upon it. He went first to see the Spanish ambassador, whose apprehensions were even more alarming than Lafayette's. Foreseeing disaster if playing with fire did not stop, Estaing appealed, apparently indirectly with the cooperation of Montmorin, to the queen, presumably a key figure in any royalist plot. Informing her of the fearsome rumor circulating in high places ("and what would happen, good Heavens, if it spread among the people?"), he begged an audience with her in order to present his view that the king's flight would be unwise. The queen granted the audience, and Estaing left it with the feeling that if any plot were afoot, it had been scotched.[20] Pernicious gossip did not subside, however. The *Révolutions de Paris* reported as a current belief that the émigrés were planning to attack France with the aid of the sov-

[19] Estaing [to Marie-Antoinette?], September 14, Ferrières, I, 264–67, and (more complete) *AP*, XIX, 390–91 (October 1, 1790). The reason for doubting that this letter went directly to Marie Antoinette, although it was intended for her ultimately is that it is probably the letter which Jefferson described as sent to Montmorin and shown by him to her; see above, n. 17. For Bertrand de Moleville's doubt that this letter ever was sent see below, p. 382, n. 115.

[20] Ferrières, I, 267. See also *Mémoires*, II, 327 n.

ereigns of Prussia, Austria, and Spain.[21] The *Patriote français* divulged (though only as malicious chatter) that some aristocrats were planning to take the king away (this time to Normandy) and launch a civil war.[22]

On September 16 Lafayette dined with some battalion commanders of the Paris National Guard and discovered that not all the conspiring was going on at Versailles. Plot was engendering counterplot. Four of the battalion commanders took their chief aside and, telling him that they were authorized to speak for all sixty battalion commanders, revealed that there was trouble ahead. Perhaps their purpose was to sound out whether he approved of what they were up to, although he thought it was to give him warning and permit him to take precautions. Part of the former French Guard, he learned, had been persuaded by some of their former officers to retake their old service as bodyguard of the king. They could watch over the king at Versailles, they thought, and counteract his intriguing advisers at the same time that they remained in the paid service of Paris, and they counted on Lafayette to give them permission to do so. A notice of their intention was circulating among all the grenadier companies urging those who wished to go to Versailles to assemble on the Place de Louis XV on the afternoon of the eighteenth.

The motives behind this venture undoubtedly were mixed. Lafayette (as well as Bailly and Saint Priest when they learned what was going on) suspected that the lack of discipline among the French Guards was not attributable to revolutionary zeal or to justifiable grievances alone but was also a result of intrigue. Among its officers, they suspected, were still a few who regretted the old honorific service in the king's household and could be persuaded or bought to do something drastic about it. Lafayette, though confident that his Guardsmen were acting out of misguided patriotism, believed that their instigators were miscalculating royalists, who were naively playing into the hands of the Orléanists, while Saint Priest thought the Orléanists were directly to blame.[23]

---

[21] No. 10, September 12–20, pp. 3–7.   [22] September 17, p. 3.

[23] For Lafayette's view see *Mémoires*, II, 297, 332–33 and n., and IV, 149 and n.; Rabaut, p. 217; and below, n. 24. For Saint Priest's see Saint Priest, II, 1–2. For Bailly's see Bailly, II, 380–82.

At this juncture Jefferson, having completed final arrangements to go home, invited Lafayette to a farewell dinner at his home. This was to be the last meeting in France of these two men, who, more than any other pair working in cooperation, had imported the American revolutionary spirit into France (insofar as the revolutionary spirit in France came from America); they were not to meet again until both were old men—in 1824. Occupied as usual with a number of other things, Lafayette arrived at Jefferson's late on the afternoon of September 17. Condorcet, Morris, and La Rochefoucauld were already waiting for him with their host. Seldom had a more illustrious group of philosophers and statesmen who were direct or indirect participants in two revolutions broken bread together.

The conversation centered on the political crisis, and Lafayette revealed the shocking development in his command: the National Guard was contemplating a march upon Versailles in order (as Morris recorded his words) "to urge the decisions of the States General." When Morris asked whether he could control his men, Lafayette replied that "they would not mount Guard when it rains but . . . would follow him into Action." Morris, who regarded the combination of the National Assembly's aggressiveness with "the King's Feebleness of Character" as likely to lead to civil war, thought to himself that Lafayette would soon have "an opportunity of making the Experiment."

Politics and hunger these days were close companions, and Morris, ever ready himself to do business, found Lafayette also "very anxious about the Scarcity of Bread." Before the dinner guests departed, Morris made an indefinite appointment to dine with Lafayette and talk about the importation of American foods. Privately, however, he felt that nothing would come of it, for Lafayette "has generally a Crowd and is but a few Minutes at Home."[24] He raised the question of subsistence again in a letter to Lafayette the next day, but still without conviction that anything would come of it."[25]

The men who had gathered at Jefferson's house to do the departing American minister honor all deeply dreaded the developing

[24] Morris diary, September 17, Davenport (ed.), I, 220–21.

[25] *Ibid.,* September 18, p. 223.

pattern of plot and counterplot. Morris was inclined to attribute impending catastrophe to the incompetence of France's leaders; Jefferson blamed aristocratic intrigue. In Morris' judgment, "This man [Lafayette] is very much below the Business he has undertaken, and if the Sea runs high he will be unable to hold the Helm. . . . If the Clouds which now lower should be dissipated without a Storm, he will be infinitely indebted to Fortune, but if it should happen otherwise the World must pardon much on the Score of Intention. He means ill to no one, but he has the *Besoin de briller*."[26]

Lafayette himself was confident, however. He asked La Rochefoucauld on returning to Versailles to inform Saint Priest as minister of the king's household that "some persons had put in the grenadiers' heads the idea of going . . . to Versailles" but that there was no need to worry "because I count upon their confidence in me to forestall that project."[27] He nevertheless considered it only prudent to take certain other precautions. He posted some of his non-paid troops on the bridge across the Seine at Sèvres with orders to impede any advance upon Versailles and informed Saint Priest that he had done so.[28] And he notified Estaing as commandant of the Versailles National Guard that "an invasion of 1,800 French Guards or malcontents" was being planned which he might not be able to prevent.[29]

[26] *Ibid.*

[27] Lafayette to Saint Priest, [September 18], *Mémoires*, II, 333 n.

[28] Saint Priest (II, 2) at a time when he was hostile to Lafayette testified to this, and it is most plausible. See also Bailly, II, 380. The "billet confidentiel" mentioned in Lafayette to unknown, "ce mardi," *Mémoires*, II, 420, may, as the editors of the *Mémoires* imply (*ibid.*, n. 1), refer to Lafayette's letter to Saint Priest of September 18 (see below, n. 29), but since the letter of September 18 was intended to indicate that all danger had passed, it could hardly have been used as a pretext to bring the Flanders Regiment to Versailles, as Lafayette's letter of "ce mardi" maintained. We believe, therefore, that this "billet confidentiel" was the one which Saint Priest claimed to have received on September 17.

[29] The date and the purport of this letter can be derived from the depositions of officers of the Versailles National Guard, *AP*, XIX, 369, 382. Lafayette apparently kept no record of it, and in his *Mémoires* (II, 331–33), going on the assumption that there was no letter to Estaing on September 17 (possibly because when he wrote his accounts—in 1790 and 1829 [see *ibid.*, pp. 95 n., 329 n., 333 n.]—he forgot about it), he implies that when Estaing took action the next morning he used (and misinterpreted) as a pretext a letter which Lafayette sent to Saint Priest only the next day, September 18 (see below, p. 295 and n.

The shock produced in Versailles by these warnings led to perhaps precipitate and, as it turned out, crucial action. Believing that Mirabeau and the Orléanists were behind the agitation in Paris, Saint Priest fearfully concluded that a large body of well-trained, hostile men would advance from Paris, while to oppose them he had at Versailles only the King's Bodyguard and the remaining Swiss Guards; perhaps the Versailles National Guard too might be counted upon, but it had no paid companies, consisting entirely of volunteers. By Louis XVI's own recent decree it was no longer permissible for regulars to be stationed inside a town without the consent of its municipal government, but Saint Priest persuaded the king's council to consider Lafayette's letter legal justification for taking emergency measures. Accordingly he sent orders to the royal Flanders Regiment (which on September 16 had already left its garrison at Douai to help escort to the vicinity of Paris the king's gift of 6,000 fusils) to continue on toward Versailles.[30]

---

32). But that later letter to Saint Priest could not have arrived in Versailles by noon on September 18 for it had not yet been written. Nor is there any persuasive reason to believe that Estaing would have either invented a letter of September 17 or falsified the one to Saint Priest of September 18. See Lafayette's letter to the Chabroud Committee, October 3, 1790, *Mémoires*, II, 333 n., and also *ibid.*, p. 331, for Lafayette's mistaken charge that Estaing made *usage irregulier et mystérieux* of his letter to Saint Priest on September 18. Lafayette's letter to M. d'Hennings, January 15, 1799, *ibid.*, III, 235, says that Lafayette informed the ministers of *agitations*, and since the letter of September 18 was intended, on the contrary, to inform Saint Priest that the agitation was over, this statement in 1799 seems to corroborate our contention (see above, n. 28) that Lafayette sent a warning to Saint Priest on September 17. See also *Mémoires*, II, 331, for another reference to a letter to Saint Priest warning of possible disorders.

[30] Saint Priest, II, 3–4, 6. For the royal forces at Versailles see below, p. 300 and n. 49. Cf. Henri Leclercq, *Les Journées d'octobre et la fin de l'année 1789* (Paris, 1924), p. 16 and nn. 3 and 4, and Tuetey, I, 102, No. 958. Leclercq argues that Saint Priest was lying when he claimed that the Flanders Regiment was ordered to Versailles only on September 17, maintaining that it had not been part of the escort of the fusils which arrived in Paris on the sixteenth. But Latour du Pin's letter to Lafayette, August 17 (Lacroix, I, 255) says: "L'intention du Roi est que le transport en soit escorté jusqu'à Compiègne par un régiment d'infanterie," and since the 6,000 weapons were gathered from more than one place and escorted by more than one military unit (*ibid.*, p. 262) and since at least some of their escort came from Douai (*ibid.*, p. 615), it seems likely that Saint Priest was not falsifying. In that case the Flanders Regiment was not ordered out of Douai (as Leclercq argues it was) expressly and only for the purpose of moving on to Versailles even before there was any threat from the former French Guards. If, however, Leclercq is correct, then Saint Priest seized upon Lafayette's warning of September 17 as a cover for action of a counterrevolutionary character already well under way.

For his part Estaing, upon receiving his warning from Lafayette, re-envisioned the dire consequences which he had but recently prognosticated to the queen if Paris grew distrustful of the court. He decided to submit to his officers the question whether the Versailles National Guards should resist the threatened invasion from Paris. After they had gathered together at noon on September 18, he dismissed all men below the rank of captain and, swearing the remaining officers to the strictest confidence, read them Lafayette's message. In the dismay that followed, the majority judged that they could defend their posts only with the aid of regular troops, and they agreed to put the matter up to the Versailles' municipal assembly—likewise in confidence.

The municipal assembly, without knowing that the Flanders Regiment already had received its marching orders, readily consented to ask the king to call in regular troops but wanted to incorporate Lafayette's letter to Estaing in its public minutes as the explanation of its decision. Estaing, however, preferred not to compromise Lafayette publicly in that way and so persuaded them to substitute in its stead a letter which he offered to get from Saint Priest. Going immediately to the Château, he got an appropriate letter—one which, without mentioning Lafayette or the French Guard, spoke of "armed men" who might come from Paris to create disorder in Versailles, and the municipal assembly annexed that letter to its minutes as evidence that it had good grounds for its action.[31] Thus, without Lafayette's knowledge, his letters, intended merely to forewarn the proper authorities of a possible danger, were made the reason or the pretext for a troop movement already under way.

Saint Priest's precaution, if it was precaution rather than counter-revolution, proved unnecessary. Despite the forebodings of Versailles and despite Morris' distrust of Lafayette's ability "to hold

---

[31] Depositions in Charles Chabroud, *Pièces justificatives du rapport de la procédure du Châtelet sur l'affaire des 5 et 6 octobre, fait à l'Assemblée nationale* (Paris, 1790), in *Procès-verbal de l'Assemblée nationale*, L, 6–7, 33–34, 35–36, 40–41, 50–51, in *Procédure au Châtelet*, III, 36–37 (J.-E. Jouanne, captain in the Versailles National Guard), and in *AP*, XIX, 369, 382; minutes of the municipality of Versailles and related documents, September 18–23, Lacroix, II, 51–54 (September 24); Leclercq, p. 18, n. 1; and *Mémoires*, II, 330–31. If Saint Priest (II, 3) was not guilty of a *lapsus memoriae*, he also persuaded the king's council to get directly in touch with the municipality of Versailles.

the Helm," the commandant general of the Paris National Guard demonstrated that at least for the time being he was not "very much below the Business he had undertaken." On September 18, he went to the Place de Louis XV at the appointed hour (3 P.M.) to meet the former French Guards who proposed to go to Versailles to claim their old posts. As well as he could make out, they meant only to help the revolutionary cause by serving both in Paris as paid National Guardsmen and in Versailles as royal bodyguards, and they counted on his approval. With a little effort he prevailed upon them to give up their project.

Upon returning to the Hôtel de Ville, with a satisfaction which he took small pains to conceal the relieved commander sent a report of his success in a note addressed to Saint Priest and intended also to be read by Montmorin. The purpose of this brief message was patent: he wanted to reassure Versailles not only that he had been able to control his men but also that the intentions of at least some of them had not been malicious: "I owe them the justice of stating that they had intended to ask my permission and that several of them thought to take a very simple step which would be ordered by me." "Four words" from him, he wrote, had sufficed to divert the grenadiers from their "whim," and the only significant effect of the whole episode had been to confirm his "idea of the inexhaustible resources of the cabalers." The king's ministers could now consider the danger passed "except as a new indication of evil intentions."[32] Lafayette obviously expected Saint Priest and Montmorin, whom he regarded as old friends sympathetic with reform, to be pleased with the outcome of the French Guard's venture. Perhaps he also meant through them to let any royalist "cabalers" in Versailles know that they were gravely mistaken if they counted upon counterrevolutionary sentiments or disaffection among his men.

Whatever Saint Priest's real intentions might have been, the fat

---

[32] Lafayette to Saint Priest, [September 18], in Chabroud, pp. 66–67; *Mémoires*, II, 333, n. 1; and *AP*, XIX, 392 (October 1, 1790). Bailly (II, 380) guessed that this letter might have been written on September 17, but he was mistaken and thereby caused Leclercq (p. 15) and others to try to attribute the chain reaction of September 17 as well as of September 18 at Versailles to this letter, which, however, could have been written only late in the afternoon of September 18.

was in the fire. With the Flanders Regiment on its way to Versailles, and ostensibly upon the request of the Versailles municipality, a step had been taken which seemed, whether it actually was or not, the beginning of another effort to use military force to repress the National Assembly and its Paris supporters. Some of the officers and men of the Versailles National Guard—Lieutenant Colonel Laurent Lecointre, commander of the First Division, foremost among them—had not approved of Estaing's appeal for royal troops, and the National Assembly, when it learned what had been done, accepted it as a justifiable police measure only after vigorous protests by some deputies. When Lafayette and Bailly were informed of Saint Priest's action, although they found scarcely a loophole for protest, they tried at once to dissuade the ministry from repeating the error of the preceding July in bringing in troops. But the Flanders Regiment was already en route, and not only had Saint Priest covered its movement with an air of duty and propriety but, in so doing, had plausibly assigned as his reason that Lafayette had appeared, if only momentarily, uncertain of his ability to control his own revolutionary forces.[33]

Within the next few days rumors grew more and more extravagant though not incredible. On September 21 a royal lieutenant named Morel came to the city hall with a report which under normal circumstances would have appeared too bizarre for a moment's serious consideration. He solemnly informed Lafayette that thousands of royalist troops and noblemen were planning to converge on Versailles, disperse the National Assembly, make off with the king to a military post, seize the Duc d'Orléans, and cut Lafayette's and Bailly's throats; some of the French Guards who recently had been prevented from going to Versailles might be implicated. If the plotters (and Morel named names) could not carry off their coup in Versailles, they planned to retire to Montargis (about 65 miles away), rally 25,000 men, and begin a civil war, the costs of which would be met by the clergy. Since in some respects this report fitted in with Lafayette's own suspicions, and

[33] Chabroud, pp. 33–36; Bailly, II, 379–82; Lacroix, II, 29 and 31–32 (September 22); *AP*, XIX, 375; Saint Priest, II, 4; and *Mémoires*, II, 332.

since his informant seemed to be "a good citizen," he did not dare to treat it lightly.[34]

Similar talk quickly circulated throughout the city, and once more the Palais Royal seethed with tales, not wholly false, and speeches, not wholly fantastic: thousands of regulars were marching on Versailles to seize the king and take him to Metz, whence he would return, supported by the émigrés and their allies, to destroy the Revolution. Some excited patriots proposed to advance at once upon Versailles and drive out the conspirators.[35] Bailly, Lafayette, and the National Guard intervened, however, and without great difficulty kept the excitement under restraint for the time being.[36]

But that was not the end. The food crisis continued acute, pushing tension closer to the breaking point. Reports that spoiled grain was being sold in the Halles brought protesting deputations to the Hôtel de Ville.[37] The distress of the unemployed led Lafayette on September 21 to hold a meeting at the Tuileries of his division chiefs, battalion commanders, and general staff to consider what they could do to alleviate hardship during the coming winter. They decided to create a fund which would be raised and administered by their wives and to which members of the Paris National Guard would be asked to contribute.

A fitting way to raise funds was to take up a collection at a now frequent ceremony in which the parish priest blessed a district battalion's flag in its church. The next day Adrienne and her son, escorted by a cavalry guard of honor, went to a flag benediction at the Church of Saint Etienne du Mont, and there she sponsored a

---

[34] Lafayette's contemporary memorandum quoted in *Mémoires*, II, 329–30 n. See also Edmond Cleray, *L'Affaire Favras 1789–90* (Paris, 1932), pp. 55–56, and Lafayette to Morel, September 30, 1789, *Révolutions de Paris*, No. 31, Feb. 6–14, 1790, pp. 34–35.

[35] [Desmoulins], *Discours de la lanterne aux Parisiens*, pp. 28–29; Julius von Wickede (ed.), *Memoiren eines Legitimisten von 1770–1830* (Potsdam, 1858), I, 61–62; Clermont-Gallerande, I, 181; Léonce Pingaud (ed.), *Correspondance intime du comte de Vaudreuil et du comte d'Artois pendant l'émigration (1789–1815)* (Paris, 1889), I, 19; and *Révolutions de Paris*, No. 11, September 19–27, p. 24.

[36] Bailly, II, 382; *Courrier de Provence*, September 21, p. 120; and *Révolutions de Paris*, No. 11, September 19–27, pp. 24–25.

[37] Bailly, II, 376, and Lacroix, I, 599 (September 16), 622–23 (September 18).

collection for imprisoned debtors. She heard her husband praised in his absence not only as one of the greatest generals of France's history but also as the father of mankind, and herself as "the protectress of the needy," who "all are her family."[38] Since Lafayette had just (September 6) turned thirty-two and Adrienne was two years younger, these figures of speech were perhaps hyperbolic, but no one seemed to mind. Praise might have been warmer still had they learned that Adrienne had ordered her household to buy and use only rye flour and dark bread during the emergency and was being counted upon by the police to care for a man wounded in the attack upon the Bastille.[39]

Despite his previous promise to attend, the "father of mankind" had been absent that afternoon from the benediction of the flag of the battalion of Saint Etienne du Mont[40] because he was concerned over the distribution of power and justice no less than of charity. Several Paris districts and neighboring towns demanded of the city hall some action to forestall suspected troop movements around Versailles, and accordingly Bailly wrote the minister of war asking for a change of marching orders for the Flanders Regiment.[41] That morning Lafayette, requested by the Military Committee to join in its deliberations, had sent back word that he was too busy to do so.[42] And his preoccupation with other matters caused him that evening to break the dinner engagement he had made with Morris at Jefferson's farewell party, giving his caller only "three words" when they finally met, although sending him off with the feeling

---

[38] *Journal de Paris,* September 23 and October 3, pp. 1204 and 1269. See also *Couplets chantés le jour de la bénédiction du drapeau du batallion de Saint-Étienne-du Mont à un repas ou assistaient Mme la marquise de La Fayette et son fils. (Par le 1ᵉʳ sergent de la 2ᵉ compagnie du batallion de Saint-Etienne du Mont),* [September 22] and [Bérenger], pp. 275–76, 278–80.

[39] Mme de Lafayette to Mme Mangin, [*ca.* October 1789], in *La Haute Loire,* LXXII, No. 105 (September 6, 1883), and Mosnier, *Chavaniac-Lafayette,* p. 69 (facsimile) and the secretary of the Committee of Police to Mme de Lafayette, September 15, Cornell University, Rare Book Room, supplement to the Blancheteau Catalogue, p. 50.

[40] See above, n. 38.

[41] Lacroix, II, 29 and 31–32 (September 22), 37, 39, and 47–48 (September 23); *Patriote français,* September 23, p. 2; *Courrier de Versailles à Paris,* September 23, p. 374; and *AP,* XI, 123.

[42] *Procès-verbal du Comité militaire,* Part I, p. 172.

that his plan for importing food into Paris would have his busy host's wholehearted support.[43]

Morris could get only those "three words" with Lafayette that evening because the commandant general had an appointment with "some law people."[44] One of the problems which, along with food shortages, suspicion of counterrevolutionary troop movements, and the policing of popular excitement, absorbed Lafayette's attention in mid-September was the tardiness of the National Assembly in considering reform of court procedure in criminal cases. Until the National Assembly took some action, the old courts had to proceed in the old way, which he distrusted. On September 12 he had learned that the Châtelet had banished Saint-Geniès for pretending to be a National Guard officer and had sent another man to the galleys for provoking agitation at the Palais Royal. Severe sentences like these, he was still convinced, were likely to make his men hesitate to make arrests, out of concern lest the accused be punished excessively. He had therefore gone to the Assembly of Representatives to ask them to petition the royal chancellor for a stay of penalties for participation in Paris disturbances until the National Assembly should take some action on criminal law procedure. The Representatives promptly accepted his recommendation, and on September 15 the chancellor granted the stay, with words of approval for "the patriotic views" of Lafayette and the Representatives.[45] Still, reform of criminal procedure moved too slowly for him, and it was probably to hasten it that on September 22 he consulted the "law people" whom Morris mentioned. The next day Lafayette urged that the Representatives petition the National Assembly to make criminal trials public at once, in the hope that justice might be done openly as well as quickly.[46]

That morning (September 23) a letter to the Paris commune from Saint Priest occasioned some consternation by speaking of the desirability of increasing rather than reducing military

[43] Morris diary, September 22, Davenport (ed.), I, 225–26.

[44] *Ibid.*

[45] Lacroix, I, 552–53 (September 12), 557 (September 13), 584 (September 15), and Bailly, II, 366–67.

[46] Lacroix, II, 39 (September 23).

measures in order to prevent interference with the movement of the Flanders Regiment. Anxiety nevertheless temporarily subsided because Latour du Pin gave assurance that only the Flanders Regiment had in fact been summoned to Versailles,[47] and Lafayette corroborated that statement in the Assembly of Representatives. Affirming that his intelligence led him to consider reports of other military measures as "more than suspect," he showed that in his mind the rumors of royal troop movements were somehow related to criminal activity. He urged the Representatives to ferret out the source of these suspect reports in order to allay the widespread uneasiness, and if a deputation were to go to Versailles for that purpose, he suggested that it also be instructed to invite the National Assembly to vote as quickly as possible a decree providing open conduct of criminal trials. The Representatives, "influenced with the same sentiments that honor the commandant general and which daily bring him new claims upon the public's gratitude," sent some of their number to Versailles for the dual purpose which he had recommended.[48]

That day the Flanders Regiment arrived in Versailles. It took the newly prescribed civic oath in the presence of the town officials and was placed under Estaing's command. The next day, when the Paris Representatives who had gone to Versailles returned, they reported that the ministers again had assured them that no regulars other than the Flanders Regiment had been ordered to Versailles, that Estaing needed that regiment because the Versailles National Guard had no paid companies, and that even with the Flanders Regiment (but not counting the King's Bodyguard and the Swiss in Versailles) the royal troops within 20 leagues (about 60 miles) of Paris numbered all together only 2,610 men. The Assembly of Representatives ordered this report printed and posted so that the mistrust of Paris and the *banlieue* might be assuaged.[49]

Reassurance came also from two cities near the northeast frontier, not far from the garrison town of Metz, which figured so menacingly in the alleged counterrevolutionary plot. A deputation

[47] *Ibid.*, p. 37.

[48] *Ibid.*, pp. 39–40.   [49] *Ibid.*, pp. 51–55 (September 24).

of volunteers from Sedan arrived on September 23 to pay its respects to the commune of Paris. Conscious of its city's strategic importance, it joined in the request that Paris provide a system of correspondence and a model of organization for the provincial National Guard units. Bailly thanked the deputation for its "assurance of fraternity," and Lafayette, praising the "patriotic zeal" of the Sedan volunteers, presented it with a copy of the Paris *Règlement*.[50] The mayor of Strasbourg, Baron de Dietrich, recently had similarly acknowledged the leadership of Paris and asked for advice on the organization of the Strasbourg National Guard. In reply Lafayette, likewise on September 23, sent him a copy of the *Règlement* and expressed his readiness to keep in touch with Strasbourg.[51] In the midst of discouraging rumors of civil war and counterrevolution Lafayette thus continued to serve as a rallying symbol of "fraternity," as the unofficial generalissimo of the National Guard of the realm.

The former French Guards, despite Lafayette's assurance to the contrary, had not given up the idea of resuming their posts in Versailles, but, for all that, there was a momentary lull in the public sense of peril. It coincided with indications that the long-awaited completion of the Paris National Guard could not be far off. The French Guard, the Basoche, and other units which had merged or were expected to merge with the National Guard all owned revered flags, which it once would have been dishonor to desert but which they now had to lay aside. Lafayette and his associates thought it appropriate to arrange an elaborate ceremony by which some of the glory of the abandoned standards would rub off onto the new. A number of the Paris battalions had by that time had their recently devised banners blessed in their parish churches, sometimes in the presence of the commandant general,[52] and the

[50] *Ibid.*, pp. 40–41 (September 23).

[51] G. V., "Une Lettre de Lafayette à Dietrich," *Revue historique de la Révolution et de l'Empire*, XIV (1919–22), 152.

[52] Lacroix, II, 94–97, and André Sevin, *Le Défenseur du roi, Raymond de Sèze (1748–1828)* (Paris, 1936), p. 163. For a large print, dedicated and presented to Lafayette, showing the sixty battalion flags see Cornell University Library, *Lafayette, an Exhibition* (Ithaca, 1964), p. 6, item 24. For the continued agitation among the French Guards, see below, pp. 313–14.

desirability of honorably retiring the colors of the vanishing veteran corps was seized upon as the occasion for a benediction of all sixty new standards.

The ceremony was set for Sunday, September 27, in the Cathedral of Notre Dame. Leclerc de Juigné, the archbishop of Paris, was invited to pronounce the benediction, and the king to send some of his palace decorations to adorn the cathedral. Saint Priest, speaking for Louis XVI, deemed it an "honor to cooperate in the dignity of a ceremony at which would be consecrated the flags of a national troop which His Majesty hopes to employ on all important state occasions," and he congratulated the National Guard and its commander on "the capital's present repose."[53] It would have been hard to contrive a ceremony better calculated to promote the esprit de corps of the new citizens' battalions, since this one, blessed with royal, popular, civic, and ecclesiastical approval, would symbolize their direct succession to the recently defunct and duly commemorated military units of the Old Regime.

Lafayette, his staff, and the Military Committee worked out the details of the program carefully.[54] On his request the Representatives appointed a special committee to assume general supervision so that the ceremony would be an act of the commune as a whole and not merely a military show.[55] The militia, who had been drilling almost daily and were reported to be making "amazing progress," now did special drills. When ten battalions constituting a division drilled as a unit, Lafayette sometimes came too. On such occasions, after they had passed in review, he inspected each company and then, drawing the men around him, talked earnestly with them about affairs of common concern.[56] The mayor and the commandant general together chose the Abbé Claude Fauchet, a

---

[53] Saint Priest to Lafayette, September 22, *Courrier de Versailles à Paris*, September 26, p. 426. See also Blancheteau catalogue, p. 46, item 151, and *Révolutions de Paris*, No. 12, September 26–October 4, pp. 3–5.

[54] *Procès-verbal du Comité militaire*, Part I, pp. 173–74 (September 23). See also *Mémoires*, II, 296–97. Lafayette gives the date here as September 24, but that is an error.

[55] Lacroix, II, 41–42 (September 23).

[56] *Révolutions de Paris*, No. 10, September 12–20, p. 10, and No. 11, September 21–27, pp. 27–28. See also *Procès-verbal du Comité militaire*, Part I, pp. 174–75 (September 23).

member of the Assembly of Representatives, to preach the sermon at the forthcoming benediction.[57]

Since the parade on that occasion was to be the first public appearance of the citizen army of Paris as a whole, some of its details, no matter how petty they might seem, could conceivably create precedents or cause jealousies. Hence several issues might become sensitive and so called for particular study. How many men from each company would take part? Of these, who would police the line of march and who march? Who would carry the colors in the parade? Who among officers of equal rank would be given priority of command? Would Lafayette take part as a military officer or as a city official? Where would the separate units and personages march and then sit or stand in the cathedral? Where would spectators be placed? Should special guests be invited by card? When would the clergy enter and the benediction begin? Lafayette found himself a sort of pageant master. Although his staff, the Military Committee, and the Assembly of Representatives discussed such matters in several searching sessions, in effect they left the final decisions to him.[58]

Some decisions were reached only on the day before the great event. The Basoche of the Palais de Justice, still unassimilated into the National Guard, was awarded the honor of maintaining order within the Palais de Justice and its neighborhood (which also was the neighborhood of the Cathedral of Notre Dame) as a final tribute to "their zeal and attachment to the common cause."[59] Some of the district battalions were so eager to cooperate that they volunteered to do duty which the carefully planned orders of the day had arranged otherwise. The District of Notre Dame, which hitherto had had the responsibility of policing the cathedral, wanted to do so on this occasion but was notified that, since this was to be a city-wide pageant, the honor would be distributed among all the battalions. The ruling that the first sergeant of the paid company

---

[57] Lacroix, I, 566, n. 1, and II, 50 (September 24), and Bailly, II, 386.

[58] *Procès-verbal du Comité militaire,* Part I, pp. 175 (September 23), 182 (September 25), 188 (September 26), and Lacroix, II, 41–42 (September 23), 50 (September 24), 85–86 (September 26).

[59] Lacroix, II, 85–86 (September 26.)

would carry his battalion's colors roused jealousy among the unpaid companies, and at the last moment (past midnight on the eve of the parade) the Military Committee, working in one room, had to send for Lafayette, working in another, to explain to several district deputations that it was too late to change, particularly since good order required uniform understandings.[60]

The weather on Sunday morning was "very fine."[61] At ten-thirty Lafayette and his staff left the Hôtel de Ville to take their assigned places in the procession. As they stepped out on the perron, they beheld sixty blue, white, and red battalion banners streaming in the morning sun. At one time Lafayette—a story went—had expressed approval of the slogan "Live free or die" which he had seen on a sapper's ax, and thereupon all the sappers had wanted to use that slogan.[62] But the battalion's standards which now waved above the muskets of 3,000 Guardsmen in cockaded hats, royal blue coats, white underdress, and gleaming boots, bore a diversity of slogans, though for the most part they blazoned liberty and devotion to a constitutional king. When they spied their commander, the massed troops saluted and spectators cheered from square, roofs, and windows. Upon the command of the division chief in charge, the officers of the color guards (of ten men each) whipped out their swords and raised them high in token of their readiness to defend their standards.

Then came the order to march. The parade moved on between 2,400 uniformed men, 40 from each battalion, drawn up in a double line and stretching all the way from the Place de Grève to the Cathedral of Notre Dame. When to the tramp of soldiers' feet and the strains of martial music the last standard had moved past them in the Place de Grève, Lafayette, his staff, and his senior officers fell in behind. The civil officials, preceded and followed by cavalry and accompanied by the Garde de Ville, joined the proces-

---

[60] *Procès-verbal du Comité militaire*, Part I, pp. 180 and 182–83 (September 25), 188 (September 26–27), 190–91 (September 28); *Chronique de Paris*, September 27, p. 139; and *Courrier de Versailles à Paris*, September 29, pp. 485–86.

[61] Morris diary, September 27, Davenport (ed.), I, 234.

[62] [Bérenger], pp. 261–62.

sion at eleven o'clock. As they reached the cathedral square, the officials closed in around the mayor, and Lafayette and his officers passed in review before them, thus evincing their deference to civil authority. Then the color guards, one by one, marched to their assigned places inside the cathedral, adorned with the tapestries sent by the king. Finally Lafayette and Bailly, the city's chosen chiefs, walked together down the aisle, flanked by thirty battalion flags on each side. The whole crowd, Adrienne and Mme Bailly among them, burst into applause as the two men took raised seats just outside the choir.

The archbishop then entered, and the service began. He celebrated mass, said a few appropriate words, and took his place at the entrance to the choir, with Bailly on his right and Lafayette on his left. Then he began the benediction of the flags. As standard followed standard in an assigned order, the audience forgot itself. Applause and cheers broke out, drums rolled, and excited riflemen fired salutes. Seldom had Notre Dame contained more noisy joy or more genuine thanksgiving. When the last standard was blessed, the officers formed a double line from the great west door to the choir steps, faced the altar, and amid a hushed assembly drew their swords, saluted their mayor and the Representatives, and solemnly repeated the oath of loyalty to nation, king, law, and commune. As their swords clicked back into their scabbards, drums rolled, trumpets blared, and muskets cracked louder than before, joined this time by the salute of cannon outside the cathedral.

The Abbé Fauchet then delivered his sermon. His theme was liberty and right, mixed with references to the impending threat of national bankruptcy and the eternal blot of poverty. He was interrupted several times by applause. Finally, after the chanting of the *Te Deum,* the cortege marched out of the cathedral, returned to the Place de Grève, and broke up. Lafayette, Bailly, and twelve of the Representatives stayed behind to dine with the archbishop.[63]

The Paris National Guard, despite the remaining gaps, seeemed at last to be a single, cohesive body, applauded by the people, sanc-

[63] The above account of the benediction of the flags is based largely on Lacroix, II, 89–91 and 94–98 (September 27), and Bailly, II, 393–95, but see also below, nn. 64 and 65.

tioned by the commune, favored by the king, and blessed by the church. The papers carried the story of the benediction for days,[64] and it lingered in official minutes and men's memories for years.[65] For all but a few skeptics the real hero of the story was "the pupil, the rival, the friend of Washington," "the young man whom two worlds claim."[66] The skeptics, however, were soon to have their day.

BIBLIOGRAPHICAL NOTES

Vol. III of Bailly's *Mémoires* is not by Bailly but by an anonymous continuator.

The *Pièces justificatives* of Chabroud's report to the National Assembly on the Châtelet investigation of the events of October 5–6, 1789, were bound (with separate pagination) in Vol. L of Francois-Jean Baudouin's (semi-official) *Procès-verbal de l'Assemblée nationale*, immediately following No. 429, October 2, 1790. On the *Procédure au Châtelet* see the "Bibliographical Notes" to Chap. XIV.

Leclercq's *Journées d'octobre* is the most detailed secondary study of the events leading up to and including October 5–6, 1789, but it is subject to correction in a number of details. See the "Bibliographical Notes" to Chapter XV.

Saint Priest's *Mémoires* are unreliable not merely because of the long interval between the events he records and his recollection of them but also because of his pronounced royalist views and dislike of Lafayette at the time of his recollecting them. His *Abrégé des circonstances du depart de Louis XVI pour Paris, le 6 octobre 1789* appended to Mme [Jeanne-Louise] Campan, *Mémoires sur la vie privée de Marie Antoinette* . . . (Paris, 1823) gives (II, 294–97) essentially the same account as his *Mémoires*, often in the same words.

[64] E.g., *Courrier de Versailles à Paris*, September 27, pp. 485–86; *Chronique de Paris*, September 27 and 29 and October 1, pp. 139, 147, 153–54; *Révolutions de Paris*, No. 12, September 26–October 4, pp. 10–14; *Patriote français*, September 28, p. 2, and September 30, p. 2.

[65] Lacroix, II, 89–91, 94–98; *Mémoires*, II, 296–97; Bailly, II, 393–95; Vaissière, pp. 22–23.

[66] *Patriote français*, September 28, p. 2; *Chronique de Paris* (September 23, 1789, p. 122), and the *Lettres à Monsieur le comte de B**** (I, 434), describing a portrait of Lafayette under which appeared the lines:

> Hic ille est juvenis, quem
> Vindicat orbis uterque
> Libertate ducem, consilioque virum.

CHAPTER XIII

"The Sea Runs High"

LATE IN August Jefferson, using a code number for the name *Mirabeau,* had expressed the private opinion that the man so designated was the chief of those who were using the Duc d'Orléans as a dupe and were exploiting the Orléans name and money for their own purposes. Jefferson's last diplomatic report from Paris again analyzed the French political situation and found it verging on civil war. As he saw it, three things tended in that direction—"the want of bread," "public bankruptcy," and the apprehended "absconding of the king." Four parties, he judged, were engaged in a struggle for power—"Aristocrats," "moderate royalists" (by which he meant the Anglophiles under Mounier's leadership), "Republicans" (meaning the group, later called Jacobins, which under Lameth and Duport advocated a weak monarchy), and "the faction of Orléans." Despite the money which he believed the Orléanist faction was spending and the support he guessed it was probably getting from foreign countries, he did not consider these "Catalines [*sic*] of the Assembly" strong, having the support of only "some of the lowest descriptions of the mob." They or the "Aristocrats" might prevail if the two wings of the "Patriotic part of the assembly"—"moderate royalists" and "Republicans"— failed to unite once more, but he expected the Patriots not to break up, because they were men of "the same honest views" and were linked by "another powerful bond of union, . . . our friend the Marquis de La Fayette," who "labours incessantly to keep them together." Jefferson deemed that friend's position so strong that neither wing would "place themselves in opposition to him."[1] Jefferson's view of party rivalry in the National Assembly at this

[1] Jefferson to Madison, August 28, and to Jay, September 23, Boyd, XV, 366, 458–60.

juncture was much the same as Lafayette's[2] and was probably derived at least in part from his.

The benediction of the battalion flags on September 27 had been part of Lafayette's program to inspire unity among the friends of the Revolution. For a short time the program appeared to have succeeded, but the response was not all sweet accord. A few saw in this military display a snare and a delusion. Loustalot, who had already warned against the military spirit which the uniform engendered, maintaining that a Guardsman was an independent citizen first and served as a soldier only as his civic duty required,[3] now held that the city-wide pageant had been unnecessary, since the battalions' flags had already been blessed in their parish churches. He reprimanded the king's ministers, who, with famine, bankruptcy, and anarchy staring them in the face, ought to have had more to do than to send ornaments to Notre Dame; their purpose must have been to woo the National Guard to join an "antipopular coalition" and keep Paris quiet while the aristocrats blocked reform at Versailles by using the royal veto.[4]

Marat too joined the discordant voices. When summoned before the Assembly of Representatives to explain an earlier denunciation of the city authorities,[5] he, without mincing words, not only defended himself but even renewed his criticism of the Assembly for, among other errors, having offered an exorbitant salary to the commandant general.[6] Nothing daunted by his arraignment by the city fathers, he too warned that the National Guard might become an instrument of the aristocracy, "transformed into automatons

---

[2] *Mémoires,* II, 334–35. This statement by Lafayette (*ca.* 1829) mentioned only "the court, the Orléanist party, and that which later took the name of Jacobin" and was silent on Mounier, apparently because the context called for a description of "intrigues" and Mounier did not appear to Lafayette to have been intriguing. See below, n. 11.

[3] *Révolutions de Paris,* No. 11, September 19–27, pp. 272–28.

[4] *Ibid.,* No. 12, September 26–October 4, pp. 2–5, 10–14. Cf. Bailly, III, 36, n. 2, and Paroy, p. 102.

[5] *Ami du peuple,* September 15, pp. 130–31.

[6] Bailly, II, 395–96; Lacroix, II, 69 and 76–77 (September 25), 100, 103–4, 105, and 106–7 (September 28); and *Ami du peuple,* September 30 and October 1 and 2, pp. 170, 183, 190–93.

under the orders of a chief" in whom "blind confidence is unpardonable and becomes a crime."[7]

These attacks were not directed specifically against the commandant general. Yet, recalling that the Compagnie de Lamour had only recently pledged unquestioning obedience to him, some journalists now expressed a lively concern lest the National Guard "become the Janissaries of a municipal Aga."[8] So there was no blinking the evidence that in the eyes of the more radical press the National Guard and the municipal authorities, because they seemed too closely allied with throne and altar, were losing some of their glamour. Even while the good will engendered by the flag benediction was fresh, touchy Guardsmen found themselves on occasion the butt of unfriendly remarks.[9]

How much of this criticism was the result of genuine political conviction and justifiable fear of counterrevolution and how much was deliberate demogoguery to promote the Orléanist cause Lafayette and Bailly could not tell, but they feared the worst.[10] Years later Lafayette recollected the critical situation at the beginning of October 1789 in curt sentences: "Three intrigues were going on at the same time: the court, the Orléanist party, and that which later took the name of Jacobin. The last two often acted together [i.e., toward the same end] rather than in concert. The Jacobins wanted to make themselves feared; the Orléanists kept under cover; the court helped them both by its mistakes."[11]

The discordant voices, however, were not yet dominant enough

---

[7] *Ami du peuple*, September 29, pp. 161–66.

[8] *Lettre à Monsieur le comte de B****, II, 102. See also *Chronique de Paris*, September 30, pp. 150–51, and above, n. 3. For the Campagnie de Lamour, see above, p. 274.

[9] E.g., *Révolutions de Paris*, No. 12, September 26–October 4, pp. 22–26, 32–33; *Ami du peuple*, September 28 and 29, pp. 154, 163–66; *Chronique de Paris*, September 29 and October 3 and 4, pp. 146, 163, 167; and [Desmoulins], *Discourse de la lanterne*, pp. 47–48 n. See also Bailly, II, 396–97, 400, 403–4, and below, n. 11.

[10] Bailly, II, 396–98, and *Mémoires*, II, 335.

[11] See above, n. 2. Lafayette meant here by *Jacobins* the followers of Barnave, Duport, and Lameth. He considered Marat and Danton Orléanists. Robespierre had not yet expressed any open opposition to Lafayette, although in 1792 he was to describe the Lafayette of 1789 as an ambitious, royalist, military intriguer: *Défenseur de la constitution* (ed. Laurent), No. 6, [*ca.* June 22, 1792], pp. 175–77.

to drown the swelling chorus of praise for Lafayette in official circles. The general esteem which he enjoyed was demonstrated when, as rarely happened, he failed to appear at his suite in the Hôtel de Ville on the day after the benediction of the flags. Immediately his colleagues worried about his health, and the Military Committee sent two of its members to his home to express their deep concern for one who "was so dear to all good citizens and so precious to the commonwealth." It turned out that he had only a slight indisposition, and he gave the deputation a most friendly reception. Thanking them for their good wishes, he promised to attend the committee's session the next morning.[12] When he appeared on the twenty-ninth, he was welcomed with "expressions of tender attachment," which he acknowledged "in terms most flattering to the committee."[13]

That day Lafayette and Adrienne made still another patriotic sacrifice. Necker had suggested that one way to stave off national bankruptcy which for months had lurked around the corner, was for patriots to make voluntary gifts to the government. The king himself set the pace by sending some of the royal plate to the mint; some leading members of this court followed suit; and then scores of devoted citizens, as individuals or as groups, made "patriotic gifts," ranging from little coins and shoe buckles to expensive gold ware. The Lafayettes sacrificed some of their silver plate, valued at 418 marcs (roughly about 22,500 contemporary livres), one of the largest donations.[14]

After his one day of respite Lafayette was quickly immersed in the routine of his office again—attending committee meetings, signing documents, deciding questions of military procedure, completing the roster of National Guard units, considering applications for commissions. Among the matters which continuing misfortune had made routine was the subsistence crisis—routine because all too familiar and not because of any regularity in handling it. The Representatives had enjoined the National Guard to see that all flour entering the city went directly to the flour market,

[12] *Procès-verbal du Comité militaire*, Part I, pp. 190–91 (September 28).

[13] *Ibid.*, p. 192 (September 29).

[14] *Journal de Paris, supplément*, October 20, p. iv.

but some of the districts had authorized local bakers to take flour from wagons at the gates or en route to the Halles, and whether so authorized or not, some bakers, and others, had raided flour shipments. Confusion and fights resulted, and soon Guard officers at the city gates and the markets appealed to the commandant general, who appealed to the Representatives, who in turn appealed to the districts. The Representatives sent out a circular begging the districts to quit giving orders contradicting their own, and they also instructed the commandant general to take the proper steps to prevent the seizing of flour on the way to market.[15] Furthermore, recognizing that looting of food shipments was a national problem, they sent a proclamation to all the towns in the Paris area enjoining stricter policing of local markets, and they petitioned the king and the National Assembly for prompt measures to assure the unhampered circulation of breadstuffs.[16]

In response to pressure from the districts, the Representatives also dismissed the old Committee on Subsistence and appointed a new one. That such acts were regarded as necessary added to the already accumulated misgivings. Almost daily protests in the Assembly of Representatives in the last days of September and the first days of October revealed that the people blamed speculating bankers and government officials for the misery they dreaded. The bakers blamed government officials and public disturbances, and government officials blamed speculators among the bankers and unknown villains who sought for selfish reasons to bring on insurrection by exploiting hunger.[17]

Lafayette's American friends hoped that the Committee on Subsistence might consider getting food supplies from the United States. Before Jefferson left Paris (armed with both a royal passport and a Paris passport, the latter endorsed by Lafayette),[18] he

---

[15] Lacroix, II, 109–11 and 114 (September 29), and Bailly, II, 398.

[16] Lacroix, II, 123–24 (September 30).

[17] See *ibid.*, pp. 57–152, *passim* (September 24–October 3); Bailly, II, 390–92, 398, 405–8; *Révolution de Paris*, No. 12, September 26–October 4, pp. 14–17, 28–29; *Ami du peuple*, October 2, pp. 191–93; *Patriote français*, October 3, p. 3; Clermont-Gallerande, I, 180; and *Mémoires*, II, 333–35.

[18] Facsimiles in Boyd, XV, facing p. 424. See also a description of them *ibid.*, pp. xxxiv–xxxxv.

had proposed to Montmorin and Necker a plan for importing salt meat from the United States,[19] and now that the excitement over the benediction of the flags at Notre Dame had died down, Lafayette himself gave major attention to the subject of food supply. One of the knowledgeable persons whom Lafayette asked to help was Ethis de Corny, who had served in the American War, was a member of the Society of the Cincinnati, and, more important, was the king's *procureur* (i.e., commissioner) in Paris.

Morris had already interested Corny in becoming a partner in a "Contract for supplying Flour to Paris,"[20] and Corny soon was "at Work on the Business."[21] Proceeding independently, Morris at last succeeded in getting enough of Lafayette's time for a long conversation on the subject. Having learned that other businessmen were interested in supplying Paris' needs, he warned Lafayette that he was becoming impatient and "in a few Days more" would "have Nothing to do with the Affair," because he suspected that the Committee on Subsistence was "casting about for Ways and Means to make Money out of the present Distress." When Lafayette suggested buying the much needed flour in England, Morris thought that importations from England could be better managed by some other man. After he left Lafayette, he called on Corny and found that his partner had received from Lafayette a proposal about food importations which both partners considered "perfectly ridiculous." They nevertheless continued the negotiations, though "tartly."[22] Meanwhile the food shortage in Paris remained unabated, and Morris' line of conduct could hardly have endeared him to Lafayette,[23] or vice versa.

On October 2 Morris again dropped in at the Lafayettes'—"to ask a Dinner," as he put it—and they talked about the by now inflammable political situation in Paris. In the course of another

[19] Jefferson to Necker, September 26, and to Jay, September 30, *ibid.,* pp. 481–83, 502.

[20] Morris diary, September 19, Davenport (ed.), I, 223.

[21] September 30, *ibid.,* p. 237.

[22] *Ibid.,* and see also *ibid.,* p. 238 (October 1).

[23] At least Lafayette later claimed that he "could not keep from smiling, along with all the people who knew him [Morris]" at his reputation for having the American virtues: Lafayette to Charles Coquerel, August 27, 1832, Indiana University Library, Ball Collection. See also Lafayette to Jared Sparks, May 10, 1832, Harvard University Library, Sparks Papers, XXXII, 109–10.

lengthy conversation Lafayette suggested that Morris confer with the new Committee on Subsistence "on Monday"—i.e., October 5—and, in order to give the conference "the Appearance of a diplomatic Affair," bring with him William Short, formerly Jefferson's secretary and now American chargé d'affaires. Morris considered this suggestion "not over wise," but he asked Lafayette to write to him and Short making the suggestion. "We shall see," Morris thought to himself, "how Feebleness will manage in arduous Circumstances," and aloud he told his host "the serious Truth" as he saw it—"that if the People of this Metropolis want, they will send their Leaders to the Devil at once and ask again their Bread and their Chains."[24] Morris later informed Short of this interview,[25] but the two men did not go "on Monday" to confer with the Committee on Subsistence, for the next Monday was October 5, and more imperious matters than Morris' contract were to rock Paris that day.

It was no secret that the former French Guards had never given up the idea of resuming their service at Versailles. Far from having evaporated with the "four words" Lafayette had addressed to them on September 18, within a week thereafter their "whim" had become a formal petition to their officers. Some of them at least sincerely regarded service at Versailles as the best way to shield a well-meaning king from his counterrevolutionary entourage, and a similar idea had spread among the rest of the National Guard and the people of Paris. Even before the impressive display of solidarity at the Cathedral of Notre Dame on September 27 Lafayette had received a letter from his battalion commanders indicating that they wished to get permission from the Assembly of Representatives to solicit for the Paris National Guard the honor of guarding the king. The old suspicion of a counterrevolutionary purpose behind such a move seemed hardly warranted in this instance, since unpaid as well as paid battalions requested it and since they expected to be allowed to proceed with not only the general's approval but also the commune's and the king's. Lafayette had submitted the battalion commander's letter to the Military Committee on September 25, but the committee, engrossed with

[24] Morris diary, October 2, Davenport (ed.), I, 238–39.
[25] *Ibid.*, October 4, pp. 240–41.

the complications attendant upon the forthcoming pageant, had postponed action upon it. While conceding that Paris' citizens generally sympathized with the battalion commanders, the committee cautioned that service in Versailles would be arduous, taking men away from their homes, and asked the commandant general to inquire more fully into the wishes of each individual battalion.[26]

Lafayette himself had already begun to wonder whether the National Assembly would not be "more tranquil" and the king "safer" if they came to Paris[27] than if they stayed in Versailles, where intrigue led to counterintrigue. The whole bitter debate over the veto power reopened with renewed intensity by Louis' continued refusal to sanction the National Assembly's decrees. He still held out on several hard-won decisions—on the series of August decrees intended to abolish certain privileges of nobles, clergy, and localities, on the Declaration of Rights, on the suspensive veto, and on the unicameral legislature. Grave popular resentment now seemed to loom from a growing conviction that he or his conservative advisers meant to use whatever power he retained for the purpose of obstructing constitutional reform. Even impartial observers could hardly fail to wonder whether the court was not intending to refuse to accept the suspensive veto itself and thus preserve the essence of the ancient absolutism.

Against that background Saint Priest's summoning of the Flanders Regiment seemed particularly suspect. To be sure, the regiment had taken the new loyalty oath, and it seemed ready to serve under the Versailles municipality and its commandant general, but was Estaing himself above suspicion? And if Louis already balked at accepting constitutional decrees, would he be any less balky with a thousand additional troops at the command of one who perhaps was his henchman? It required no great stretch of the imagination to envisage the more daring or more desperate at Versailles as contemplating a coup d'état supported by the Flanders Regiment, the King's Bodyguard, and loyal volunteer noblemen as well as, if the conspirators were clever and lucky enough, the Versailles National Guard.

[26] *Procès-verbal du Comité militaire*, Part I, p. 180 (September 25).

[27] *Mémoires*, II, 298, 349. See also Leclercq, p. 20.

Lafayette did not have to depend wholly on plausible surmises to gather that something not to his liking was going on at Versailles. Even if he had not wholly trusted his judgments from circumstantial evidence, he had some corroborating oral testimony. Lieutenant Morel came back to see him on September 30. The court conspiracy, Morel testified (though admittedly on hearsay evidence), was making headway; the king had not yet become involved directly, but the queen already was; so were Saint Priest and—what must have been hard for Lafayette to believe—Estaing; several generals and deputies of the National Assembly were also implicated, and they had procured arms.[28] Whether or not he believed his informant, Lafayette now provided him with a written but secret document authorizing him to look upon himself as an officer in the National Guard with the special assignment of spying out all he could about the alleged conspiracy.[29]

When Lafayette thus on his own authority appointed a secret intelligence officer for the National Guard, he was departing from his practice of naming officers only with the consent of the civil authority. That he was deliberately doing so seems to explain why the document states that he was acting as both "one of the representatives of the nation and a general of the army I have the honor to command."[30] He now had the beginnings of an independent, private intelligence system. About this time too he hired Coulon de Thévenot, who had devised a system of stenography, to sit in the National Assembly's meetings and provide him with full reports.[31]

[28] *Mémoires*, II, 330 n.

[29] This authorization was published in *Révolutions de Paris*, No. 31, February 6–14, 1790, pp. 34–35.

[30] See above, n. 29.

[31] *Chronique de Paris*, September 30, p. 51. These associations (Morel and Coulon) are the only basis we have found for a statement sometimes encountered—e.g., Anatole de Gallier, "Emeutiers de 1789," *Revue des questions historiques*," XXXIV (1883), 125; Alfred Bougeart, *Les Cordeliers* (Caen, 1891), p. 158; Manuel Lecoq, *La Conspiration du marquis de Favras, 1789–1790* (Paris, 1955), p. 15, and Ludovic Sciout, *Histoire de la Constitution civile de clergé (1790–1801)* (Paris, 1872), II, 438—that Lafayette as early as August 1789 inaugurated a spy system. He did in fact tap a considerable sum put at his disposal by the Comité des Recherches for intelligence purposes, but this fund seems not to have been used before October; see above, p. 258, n. 3.

With probably no better sources of information to go on, the more popular journalists had likewise been denouncing a royalist plot. When at the close of September the National Assembly chose as its president the (by Jefferson's analysis) "moderate royalist" Mounier—the very man who had led the fight for the absolute veto and the bicameral legislature—these journalists saw in the choice fresh evidence that the aristocrats had gained the upper hand in the National Assembly.[32] Mounier's election was all the more disturbing to the opponents of the veto because the conflict over that issue had by this time moved from political sparring into an earnest fight. The National Assembly once more had sent for the king's approval the decrees which it had so far adopted and he had refused to sanction, but by October 4 no reply was yet forthcoming from the palace. Whether Louis himself or only certain aristocrats around the throne were resisting the Revolution, Lafayette was beginning to believe the situation, bad though it was, was made to look worse because of the weakness of the royal ministers. Even Necker, the most popular among them, Lafayette had become persuaded, was "a terrible man for words but not deeds."[33]

With a recalcitrant king, a veto-advocating president of the National Assembly, and an overrated popular champion in the ministry, the Patriots had good reason to be concerned for the Revolution, and by the same token the court party had good reason to hope for victory. Much depended upon the citizens' army in Paris. Somewhere during these uncertain days Lafayette himself became a direct target of the court party's aim to pilot the Revolution into whatever channels it chose. No less a personage than the royal minister of foreign affairs, the Comte de Montmorin, came to see him. Though they had long known each other well, this was no ordinary friendly visit. Montmorin had consistently urged the royal family to have confidence in Lafayette, believing, or perhaps only professing to believe, that he was a loyal subject

---

[32] *Révolutions de Paris*, No. 12, September 26–October 4, 1789, pp. 26–27, and *Ami du peuple*, September 30, p. 172. See also Bailly, II, 397.

[33] Lafayette to unknown, [*post* September 18], *Mémoires*, II, 328.

ready to defend the king's position against the forces undermining it.[34] Montmorin now spoke to Lafayette about his fears of the Orléanists (who presumably were thinking of some sort of regency such as the present duke's great-grandfather had exercised in the minority of Louis XV). To counteract Orléans' supporters, would Lafayette consider some extraordinary rank? Perhaps that of "marshal of France" or "constable of France" (ancient and glorious titles which no one had held since the early seventeenth century)? Or even "lieutenant general of the realm" (a title implying exceptional powers such as at crucial emergencies in France's history had been given to a paladin designated by the king)?

Lafayette thought he detected in this flattering offer a gambit not only to offset Orléanist intrigue but also to buy him off and put him safely in the royalist camp, and he hastened to make his position clear. Such a post, he replied, would enhance neither his prestige nor his determination to defend the king against conspiracy. If, however, the court was concerned about plots from hidden quarters, he had a positive suggestion to offer: let His Majesty of his own accord come from Versailles to Paris, where the National Guard would make every effort to watch over his safety.[35]

Lafayette considered the matter ended there. He mentioned it only to his wife and a few friends,[36] repeating to at least one of them that he had no ambition beyond retiring to his Auvergne estate once France had secured a constitution.[37] But it did not end there. Mounier too came to see him, some time later, and raised the question of the constableship again, but Lafayette did not

[34] See Marie-Antoinette to Mercy, [July, 1789], Feuillet de Conches, *Louis XVI, Marie-Antoinette et Madame Elisabeth, lettres et documents inédits* (Paris, 1865), I, 230–31; Bertrand de Moleville, *Mémoires*, I, 93, and *Histoire*, II, 191–92, and IV, 327; and *Mémoires*, IV, 169–70.

[35] *Mémoires*, II, 297–98. See also Bouillé, *Mémoires*, pp. 124–25, and Saint Priest, "Abrégé," p. 305. For Mounier's perhaps contradictory testimony see below, n. 39.

[36] *Mémoires*, II, 298. See also below, n. 42. The so-called *Mémoires de Condorcet* (II, 83) put in Lafayette's mouth words which (except for an anachronism about going to Holland to make a revolution) correctly reflect his attitude.

[37] Bouillé, I, 124–25.

yield to pressure even from the president of the National Assembly,[38] though he gave Mounier to understand that he would never consent to making the king come to Paris by force.[39]

Morris, who shared with Bishop Talleyrand and the lady's husband the affections of the Comtesse de Flahaut, who seemed to know everyone worth knowing, possibly had wind of what was going on. At any rate, on one of his several visits to Lafayette to promote his food contract, while waiting, detained as usual, to see the general, he found that some of the members of Lafayette's military family "at least *wish* well to the Noblesse." After dinner on that occasion Morris urged Lafayette to share that wish. The commandant general, he contended, must "immediately discipline his troops and make himself obeyed" and must beware of depending upon the affection of a nation "used to be governed," lest he become "the dupe" of his own popularity. The party of the king was, according to Morris, "the only one which can predominate without Danger to the People," and Lafayette ought to "attach himself" to that party.[40]

At one point during the conversation (if such it was; from Morris' account it sounded more like a monologue) he thought Lafayette's expression changed. This was when Morris was criticizing the lack of discipline in the National Guard, and he attributed the change of expression to his host's feeling of guilt over having "given the Command to Officers who know Nothing of their Business." The conversation digressed, however, when Filippo Mazzei, Italo-American physician and diplomatic agent, joined the two men.[41] Even if Morris was ignorant of the court's brilliant offer to Lafayette, he could nevertheless have done very little more to persuade him to accept it. But Morris probably over-

---

[38] *Mémoires,* II, 298.

[39] Mounier in *Procédure au Châtelet,* III, 71, says: "On avoit eu projet de forcer le roi de se rendre à Paris . . . et plusieurs fois aussi M. de la Fayette . . . m'avoit déclaré, ainsi qu'à autres personnes, qu'il ne consentiroit jamais à cette mesure." We take this to mean not that Lafayette expressed opposition to the king's coming to Paris but to his being forced to come.

[40] Morris diary, October 2, Davenport (ed.), I, 238–39.

[41] *Ibid.,* p. 239.

estimated the weight of his words with Lafayette. Having confidence in his subordinates—experienced soldiers like Gouvion, Dumas, and La Colombe—and being contemporaneously censured by Loustalot and Marat because the National Guard was too thoroughly disciplined for a citizen army, its commander might well have had a different feeling from that which Morris divined, perhaps a mixture of indignation and amusement of the kind that a self-confident general might feel in reaction to conflicting civilian reproaches. In actuality, Lafayette privately looked with a certain sense of humor upon the secret but flattering proposals and public but gratuitous advice he was receiving on all sides.[42]

In addition to being Paris' leading police officer, the National Guard's leading candidate for *generalissimo,* and a coveted prize in the competitive bidding of France's rival political groups, Lafayette also played an active part, though *in absentia,* as a member of the National Assembly. He kept in touch with what went on at Versailles through official correspondence and the occasional deputations that went back and forth between the two cities, as well as through Coulon de Thévenot. One of the few projects before the National Assembly which he had himself initiated still hung fire—a new code of criminal procedure for the city's court. As the courts waited for the National Assembly to adopt a new criminal procedure, the problem of how to deal with the men detained for trial grew more acute. Bailly's warning that tampering with the existing system of punishing disorder would only make matters worse by stalling the wheels of justice[43] had proved all too true. Saint Huruge's friends, prominent among them being Danton's District of the Cordeliers, were becoming more and more clamorous for his release. One of their pamphlets was so vehement an

---

[42] Lafayette to [Mme de Simiane?], [*post* October 6], *Mémoires,* II, 414. This letter was obviously written after October 6 despite Lafayette's claim (*Mémoires,* II, 298) that, having told his wife and some friends about Montmorin's offer on "the very day" that it happened, he never spoke of it again until Bouillé (see above, n. 35) revealed it. It is also possible but less probable that this letter was written to Mme de Tessé, to whom (despite his claim never to have spoken of it again until a later date) he wrote in 1797 (*Mémoires,* IV, 406): "As you know, I refused to be royalized for a constable's sword."

[43] Bailly, II, 361–62, and see above, p. 248.

attack on Lafayette and Bailly that Saint Huruge himself hastened to disown it.[44] Besenval's friends were not equally clamorous, but his case called for more immediate attention because his keep consumed some of the limited funds available for maintaining Guardsmen on duty outside the city walls.

The National Assembly, trapped no less than Lafayette and the commune of Paris in the maelstrom of revolution, could give consistent and prolonged consideration to only a few of the problems which cried for attention. On September 29 it finally received a committee report on criminal procedure. The report, praising "the enlightenment of the capital and of the soldier-philosopher who commands its citizen militia" for initiating a movement to reform criminal procedure, proposed a program along the lines Lafayette had suggested, but it led to no immediate action. On September 30 Lafayette again raised with the Paris government the need for relief from the burden of guarding Besenval,[45] thus bringing on in Paris a renewed discussion of the general issue of reform of criminal procedure.

In view of the city's sullen mood, the Representatives felt that "the disastrous inaction of the judicial authority," "the enforced silence of justice," and the seeming "impunity for all offenses" had produced "a terrible situation which, if it lasted, would undoubtedly bring ruin to the capital." So once again the Representatives sent off a deputation to Versailles. It was instructed to neglect no measure to forestall "the imminent danger which threatens the capital if the guilty can much longer indulge in the belief of immunity."[46] On October 2 the Paris deputation presented its memoir on the subject at Versailles, and it was informed by President Mounier that the National Assembly expected to take up its own

---

[44] *Mémoire à consulter et consultation pour le marquis de St. Huruges* [sic] *contre les sieurs Bailly et La Fayette* (Paris, 1789). See also Victor Fournel, "Palais-royal sous la Révolution: Saint-Huruge," *Revue de la Révolution*, VI (1885), 336–37. For Saint Huruge's repudiation of this attack see *Chronique de Paris*, September 29, p. 147, and *L'Observateur*, September 27, p. 164. See also *Révolutions de Paris*, No. 12, September 26–October 4, p. 26, and *Patriote français*, September 20, p. 2, and October 1, p. 4.

[45] *Procès-verbal du Comité militaire*, Part I, pp. 194–95 (September 30), and Lacroix, II, 122 (September 30).

[46] Lacroix, II, 121–25 (September 30).

committee's report soon. In fact, a debate on that report began the next evening but only to be dropped because of the more importunate problem of food shortage.[47]

Thus at the beginning of October Paris was faced simultaneously with famine and with collapse of its ordinary system of justice. In the current climate of intrigue within intrigue no steadying force seemed available to preserve calm, and no one could be certain what was a generally acceptable system of court procedure. Meanwhile cauldrons bubbled. The royal family was collaborating with aristocrats, even if itself sometimes hesitant or pulling in divergent directions. The advocates of strong monarchy like Mounier were attempting to win cooperation from inflexible advocates of limited monarchy like Lafayette. Lafayette himself was still trying to preserve national unity by teaming together the two groups which Jefferson called "moderate royalists" and "Republicans," but they were finding it harder and harder to work smoothly in harness. The Orléans clique hoped that the harder the others tried, the sooner they would fail and its turn come. And incessant rumors of intrigue and conspiracy ran from newspaper to newspaper and from ear to ear in Paris stirred up by frightened or reckless journalists and district politicians, whether patriots or self-seekers. The dependability of the one potential military defender of order in a collapsing regime, the National Guard of Paris, was itself being severely undermined by its avowed desire to take up the duty of guarding the ambivalent king in Versailles—a point on which its civil superiors, the Military Committee, were hesitant. And who could be certain which side its commander, the Marquis de Lafayette, even if he was not venal, would take?

On October 1, in accordance with established military courtesy, the officers of the King's Bodyguard gave a banquet to welcome the officers of the Flanders Regiment to Versailles. It took place in the Salle de l'Opéra of the Château and was attended also by officers of other units stationed in Versailles, and by twenty men

---

[47] *AP*, IX, 213–19 (September 29), 239–40 and 339 (October 2), and Lacroix, II, 150–51 and 155–56 (October 3). For the earlier efforts to get action on the reform of criminal procedure, see above, pp. 248, 299–300.

selected from all ranks of the Versailles National Guard. It also attracted a number of onlookers. Toasts and vivas were offered to the king, the queen, and the royal family but none to the nation, and the omission could not easily be assumed to have been due to oversight.[48] The king, the queen, and their two children joined the banqueters for a short while, and their presence led to displays of elation, the orchestra playing some sentimental pieces, perhaps appropriate to the occasion but certainly conveying royalist overtones. When Louis and his family left, the banqueters joyfully gamboled under the king's balcony. A few, perhaps more convivial and certainly more boisterous than the rest, stayed longer and, nearing the queen's apartment, shouted: "Long live the king! Down with the Assembly!"

For the next few days demonstrations of good will toward the royal family recurred in Versailles. On October 2 the queen received a deputation from the Versailles National Guard that came to thank her for a gift of some flags she had presented to them. On October 3 the King's Bodyguard invited to dinner as its guests several scores of Versailles National Guards, and, on this occasion too, toasts were offered to the several members of the royal family, although this time also to the nation, the National Assembly, the National Guard, and other military corps. And on October 4 the Versailles municipality, with the National Guard acting as hosts, regaled the staff of the Flanders Regiment, toasting the nation as well as the king and the queen. That loyalty to Louis XVI and his family was conspicuous on all these occasions was beyond dispute; that at least some of the participants felt a kind of loyalty to Louis XVI and his family which was incompatible with loyalty to the National Assembly and the nation could easily be supposed; but that these demonstrations of loyalty were not spontaneous but were rather from the first carefully designed as part of a counterrevolutionary plot was then and still is a moot question. Many Parisians, however, were in no mood for such niceties.[49]

Lafayette himself promptly received a probably realistic account

[48] Estaing to Marie Antoinette, October 7, *AP*, XI, 390.

[49] See below, "Bibliographical Notes," p. 328.

of what had happened at Versailles,[50] but frightening or infuriating rumors arrived elsewhere, and as early as October 2 things again began to get out of hand in Paris. Journals and cafés gave wide publicity to a conviction that in the midst of widespread scarcity of food the officers of the King's Bodyguard had tendered to the Flanders Regiment an extravagant reception which the king and queen had perhaps arranged and had in any case attended, that some of the officers had exchanged their tricolor cockades for white ones, that some soldiers at the banquet had even put on a black cockade (black being the color of the Habsburgs, Marie Antoinette's family).

The reports grew more appalling on the following day. White cockades, they ran, were being distributed in Versailles and appeared often at court; the Flanders Regiment had gone over to the aristocracy; and inebriated Bodyguard officers had insulted officers of the National Guard of Versailles as well as the tricolor cockade. There was enough semblance of truth in all these reports to convince those ready to be convinced, and by October 3 many in Paris believed that the king and the queen had attended an orgy where the tricolor cockade had been trampled under foot! Could anything show more plainly than such outrages the court's intention to undo the Revolution?

Day after October day, amid want, unemployment, high prices, and complaints about court procedure, dark rumors of troop movements, of counterrevolutionary rallies, and of market speculation fed upon one another, causing anxiety and indignation to grow. On October 3 an attack upon the stores of the Ecole Militaire seemed imminent, and the Representatives sent a deputation to calm the unruly throng. The threat continuing, they asked the commandant general to deal with it, and before the danger of riot passed, the mayor, accompanied by another contingent of Representatives, had to put in an appearance.[51]

[50] Lafayette to Dumas, 10 germinal [1800 or 1801], Musée Calvet of Avignon. Lafayette says here that one of his aides, named Peyre, gave a report of the "fameux repas" at his house in Dumas' presence. The *Almanach royal* for 1790 lists no officer named Peyre on Lafayette's staff (pp. 427–32), but apparently at this time some temporary volunteer officers were not formally listed.

[51] Lacroix, II, 150–51 (October 3), 185–88 (October 6), 193–94, and *Chronique de Paris,* October 4, p. 167.

October 4 was a Sunday. As had become customary, Lafayette reviewed a National Guard division that day on the Champs-Élysées, where five thousand uniformed and armed men impressed some of the spectators as admirable representatives of a redoubtable army always ready to assure the triumph of the Revolution.[52] At the close of the review the men were ordered to report to their captains' quarters to receive the commander's approbation and to renew their pledge of loyalty.

As the review broke up, there came a foretaste of what some feared and others hoped. An indiscreet Guardsman had decided to wear both the colors of the Revolution and the colors of his queen—but he had put the black cockade above the tricolor one! Indignation led to altercation, and his company, drawing up in order before the commandant general, presented the case for his consideration. Stickler for law that he was, Lafayette could cite no regulation that would forbid a Guardsman to wear the queen's colors, but he insisted that a Guardsman owed his first loyalty to the nation and therefore must at least wear the tricolor cockade above the black one. The soldier changed his cockades around, and the episode seemed ended. Lafayette returned to the city hall.[53]

The orderly way, however, in which a company on review by its general had acted was no criterion of how an undisciplined mob might act if it encountered wearers of the black cockade. Arrived at the city hall, Lafayette went to the Assembly of Representatives to report the measures he had already taken to preserve order and to get explicit emergency instructions in the event of disturbance. The Representatives approved of his "prudence and wisdom," invited him to continue his "vigilant pains," and left to him the choice of the means to prevent disorderly encounters.[54]

Disorder was not long in coming. White cockades and black cockades appeared upon the streets, tempers rose, and the city seemed to be on the verge of riot. When the Assembly of Representatives met for its evening session on October 4, a deputation came

---

[52] *Annales patriotiques et littéraires,* October 6, p. 1, and *Chronique de Paris,* October 6, p. 175.

[53] *Chronique de Paris,* October 6, p. 175, and *Deux Amis de la Liberté,* III, 148.

[54] Lacroix, II, 160 (October 4).

from the District of Petit Saint Antoine to request a full investigation of "the confederation which seems to be forming" as evidenced by the reappearance at Versailles of the black cockade. The Assembly decided to send its own orders to the districts: paid companies were to remain under arms, and battalion commanders were to rally as large a number of patriotic citizens as possible, whether Guardsmen or others. The Representatives then decreed: "The cockade of the colors red, blue, and white is the only one citizens ought to wear," and it forbade any other, requiring the commandant general to enforce its decision.[55]

But misery, intrigue, and distrust could not be forbidden by decree or policed as easily as wearing of the black. Uneasiness probably would have remained even if there had been time enough to repress the display of royalist sympathies. Time had run out, however. Hardly had the Representatives decided to post their order forbidding other than tricolor cockades than a deputation from the District of Saint-Magloire entered the Grande Salle, requesting the commandant general to give the "superior orders" required by "the alarming circumstances."[56] No one among the Representatives could have assumed that other districts were less concerned. As a matter of fact, the District of Bonne Nouvelle had already sent deputies to consult with other districts on the reports about Versailles.[57] And the District of the Cordeliers adopted a long resolution which it circulated among the other districts, proposing that the commune instruct the commandant general to go ask the king to send the Flanders Regiment away and to permit "the citizens of Paris" to share with "their brothers of Versailles" in guarding the royal palace.[58]

Throughout that day, October 4, nervous gatherings at the Palais Royal had talked of bread and conspiracy, and of an advance upon Versailles to get the one and prevent the other. Some women

[55] *Ibid.*, pp. 160–61.

[56] *Ibid.*, pp. 161–62.

[57] *Ibid.*, p. 162.

[58] [V. M. Daline and Georges Lefebvre (eds.)], "Un inédit de Babeuf. Sa 'Correspondance de Londres' (1er–8 octobre 1789)," *AHRF*, XXX (1958), 42–44. See also *Deux Amis de la Liberté*, III, 149–50, and Mathiez, "Les journées des 5 et 6 octobre," *RH*, LXVIII (1898), 292.

vehemently announced their intention to go to Versailles in the morning and ask for bread, but the night passed without public violence. With the coming of daylight, however, things began to happen, and they happened so fast that Lafayette always believed that they were manipulated by unseen hands, and he blamed the Orléanists.[59]

Whether or not men with ulterior motives were operating secretly behind the scenes, the excitement of the preceding days ought to have impelled the responsible authorities to take extraordinary measures like those which recently had kept Saint Huruge from marching to Versailles and had contained the "whim" of the former French Guards. But only insufficient measures were taken—an astonishing lack of foresight, which led subsequently to suspicion that Lafayette, either to counteract royalist intrigue or to increase his own power (or both), had wanted a show of force by Paris against Versailles and so had deliberately remained inactive, letting mischief take what course it willed.[60] Such studied inaction, however, would have been a blatant contradiction of Lafayette's announced policy—to keep order in Paris and preserve the freedom of the National Assembly's discussions. Nor was it in keeping with his public character, whether sincere or posed, whether conscious or subconscious: double-dealing was not a method Washington would have used. When the outcome proved, however, that Lafayette had stumbled into an increase of power, that he had still more greatness thrust upon him, the suspicion arose retrospectively among the resentful, the envious, and the puzzled that he must have been both a clever conspirator and a subtle hypocrite who had cunningly planned it that way.

More likely, the failure to take wholly adequate police measures in face of a widespread and publicly proclaimed menace to peace and order was due to overconfidence. Lafayette was probably better informed than most others on what had actually happened at Versailles in those early days of October, and his information might

[59] Lafayette to unknown, [October 6], *Mémoires*, II, 411; Short to Jay, October 9, Boyd, XVI, 4, n. 2 (probably derived from Lafayette); Lafayette to Mounier, October 23, *Mémoires*, II, 416. See also *ibid.*, pp. 335, 357, 361–62, and III, 233–35.

[60] See below, "Bibliographical Notes," Chap. XIV, p. 350–51.

well have made him feel that, however outrageous the royalist demonstrations at the Château might appear, they were not a genuine threat to the Revolution and therefore called for no belligerent reaction in Paris. His very lack of proof of an Orléanist plot, while it did not diminish his suspicions of it,[61] probably made him underestimate the strength of its following. His unquestionable popularity (as well as Bailly's) must have led him to calculate that, regardless of how hungry or alarmed or misguided Parisians might get, few of them would hold the Hôtel de Ville responsible for their discontents. And if the discontented were to turn their wrath against the aristocrats at Versailles, his very success in handling insurgence on previous occasions would have reinforced his confidence, already expressed more than once, that he could control not only his uniformed men but also the civilian population. So, underestimating the impact of discontent, deprivation, resentment, and perhaps conspiracy upon the multitude, overestimating his ability to maintain order if it were gravely endangered, and possibly also not altogether averse to a non-violent demonstration in favor of extracting royal sanction of the sidetracked constitutional decrees, he took what events soon were to prove to have been too little precaution to meet the turmoil which came with the break of day on October 5. He apparently reinforced the ordinary patrol of the city-hall square with less than one battalion of the National Guard. Ermigny was left in command, and some Representatives stayed at the Hôtel de Ville all night.[62]

---

[61] Lafayette to Mounier, October 23, *Mémoires*, II, 416.

[62] Leclercq (p. 44, n. 6) accuses Lafayette of *incurie* and implies a serious dereliction of duty, and he cites three sources for this charge. Two of them, however, not only are hearsay witnesses (Ferrières, I, 285, and the continuator of Bailly's *Mémoires*, III, 84) but moreover their testimony does not support the charge. And the third (Thiébault, I, 240) indicates that while no extraordinary precautions were taken in time so far as he knew (but he was not at the city hall—he was a member of the National Guard battalion of the Feuillants), part of a district battalion was there to reinforce the regular guard when the Hôtel de Ville was attacked. Ferrières also mentions "a strong detachment of national militia posted upon the perron of the Hôtel de Ville," and the Bailly continuator speaks of "a dense battalion drawn up in a square in front of the Hôtel de Ville" at the first attack. Hence, so far as these witnesses have any validity at all, their testimony tends to show that Lafayette took some extra precautions, which only the outcome proved to be inadequate. For the Representatives who stayed overnight, see p. 329 and n. 1.

BIBLIOGRAPHICAL NOTES

The account given above of what happened at Versailles on October 1–4 depends in part upon studies by Leclercq (pp. 25–31) and Mathiez. Mathiez wrote his series of articles in *RH*, entitled "Etude critique sur . . . 5 et 6 octobre" (LXVII, 241–81; LXVIII, 258–94; LXIX, 41–66) in 1898–99. Convinced that there was a maniplated royalist plot, he argued that the tricolor cockade was in fact deliberately discarded if not actually trampled. Leclercq subsequently (1924) made an earnest effort to sift reality from rumor and came to the conclusion that what happened those days at Versailles was a spontaneous show of royalist feelings, and he maintained (pp. 28–29, n. 7) that a careful assay of the evidence did not justify a conclusion that the tricolor was trampled. For our purposes what was thought in Paris to have happened in Versailles is more important than what actually happened.

CHAPTER XIV

October 5

B
Y EIGHT O'CLOCK in the morning of October 5 groups of women had gathered in the Place de Grève, and soon they presented themselves at the door of the Hôtel de Ville demanding to see the mayor and the Representatives. They were apparently primarily concerned about bread. Since the mayor had not yet arrived and since the Representatives, except the few who had remained all night, were kept by threats or dissuasion from entering the city hall, the women waited. As they waited, someone rang the tocsin of alarm from the city-hall belfry, and more women, and some men armed with pikes and other impromptu weapons, came pouring into the Place de Grève. From about nine o'clock on, the square began to fill, and as the crowd swelled, fear of violence grew.

As long as women made up the majority of the crowd, the National Guard on duty made no serious effort to resist it. The women were boisterous but, for the most part, not destructive, and they even helped Ermigny keep marauders out of the city hall. But about 10 A.M. some of them denounced the tardy city officials as bad citizens who deserved to be lynched, "Bailly and Lafayette most of all,"[1] and indignantly set off for Versailles. Then some of the rest lost patience, became disorderly, and forced their way into the Hôtel de Ville by a back door. They began to pillage it, breaking into the jail and the safes, attempting to set fire to the building, and threatening bodily harm to several they encountered who had incurred their displeasure.[2]

[1] *Procédure au Châtelet*, I, 118–19 (testimony of Stanislas Maillard), and Lacroix, II, 165–66. See also *Révolutions de Paris*, No. 13, October 3–12, pp. 9–10.

[2] *Procédure au Châtelet*, I, 31, 58–59, 66–67, 71–72, 75, 78, 87, 117–18, and Lacroix, II, 165, 167. See also *Révolutions de Paris*, No. 13, October 3–12, pp. 9–10.

By that time the National Guard staff was on the alert. Gouvion, who meanwhile had taken command, called up reinforcements, while Ermigny with some mounted men barred the entrance to the Hôtel de Ville. Before noon adequate reinforcements arrived, temporarily reducing the crowd to a frustrated mass, which for the time being could do no more than shout.[3]

Lafayette did not arrive at the city hall from his home on the Rue de Bourbon until about 11 A.M. About nine o'clock he had first learned what was going on. Moreau de Saint-Méry, upon attempting to go to his post as president of the Assembly of Representatives, had been stopped by some National Guardsmen, who recognized him and advised him to go elsewhere. He immediately went to Lafayette's house, and he and another Representative were probably the first to inform the commandant general what was happening at the Hôtel de Ville.[4] The commandant general immediately determined to make no concessions to the demonstrators.[5] Leaving his home upon the first word of disorder, he made his way slowly through crowded streets and squares to the Hôtel de Ville. It apparently took him somewhere in the neighborhood of two hours to get through the gathering throngs, and when he arrived he found the crisis already seemingly passed and the interior of the city hall free of invaders.[6]

Shortly after his arrival, with Lafayette presiding, the few Representatives who had been at their posts all night or had succeeded in making their way through the square gathered in the meeting

[3] Lacroix, II, 168–69.

[4] Moreau de Saint-Méry, *Mémoire justificatif* (Paris, 1789), pp. 28–29n. See also Elicona, p. 62.

[5] *Mémoires* (II, 336) says that "from 9 A.M. to 4 P.M. he did not change his mind," but cf. *ibid.*, p. 337, and III, 235, where he speaks of resisting for "eight hours"—i.e., from 9 A.M. to 5 P.M.

[6] *Ibid.*, II, 335–36. Lafayette (p. 336) says that "vers onze heures" he was in the meeting room of the Police Committee, but in the minutes of the Representatives (Lacroix, II, 168) it is put "vers midi." See also below, nn. 7 and 9. It is indeed strange that no one testified to seeing Lafayette on the streets before he entered the Police Committee's room, but that lack of testimony does not seem sufficient reason for doubting his own statements on several different occasions that he was occupied with the outbreak from the moment that he heard of it, around 9 A.M.: see *Mémoires*, II, 336, 346, and III, 235; Lacroix, II, 169; and Short to Jefferson, October 8, Boyd, XV, 511 (probably derived from Lafayette).

room of the Police Committee.[7] Word came to them that some of the National Guard, under the leadership of Antoine-Joseph Santerre (a brewer of the Faubourg Saint Antoine, destined himself one day to be general of the National Guard), were acting in a high-handed fashion. They had gone to Bailly's home to persuade him not to go to the city hall and had offered him a place of safety in the country. Lafayette always believed that Santerre was "an instrument of the Orléanist faction."[8] Upon the advice of the Police Committee the assembled Representatives decided to send an armed escort to fetch Bailly, and Lafayette provided it.

While they waited for the mayor to come, the Representatives debated the causes and the probable consequences of the riot. Only about noon did they learn that a concourse of people "appeared to have" started out for Versailles—as in fact they had, two hours earlier—and they undertook to notify the National Assembly and the king's ministers of this alarming development. They designated a young Representative named Claude-Toussaint Fissour to carry this message to Versailles, and Lafayette proceeded to dictate a draft of it to him.[9] What he dictated was the first (and probably the most reliable) extant record of the day's events up to that time. The Representatives, it stated, knew of "no pretext for this outbreak other than the sudden agitation roused by the cockades of colors differing from those of the Hôtel de Ville," an agitation "which the fear of bread shortage had made more dangerous." Some people, the message warned, had found some arms at the city hall and seemed to be headed toward Versailles. But with characteristic self-confidence Lafayette continued: "Already M. le Commandant Général has restored order in the Hôtel de Ville [without mentioning Ermigny's or Gouvion's valiant services in his absence] and is engaged in restoring quiet in Paris,"

[7] As noted in n. 6, Lacroix, II, 168, puts this meeting "vers midi" and Mémoires, II, 336, puts it "vers onze heures," whereas a Representative (Poursin de Grandchamp) in Procédure au Châtelet, I, 87, puts it "vers une heure ou une heure et demi." On the testimony of Lacroix and Fissour (see below, n. 9) we think it took place about noon. Lafayette's statement came too many years after the event (ca. 1829) to be precise, and we find it easy to suppose that Poursin de Grandchamp, who had just escaped lynching, might have been confused.

[8] Mémoires, II, 336.

[9] Ibid.; Lacroix, II, 168–69; and Procédure au Châtelet, I, 75 (testimony of Fissour).

although the danger, he admitted, still seemed serious, for "it appears that the insurrection arises at the same time among people in different quarters," is "premeditated," and is "far from over."[10]

That the insurrection was "far from over" soon was manifest. Even before Fissour could start off toward Versailles, there came a loud knock on the door of the meeting room where Lafayette and a half-dozen or so Representatives had gathered. It came from a group of grenadiers, who firmly asked leave to talk to their commander, and he went to the door. Their spokesman was an articulate lieutenant named Mercier. In the course of a calm but animated conversation it came out that they represented all six companies of grenadiers, who trusted Lafayette but believed he was being duped. In their opinion, the people were hungry, the Committee on Subsistence was incompetent, and the National Guard would not fire "on women begging for bread." Moreover, Versailles, they were convinced, was in the hands of the National Guard's enemies, and so they intended to go there to "wipe out the Bodyguard and the Flanders Regiment, who had trampled on the national cockade." If the king was "too feeble to wear the crown," then he ought to lay it down and let his son reign in his stead.[11]

Lafayette thought he detected in all this the hand of a conspirator: someone must have put his men up to asking that the dauphin be made king—which, since the dauphin was a child of four, would mean a regency.[12] The grenadiers themselves used

[10] Lacroix, II, 169.

[11] The above account rests chiefly upon Fissour's affidavit, *Procédure au Châtelet*, I, 75. Other witnesses report other words, though of much the same tenor, but it is not clear whether they were reporting different parts of the same conversation or different versions of the same parts with varying degrees of accuracy: see *ibid.*, pp. 12, 18, 59–60, 72. Some of these statements are hearsay, but none of them is contradictory of the above account in an essential way. Lafayette was a first-hand witness, of course, and his *Mémoires* (II, 336–37) essentially support our account, but they were written forty years later.

[12] Lafayette forty years later had persuaded himself that when the grenadiers mentioned a regency, they naturally thought of him as regent. But his memory seems to have betrayed him—perhaps not because he wanted to be regent (his acts past and to come showed that he probably did not want to be) but because he would have been pleased if his men had thought that he should be. Since, however, on October 5, 1789, he was convinced that he was face to face with an Orléanist plot, it is highly unlikely that he could have imagined that the Orléanists were demanding him as sole regent and that his men were simply repeating that Orléanist demand. See *Mémoires*, II, 336–37. For the date of the writing of this passage, see *ibid.*, pp. 95, n. 1, and 329, n. 1.

the unfamiliar phrase "a council of regency," and that phrase in Lafayette' mind could mean only that they had been coached to parrot "expressions which seemed in their mouths only repetitions of what they might have heard."[13] Still, whether that phrase was parroted or spontaneous, whether they wanted Orléans or some other as regent, one thing was clear: the grenadiers now meant to go to Versailles with or without Lafayette's approval. And if they, the picked men in the force which he was counting upon to police violence and restore order, joined "the insurrection," who would police the police?

Lafayette tried to dissuade the grenadiers from their purpose this time as he had done before. For about an hour he expostulated with Mercier and his companions, and for an hour they persisted: they would give the last drop of their blood for him, but the people were unhappy.[14] Still hoping to win his grenadiers over, he went with Mercier and his companions down into the square to talk to the others. "His gentleness and his eloquence," his "admirable calm" did no good.[15] With Mercier still acting as spokesman, the grenadiers insisted that the source of the evil was at Versailles: "General, we must go to Versailles. All the people want us to."[16] When Lafayette asked whether they really meant to make war on the king, Mercier replied that they expected Louis, whom they loved, not to run away but to go along with them; yet if he did run away, "we have the dauphin."[17] As Lafayette continued to harangue them, he was interrupted again and again by cries of "To Versailles! To Versailles!"[18]

Since he had previously assumed that the grenadiers would

---

[13] This passage is from Lafayette's testimony given to the Châtelet on April 27, 1790: *Procédure au Châtelet*, II, 38. Jean-Louis Brousse-Desfaucherets, secretary of the commune, also said (*ibid.*, I, 59), but on hearsay evidence, that the grenadiers spoke of "a council of regency." Other hearsay evidence used the same phrase and none the word *regent* alone. Fernand Caussy, *Laclos, 1741–1803* (Paris, 1905) argues (pp. 118–20) that Abbé Fauchet as an Orléanist had that morning tried to compromise Lafayette by proposing him as regent, but Caussy is inexact and unconvincing.

[14] Affidavit of Bernard Peyrilhe, Representative, *Procédure au Châtelet*, I, 18.

[15] Affidavit of Paul-François Lourdet, Representative, *ibid.*, p. 174.

[16] Jean-Pierre Marquié, lieutenant of grenadiers, *ibid.*, p. 116.

[17] *Ibid.*

[18] *Ibid.*, pp. 59 (Brousse-Desfaucherets), 72 (Lourdet).

follow him under fire, Lafayette might well have been painfully astonished at their display of independent spirit. But, if .so, he covered up his astonishment, and perhaps believing that he had "mastered their boiling but still submissive impatience,"[19] he re-entered the Hôtel de Ville. There he gave final instructions to Fissour, who, thus delayed until two o'clock, started off for Versailles.[20]

By this time Lafayette had four separate though interrelated sources of disturbance to deal with. The first was that of the women, primarily moved by the scarcity of bread, who had set out for Versailles in the morning, their number becoming larger and larger as they moved toward Versailles. They took along a few cannon, and they were joined by some men, at least several of whom were thought to have been disguised as women. They committed some acts of cruelty and violence on their way, but they killed no one. The second source of disturbance was made up of small groups, some hostile and some perhaps merely curious, who at different times and from different points of the city had been going off separately to Versailles. The third was the steadily growing and increasingly menacing mass of haphazardly armed men who milled around the Place de Grève—some for one purpose and others for another, although Lafayette himself was most fearful of the Orléanist among them. The fourth was the grenadiers themselves who out of regimental pride, resentment of imagined or real insults to their new colors, and apprehension of danger to the popular cause wanted to resume responsibility, whether in Versailles or Paris, for the king's person.

About those who had already gone off in the morning Lafayette, having sent due notice to Versailles, preferred to do nothing or very little, apparently hoping that they would be kept in order by the forces available there.[21] About the small, separate groups he seemed to have only a vague idea and no serious concern. It was clearly his duty, however, as a police officer to prevent the third

---

[19] Lafayette to Hennings, January 15, 1799, *Mémoires,* III, 236.

[20] *Procédure au Châtelet,* I, 75–76 (Fissour).

[21] Thiébault, I, 240–41, says that his battalion received an order to block the passage to Versailles but that that order was apparently not city-wide.

group, a huge throng made up largely of politically motivated and angry men, with whom his grenadiers seemed ready to fraternize, from going to Versailles if he could. And if the grenadiers themselves went off without permission or order, they would be in mutiny and the whole military edifice which he had labored for nearly three months to erect would come tumbling down, crushing his reputation and his cause. At all costs he had to preserve some semblance of military decorum, and if he could do that, perhaps he and the National Guard could together, as on previous occasions, prevent a Paris mob from invading the precincts of king and National Assembly.

Having sent off Fissour, the harassed commandant general returned to the handful of Representatives in the meeting room of the Police Committee. The meeting, once again "in the presence of the Marquis de La Fayette," turned its attention to mitigating the causes of popular unrest. Even if (as Morris had implied) the city authorities had not fully appreciated before that vigorous measures were imperative to bring food into the hungry city, they appreciated it now. They instructed Lafayette (apparently assuming that he still had control of his men) to strengthen the guard at the city gates through which convoys of grain were expected and to send a special contingent to Mantes, where a detachment of still undisbanded Basoches was trying unsuccessfully to prevent the pillage of a shipment of flour, in order to reclaim and deliver as much of it as possible. He himself recommended that he be authorized to use "all the military means in his power" to promote the threshing, milling, and transportation of breadstuffs—whereupon the rump Assembly required his division chiefs to dispatch contingents to rural areas, specified for each of them, in order to buy wheat at a fixed price (subject to adjustment in cases of dispute) and have it milled and delivered to Paris as promptly as possible. Orders went immediately to the heads of the six divisions and the sixty battalions to send ten detachments of twenty men from each battalion (12,000 men in all) to hunt for wheat all over the neighboring countryside[22] (a striking precedent for the Paris Revolutionary Army of the Terror of 1793–94). Such measures, if

[22] Lacroix, II, 169–70.

taken earlier, might have prevented wide-scale disorder but now were too little too late.

The crowd in the Place de Grève had meanwhile become a teeming mass, still orderly but armed and excited. Many of the newcomers were National Guard units carrying their banners; many were unorganized men armed with pikes and other make-shift weapons, ready to join in whatever course the Guard took. Shouts of "Bread!" had now given way entirely to shouts of "On to Versailles!" As the afternoon wore on, they grew more frequent, more strident, and more ominous. It began to rain, a cold October rain.

All this while the contingent that Lafayette had sent to fetch the mayor was making its way back to the Hôtel de Ville, and it finally arrived escorting Bailly and some Representatives as well. Upon entering the Place de Grève Bailly and the Representatives with him appealed to the soldiers in the swarming square to remain calm, but the appeal had no apparent effect.[23] After the mayor entered the city hall, the Assembly went to its usual meeting place, the Grand Salle, and attempted to resume the business of the day.

But to no avail. The cries from the throng outside grew more and more clamorous, and Lafayette decided to try again to exert his influence, hoping that the measures just decreed to alleviate the bread shortage in Paris would make a favorable impression.[24] Taking some of his staff officers with him, he went out to the Place de Grève. For better effect he mounted his white horse and rode among the grenadiers. He reminded them of their oath and, professing his continued reliance upon their loyalty, pledged in return his own readiness to die in defense of liberty. Gallant words like these would once have brought loud cheers, but now they made small difference, and the crowd remained unappeased, shouting: "To Versailles! To Versailles!"[25] Rain, hunger, and mounting

---

[23] *Ibid.*, pp. 170–71; *Mémoires*, II, 336; and *Procédure au Châtelet*, I, 87 (Poursin de Grandchamp).

[24] Lacroix, II, 171.

[25] *Mémoires*, II, 336; Lacroix, II, 171; and affidavits of René-Remi Magin, National Guardsman, Thomas-Louis Bremont, National Guard captain, and Jean Lourdet de Santerre, Representative, *Procédure au Châtelet*, I, 23, 31, 74. The account of Lafayette's harangue rests on the testimony of Magin alone but seems corroborated by the circumstances and conforms with Lafayette's characteristic style.

fatigue, in fact, only made the shouts more sullen, and some of the more brazen men in the square became openly murderous. They aimed their guns at the general on the white horse and lowered the street lamps,[26] from which in recent months more than one victim of popular fury had dangled. At intervals one or another of Lafayette's aides rushed into the Grand Salle to warn the Representatives that his life was in danger.[27] One of the more conspicuous grenadiers demanded that the National Guard leave for Versailles under its own leaders if Lafayette would not go with them.[28]

Until four o'clock and beyond uniformed men pleaded, protested, threatened, and nearly came to blows and bloodshed, the grenadiers arguing that they must all go and Lafayette and his staff arguing that they must all stay. Nevertheless, the grenadiers did not leave, and Lafayette did not yield. But how much longer could open and perhaps bloody mutiny be staved off?

By that time, without Lafayette's realizing it perhaps, he no longer had actual control of the situation. Armed men had for hours stood herded behind the National Guard in the square and the adjoining streets. These men were constrained by no oath or military discipline, and by two o'clock some of them had already had enough of dallying in the rain. So the more angry, indignant, and desperate patriots as well as the more ill-intentioned politicos among them began their trudge to Versailles without the National Guard, trying to catch up with other groups that had already moved off from other parts of the city. Together they formed a poorly armed but large and terrifying band intent upon invading Versailles in search of bread and in defense of the Revolution. Their departure was not known inside the city hall, for the confusion and congestion in the Place de Grève interfered with communication.

Lafayette learned of this crucial development only sometime between four and five o'clock as, mounted amid his discontented men and steadfastly refusing to let them march, he was being

---

[26] *Mémoires,* II, 336. See also *Procédure au Châtelet,* I, 156 (which, however, is hearsay).

[27] *Procédure au Châtelet,* I, 68 (Blois).

[28] *Ibid.,* p. 23 (Magin).

menaced with mayhem.[29] Up to that moment he might perhaps have preferred to die at the hands of mutineers for upholding civic authority and military discipline rather than consent to their violation, as he saw it, of their oaths of loyalty to nation, king, law, and commune. But a frightening horde of men and women were now known for a certainty to be on their way to Versailles, perhaps to defend the Revolution but at the same time perhaps to endanger lives and property. Would it be wise to persist stubbornly in the attempt to keep the Paris National Guard from going to Versailles either to act as the king's bodyguard there or to bring him to Paris? Or was it better for their commander to go with them, thus certainly avoiding personal danger and perhaps also diminishing the destruction that a mutinous army might wreak? Was it his duty to die, if need be, while trying to uphold law and order rather than to yield gradually to his men's demands while trying to exert some restraint upon them?

If Lafayette had thought that he could no longer control his troops or that, even if he went along with them, they would foment rather than contain disorder, perhaps honor would have dictated death rather than submission. But he did not appear to think, despite eight hours of continuous turmoil, verging toward the end on mutiny and homicide, that any but a few of his own men were disloyal. Considerations like these finally won out, and he decided to ask the civil authority for formal approval that the Guard go to Versailles—for the very permission which until then he had himself refused to grant. Since he was practically a prisoner of his own army, he sent an aide to tell the Assembly of Representatives that it was no longer possible to resist the people's demands.[30]

[29] *Mémoires*, II, 337, 347, and III, 236; Comte de Ségur, *Mémoires ou souvenirs et anecdotes* (Paris, 1825–27), pp. 449–50; *Procédure au Châtelet*, I, 74 (Lourdet de Santerre); and Lacroix, II, 171.

[30] Lacroix, II, 171; Godard, p. 69; Ségur, III, 449–50; and *Mémoires*, III, 236. It has become part of the Lafayette legend that he himself went back into the Hôtel de Ville to get his orders. An aquatint of 1790 shows him "descending from the Hôtel de Ville with the orders to leave for Versailles"; see F. L. Bruel (ed.), *Un siècle d'histoire de France par l'estampe, 1770–1871. Collection de Vinck* (Paris, 1914), II, 437–38, No. 2966. In the University of Chicago Library, Rare Book Room, Lafayette Collection, there is a scrapbook (Vol. XIII) believed to have been assembled by Anastasie, Lafayette's oldest child, which contains some issues of a periodical called *Evénements*, each issue of which, long after the events, was made up to look like a newspaper reporting contempo-

Inside the city hall the Assembly of Representatives had been waiting. If Lafayette were sacrificed, they feared that no one could control the mob and soldiers, and then fighting between Parisians and whatever forces the court could muster probably would cause blood to flow on the road to Versailles and in the Château itself. Moreover, what had just been merely a fearful uncertainty was now known to be an actuality: despite Lafayette, desperate men and women were unmistakably on their way to Versailles in large enough numbers to constitute a serious menace. It was obviously the duty of the commune to keep this "large part of the people" in order, if possible, and to defend them, if necessary, and in any event to aid a neighboring city in distress.

If now the Paris commune with proper decorum were to instruct its National Guard to march to Versailles, everyone might still save face: the superiority of the civil authority to the military would seem to have received the proper deference; military discipline would appear to have been correctly observed; Lafayette would neither as an intimidated leader be obliged to follow his defiant men nor as a pitiful corpse be left dangling from a lamp post on the Place de Grève; and, what was more, order might yet be preserved. And so, professing confidence in the Paris National Guard's "zeal and loyalty" to prevent or to repress disorder and pointing to "the desire of the people" and "the representation made by the commandant general that it was impossible to refuse to comply with it," the Assembly passed a resolution which "authorized the commandant general and indeed ordered him to go to Versailles," taking the necessary precautions for the safety of the city he would leave behind.[31] The Representatives sent four of their own number along with the expedition, to betoken the civil authorization of the militia's advance and to make certain requests of the king, prominent among them being that he come to live in Paris.[32]

raneously a gala day of the Revolution. One of these issues is entitled "Evénement du 5 Octobre 1789." It speaks dramatically of Lafayette's demanding orders of the commune and returning to the square amid shouts of joy. No contemporary evidence supports this bit of histrionics.

[31] Lacroix, II, 171, and Godard, p. 70. See also *Procédure au Châtelet,* I, 68 (Blois).

[32] Lacroix, II, 171, which at this point does not specify the Representatives' demands, but see below, Chap. XV, p. 358.

A little before five o'clock Lafayette, still on horseback in the Place de Grève, received the instructions of the Assembly and at last gave the order to march. From the streets to the west of the city hall a semiarmed, uniformed host moved out first, preceding a military formation of four companies of grenadiers and fusiliers who acted as a vanguard, under the command of the Duc d'Aumont, lieutenant general in the royal army and the most experienced division commander of the Paris National Guard.[33] Somewhat later the rest of the National Guard available in the Place de Grève, flags flying and drums rolling, followed.[34] Those nearest Lafayette opened a passage for his mount, and with its commander as "the prisoner of his troops and the mob which followed them,"[35] the army of Paris started on its way. In a driving rain it marched to the Quai Pelletier (now part of the Quai de Gesvres), past the Pont Neuf, the Tuileries, and the Place de Louis XV, and on to the road to Versailles, greeted by loud shouts of approval from thousands of throats. Lafayette noted particularly a "group of elegantly dressed spectators" on the Tuileries terrace who joined in the cheers.[36] Seemingly in command of his men once more, he showed his pleasure, smiling at the cheering onlookers—in token of his readiness, the journalist Loustalot presumed, to follow the will of the people. Loustalot, as he watched the procession file by, inwardly mused: "March on, good citizens, you carry with you the destiny of France. . . . Save our king, save our deputies, uphold the national majesty."[37]

Since Gouvion went along with Lafayette as chief of staff, the

---

[33] Affidavit of Lecointre, Chabroud, *Rapport, pièces justificatives*, p. 23.

[34] See below, n. 37, and J.-G. Wille, *Mémoires et journaux*, ed. Georges Duplessis (Paris, 1857), II, 244.

[35] Short to Jay, October 9, Boyd, XVI, 4, n. 2. Short was probably not an eyewitness, but he most likely had learned from Lafayette among others about what happened. See also *Procédure au Châtelet*, I, 31 (Bremont).

[36] *Mémoires*, II, 337–38. For evidence of the rain see Wille, II, 224–25.

[37] *Révolutions de Paris*, No. 13, October 3–12, pp. 13–14. The account of Loustalot is not first-hand for what happened on the Place de Grève, although a number of contemporary and later accounts borrowed from it unconscionably. Loustalot was at the Place de Grève early but only briefly. He was, however, on the Quai Pelletier when the march to Versailles began. See his affidavit, *Procédure au Châtelet*, II, 56–57. See also *ibid.*, pp. 26–27, and *Mémoires*, II, 337–38.

Representatives put Jean Charton, commander of the First Division, in charge of the units of the National Guard which remained in Paris. They were so few as to raise some concern that they might not be adequate, even if willing, to cope with the city's restless population.[38] As the news of the grenadiers' departure spread, several National Guard units which had so far stayed in their district quarters decided to catch up with them.[39] In the end, by far the greater portion of the Paris Guard (together with their civilian cohort they were said to number 20,000 men)[40] chose to set off for Versailles. The motley civilians were, so far as possible, persuaded to keep in the center of Lafayette's line of march.

The hours of indecision had obviously passed, and once more a force of Paris activists was out to capture its king, this time not waiting for him to come of his own accord. Whatever the subterfuges, this was all but civil war. The demands of an amorphous mob or series of mobs earlier in the day had now become the formally proclaimed purposes of the city's official representatives, punctuated by the tramp of armed and determined thousands.

The Assembly of Representatives decided to remain in session until assured of tranquility in Paris and until informed of what was happening in Versailles. While it waited anxiously for news, others excitedly mulled over the more dramatic episodes of the day.[41] Morris, somewhat apprehensive but not at all astonished, learned that Lafayette had "marched by Compulsion, guarded by his own Troops who suspect and threaten him." He believed Lafayette to be in a "dreadful Situation," having been "obliged to do what he abhors or suffer an ignominious Death, with the Certainty that the Sacrifice of his Life will not prevent the Mischief." At supper that evening Morris agreed with his companions that

---

[38] Lacroix, II, 171–72. For the concern about order in Paris, see below, p. 367 and n. 52.

[39] Affidavits of several National Guard officers, *Procédure au Châtelet*, II, 129, 154, 184, and Thiébault, I, 241–42. Thiébault's much later testimony does not quite agree with that of his captain in *Procédure*, II, 154.

[40] Report of [Louis] Lefèvre and [Broussais] de la Grey to the Assembly of Representatives, October 5 [*sic*, for October 6], Lacroix, II, 183.

[41] Lacroix, II, 171; Morris diary, October 5, Davenport (ed.), I, 243–44; and Fernan Nuñez to Floridablanca, October 6, Mousset, p. 87.

"our Parisians will be beaten and we consider it as fortunate that they are gone." Returned home, he entered in his diary: "From this Day forward the french Army will return to its Sovereign," if the Flanders Regiment would, as expected, "do their Duty this Night."[42] Undoubtedly that entry reflected the thinking of some of the "elegantly dressed" who had not joined the crowd that had cheered Lafayette on the Tuileries terrace.

When he had started out, Lafayette no more than Morris knew what was actually going on in Versailles. What if the news of an armed invasion from Paris, which must have already reached the king, should induce him either to flee or, more likely, to resist? If resistance had already been decided upon, a royal force could be expected to try to hold the bridge across the Seine at Sèvres. Hence, when Lafayette's forces reached Auteuil, then a few miles outside of Paris, he sent on ahead two officers, one named Villars and the other Antoine Desperrières. They were to see if the bridge at Sèvres was defended by the king's troops, and if so they were to return. If the way lay open, however, they were to go on to Versailles and tell President Mounier and the royal ministers that the Paris Guards had no hostile purpose but were coming with the intention of maintaining order and respect for the king.[43] Such advance notice, at least implicitly, betokened the hope that the king's defenders would refrain from firing upon the Parisians who had gone ahead, for if they did, the former French Guards would feel honor-bound to engage them, and a bloody battle would be unavoidable. The two officers did not return but went on to deliver their message, and so Lafayette was led to assume that the bridge at Sèvres was unguarded.[44]

Versailles is almost twelve miles from Paris, a distance which

[42] Morris diary, October 5, Davenport (ed.), I, 243–44.

[43] *Mémoires*, II, 338; Saint Priest, II, 13–14, 86–87; *Procédure au Châtelet*, I, 76 (Fissour); Montlosier, I, 289; A. Lameth, I, 150; and Mounier, *Appel*, p. 162. For our spelling of Desperrières' name, see Maleissye (pp. 104–5), who knew him and thought "he possessed all the vices" but nevertheless believed a rather fantastic story he is alleged to have told to the effect that Lafayette himself instigated the uprising of October 5.

[44] Paine (Everyman ed.), p. 37, and Short to Jefferson, November 3, Boyd, XV, 531. Paine says (p. 37, n. 1) that he got his information directly from Lafayette, and so probably did Short.

normally took three or four hours to cover on foot. The rain stopped about eight o'clock, and the moon came out,[45] but mud and wind, the non-paid guards' inexperience, and Lafayette's deliberate caution made progress slow, and it took between six and seven hours to cover the distance that day.[46] The bridge across the Seine at Sèvres was approximately halfway between the two cities. Lafayette looked upon crossing the river as the decisive step —as he afterward called it, his "Rubicon." He stopped his army there for a brief spell, but once across he ordered his men to push on against whatever opposition they might encounter. They had advanced only briefly, however, when word came to him that he need fear little opposition, for the men of the Flanders Regiment (but not their officers) sent to request his orders, and he enjoined them to remain in their barracks.[47] With the Flanders Regiment thus neutralized, Lafayette's forces were not likely to encounter resistance before they reached Versailles, and possibly not even there. He immediately sent word to his anxious wife, and he asked her to inform others who might be interested, that the Flanders

---

[45] Affidavits of several witnesses, *Procédure au Châtelet*, I, 268, 156, and III, 25. This testimony about the weather at Versailles, presumably that between Paris and Versailles, did not vary markedly.

[46] This description of the difficulties of the march is derived largely from Thiébault, I, 244, but his battalion started out later than the main body and arrived later. See also above, n. 39. Camille Desmoulins in *Révolutions de France et de Brabant*, No. 47, [*ca.* October, 1790], p. 368, intimated that it took Lafayette, whom he dubbed "Fabius Cunctator," nine hours to cover the distance on his white horse, but he was obviously caricaturing.

[47] *Mémoires*, II, 338. The anonymous but apparently well-informed royalist author of *Les Forfaits du 6 octobre ou examen approfondi du Rapport de la procédure du Châtelet . . . par M. Charles Chabroud . . suivi d'un precis historique de la conduite des Gardes-du-corps* (Paris, 1790), II, 126–27, claimed that Orléanist money bought off the Flanders Regiment. So did the Marquis de Paroy; see his letter to his wife, October 6, in "Journées des 5 et 6 octobre 1789" *Revue de la Révolution: documents inédits*, I (1883), 2. But Lafayette stated that testimony to that effect had been proven false: see *Mémoires*, II, 349–50. The *Révolutions de Paris*, No. 13, October 3–12, p. 17, as well as the continuation of Bailly (III, 103), which depends upon it, says that Lafayette addressed his soldiers at Sèvres as they marched past and that the soldiers made him continue in a carriage to save him from the rain and fatigue, but the author of neither of these accounts appears to have been present, and no reliable eyewitness corroborates them. Claude Fournier l'Américain perhaps was present, and he speaks of a carriage in which he thought Lafayette was riding, but he was not allowed to make certain: see F.-A. Aulard (ed.), *Mémoires secrets de Fournier l'Américain* (Paris, 1890), pp. 30–31. Desmoulins (who perhaps was no eyewitness either) claimed that Lafayette rode his white horse: see above, n. 46.

Regiment had been won over and there was no longer any need to worry.[48]

Meanwhile, Versailles had been in confusion. At the opening of the session of the National Assembly that morning Mounier had announced the unwelcome but not unexpected reply of Louis XVI to the National Assembly's renewed request for sanction of the Declaration of Rights and the proposed articles of the constitution: he would consider acceptance only on certain conditions, chief of which was that full executive authority be left in his hands. Even as the National Assembly was considering its next step the first, unofficial reports of disorders in Paris arrived, and shortly thereafter (though probably not therefore) the National Assembly decided to demand of the king a sanction "pure and simple" of the Declaration and the constitutional articles.[49] The same kind of unofficial reports induced the court to summon Louis hastily to the Château from his daily chase. Estaing was put in charge of defending the Château and engaged most of the day, apparently quite ineffectually, in military preparations.

The women who had set out from Paris in the morning to seek bread reached Versailles about 3:30, after more than five hours of trudging. At first they were comparatively orderly, but as they were joined by hundreds of others, wet, cold, hungry, and resentful, their patience wore thin. Upon arrival, some of the wretched aggregation went to the Château, threatening its defenders, howling against the queen, and trying to force their way into the king's presence. Despite a good deal of provocation and shooting, only two horses were killed, their riders hurt, and only one officer of the King's Bodyguard was fatally wounded. Other Parisians swarmed into the Salle des Menus Plaisirs, clamoring for bread and for speed in the work of the National Assembly.

---

[48] That Lafayette notified Mme de Lafayette of the Flanders Regiment's submission is obvious from Lafayette to unknown, [October 6], *Mémoires,* II, 411, and see Chap. XV, n. 54. Clermont-Gallerande (II, 174–75) gives a text which he says is that of a note of Lafayette to Adrienne which came to him "by extraordinary chance." It seems authentic, but Clermont-Gallerande's argument that its reporting the submission provides convincing proof that Lafayette conspired to kidnap the king seems a non sequitur.

[49] *AP,* IX, 342–46.

These remonstrances retarded the business of the Assembly, but their relevance was all the more pointed because now, having heard the protests from Paris, the Assembly added to its request for the king's "pure and simple" sanction of its decrees a plea for help in provisioning Paris. A deputation headed by Mounier and surrounded by the women of Paris went off to the Château to present this petition.

The first official messenger to arrive in Versailles from the Paris commune was Representative Fissour. Though impeded and even unceremoniously halted by the marchers on the road, he was able after only a few hours' ride, to reach the Salle des Menus Plaisirs —about 5:30. He went to the Assembly first and then to the Château. By that time Mounier was engaged at the Château in trying to get a "pure and simple" sanction from Louis XVI. Encountering difficulty in both the Salle des Menus Plaisirs and at the Château in finding proper persons to entrust with his message, Fissour was able to hand his message to Necker and thereby complete his mission only a considerable time later. On his way out of the Château he met Desperrières (and presumably Villars too) whom Lafayette had sent from Auteuil well after five o'clock.[50]

For hours the king and his advisers had been wavering on what to do. As usual, the royal retinue was divided, Saint Priest suggesting either resistance or flight, Necker opposing both, and the king unable to make up his mind. So only confused and self-defeating measures had been taken to put the Château in a state of defense, leading to the needless exposure of the King's Bodyguard to the attack, still mostly verbal, of the Parisians. The messages which Desperrières and Villars brought from Lafayette (somewhere between nine and ten o'clock), though intended to allay Versailles' fears, only confirmed its most cynical suspicions: Paris this time was on the offensive not in improvised and amorphous groups but in disciplined and well-armed array.[51] Saint Priest, dreading

[50] *Procedure au Châelet,* I, 76 (Fissour), See also the affidavit of Noel-Joseph-Madier Demontjau, deputy in the National Assembly, *ibid.,* p. 268.

[51] Desperrières' message is probably the one of which Felix Faydel, secretary of the National Assembly in 1789, speaks in a letter of 1814, quoted in Baron de Maricourt, *En Marge de notre histoire* (Paris, 1905), p. 166. If so, Faydel's belated account of it contains some excusable, not important inaccuracies. It may, however, be evidence of a third message.

the worst, renewed the suggestion that the king flee, and carriages were actually ordered to be ready to take the royal family to Rambouillet. But in the end Louis decided that he simply could not permit himself to become a fugitive king, and so he stayed.[52]

All this time Mounier had been waiting in the Château with the delegation of the National Assembly for the king's "pure and simple" approval, and he was there when Desperrières arrived. With the King's Bodyguard already under desultory fire and with a veritable army advancing from Paris, further resistance would obviously be ill advised, and so Louis gave his unconditional sanction to the waiting president of the National Assembly. The revolutionary element of Paris thus scored a major victory even before Lafayette's arrival. Mounier was outraged by the threat of armed force against the king's veto, and he was ready to raise the question whether the National Assembly ought not to denounce the Paris militia for having usurped "the right to come to Versailles, with weapons in hand, to dictate the law to the king."[53] But when he returned to the Salle des Menus Plaisirs, he found the Assembly disorganized by the roisterers from Paris, and when he got the meeting going again, he was content to announce the king's "pure and simple" acceptance of the Assembly's decrees.

Aumont's vanguard arrived in Versailles about ten o'clock.[54] The king had ordered his Bodyguard not to fire, and so, having formally challenged Aumont's advance, it retired without resistance to posts within the Château gates. While waiting for the main body to come up, Aumont posted his men outside the Château in the huge square known as the Place d'Armes, into which the main avenues of the town lead. There, from Lieutenant Colonel Lecointre and another Versailles National Guard officer

[52] Saint Priest, II, 10–17; Mounier, "Exposé," AP, IX, 575–76, and Appel, p. 162; and Maleissye, p. 114.

[53] Mounier, "Exposé," AP, IX, 575–76. Mallet du Pan's statement that Mounier immediately urged Necker to go with the other ministers to the Assembly and denounce Lafayette as a traitor is based upon his delayed recollection of a conversation long after October 5 with Mounier: Mallet du Pan, Mémoires et correspondance, ed. A. Sayous (Paris, 1851), I, 182 n. It has no corroboration, however, in contemporary evidence.

[54] AP, IX, 348.

who accompanied him, Aumont received assurance of their co-operation.[55]

About an hour later Lafayette's command neared Montreuil,[56] now a faubourg of Versailles, then a village at the eastern end of its Avenue de Saint Cloud. Here he halted his army, and reminding them that they had sworn, among other things, "loyalty to the king despite cabals,"[57] he administered to them in addition "a pledge to respect His Majesty's residence."[58] If any of the soldiers who but a few hours earlier had been defiant now objected to taking that pledge, none of the many witnesses who subsequently testified to these events recorded his objection. Meanwhile, the same officers of the Versailles National Guard who had promised Aumont cooperation, learning of Lafayette's arrival, rode to Montreuil to put themselves at his disposal—only to find the Comte de Gouvernet, son of the minister of war and second in command of their unit, had anticipated them. Lafayette ordered Lecointre to instruct his men to receive their Paris comrades "with distinction."[59] Everything concurred to make plain that the Paris militia could count upon the Versailles militia as allies rather than as foes.

Between ten and eleven o'clock the remonstrants at the Salle des Menus Plaisirs along with the deputies who were still at their places had taken a respite to find something to eat. During that

[55] Chabroud, *Rapport, piéces justificatives*, pp. 22–23 (Lecointre), and *AP*, XIX, 375.

[56] Lacroix, II, 182.

[57] Lafayette to unknown, [October 6], *Mémoires*, II, 411.

[58] Lefèvre and De la Grey to the Representatives, [October 6], Lacroix, II, 182. Lafayette's affidavit (*Procédure au Châtelet*, II, 37) and also his *Mémoires* (II, 339) described the oath as "to the nation, the law and the king." Short, who probably got his information from Lafayette, described it in a letter to Jay, October 9 (Boyd, XVI, 4 n.) as "to the National Assembly and to the King." We think, however, that in a formal report two official witnesses to a governmental body within a day of the events reported were not likely to invent an unusual wording for an oath, whereas Short in an informal letter after several days' interval and Lafayette in testimony given (in one case) several months and (in the other) several decades later were more likely to let slip a wording which even at the earlier dates was already a cliché (though probably not yet with "the king" in the last place). Whatever the wording, however, the intent of the oath is clear: it reminded the Guards of their duty to preserve property and order. Ferrières, p. 318, n. 1, says that the oath was taken at Viroflay, but he was not a first-hand witness.

[59] See above, n. 55.

hour a Paris National Guard officer came to announce to Mounier that Lafayette would soon arrive and would wait upon the National Assembly. Mounier sent back word of the king's unconditional acceptance of the National Assembly's decrees, obviously intending that the Paris army should know of the royal compliance and presumably be somewhat mollified.[60] About the same time Louis himself took the same precaution, sending an officer to state that His Majesty was glad to know that Lafayette was coming and had accepted *"his* [Lafayette's] declaration of rights."[61] Lafayette relayed to the anxious commune the news of this friendly message by a second messenger, an officer who had promised the Paris Representatives to catch up with him and bring back a report on how things were going. The officer reached Paris with his heartening tidings only at 3 A.M. Much relieved, the Representatives saw in the king's concession a token that "the course which the citizens of Paris had taken would have a fortunate outcome."[62] Once more Louis XVI and the people of Paris seemed to be allies against a common enemy, the counterrevolutionaries.

Meanwhile, with confidence in his men restored, Lafayette had advanced from Montreuil. The civilians with pikes, knives, and other impromptu weapons, who at times had scattered all over the line of march, had been persuaded to fall back again so that the grenadiers and fusiliers could take the lead. Lafayette's army had so far advanced only slowly—so slowly that hostile observers believed he was marking time in order to permit an opportune crisis to develop in Versailles.[63] Actually, insofar as the delay was not due to rain, mud, darkness, and the inexperience of his men, its purpose seems to have been less contrived. It gave the battalions which had made a late start a chance to catch up with him, and it provided simple military precautions against the

---

[60] Mounier, "Exposé," *AP*, IX, 576, and *Appel*, p. 163.

[61] *Mémoires*, II, 331. The underlining is probably Lafayette's rather than the king's. Leclercq (p. 102, n. 5) thinks that "this assertion [of the *Mémoires*] is devoid of all truth," but see the Marquis de Vergennes to M. de Bellejeant, October 6, Vaissière, p. 96, and also below, n. 62.

[62] Lacroix, II, 173, 174, and Godard, p. 71.

[63] Ernest Daudet (ed.), *Mémoires du Cte Valentin Esterhazy* (Paris, 1905), pp. 252, 253, 258. See also "Bibliographical Notes," pp. 350–51, below.

possibility of attack, which until the submission of the Flanders Regiment and the Versailles National Guard Lafayette had with some reason apprehended.[64] Now that effective resistance had evaporated, he moved as fast as he could. Even so, it took his enormous force marching six abreast at double time a full hour to pass a watching deputy's house.[65] Another deputy, worn out by the day's trials, upon hearing drums and learning that Lafayette was at the head of the soldiers who were parading through Montreuil, felt assured that order would now prevail.[66]

When the army of Parisians began to move out of Montreuil, it had only a short distance left to go. It tramped down the Avenue de Paris by torchlight and moonlight, impressing onlookers with its train of artillery, its good order, and, except for the rolling drums, its silence.[67] It was prepared to meet attack if attack should come, but it expected no serious opposition, and it encountered none. As the Paris force moved up, some shots rang out—fired, Lafayette supposed, by persons intending to provoke an uneven contest—but they were ignored.[68] When it had drawn close to the Hôtel des Menus Plaisirs, it halted. Satisfied at last that there would be no battle, Lafayette left his men in the charge of his senior officers and, accompanied by two of the Paris Representatives, Broussais de la Grey and Louis Lefèvre, went to pay his respects to the National Assembly.[69] It was almost midnight now.

BIBLIOGRAPHICAL NOTES

A great deal of the confusion in the secondary accounts of Lafayette's activity on October 5 arises from the failure of some historians to distinguish between evidence and inference, between direct and hearsay evidence, and between good and bad direct evidence. Some historians have accepted as good

[64] Lafayette to unknown, [October 6], *Mémoires*, II, 411.

[65] Gaultier to his constituents, October 6, Mège, *Gaultier*, II, 283.

[66] *Procédure au Châtelet*, I, 169 (Malouet).

[67] Depositions of eyewitnesses, *ibid.*, p. 233, and II, 141, 209, and III, 53, and Montlosier, I, 293. One witness (*Procédure au Châtelet*, II, 21) testified that he heard drums coming by two avenues, that of Saint Cloud and that of Paris, but he was perhaps referring to the separate advance of the vanguard and of the main body. No other direct witness indicates that Lafayette's main body was divided into two lines of march.

[68] *Mémoires*, II, 338-39.

[69] *Procédure au Châtelet*, II, 39 (Lafayette), and III, 73 (Mounier), and Lacroix, II, 678.

evidence, whenever it fitted into some preconceived notion, the accounts of newspapers (which at that time notoriously copied from, if indeed they did not embroider upon, each other, frequently regardless of whether what they copied was reliable) and memoirs of contemporaries (whether or not speaking about events actually witnessed and whether or not suffering from *lapsus memoriae*). Largely as a result of this exploitation of evidence to bolster preconceived notions, the descriptions of the role of Lafayette on October 5 conveniently fall into three classes: (1) those who make him out to have been an impeccable paladin, (2) those who think he was a fool, and (3) those who think he was a knave.

The major source of the paladin school is Lafayette's own *Mémoires*. They at least have the advantage that Lafayette was a first-hand witness of his activities and was usually able and willing to tell the truth. While the accounts in his *Mémoires* of his role on October 5 were written years after the events they record, the *Mémoires* also give letters written by him close to the events, and in a number of instances his later recollections, inexact and self-centered though they sometimes were, are borne out by his earlier testimony at the Châtelet investigation and by other first-hand testimony. We have tried to accept none of his recollections which does not have good corroboration, direct or circumstantial. In general, we have carefully excluded hearsay evidence except as supplementary to direct evidence, and we have limited inference to *what must have happened* rather than *what may have happened*.

The major sources of the fool school are a number of contemporary journalists, pamphleteers, and memoirists who gave rise to the cliché regarding Lafayette and his army that "he was their leader, so he followed them." This attitude was perhaps most pointedly portrayed in a contemporary caricature entitled "Depart du général parisien pour la fameuse nuit du 5 au 6 octobre," showing a well-caparisoned horse with a human head unmistakably resembling that of Lafayette being led from the Hôtel de Ville by a crowd with improvised weapons, the head saying, "My friends, take me, please, to Versailles to sleep." Charavay (p. 189) gives a reproduction of this caricature. See also Hippolyte A. Taine's *French Revolution*, trans. John Durand (New York, 1885–97), I, 102–3: "Being their chief it is pretty plain that he must follow them." Taine here, as in general, has presented a cynical view of the French Revolution.

The knave school divides into two parts. One of them portrays Lafayette as working with some other conspirator like Orléans; see, for example, M de Lescure (ed.), *Mémoires de M. le baron de Goguelat sur l'émigration (1791–1800)* (Paris, 1877). The other portrays him as, for different reasons—jealousy of Estaing (Rivarol, pp. 255–56) or desire to make the king his prisoner (among others Maleissye, pp. 103–5; Elliot, pp. 38–39; and Thiébault, pp. 249–50)—instigating the near mutiny on the Place de Grève. See also below, Chap. XV, n. 12. The knave thesis rests almost entirely on hindsight inferences by memoir writers. Heinrich von Sybel gave it currency in Germany (see his *History of the French Revolution*, trans. W. C. Perry [London, 1867–69], I, 122–32), and it was presented at length in Wilhelm Güthling, *Lafayette und die Überführung Ludwigs XVI von Versailles nach Paris* (Halle, 1930). Nevertheless, thousands were direct witnesses of Lafayette's behavior on October 5, and the testimony of scores of them are available in the *Procédure au Châtelet* and elsewhere. Fournier l'Américain (not an unbiased witness) was the only one we have found among them who claims to have directly witnessed anything but more or less fitting and honorable behavior on Lafayette's part on that occasion; the attribution of ulterior motives to him rests otherwise on restrospective hearsay or inference.

Ségur's *Mémoires* give what appears to be a thoroughly plausible account of a conversation in November 1789 with Lafayette about the events of October 5 and 6.

There is a good deal of disagreement among witnesses on the exact time at which certain events occurred. Therefore we have usually indicated approximate times. We think that the sequence of events, which is more important than their exact timings, is correct as given above.

The *Procédure au Châtelet* contains nearly four hundred *dépositions* (a word which corresponds more to the word *affidavits* than *depositions* in American usage). Each *déposition* (except those taken in a distant city and published at the end of Part III) is numbered in Roman numerals and is often cited by its Roman numeral, but as some *dépositions* run to several pages and as Roman numerals in the 300's sometimes require as many as eleven capital letters, we have preferred to use the volume and page numbers. Even though the volumes are not numbered, each of the last two volumes being entitled *Suite de la Procédure criminelle instruite au Châtelet de Paris*, their sequence is easily determined by the successive numbering of the *dépositions.* tions.

Maurois (p. 211) thinks the letter of Lafayette dated *ce mardi* [October 6] in *Mémoires*, II, 411, is to Mme de Simiane. We think it somewhat unlikely that even if that lady were in Paris rather than Versailles on October 5–6, Lafayette would have expected his wife (as the letter indicates he did) to keep her informed of his movements. It seems more likely that the letter was to someone at the Hôtel de Ville—perhaps Bailly or Moreau de Saint-Méry, who was by this time a personal friend as well as a high municipal official: see Elicona, pp. 45, n. 1, and 69–70.

CHAPTER XV

October 6

BY THE TIME Lafayette left the main body of his troops on the Avenue de Paris he must have fully recovered his self-confidence, if indeed he had ever lost it. He had come to Versailles under legal cover, on the orders of the Paris commune. He had reassured himself of his men's discipline and of their sense of responsibility for order. He had ascertained that no resistance would be encountered from the king's forces or from the Versailles National Guard. The president of the National Assembly had seemed, if only by implication, not to object that he had come to Versailles with his army, and the king had explicitly expressed his pleasure. The Declaration of Rights and the National Assembly's other constitutional decrees now had a pure and simple royal sanction. Some Parisians, notably a party from among the first women who had come seeking bread, had already gone home, satisfied with a small supply sent by the king and the promise of royal solicitude about their food problems. If indignities had been suffered and a Bodyguard officer fatally wounded, no one had yet been killed, and the prospect of a bloody clash seemed far more remote than it had that afternoon.

Nevertheless all was not serene. The former French Guard still wanted to regain its posts in Versailles, and the demand for more bread for Paris remained essentially unanswered. An angry multitude, made no more docile by fatigue, hunger, and the prospect of a hard night in improvised lodgings at Versailles, still nursed their grievances against the queen, the aristocrats, the King's Bodyguard, the Flanders Regiment, and the wearers of white or black cockades.

Hence Lafayette still had to contend with a tense and delicate situation. It would require tact combined with force, cajolery combined with strength, to bring the antagonists together without a fight—attackers with defenders of the Château, National Guard with King's Bodyguard, populace with aristocrats and court. The decisions were now Lafayette's to make, and he was in a peculiarly strategic position to make them. As a court aristocrat but a liberal leader, as a general in the royal army but a member of the National Assembly, as a popularly elected official of the city of Paris but the one responsible for the preservation of order in that city, as commander of a citizens' army but an army of which the paid companies were veterans from the army of the Old Regime he had firm ground from which to exert authority, perhaps even to expect to inspire confidence, on all sides.

When Lafayette dismounted and entered the hall of the National Assembly a little before midnight of October 5, the Salle des Menus Plaisirs was still overrun by men and women from Paris. Mounier, upon returning from his mission to the king, had sent out a call to the deputies to resume their places, and they were coming in. A handful of them, clustered around their presiding officer, were valiantly trying to maintain the dignity of the nation's representative body. Lafayette entered the chamber alone. Although he had not attended the National Assembly since July 15, he was still a member, and he had every right to be there.

Mounier, genuinely displeased that soldiery had come with a show of force, probably had not ceased to worry about its intentions, but Lafayette promptly made his position clear. The army of Paris had no belligerent purpose, he declared; it had sworn allegiance to the king and the National Assembly, and it had promised to permit no violence.[1] He indicated that the imminence of famine and the resentment over the Bodyguard's royalist banquet had provided "the factious" with an inflamed following. They had distributed a huge amount of money, he claimed, and he had

---

[1] Mounier, "Exposé," *AP*, IX, 576. Mounier says here and in *Procédure au Châtelet* (III, 74) that Lafayette claimed to have administered the oath to his troops *plusieurs fois*, but we have found credible evidence of only one time on this march. Lafayette might, of course, have been referring to oaths administered on previous dates as well as on this one when talking to Mounier. See also Mounier, *Appel*, pp. 165–66, and *Procédure au Châtelet*, II, 37 (Lafayette).

been caught off guard by the resulting demand, especially among his own paid troops, for an advance upon Versailles.[2]

If Lafayette and his army were peacefully inclined, Mounier then wanted to know, what did they really want? Lafayette answered that whatever his men's motives had been on starting out, they now meant to impose no law; to calm the public indignation, however, it might be wise of the king to send away the Flanders Regiment, to allow the former French Guard to resume its service as part of the royal bodyguard, and to say a few words publicly in favor of the national cockade.[3]

With these pacifying remarks, Lafayette left with the two Paris Representatives, Lefèvre and De la Grey, to go see the king. Outside the Salle des Menus Plaisirs his staff joined him, and they rode together to the Place d'Armes. Aumont's van was still there, the main body and the rest of the Paris National Guard stretching along the Avenue de Paris all the way back to the Hôtel des Menus Plaisirs, with latecomers steadily arriving and as they arrived, being required to renew their loyalty oath.[4] From the Place d'Armes, Lafayette proceeded on foot toward the outer court of the Château, the Cour des Ministres. When the grenadiers near the Château saw their commandant's party head toward what well might prove to be an enemy trap, several of them, without orders, left their places to share his danger. Staff, grenadiers, Representatives, and Lafayette presented themselves at the locked gate to the Cour des Ministres and asked to be admitted. The officers in charge of the King's Bodyguard at that point sent to His Majesty for instructions, and a delay ensued.

Inside the Château the king, surrounded by a throng of courtiers, was expecting Lafayette to make his entrance at any moment. When it was known that Aumont's vanguard had arrived, Louis had requested Mounier to bring to the palace as many dep-

---

[2] *Procédure au Châtelet*, III, 74 (Mounier). In his earliest extant account ("Exposé," *AP*, IX, 576) Mounier dropped his testimony on this point to a footnote and gave as his source not Lafayette but "quelq'un d'une très haute considération," but in his affidavit for the Châtelet and in his *Appel* (see above, n. 1) he named Lafayette as the source.

[3] In his "Exposé" (*AP*, IX, 576) Mounier did not mention the demand concerning the former French Guard, but he did so in *Procédure au Châtelet*, III, 74, and *Appel*, p. 166, n. 1.

[4] *Procédure au Châtelet*, I, 97 (Ambroise Guerin, Paris National Guard).

uties of the National Assembly as would come, in order that they might together face a general whose intentions were still unclear and might be belligerent, but the deputies had not yet reached the Château. Among the king's retinue clustered in the large waiting room known as the Oeil-de-Boeuf were Gouvernet, who had gone to the Château apparently while Lafayette was at the National Assembly, and Mathieu Dumas. Dumas was now acting as director-general in the Ministry of War under Latour du Pin, who was Gouvernet's father, but he was also an officer in the Paris National Guard and was wearing its uniform. When the king gave the order to admit Lafayette, they went down to the gate to meet him.[5] Better messengers could hardly have been chosen, for, being intimately associated with the court, the royal ministry, the army of the Old Regime, and the new citizens' armies, they symbolized a possible union of the forces which but a short while earlier had been at swords' points.

The grenadiers were still reluctant to allow their general to enter the Château without them, some perhaps because they did not trust him but nearly all because they did not trust his enemies. After about half an hour of pleading and cajolery, Dumas and Gouvernet seconding his pleas, Lafayette persuaded his friends that his honor and theirs required him to give to the king proof of their devotion.[6] To a captain of the Swiss Guards who frankly admitted his astonishment that Lafayette was willing to take such a risk alone he replied, with the gallantry characteristic of the *guerre en dentelle* tradition, that he would always feel safe among "the brave regiment of Swiss Guards."[7] When finally his grenadiers let him go and the non-commissioned officer at the gate opened it a little to let him in, his friends still tried to retain him, holding on to him through the grill. He freed himself only with difficulty, and accompanied by the two Representatives from Paris, who received permission to enter the palace with him,[8] and almost carried by Gouvernet and Dumas (he was so exhausted), he made

---

[5] La Tour du Pin, I, 221, and Dumas, I, 103–7.

[6] Dumas, I, 106.

[7] *Mémoires,* II, 339.

[8] Dumas, I, 106–7, and Lefèvre and De la Grey, [October 6], Lacroix, II, 182.

his way toward the inner courtyard, the Cour Royale. On passing through the gate to the Cour Royale, he charged the Bodyguard sentinel on duty to warn his comrades to be discreet and do nothing to make a bad situation worse.[9]

Though "covered with mud from head to foot,"[10] Lafayette went with his four companions directly to the king's apartment. In the guardroom and the antechambers on their way they encountered ladies and gentlemen of the court, ministers, deputies of the National Assembly, servants, guards, and officers, all brought together by duty, curiosity, or apprehension. Among them were close friends and relatives of Lafayette, including Adrienne's father, the Duc d'Ayen, who, though off duty, as a captain of the King's Bodyguard probably would have been ready to defend his monarch even against his son-in-law if necessary. If some of them were relieved that Lafayette had come,[11] others were uneasy, still wondering whether he did not have ulterior motives in presenting himself with an army at his back, whether he himself had not manipulated the disturbances in Paris in order that they serve him as a pretext for "protecting" Versailles.[12] A hush fell upon the gathering as Lafayette and his companions entered. "Lafayette had a very calm air," wrote Mme de Staël, who watched him enter, and "no one ever saw him otherwise."[13] One of the less relieved dignitaries sneered: "Here comes Cromwell!" To which Lafayette retorted (and the readiness of the retort possibly betrays that he

[9] Chevalier Desplas to Comte d'Agoult, March 3, 1790, Vaissière, p. 111.

[10] Marquis de Paroy to his wife, October 6, "Journées des 5 et 6 octobre 1789," *Revue de la Révolution: documents inédits,* I (1883), 3.

[11] Mme de Staël, *Considérations sur les principaux événemens de la Révolution française,* ed. Duc de Broglie and Baron de Staël (Paris, 1818), I, 341, and Ambassador Stael-Holstein to Gustavus III, October 8, *Correspondance diplomatique du baron de Stael-Holstein,* ed. L. Léouzon le Duc (Paris, 1881), pp. 132–33.

[12] See, for example, A. Rivarol, *Oeuvres complètes* (Paris, 1808), IV, 278–89, 324; Maleissye, pp. 103–5, 108–10, 136; Tarante, pp. 2–5; Clermont-Gallerande, II, 174–75; Mme de Ménerville, *Souvenirs d'emigration: 1791–1797* (Paris, 1934), p. 28; Wickede, I, 97–98; and Thiébault, I, 249–50. Cf. *Ami du peuple,* September 25, 1790, p. 12; October 4, 1790, pp. 1–10; October 6, 1790, pp. 1–7; October 8, 1790, pp. 3–7; and October 17, 1790, pp. 5–8; and *Orateur du peuple,* No. 6, [October 1790], pp. 45–46.

[13] Staël, I, 341.

had been thinking of the parallel himself): "Cromwell would not have come alone."[14]

The court, which but hours before had been on the verge of flight and which even now was making concessions only under duress, still scrupulously observed its traditional etiquette. While some of the deputies of the National Assembly who were present were kept out, Lafayette and the Paris commissioners were formally ushered into the king's inner sanctum by His Majesty's chief valet-de-chambre.[15] Provence, Estaing, Necker, and several other personages were there with the king, who received Lafayette and the commissioners in a dignified, friendly fashion.[16] Addressing Louis directly but making no demands and contenting himself with explaining why he had come, Lafayette made a little speech which he had probably mentally rehearsed beforehand: he and the deputies of the commune of Paris had presented themselves in order to show their love for the king's sacrosanct person and to assure him that they would shed the last drop of their blood for his safety; 20,000 armed men were out on the avenues of Versailles in obedience to the popular will; there had been no way to keep them from coming to Versailles, but he had persuaded them to take an oath to remain under the strictest discipline.[17]

---

[14] *Mémoires*, II, 339. See also Dumas, I, 107. Apparently the analogy with Cromwell was contemporaneously in several people's minds. In a pamphlet entitled *Le Cheval blanc et les frères bleus* (meaning "Lafayette and the National Guard") Lafayette is compared to "ce Cromwell qui de la nation la plus libre de l'univers fit un peuple d'esclaves." It is possible, however, that this pamphlet appeared after rather than before October 5.

[15] *Procédure au Châtelet*, II, 49 (Thierry de Ville d'Avry, chief royal valet), 77 (Marquis de Vaudreuil, deputy in the National Assembly).

[16] Lefèvre and De la Grey in Lacroix, II, 182–83, and *Mémoires*, II, 339. See also the account of the king's master of the horse, Marquis de Cubières (as reported in the Morris diary, October 24, Davenport [ed.], I, 269, and as quoted in Baron de Maricourt, *En Marge de notre histoire* [Paris, 1905], pp. 149–50), and Paroy's letter to his wife, October 6, *loc. cit.*

[17] Our account is based upon the earliest report of this speech by direct witnesses. It is that of the two Representatives, dated by what must be an error October 5 (for October 6) at 4 P.M. (for 4 A.M.) (Lacroix, II, 182–83). Theirs was a formal statement by officials to the body to which they were responsible, made within hours of the event narrated. Paroy's letter (*loc. cit.*) was begun at 5 P.M. (although it was finished only about midnight; see *ibid.*, p. 7), and he was not a direct witness of the interview, having been in an outer room. The "Souvenirs inedits" of the Marquis de Cubières, quoted in Maricourt, pp. 149–50,

The king and his brother then asked the commissioners what the commune wanted, and "with the most profound respect" they presented the points which they believed summed up the demands of "an immense number of people." These were that he confide to the National Guard of Paris and of Versailles alone "the guarding of his sacred person," that special ministerial communiqués promise the people of Paris a supply of food during the approaching winter, that a court system be provided which would speed up the trial of prisoners, that the king cooperate with the National Assembly, and that he take up residence in the Tuileries, "the most beautiful palace of Europe in the midst of the largest city of his empire and among the most numerous part of his subjects."

Some of these demands, having been anticipated, had already been complied with, for Louis, even before the Representatives presented them, had sanctioned the Declaration of Rights and the proposed articles of the constitution and had instructed his ministers to confer with the Paris officials on the capital's food problem. He now granted most of the rest. The request that the National Guard of Paris and Versailles alone serve as his bodyguard was perhaps unexpected, for up to that point the most that the French Guard seemed to have openly demanded was to resume the service which in the past it had shared with other royal guard units. The Representatives' demand seemed to be an innovation, tantamount to asking for the removal of those units other than the Versailles National Guard that had participated at the Château in the recent demonstrations of royalist sentiment. And so Louis demurred, though only slightly, asking Lafayette and Estaing to confer on the subject and promising willingly to follow their joint advice. Mentioning his having earlier that evening signed the constitutional

---

although first-hand, appears to have been written at least a few days after the event (cf. Morris diary, I, 259), but except for its allegation of whimpering by Lafayette and severity on the part of Louis XVI, both uncharacteristic, it does not essentially contradict the Representatives' account. All the other reports of what Lafayette said are, if by eyewitnesses, remote recollections—e.g., Saint Priest, II, 17—or hearsay—e.g., "Rapport du Comte de Salmour," October 9, Jules Flammermont (ed.), *La Correspondance des agents diplomatiques étrangers en France* . . . (Paris, 1896), p. 265. Hence they are less trustworthy, even though commonly cited as if reliable in secondary accounts of October 5–6.

decrees, he implied his readiness to accept reform of criminal procedure also. Only on the suggestion that he go to Paris to live did
he fail to give or imply an answer, and the point led to a discussion
among those present (in which, however, Lafayette, presumably
out of deference to the civil authority and the desire to avoid the
semblance of a military coup, apparently did not take part). When
the Paris commissioners finally left the Château, they were greatly
encouraged, feeling that "their mission would have a happy ending."[18]

When Lafayette left the royal presence,[19] he had been on the
alert for many hours, "probably without food and amid many perplexities." Saint Priest, even long after he had ceased to feel kindly
toward the commandant general, conceded that Lafayette was at
that point entitled to go off and get some rest,[20] leaving a subordinate to supervise the preservation of order. But the Paris commander had been charged by the king to deal with the Versailles
commander on the demand that their two commands alone serve
as the palace guard. Hence, he had to settle that matter first. He
had good reason to expect to get authority to take over at once the
precincts of Versailles up to the grillwork which enclosed the inner
Cour Royale, for these were the posts formerly policed by the
French Guard.[21] But the quondam French Guard had no traditional claim to exclusive charge of both the exterior and the interior
precincts, and apparently Lafayette did not request that the honor
and responsibility by patrolling the interior be granted to them
immediately.

In any case, if, feeling bound by the two Representatives' request,
he asked that only the two National Guard units serve as the royal
bodyguard, supplanting the King's Bodyguard, the Cent Suisses,
and the Swiss Guard in the Château that very night, that permis-

---

[18] Lefèvre and De la Grey in Lacroix, II, 183.

[19] Chevalier de la Serre, non-commissioned officer in the royal army (*Procédure au
Châtelet*, II, 82) puts this at 11 p.m., but it must have been later.

[20] Saint Priest, II, 17. See also *Procédure au Châtelet*, I, 209 (Michel-Louis de Marcenay,
of the King's Bodyguard).

[21] *Mémoires*, II, 347.

sion was refused,[22] and he had to rest content with permission for the National Guard to police only the outer posts.[23] He assumed command of these himself, relieving Estaing of those posts immediately.[24] Hence his responsibility stopped at the iron gate and fences of the Cour Royale but included the outer areas, in which restless Parisians were still milling about. The courts and gardens beyond the grille around the Cour Royale as well as the interior of the Château remained under the supervision of the king's other guards.

Before leaving the Château, Lafayette spoke confidently to several bystanders, evidently meaning to reassure them and to make certain himself of the adequacy of the interior guard.[25] The Comte

[22] Mme de Staël stated long afterward (I, 341) that Lafayette asked for the interior posts and was refused, but no testimony close to the event suggested such a request. Comte Lavalette, who on October 6 was a Paris National Guardsman at Versailles but was probably not a witness to the transactions involved, wrote subsequently that Mme de Staël was right: *Mémoires et souvenirs du Comte Lavalette* (Paris, 1831), I, 29. The deputies Alexandre de Lameth (I, 152) and Montlosier (I, 295–96), though also at Versailles on October 6, probably were not direct witnesses either, but they quote her account with approval. Dumas (I, 107–8), without stating, however, that Lafayette asked for the interior posts, decried "a vain etiquette" which led to refusing "direction of all measures" to the one "who alone could insure their success." Lafayette (*Mémoires*, II, 347 and n.) suspected long afterward that the king wanted his own men to police the garden side of the Château because until 2 A.M. he had not fully decided not to flee by the garden to Rambouillet; see also the first page of an autograph note by Lafayette on Montjoie's *Conjuration de Philippe d'Orléans* in the Lafayette Archives, Cornell University Library, Carton V (microfilm). In his midnight interview with Louis XVI, however, it appears (*Mémoires*, II, 339–40) that Lafayette did not consider it appropriate to engage in politics by endorsing the commissioners' demands for the interior service or any other concessions.

[23] *Procédure au Châtelet*, II, 37 (Lafayette), and *Mémoires*, II, 347.

[24] Estaing's testimony at his trial before the Revolutionary Tribunal, March 29, 1794, quoted in J. J. R. Calmon-Maison, *L'Amiral d'Estaing* (Paris, 1910), p. 423.

[25] Though sometimes suspect, the witnesses seem to agree, even when they doubt Lafayette's sincerity or competence, that such might have been his announced purposes. Marcenay (*Procédure au Châtelet*, I, 209) claimed to have overheard a few (not very meaningful) words of a conversation of Lafayette with Lally-Tollendal, and several others record more or less plausible remarks which Lafayette is alleged to have made on his way to or from the king's apartment: Desplas to Agoult, March 3, 1790, Vaissière, p. 111; Wickede, I, 98; and *Procédure au Châtelet*, II, 70–71 (Chevalier de Valory, of the King's Bodyguard). The deputy Baron de Batz (*Procédure au Châtelet*, II, 48) reported similar remarks but by an officer who accompanied Lafayette, not Lafayette himself. The only such report which seems to be somewhat (but not wholly) implausible is that of A. N. Chauchard and Pierre Deroux, officers in the king's army (*ibid.*, I, 158, 164), who said that they overheard Lafayette apologize to the Duc d'Orléans for not answering a letter. Cf. Chabroud's *Rapport*, p. 81. The reason their report may be suspect is that Deroux seemed to be quite uncertain of his testimony.

de Luxembourg was the captain of the King's Bodyguard on duty that day. In reply to Lafayette's specific question he claimed that his men had taken the necessary precautions to protect the Château on the garden side, but to make doubly sure Lafayette and Dumas went to the balcony facing the garden to see for themselves. They saw a large detachment which they took to be the main force of the King's Bodyguard drawn up on the lawn. Convinced that the detachment was sufficient to defend the garden side of the Château, Lafayette then left.[26]

At he passed out through the grille of the Cour Royale, the commandant general paused to make a gesture not expected of generals in an aristocratic army; he shook hands with the non-commissioned officer who had let him in and now was letting him out and with the sentinel on duty at the gate.[27] He then went back to his men, still lined up along the Avenue de Paris,[28] and sent an officer down the line to carry the cheering news that His Majesty had vested in the National Guard the coveted custody of the exterior posts.[29] He and Gouvion and their staff thereupon proceeded to station men to do sentinel duty at the restored posts.[30]

The rest of the Paris National Guard busied itself finding quarters for the night—the old barracks of the French Guard, churches, royal stables, private homes. By 2 A.M. most of the battalions had been fed and housed somehow, and except for spasmodic flare-ups quiet seemed to have settled over Versailles.[31] A large number of Parisian men and women, however, remained in the town. Although the military patrols found them peaceful and they were trying to get such sleep as the city's limited facilities permitted, they were mostly out of doors, and an autumnal night offered small promise of comfort or rest.

[26] Dumas, I, 107–8, and *Procédure au Châtelet*, II, 37 (Lafayette).

[27] *Procédure au Châtelet*, II, 7 (P.-L.-E. Charmont, of the King's Bodyguard) and Desplas to Agoult, March 3, 1790, Vaissière, pp. 110–11.

[28] *Procédure au Châtelet*, I, 194 (Vicomte de la Chatre, deputy).

[29] *Ibid.*, II, 37 (Lafayette). See also *ibid.*, I, 261 (C.-F.-M. d'Ogny, commandant of the Battalion of Saint-Eustache).

[30] *Ibid.*, II, 37 (Lafayette); Dumas, I, 108; and *Mémoires*, II, 340, 347–48.

[31] See (among others) the affidavits in *Procédure au Châtelet*, I, 31, 55, 97, 112; II, 31–32, 48, 82, 116, 121, 129, 154; and III, 18.

Though several others had already remarked how exhausted and disheveled he looked, Lafayette, having tried to provide for his posts and his men as adequately as conditions allowed, returned to the National Assembly to speak to President Mounier. Tired men were still in session there, making an effort, continually interrupted by an unmanageable gallery, to discuss a code of criminal procedure such as Lafayette had recently requested and the Representatives' commissioners had just included in their requests of the king. This time, preferring not to interrupt the debate and give an excuse for adjournment, the president sent Clermont-Tonnerre and Lally-Tollendal to speak to Lafayette. And when the two deputies returned saying that the Paris commander was certain all was well, the Assembly at last adjourned for the day.

That was about 3 A.M. Mounier left the Salle des Menus Plaisirs accompanied by another deputy, Comte de Virieu. At the door he imparted to Lafayette his readiness to reopen the session if the least reason existed to apprehend further disturbance, but the general repeated his assurances: order had been restored, all the necessary steps for preserving it had been taken, and since Mounier must be worn out, they could all go to bed, as he himself intended to do. The area around the Château did indeed seem peaceful and reassuring. Accordingly, having agreed to meet Mounier (perhaps together with Adrien Duport) after a few hours' rest and confer on the state of affairs, Lafayette went along with the Comte de Virieu, a fellow deputy, to escort the president home.[32] On the way he expressed to Virieu his conviction that the evils of the day were the machinations of a cabal which they had both long suspected.[33] Lafayette's intentions seemed clear: if all went well, he hoped that the Duport and the Mounier wing of the Patriot group might yet join forces to combat the alleged cabal.

Arrived safely at home, Mounier went to bed, sick and spent, and did not wake up again until eight or nine o'clock,[34] but Lafayette still had a job to do, no matter how worn out he might look or feel. He now returned to the Château to report to the king that

[32] Mounier, "Exposé," *AP*, IX, 576–77; *Procédure au Châtelet*, I, 216 (Virieu), 222 (J.-F. Ange d'Eymar, deputy), 244 (Henri de Longuêve, deputy); II, 36 (Duport), 37 (Lafayette); and III, 75–76 (Mounier); and Mounier, *Appel*, p. 169.

[33] *Procédure au Châtelet*, I, 216–17 (Virieu).

[34] Mounier, "Exposé," *AP*, IX, 577.

the National Guard was at its posts and order prevailed. Between Lafayette's earlier visit to the Château that night and his second call upon Mounier a deputation from the National Assembly, upon the king's request, had come to the palace and gone. While the deputies had been there, Louis explained that he had invited them to come before Lafayette had arrived, in the hope that they might together present a united front against the expected aggression of Paris, but since Lafayette had arrived before them, he no longer had anything to tell them except that he had no intention (despite a widespread belief to the contrary)[35] to flee from Versailles. When the deputation withdrew, Louis, apparently feeling the emergency had passed, retired. By the time Lafayette returned to the Château, His Majesty was apparently already in bed. At any rate, the royal attendants refused to disturb him,[36] and so Lafayette simply left word that all was well. Upon receiving this report the king ordered the reception rooms cleared, and the calm of night at last settled upon the palace.

Marie Antoinette, whom Lafayette had not seen at all so far, was less given to wishful thinking than her husband. She, after all, disliked the Revolution much more than he and had been vehemently denounced, not only by some Paris politicians but also by Cassandra voices in the National Assembly, as a fomenter of counterrevolution. The Parisians in the Versailles streets had made no secret of their special animosity toward her, and she believed no good would come from confidence in a revolutionary like Lafayette, whom she suspected of not telling the truth about his reasons for coming to Versailles. Yet, since he had pledged himself to the king before so many witnesses, she felt he was honor-bound to preserve discipline among his men, who appeared to her obviously devoted to him. So she too, shortly before three in the morning, retired to her apartment.[37]

[35] *Ibid.*, p. 576. On the king's not deciding definitely whether to flee until 2 A.M., see *Mémoires*, II, 347 and n., and above, n. 22.

[36] *Procédure au Châtelet*, II, 37 (Lafayette), and III, 53 (J.-C. Rabel, royal servant); *Mémoires*, II, 340, 348, and III, 236; and a report of a statement by the Duc de Guiche in M. d'Albignac to Agoult, January 10, 1790, Vaissière, p. 108.

[37] Campan, II, 75. Although Mme Campan's memoirs, as memoirs frequently do, show a faulty memory, in this instance her eyewitness account is corroborated by circumstantial evidence and by Ségur's report of a later conversation with Marie Antoinette: Ségur, II, 458–59.

Upon leaving the Château for the second time, Lafayette set out for the Hôtel des Gardes-du-Corps, the barracks of the King's Bodyguard, which the Paris National Guard had taken over immediately after its arrival. At the Château he had been told that some of his men were engaged in pillaging arms there and a fight was going on which the officers in charge had not been able to control. Accompanied by his aide Jauge, Lafayette rode toward the barracks with the Comte de La Marck, a close friend of the court, in La Marck's carriage, the only one available at that hour. Before they had gone far, a group of people stopped the carriage, and when Lafayette asked what they wanted, they retorted: "The heads of the Bodyguards." When he asked them why, they accused the Bodyguards of having trampled on the national cockade, an outrage which must be punished. Lafayette told his aide to give them some money, and he himself adjured them to remain quiet and leave the matter to him. Pacified by the money and Lafayette's persuasiveness, they let the carriage move on.[38] As it approached the barracks, however, the crowd became thicker, and the carriage at one point could hardly get through. At that point Lafayette learned that his men at the Hôtel des Gardes-du-Corps had meanwhile established a good rapport with the men of the King's Bodyguard there. So he asked La Marck to drive him back to the main gate of the Château.[39] The royal guards at the barracks seemed safe, but the episode showed, all the same, that the King's Bodyguard was still the target of a deep resentment, even if things appeared for the time being well in hand.

Lafayette's staff had established headquarters at Adrienne's grandfather's house, the Hôtel de Noailles, on the Rue de la Pompe, where Lafayette had lived when he was actively a deputy at Versailles. It was a good location for headquarters, since it was close to the National Guard units stationed on the Place d'Armes.[40]

[38] La Marck in Bacourt, I, 116–18, gives a full account of this episode, which, however, is mistaken about the hour it occurred. See also *Procédure au Châtelet*, II, 70–71 (Valory), and *Les Forfaits du 6 octobre*, II, 287–88. That the Paris National Guard immediately took over the Hôtel des Gardes-du-Corps rests on the testimony of Lacointre (*AP*, XIX, 375).

[39] Bacourt, I, 117–18, and *Procédure au Châtelet*, II, 37 (Lafayette), 71 (Valory). For the conflict at the Hôtel des Gardes-du-Corps see A.M.—, *Relation très exacte des événements des 5 et 6 octobre par un témoin oculaire et désinteressé* [Paris, 1789], p. 27.

[40] Dumas, I, 108; *Mémoires*, II, 340, 348; and *Procédure au Châtelet*, I, 156–57 (Chauchard), and II, 37 (Lafayette).

. On his way to the Hôtel de Noailles Lafayette, now accompanied by Dumas, entered the Cour des Ministres once more, having decided to call upon Montmorin, who, like other ministers, had a suite facing upon that court. It was now about four o'clock.[41] Dumas left him at Montmorin's and went on to the Hôtel de Noailles.

Lafayette stayed at Montmorin's for an hour or more, and while he was there, the Comte de Luxembourg also came in. At least one subject of their conversation was the patent hostility of the people of Paris toward the royal bodyguard.[42] Something had happened which Lafayette, and perhaps Luxembourg, did not know but which would probably have convinced them, if they had known about it, that dividing the command of the forces guarding the Château was a grievous error. Luxembourg's subordinate officers, whether because they wished to avoid a clash with the populace or because they were expecting to escort the king to Rambouillet, had sent a large contingent to the Trianon Palace, which though still on the extensive Château grounds was a considerable distance from the palace itself.[43] By the time Luxembourg and Lafayette met at Montmorin's residence it was clear that the king would not take flight,[44] and Luxembourg apparently was more concerned, now that the Paris National Guard had the situation under control, that it might join in an assault upon his men than that the mob might assail the Château.

The King's Bodyguard, still duty-bound to observe the royal order not to fire, was indeed in danger from the unconcealed sympathy of some National Guards with the populace, and yet its duty was not to save itself but to defend the interior of the Château. The withdrawal of a large part of its total force from the immediate vicinity weakened the palace's inner defenses. Outside the Château the Basoche was on patrol from four to five, at four that morning a few men occupied the Place d'Armes, and a mounted National

---

[41] Dumas, I, 108; *Procédure au Châtelet*, II, 37 (Lafayette); and *Mémoires*, II, 340, 348, and III, 236. Lafayette years later (*Mémoires*, II, 340) said that he went to Montmorin's about daybreak, but this is imprecise.

[42] *Procédure au Châtelet*, II, 37 (Lafayette).

[43] Affidavits of several bodyguards, *ibid.*, II, 71, 149, and III, 25; *Mémoires de Weber, frère de lait de Marie-Antoinette* . . . (Paris, 1885), p. 239; and Vaissière, pp. 108–10.

[44] See above, n. 22.

Guard officer was in charge in the Cour des Ministres, but only the usual number of sentinels stood guard inside the grille of the Cour Royale.[45] Obviously nearly everybody counted upon the effectiveness of Lafayette's policing of the outer posts, and, in fact, except for the absence of the contingent of mounted bodyguards assembled at the Trianon (later that morning moved to Rambouillet), the Château was guarded as well as, but no better than, it had regularly been before the French Guard had gone over to the Revolution. The officers of the King's Bodyguard, except a few on call, apparently felt that everything was safe; at any rate, they went to spend the night as usual, some of them outside the Château.[46] Luxembourg and Lafayette doubtless thought they had done their full duty; French mobs had yet to learn to attack a royal palace.

No eyewitness other than himself has left direct testimony on what Lafayette did at Montmorin's,[47] but conceivably eighteen hours of unremitting, strenuous, enervating toil and harassment took their toll, and he closed his eyes for a spell. At any rate, about five o'clock, he left Montmorin's and, after going about "a hundred paces," arrived at the Hôtel de Noailles.[48] Everything seemed shipshape in the courtyards as he passed, and he felt confident that "all" was "calm."[49] He mounted the stairs to his staff headquarters on the second floor. Bone-tired, hungry, and unkempt, he spoke with

---

[45] *Procédure au Châtelet*, II, 60 (Charles de la Lain, of the Versailles National Guard), 70, (Valory), 125 (Francois Laurent, commander of the Basoche). See also Dumas, I, 111–12. On whether any of the gates were open and which ones see Mounier, *Appel*, pp. 174–75. There was also an unguarded staircase which escaped notice; see Saint Priest, II, 18–19. Maleissye (pp. 109–11) claims that Lafayette carefully arranged for a careless patrol, but his story is not corroborated by any available testimony and is contradicted by details (but given on hearsay evidence) in Mounier, *Appel*, pp. 174–75.

[46] *Mémoires*, II, 344, 350; III, 237; and IV, 203. In "Evénements des 5 et 6 octobre 1789," contained in *Les Forfaits du 6 Octobre*, the anonymous author defends the King's Bodyguard (II, 256–63) and, repudiating the charge that "all the officers" went to bed, nevertheless shows that it was commonly believed that they did so (p. 263, n. 75).

[47] La Marck in Bacourt, I, 118, claimed that Montmorin told him (1) that Lafayette assured him (Montmorin) that all was well—which is quite plausible—and (2) that Lafayette remained at Montmorin's for only a quarter of an hour. Dumas and Lafayette, being in a better position to know, give more reliable testimony than the résumé of Montmorin's words by La Marck, who is anxious to show that Lafayette had time to get "several hours of rest" at the Hôtel de Noailles.

[48] Dumas, I, 108.

[49] *Procédure au Châtelet*, II, 37 (Lafayette).

Gouvion and Dumas, while a servant brought him food and another dressed his hair. Gouvion, who had just inspected the National Guard posts, reported that "everything was perfectly tranquil—and that the horde of women and bandetti . . . was dispersed."[50]

It was high time to consider taking "some urgent measures regarding Paris."[51] Lafayette and Gouvion were anxious about the policing of that city, where only part—mostly the unpaid part—of the National Guard was available, perhaps inadequate for a routine day and certainly for one on which, as expected, the king would agree to go there. So Gouvion undertook to ride back to Paris at the break of day.[52] In preparation, he lay down across Lafayette's doorway to snatch a few minutes rest, if possible, or to be ready for any emergency, if necessary. Shortly afterward, stepping over the sleeping Gouvion, Dumas left, while Lafayette was still having his hair dressed. By the time Dumas passed through the Cour des Ministres, it was daylight.[53]

Somewhere between the time Lafayette saw the king and daybreak, he found a moment to write a few lines to tell what had happened after his arrival in Versailles. Everything, he reported, had gone "better than we could have guessed"; the good will of the troops had prevented the lawlessness which he now admitted he at first had dreaded. The king, he was glad to say, had received him well, and the royal sanction of the constitutional provisions and the adoption of the national cockade would have the desired effect. He himself, he proudly asserted, had that day done good service for the king. And at last: "Good morning! I am falling asleep. . . ."[54]

For nearly twenty consecutive hours now Lafayette, out of a

---

[50] Dumas, I, 108.   [51] *Mémoires*, III, 236.

[52] *Procédure au Châtelet*, II, 36 (Duport), 78 (Gouvion).

[53] Dumas, I, 108.

[54] The ellipsis, as given above, is in the contemporary manuscript copy; Lafayette to unknown, [October 6], Cornell University Library, Lafayette Archives, Box 2, (p. 45 of the bound set of copies of letters said to be to Mme de Simiane). Presumably to avoid giving ammunition to those who alleged that Lafayette had slept through the initial eruption, the printed version (*Mémoires*, II, 411) omitted the last words quoted. Lafayette perhaps forwarded this letter to the Assembly of Representatives by C.-F. Desmousseaux, one of the Representatives who accompanied him to Versailles; Desmousseaux returned and reported to the Assembly of Representives about 6 A.M. on October 6 (Lacroix, II, 178),

high sense of duty and patriotism, had braved lynching, mutiny, misunderstanding, charges of treason, and—for him perhaps the least willingly taken risk—unpopularity. While haggard and worried, he had remained vigilant even if, for obvious reasons, several who had seen him in the course of the morning assumed that he had gone to bed.[55] If he was now planning to get some repose,[56] he had earned it. He had taken nearly every reasonable precaution to see that his command performed its duty, and if the royal family was still in any danger, a critical observer might have judged that in part the reason was his failure to expect the unexpected but, more likely, was the weakness at posts which the king had seen fit not to place under Lafayette's command.

The French Guard had in the old days been accustomed to open the outer gate to the Cour des Ministres mornings at 5:30, and they did so now. About six o'clock, when the sentinels of the King's Bodyguard at the inner gate were changed, the Place d'Armes still seemed quiet. With daylight, however, the Parisians became active again, and finding the outer gate open, some of them wandered into the Cour des Ministres.

Suddenly came pandemonium and massacre.[57] Some men— patriots doubtless in their own estimation; "armed bandits . . .

and another Representative (Desfaucherets) subsequently testified that Desmousseaux brought a letter from Lafayette (*Procédure au Châtelet,* I, 61). If he did, however, we doubt that it was the one here under consideration because this one is too informal in tone, because Desmousseaux reported that the National Guard was patrolling both the interior and the exterior posts at Versailles (something he probably would not have thought if he had been briefed by Lafayette), and because the minutes of the Assembly of Representatives would doubtless have noted that Desmousseaux had brought a letter from the commandant general if he had indeed brought one. We think it more probable that Gouvion carried this letter to Paris and that while it was not addressed directly to the Representatives it was to some Paris official who knew Lafayette and his concern about his army well—perhaps Bailly or Moreau de Saint-Méry. It is highly unlikely to have been addressed to Mme de Simiane, who was in Versailles and had no need (as the letter assumes its recipient did) to learn what was going on there from Lafayette's earlier letter to Mme de Lafayette in Paris.

[55] *Procédure au Châtelet,* II, 3 (Sieur de Blaire, alternate deputy); Hézecques, pp. 288–89; *Life and Letters of Madame Elisabeth of France,* trans. K. P. Wormely (Boston, 1902), p. 211; Malouet, I, 345 and n.; Rivarol, *Mémoires,* pp. 296–302; Bacourt, I, 116–19; and La Tour du Pin, I, 224.

[56] *Mémoires,* II, 348, and III, 236–37.

[57] *Procédure au Châtelet,* I, 98 (Guérin), and II, 129 (Joseph La Combe, captain in the Paris National Guard).

egged on by secret maneuvers" according to a subsequent indictment of the Paris procureur-syndic[58]—somehow found access to the inner courtyards. Among them was at least one National Guardsman. They entered the gate of the Cour des Princes, which was customarily left open but should have been patrolled at least on the outside by the National Guard, and perhaps by other gates as well.[59] By the adjoining Passage de la Voute they made their way to the innermost court, the Cour de Marbre, which the royal apartments looked out upon. There one of the intruders fell, apparently fatally injured—whether shot by a bodyguard or by accidentally falling and cracking his skull on the marble floor is not clear.[60] Persuaded, however, that he had been shot, his comrades fell upon the nearest bodyguards, overpowered them, and killed one of them. A mob then poured into the palace by the marble staircase and made for the queen's apartment. Only because a second bodyguard gave his life and several others risked theirs to stem the onslaught did the queen have time to flee to the king's apartment and safety. Meanwhile other enraged Parisians fell upon bodyguards wherever they could find them, and the bodyguards, outnumbered, without commissioned officers, and generally obeying the king's order not

---

[58] Quoted in *Mémoires*, II, 353 n. Lafayette in 1799 (*ibid.*, III, 237) described them as "brigands hidden in the groves." He also quoted (II, 353 n.) the statement of the procureur-syndic (December 1, 1789) that the eruption came "by the interior passages of the garden." Dumas (I, 111–12) also thought so. The only direct evidence we have found, however, to indicate that the first eruption might have come from the Château gardens was in the affidavits of several servants of the queen and one royal bodyguard; *Procédure au Châtelet*, I, 139, 154, 155, 200. These witnesses heard people on the terraces about 6 A.M., but it does not necessarily follow that these people came in from the garden. Other sources indicate that they came in from the Cour des Princes: see below, n. 60.

[59] *Procédure au Châtelet*, I, 250 (Comte de Saint Aulaire, officer in the King's Bodyguard), II, 7 (Charmont), and III, 65 (C.-L. de Lisle, bodyguard), and *Les Forfaits du 6 octobre*, II, 258, n. 74, and 307–8. Cf., however, *Procédure au Châtelet*, III, 68–69 (A.-P. de Raymond, bodyguard), who says that the King's Bodyguard patrolled the grille of the Cour des Princes—apparently, therefore, on the inside.

[60] *Procédure au Châtelet*, I, 36, 39, 64, 65, 199, 200, 250; II, 7, 66, 144; and III, 16, 33, 65, 68 (bodyguards); *ibid.*, I, 55, 98, 116; II, 124–25, 129, 167, 184, 185; and III, 18 (National Guards); *ibid.*, I, 116, 134, 211–12; II, 3, 77, 181; and III, 30, 53–54 (other witnesses). See also *AP*, XIX, 376 (Lecointre); Paroy, *Mémoires*, p. 121; and La Tour du Pin, I, 225–28. It seems more likely that the man was shot, and probably by a royal bodyguard, although the Chevalier de Fougères, non-commissioned officer in the King's Bodyguards, vigorously denied that any bodyguard fired any shot throughout October 5–6; see his *La Conduite des Gardes-du-corps dans l'affaire qui se passa à Versailles les 5 et 6 du courant* [Paris, 1789], pp. 8–9.

to fire, defended themselves as best they could, those inside the Château slowly retreating from room to room.

Aumont seems to have been nowhere around,[61] but some other officers of the Paris National Guard companies outside the Cour Royale could see different parts of the seething populace, and when they heard the roar and some shots, they took action. One of the first companies to march to the defense of the palace was the grenadiers of the First Division under Captain Charles Cadignan, and among the non-commissioned officers who distinguished themselves on this occasion was a young sergeant of that company, the future General Lazare Hoche.[62] Captain Jean-Etienne Gondran, of the Battalion of Saint Phillipe du Roule, led his center company, which had been joined by about fifty volunteers, immediately through the main gate into the Cour de Marbre (which was beyond the National Guard's jurisdiction) and got his men—though only after a dramatic appeal to their honor—to move to protect the palace and the bodyguards there.[63]

At the Hôtel de Noailles, shortly after Gouvion had left for Paris, the officer and sentinels on duty gave the alarm. Not waiting for a horse to be saddled,[64] the dismayed commandant general, followed by some of his men, rushed toward the Château, pushing through the crowd. Even before he got there, acting under their captains the available National Guard units had begun to gain control in the Cour de Marbre. Although impeded by royal bodyguards who distrusted their intentions and by a compunction that constrained them to get the king's permission to take up posts so close to his person, some of them were even inside the palace, clearing out intruders or keeping the people from bursting in again.[65] On his way to the Château Lafayette dispatched orders to

---

[61] *Procédure au Châtelet*, II, 3 (Lucas de Blaire).

[62] *Ibid.*, p. 37 (Lafayette), and *Mémoires*, II, 340, 348, and III, 236–37. In *Mémoires*, III, 237, Lafayette implies that Cadignan acted upon his own initiative at the first signs of trouble, but *ibid.*, II, 348, he says Cadignan acted under his orders. The statement in Vol. III is of 1799 and that of Vol. II is of 1814. The earlier statement seems more acceptable.

[63] *Procédure au Châtelet*, I, 55 (Gondran).

[64] *Mémoires*, II, 340 and 348.

[65] *Procédure au Châtelet*, II, 77 (Vaudreuil), and *Mémoires*, II, 340.

the other battalions to come up as fast as they could, hoping by the maneuver used before in the Place de Grève to edge the crowd out of the Cour de Marbre.[66]

To the mass that still raged outside the Château, the body-guards were the object of most passionate hatred. Several of them had already been taken captive, and infuriated men fell upon these hapless "culprits," meaning to drag them off to "execution." As Lafayette hastened on foot to the Château, he learned of the intended lynchings. Mounting the first horse that was brought up, he galloped toward the spot where a vengeful band was mis-handling a few disarmed captives. As his horse clattered toward them, he passed some of those who had assaulted the King's Body-guard in the Cour de Marbre and in the queen's apartment and who were now triumphantly parading to Paris with their trophies —among them the heads of the two fallen bodyguards stuck on the ends of pikes. More appalled at what might happen than at what had happened he did not stop, and the ghastly trophies continued undisturbed to Paris and the Palais Royal Garden, where they were exhibited for a few hours until the authorities intervened and dis-posed of them.[67]

Upon reaching the place where the "executioners" were prepar-ing their "culprits" for their fate Lafayette ordered the captors to release the intended victims. An enraged ringleader of the mob turned to his followers and shouted to them to kill the comman-dant general[68] (and that ringleader was not the only one that day to make that demand).[69] Lafayette ordered the bystanders to arrest

[66] *Procédure au Châtelet*, I, 55–56 (Gondran), and II, 37–38 (Lafayette), 77 (Vau-dreuil), 184 and 185 (C.-H. Plantade and F.-L. Duperry, volunteer members of the Paris National Guard); *Mémoires*, II, 341, 348, and III, 237; Count Miot de Melito, *Mémoires*, trans. General Fleischmann (New York, 1881), p. 15; and Saint Priest, I, 18.

[67] *Procédure au Châtelet*, II, 38 (Lafayette), and *Mémoires*, II, 353–54. Lafayette (*Mémoires*, II, 353) denied that the heads were carried in front of the carriage which took the king and his family to Paris later that day, as sometimes was alleged, and Mme de Staël (I, 345) says that the return to Paris was deliberately routed through the Bois de Boulogne to avoid any such encounter.

[68] *Mémoires*, II, 348–49.

[69] *Procédure au Châtelet*, I, 145 (Elisabeth Girard, bourgeoise), and II, 97 (Marie-Marguerite Andelle, worker), 156 (J.-L. Desmottes, aide to Lafayette), and Chabroud, *Rapport, pièces justificatives*, pp. 54–55 (Widow Ruvet).

the man, and his peremptory tone brought obedience. Some of them seized the agitator and dragged him by the heels, his head bouncing on the paving stones, toward Lafayette.[70] Yet the grenadiers made no move to rescue the doomed bodyguards. Taken aback, Lafayette lashed out at his men: he was grieved to hear that some of the royal defenders had already been killed; but, he protested: "I have given the king my word that the Bodyguard will suffer no harm," and if the grenadiers considered him capable of commanding them, they must begin by obeying him. Reluctantly persuaded, the grenadiers rescued the guards from their captors.[71] It was hardly an edifying situation for a commanding general to find himself in—begging his still resentful men to do their patent duty and not put him in the unenviable position of breaking his word of honor. But at length Lafayette succeeded, and none of the king's several palaces was to be subjected to sanguinary attack again until the monarchy collapsed altogether on August 10, 1792.

Other mobs were running loose over other parts of the palace grounds and in the town, being kept from looting the stables and from attacking bodyguards by nearby National Guard contingents acting independently.[72] In the end, although a number of bodyguards were captured and threatened with death, after the onslaught at the Cour de Marbre and the queen's apartment not another one was lynched.[73] As other units of the National Guard

[70] *Mémoires*, II, 349.

[71] The speech as given here is taken mainly from *Procédure au Châtelet*, II, 183 (Emery de Guillement, retired lieutenant). See also A.M.——, p. 31, and the letter of one of the rescued bodyguards, February 16, 1790, Braibant, p. 89, No. 259. Saint Aulaire gave a somewhat similar version (*Procédure au Châtelet*, I, 251–52) but on hearsay evidence. Other similar versions rely on even more indirect testimony—e.g., Ferrières, I, 326, and *Procédure au Châtelet*, III, 72 (Mounier). For other details given above see also *Procédure au Châtelet*, I, 110 (Alexis Grincourt, Versailles merchant), 116 (Marquié), 176 (Pierre Bisson, servant), 178 (Jean Blanchoin, servant), 197–98 (F.-N. Gueroult du Berville, bodyguard), and II, 117 (L.-A. Berthier, in October 1789 chief of staff of the Versailles National Guard), 156 (Desmottes).

[72] Thiébault, I, 243, and *Procédure au Châlelet*, II, 130 (La Combe).

[73] *Procédure au Châtelet*, II, 42–43 (Ayen). See also *ibid.*, I, 110 (Grincourt), 116 (Marquié), 197–98 (Gueroult du Berville), and II, 38 (Lafayette), 77 (Vaudreuil), 117 (Berthier), 155–56 (Jean Doazant, captain in the Paris National Guard), 164–65 (Louis Priere, concierge), 183 (Guillemet), 250–51 (Saint Aulaire); *Mémoires*, II, 341, 348–49; and Thiébault, I, 243.

came up, the mob in the Château courtyards grew calmer and the Guard seemed to gain full control. Lafayette himself induced some men and women to withdraw by the main gate.[74] Nevertheless, the crowd did not disperse.

About eight o'clock[75] a lull in the tohubohu permitted Lafayette finally to dismount and go inside the Château. Before he got there, the king, in response to the insistent demand of the crowd, had already gone out on the balcony and had received an ovation.[76] On the way to the royal apartment, the commandant general found that Gondran had re-established order inside the palace and that National Guards were going about their duty, preserving life and property in a soldierly manner. The general commended them for their brave conduct and once more called upon them to protect the royal family and its guards.[77] The Oeil-de-Boeuf was crowded with courtiers and deputies who had rushed up upon learning of the assault, and the three remaining Paris Representatives also were there.[78] No one hailed Lafayette as Cromwell now.

Riots might come and go, but court etiquette seemed to go on forever; a court officer advanced to meet the welcome general and solemnly announced: "Monsieur, the king accords you the right to enter his cabinet."[79] On entering the royal sanctum Lafayette found the king's family there—Louis' queen, children, sister, brother, and aunts.[80] Apparently all breathed a little more easily now. At 9 A.M., when Lecointre, commanding a detachment of

---

[74] *Procédure au Châtelet*, II, 38 (Lafayette).   [75] *Ibid.*, II, 183 (Guillemet).

[76] Report of Representative J.-J. Rousseau (who had gone to Versailles to see Lafayette on a private matter; see Lacroix, II, 184), delivered to the Assembly of Representatives by Representative Nicolas de Bonneville, October 6, *ibid.* This report was soon confirmed by a letter from Lafayette to Bailly: *ibid.* p. 185. That this first appearance of the king on the balcony must have happened before Lafayette entered the king's apartment is deduced from Paroy's letter to his wife, October 6, *loc. cit.*, p. 5. Paroy makes clear that Lafayette joined the royal party only a little before the king's next appearance on the balcony.

[77] *Mémoires*, II, 341.

[78] *Ibid.*, I, 56 (Gondran), and II, 36 (Duport), 38 (Lafayette); *Mémoires*, II, 341; Rivarol, *Mémoires*, p. 309; Montlosier, I, 298; and Saint Priest, II, 190.

[79] *Mémoires*, II, 342 n.

[80] *Procédure au Châtelet*, I, 264 (Marquis de Digoine, deputy), and II, 182 (Guillaume de Prioreau, officer in the royal army).

the Versailles National Guard on the Place d'Armes, asked for orders, Lafayette had no need to give any (although he later requested a contingent to reinforce one of his Paris companies).[81]

By that time Saint Priest had made his way by a secret (and also unguarded) stairway to the king's apartment. Although he had already roused Lafayette's antipathy by his animosity,[82] he subsequently testified that he found Lafayette busily engaged in restoring calm. The king seemed to Saint Priest especially dazed as the rumbling of the crowd and the crack of occasional shots continued to reach his windows from the court below.[83] Would not His Majesty, Lafayette now asked, allow the National Guards who were inside the king's apartment to repeat their oath of loyalty? Louis consented, and he and Lafayette went into the Oeil-de-Boeuf and nearby rooms, where Gondran and his company, aided by other Guardsmen who in the meantime had joined them, had taken charge. Louis explained to them that his Bodyguard was not guilty of the alleged charges, and, deeply moved, the Paris Guardsmen, largely grenadiers, swore to perish to the last man for their king.[84] To those who were former French Guards this oath in His Majesty's presence was a notable victory—a marked royal preferment beyond their previous status as guardians of peace only outside the Château. To Louis it represented a concession to soldiers who had left his service to join the Revolution—a concession which possibly only the danger of the moment would have wrung from him.

It was now past ten o'clock. Four bloody hours had been added to the long stretch since dawn of the preceding day during which some of the National Guard had been continuously under arms. What was now to be done? Outside the king's apartment a sullen swarm only precariously daunted by the fixed bayonets of the Guards drawn up in their midst, still filled the Cour de Marbre,

---

[81] "Déclaration de Lecointre," *AP*, XIX, 376.

[82] Lafayette to unknown, "ce mardi," *Mémoires*, II, 420.

[83] Saint Priest, II, 19.

[84] *Procédure au Châtelet*, I, 56 (Gondran), and II, 38 (Lafayette), 77 (Vaudreuil), and *Mémoires*, II, 349.

now setting up a howl, repeated again and again: "The king on the balcony!" and "The king to Paris!"[85]

Fearful for His Majesty's safety, Saint Priest recommended that the king yield to the popular clamor.[86] Louis consulted the queen and his other advisers in his inner sanctum. While Lafayette went in with them, he took special pains not to become involved, obviously in order to avoid a charge of having unduly influenced the royal decision.[87] When they emerged from the king's cabinet, Louis stepped out on the balcony again, this time accompanied by the queen, the royal children, Necker, and Champion de Cicé, with Lafayette standing between the royal couple. Prolonged cheers greeted them, and when Louis could make himself heard, he promised to go to Paris with his wife and children, confiding "to the love of my good and faithful subjects what is most precious to me." A lusty roar of "Vive le roi!" greeted his announcement, re-echoed from corner to corner as the news traveled down the courts to the Place d'Armes.[88]

Lafayette, confident that the people though "sometimes misled," would "listen to the voice of reason and honor" and that from experience he knew how to speak to them, then signaled with his hat for quiet, and when he could make himself heard, candidly rebuked them for being led astray by factious men, enemies of the Revolution and of liberty. His words momentarily had the desired effect, and shouts of approval went up from the assemblage.[89]

When he could be heard again, Louis, once more the kind if ineffectual patriarch, asked pardon for his royal praetorians: "My Bodyguard has been maligned. Their loyalty to the nation and to

[85] Lacroix, II, 184 (Rousseau), and Paroy, *loc. cit.,* p. 6.

[86] Saint Priest, II, 19–20, and *Procédure au Châtelet,* II, 62 (O.-G.-L. le François Derosnet, equerry).

[87] *Mémoires,* II, 349, and Saint Priest, II, 89. Paroy in his letter to his wife of October 6, *loc. cit.,* says (p. 5) that the queen led Lafayette into the council room, but it does not necessarily follow that even if she did, Lafayette participated in the council.

[88] Lacroix, I, 184–85 (Rousseau). Paroy does not mention the king's promise to go to Paris at this point; see below, n. 102. See also *Procédure au Châtelet,* I, 31 (Bremont).

[89] *Procédure au Châtelet,* II, 38 (Lafayette); *Mémoires,* II, 341; Saint Priest, II, 89; Dumas, II, 109; and Paroy, *loc. cit.* Paroy says that Lafayette got the people to raise their hands and swear loyalty, but no other witness mentions a formal oath-taking.

me ought to preserve for them the esteem of my people."[90] Then, withdrawing a little, he asked Lafayette to do something for his guards, and together with the three Representatives of the Paris commune, the general presented a non-commissioned officer of the King's Bodyguard to the assemblage, embracing him and giving him his own tricolor cockade to wear.[91]

Could *mise en scène* have been more spectacular? General and non-com, tricolor and royal uniform, King's Bodyguard and National Guard merged in embrace under the eyes of the king and his court and a square packed with penitent subjects! No wonder ill-wishers were subsequently to contend that Lafayette had staged the whole thing. If he had stayed up nights rehearsing for this moment and had hired his own claque, it could hardly have turned out so well. Those who but hours before had sought to slaughter bodyguards now applauded, and thousands of throats grew hoarse with shouts of "Vivent les gardes-du-corps!"[92] Nearby bodyguards, in token of their submission and good will, removed their white sashes and threw away their caps with white cockades and replaced them with caps which National Guardsmen took off their own heads and gave them.[93] Lafayette then urged the crowd to break up and go back to Paris, and the king's party, still acclaimed, returned indoors.[94]

[90] For the king's and Lafayette's appearances and speeches on the balcony we have leaned upon the report of Rousseau to the Assembly of Representatives (Lacroix, II, 184–85) and Paroy's letter (*loc. cit.*). They corroborate each other generally, but when they do not, we have followed Rousseau as being the earlier and probably more detached witness. Moreover, the details of Rousseau's report were said to have been "confirmed by a letter addressed to the Mayor by the Commandant General" (Lacroix, II, 185). Unfortunately we have not seen this letter, and its contents are not further indicated in the minutes of the Assembly of Representatives. It may be the one which Mme Elisabeth warned Lafayette to take out of the files (but, if so, it was probably not Lafayette who removed it; see below, p. 380.) See also *Procédure au Châtelet*, I, 31, 135, 165, and Miot de Milito, p. 16.

[91] See above, n. 90. In *Mémoires*, II, 341, Lafayette gives these episodes in a wrong chronological order. He puts the embracing of the bodyguards after the queen's appearance alone on the balcony—which none of the more contemporary sources does.

[92] Letter of October 8 quoted in *AHRF*, XXX (1959), 367; Lacroix, II, 185 (Rousseau); *Mémoires*, II, 341; and *Procédure au Châtelet*, III, 78 (Mounier, whose account here, however, is heresay).

[93] *Procédure au Châtelet*, I, 135, 162, and II, 211 (M.-J.-A. Pulieux, bodyguard) and III, 17 (P.-C. Bellanger de Rebourceaux, bodyguard); Miot de Melito, p. 16; Mme de Staël, I, 346; and Fougères, p. 10.

[94] Paroy, *loc. cit.*

The crowd did not break up, however, and soon murmurs arose once more. This time the mob called for the queen, and in tones which were not altogether friendly. Lafayette was inside the king's apartment, talking to Adrien Duport, who had just come in.[95] He now decided upon a daring gesture. "Madame," he asked the queen (as he, probably overglamorously, remembered their conversation years later), "what is your personal intention?" Marie Antoinette replied, with a spirit that Lafayette recalled as magnanimous, that she knew the fate which awaited her, "but my duty is to die at the king's feet and in my children's arms." "Then, Madame," he rejoined, "come with me." The queen shrank back a little. "What! Alone on the balcony! Haven't you seen the gestures they have made at me?" "Yes, Madame," he said, admitting to himself (as he afterward recollected) that the gestures had been frightening; "Come along."[96] If his memory did not play him false, he was again the self-confident leader trusting to his intuition, his luck, and his popularity, as well as his National Guards, who lined the sides of the courtyard. And yet what he suggested might well have frightened Marie Antoinette, for the National Guard had only a limited control over the people, massed together in its center, and a single misguided patriot or (if Lafayette's own suspicions were correct) an *agent provocateur* could have aimed a shot at the queen or started a contagious protest which might have led to a worse catastrophe than had yet occurred.

Whether prompted by the histrionic words of Lafayette or her own pride, Marie Antoinette was equal to the occasion. Carrying the little dauphin and leading his bigger sister by the hand, she stepped out on the balcony with the commandant general.[97] Probably the queen had learned that once her famous mother with her infant son in her arms had won recalcitrant Hungarian magnates to her side. But those Marie Antoinette now had to face were not

[95] *Procédure au Châtelet*, II, 36 (Duport).

[96] Lafayette's account (*Mémoires*, II, 341) is largely corroborated by *Procédure au Châtelet*, I, 264 (Digoine). See also Necker, IX, 270–80. Ferrières (I, 327–28) and Mounier (*Appel*, p. 190) give somewhat similar but hearsay accounts.

[97] *Procédure au Châtelet*, I, 264 (Digoine), and II, 62–63 (Derosnet), and Mme Campan, II, 81.

magnates, and the first impact was not friendly. That "the Austrian" should appear to be seeking refuge as the mother of the future king of France instead of standing on her own feet created an unfavorable reaction. "No children!" some of the crowd yelled.[98] The proud queen took the children inside and came back alone. When she reappeared, obviously mastering her fright, the murmur was deafening, but its causes were confused. Witnesses claimed to have seen or heard threats of shooting, but if anyone took aim at the balcony, no one actually fired.[99] Still accompanying her, Lafayette tried to talk, but he could not make himself heard above the roar.[100] If some much later testimony is correct, he intuitively performed a *beau geste* which he subsequently claimed was "risky but decisive"—a gesture which under the teetering of public reaction only a court noble who could count upon wide popular support could have carried off without exciting disapproval: he bowed low and kissed his queen's hand. Lafayette afterward claimed that the effect was electric, that instantly the rumble of dissatisfaction changed into a cheer: "Vive le général! Vive la reine!"[101]

Whatever it was that altered the mood of the crowd, after a few moments of terrifying uncertainty the queen left the balcony and returned to her family not only unharmed but triumphant. It was now about eleven o'clock. The cries of "The king to Paris!" "The king to Paris!" never subsided. There seemed to be nothing left to do but to make known the hour of the king's departure for Paris. Again Louis took council with his ministers, and then he, the

---

[98] The only Châtelet witness to mention the unfavorable reception of the queen was Derosnet (*Procédure au Châtelet*, II, 62–63), who does not mention a shout of "No children," but it is mentioned in several memoirs of eyewitnesses, including Campan (II, 81), Tourzel (I, 38), Hézecques (pp. 292–93), Hue (p. 133), and Weber (p. 276).

[99] *Procédure au Châtelet*, III, 21 (Jeanne-Antoine Bessous Tillet, restaurant keeper); Weber, p. 258; and Paroy, *loc. cit.* Cf. Mounier, *Appel*, p. 190, and Ferrières, pp. 327–28 (both hearsay).

[100] Jeanne Martin-Lavarenne, wife of a concierge, was the only witness who claimed to have heard him (*Procédure au Châtelet*, I, 135). She reported him to have said that the queen was sorry about what had happened, admitted that she was mistaken, and now promised to be as devoted to the people "as Jesus Christ is to his church." Despite the spectacular circumstances, these words seem out of character for both Marie Antoinette and Lafayette.

[101] *Mémoires*, II, 341, 349, and Lacroix, II, 185 (Rousseau). See below, Appendix IV.

queen, and Lafayette once more stepped out on the balcony, where Lafayette announced, and Louis confirmed, to a rejoicing multitude that expressed its gratitude with shouts and shots that His Majesty would fulfill his earlier promise that very day and would start out about noon.[102] Lafayette ordered his First Division to set off immediately,[103] and the king's court, guards, and servants prepared for the trip, which, despite the excellent weather,[104] promised to be a hard one. In the new atmosphere of harmony inside and outside the palace, the danger to the king's guards had passed. They were scattered about the Château and the town, some of them still in the protective custody of the Paris troops.[105]

Within the king's apartment, once the balcony scenes had ended, the first feeling was one of relief. Mme Adélaïde, one of the king's aunts, kissed Lafayette and thanked him for what he had done for her "poor nephew,"[106] and even the queen felt that "no matter what she had against him, . . . he had gone to our rescue and given us the most essential service."[107] If any members of the court felt that they had been humiliated and betrayed, they did not yet express such feelings openly.

Lafayette now had to make preparations for a host he later estimated at 60,000[108] to march a distance of about twelve miles. Not certain that the Paris commune would be informed through other observers, he wrote to Bailly about what had happened so that the city might not be caught unaware of its new honors and

---

[102] Mme de Staël, I, 347, and Dumas, I, 109. Paroy *(loc. cit.)* gives the impression that the decision to go to Paris was reached only just before this third appearance of the king on the balcony, for he mentions no earlier promise to do so. Again we follow the Rousseau report (Lacroix, II, 184–85), which was apparently sent from Versailles before this last announcement, which in his turn Rousseau did not mention, quoting instead the promise the king made at his second balcony appearance—to go to Paris but at no precise time.

[103] *Procédure au Châtelet,* I, 31 (Bremont). See also *ibid.,* p. 135 (Martin-Lavarenne). Miot de Melito (p. 16) says that Necker made the announcement and that Lafayette confirmed it.

[104] Staël, I, 345. Wille, II, 227, 229, however, says that it rained when the procession reached Paris and marched to the Hôtel de Ville.

[105] Mounier, *Appel,* pp. 188–90; *Précis historique de la conduite des Gardes du Corps du Roi* (Paris, 1789), p. 11; and Chevalier d'Arbonneau to Agoult, February 25, 1790, Vaissière, p. 118.

[106] *Mémoires,* II, 343–44, 349.

[107] As quoted by Ségur, II, 458.   [108] *Mémoires,* II, 342.

responsibilities and might prepare a decent reception for the royal family.[109] He tried to induce the Paris populace to march off ahead so as to sandwich them between his already departed First Division and the several battalions which would follow, reserving the rest of his forces as an escort for the royal family and its retinue.[110]

A legal technicality presented some embarrassment at this point. The Paris government required a passport signed by some proper authority for moving from one's accustomed abode into the capital, and members of the royal household were no exception to that rule. Lafayette's signature was obviously a better guarantee of safe conduct for those seeking to enter Paris from Versailles than that of a compromised minister or some other royal agent, and so courtiers who a short time ago had been ready to spurn him as a Cromwell now begged for his signature. Sitting at a table in the king's cabinet, he signed scores of passports, among which doubtless several belonged to aristocrats whose openly expressed gratitude was probably not unmixed with hidden resentment.[111]

One of these petitioners, however, remained genuinely grateful for a long time. Louis had intended that his sister, Elisabeth, should accompany his aged aunts to their château at Bellevue, which was about half way to Paris and much safer, rather than go to Paris with the rest of the family, but preferring Paris, she asked Lafayette to intercede for her, and the king finally complied. She was one day to return the favor by warning Lafayette to remove from the record a letter which his enemies were intending to include in a dossier they were preparing for the time when the counterrevolution would set in and he would be tried for treason—to which warning Lafayette replied that he had written no letter he was ashamed of, and he did nothing about it.[112]

Having provided the king's courtiers with passports, Lafayette

---

[109] Lacroix, II, 185.

[110] *Mémoires*, II, 343.

[111] *Ibid.*, p. 342; *Procédure au Châtelet*, III, 32 (H.-P.-G. Santerre, officer in the Versailles National Guard); and Comte de Mercy-Argenteau to Marie Antoinette, October 6, *Feuillet de Conches*, I, 251.

[112] *Mémoires*, II, 344, and M. Regnault-Warin, *Mémoires pour servir à la vie du général La Fayette et à l'histoire de l'Assemblée constituante* (Brussels, 1824), p. 77 of "pièces justificatives" in Vol. II.

took steps to clear the atmosphere at Versailles. Captain Gondran brought him the officers of the Flanders Regiment, who had not yet given any open sign of approval of their men's compliance with Lafayette's orders the night before, and Lafayette instructed him to do what he could to effect a reconciliation between them and their men. Gondran was able to do so after the officers consented to take the civic oath. That occasion gave the regiment's commander a chance to complain that its colors had been seized in that morning's uproar by a company of the Paris National Guard. Lafayette wrote out an order that they be returned immediately (although they actually were returned only after great pains on the part of the officer who went to get them).[113] To prevent deterioration of the soon-to-be-deserted Château, Lafayette commanded Lecointre as the highest responsible officer remaining behind with the Versailles National Guard to occupy its outer squares and its gardens,[114] while Captain Gondran and his Paris National Guard company in keeping with the new state of things, replaced the King's Bodyguard in the interior.

By one o'clock the king and his family were ready to leave Versailles, and the main body of the Paris National Guard, drawn up along the Avenue de Paris, received the command to march. In its midst was a long train of wagons filled with flour from the palace bins. The king's carriage, escorted by Lafayette and Estaing and filled with members of the Bourbon family, followed. Behind the king's carriage came those of other residents of the Château and of a deputation that the National Assembly had voted to send along with the king. A contingent of the Paris Guard brought up the rear. Trailing beside the troops all along the line were thousands of Parisian men and women, some of them too bedraggled to rejoice, some of them shouting victoriously to spectators massed along the road: "We are bringing back the baker, the baker's wife, and the baker's boy." Triumph and hope, bread and politics, confidence and contempt, were mixed up in that metaphor.

The loaded wagons made progress slow. As they rode along,

---

[113] *Procédure au Châtelet*, II, 21–22 (Comte de Montmorin, major in the Flanders Regiment); *ibid.*, p. 56 (Gondran); and Mounier, *Appel*, pp. 198–99.

[114] Lafayette to Lecointre, October 6, Tuetey, I, 383, No. 3445.

Lafayette and Estaing had a chance to talk about the events of the last forty-eight hours. Estaing, whose loyalty to the queen was deep, hoped that she would now have a chance to regain the affections of Paris, and he thought Lafayette should give her an opportunity to do so. Lafayette indicated that he would try; the horrifying events of the day, he confessed, had made him a royalist. Since Lafayette had been a royalist all along, what he meant was that he now believed more firmly than ever that since the general will might be misled by ambitious men, the reigning monarch must be defended against those planning to replace his dynasty with another. Estaing the next day wrote to the queen urging her and the king to draw profit from disaster not only by trusting Lafayette but by actually showing that they trusted him.[115]

As soon as the authorities in Paris learned what had happened at Versailles, they broadcast that the royal family was coming and that the King's Bodyguard, having taken the civic oath, had "as brothers merged under the flags of the Paris National Guard." They also passed a resolution acknowledging indebtedness to Lafayette's "prudence and wisdom" for "the happy outcome" in Versailles, sending a Representative to carry this expression of appreciation to the commandant general.[116] Earlier that morning some of the very women who had initiated the outburst of the previous day proposed to meet the returning hero with a crown of laurel and at Viroflay joined the throng accompanying the king.[117]

When the cavalcade neared the city gates, Lafayette sent an aide ahead to inform the Hôtel de Ville of the king's approach. Finally, after about a six-hour trek, stopping at various points to allow those on foot to rest,[118] the weary caravan reached the city's outskirts, where the mayor and his party met it. Thanking the king for having come to make Paris his permanent home and for his efforts to relieve the city's famine, Bailly, for the second time

---

[115] October 7, *AP*, XIX, 390; Calmon-Maison, p. 389; *Mémoires*, III, 201; and Lafayette to unknown, *ca.* 1816, *ibid.*, VI, 7. Bertrand de Moleville, *Histoire*, II, 271, doubts that Estaing's letters were ever sent to the queen, but he does not deny that they were written.

[116] Lacroix, II, 185, 194–95.

[117] *Procédure au Châtelet*, I, 132 (Maillard).

[118] Vergennes to Bellejeant, October 6, Vaissière, pp. 96–97.

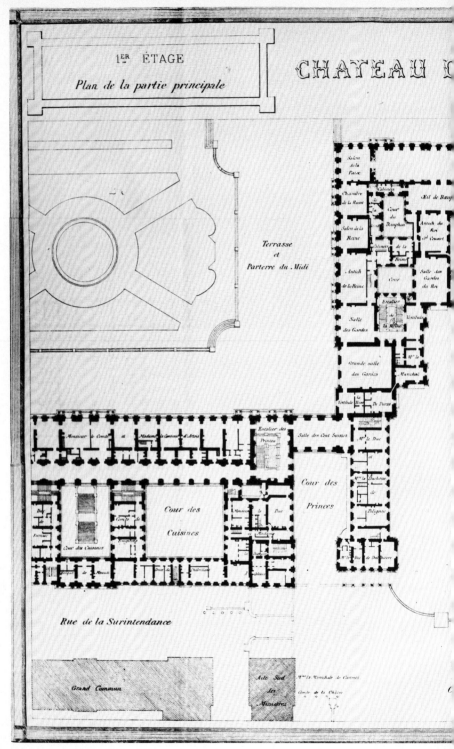

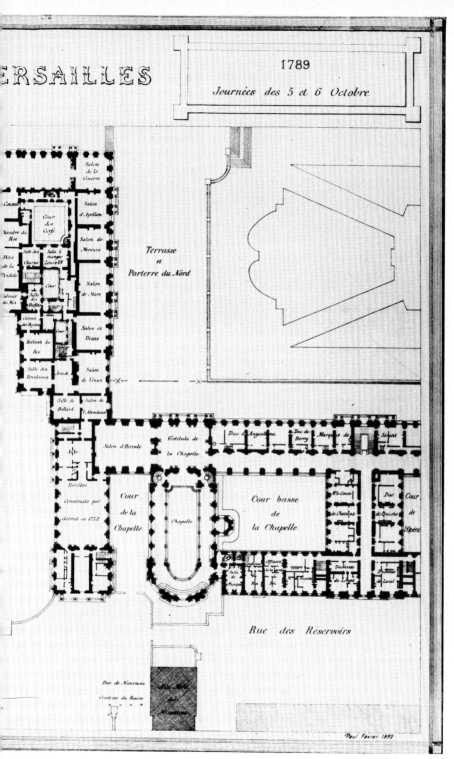

within three months, presented him with the keys of the city, and in response Louis tactfully expressed his constant "pleasure and confidence" in finding himself "among the citizens of my good city of Paris.[119] Since the commune had made plans to receive him formally before he finally installed himself at the Tuileries Palace, Louis, yielding, despite fatigue, to pressure from Bailly and Lafayette, consented to go to the Hôtel de Ville first.[120] Marie Antoinette thought that perhaps she ought to head directly for her new home, which was on the way, and she consulted Lafayette on that matter. He in turn consulted Moreau de Saint-Méry, who thought she had better stay with the rest, for it was already dark and the crowds were thick and still excitable; although he hoped that the queen as one of the royal suite would reach the Hôtel de Ville unharmed, he doubted that she would be able to get safely to the Tuileries alone.[121] The queen and her tired, hungry children went along to the Hôtel de Ville.

With all the dash that their fatigue, encumbrances, and long stretch of duty would allow, the National Guard now proceeded in marching order down the streets of Paris. It was already dark, but the city was bright, for a joyous people had "illuminated" it, with street lanterns at their brightest and house windows lighted up by lamps, torches, and candles. The streets were lined by a double column of Guardsmen. From time to time bystanders threw taunts at the royal carriage, but they were usually drowned out by shouts of "Vive le roi!" (especially in the good residential area of the Faubourg Saint Honoré), and applause for the city's troops was general.[122] A wounded soldier of the King's Bodyguard was con-

[119] Lacroix, II, 189–90.

[120] Memoirs of the Duchess de Tourzel, governess to the children of France . . . (London, 1886), I, 42.

[121] Mémoires, II, 343 n.

[122] Wille, II, 227–29; Staël, I, 345; unknown to Artois in Maury, p. 302; and several contemporary letters of royal bodyguards and others in Vaissière, pp. 97, 116, 120–21, 125, 149–50. See also above, n. 67. While the populace doubtless was not sedate, the immediately contemporaneous accounts say little about drunkenness and frenzy, which are frequently imputed to those who marched from Versailles to Paris on October 6. For examples of later, probably indignantly exaggerated, accounts see Baron Imbert de Saint-Amand (ed.), Journal de Marie-Thérèse de France, duchesse d'Angoulème [daughter of Louis XVI], 5 octobre 1789–2 septembre 1792, corrigé et annoté par Louis XVIII (Paris, 1893), pp. 3–12; Weber, pp. 277–79; and F.-R. Chateaubriand, Mémoires d'outre-tombe, ed. Edmond Biré (Paris, [1899]), I, 280–81.

ducted by a National Guardsman to Lafayette's house, where Adrienne took every possible care of him, and in a few days he recovered.[123]

About 8 P.M. the royal family and its escort reached the Place de Grève, where the congestion was so dense that the procession could move only slowly through the narrow path the National Guard opened before it. So the king and his family, leaving their carriage, continued on foot to the Hôtel de Ville, Lafayette and the deputies of the National Assembly following behind him. The Garde de la Ville had been accorded the honor of policing the city hall's doors, and a select group of the National Guard policed the interior. When the party reached the Grande Salle, the king was seated on a hastily prepared dais, surrounded by his family, and Bailly and the Representatives likewise took their places in front of an over-flowing audience. While the dauphin slept in his governess' arms, citizens and royal family listened to appropriate speeches. At one point, when Bailly was quoting the king's words at the city barrier indicating the royal "pleasure and confidence" in returning to Paris, he left out the words *and confidence* and was gently corrected first by the queen and then by the king. The royal couple's good humor and Bailly's tactful compliment to the queen in making the correction she had indicated brought cheers from the auditors. An announcement that the National Assembly would soon follow the king to Paris brought more cheers, and other marks of warm approval frequently punctuated the ceremony.

When the speeches were over and the applause died down, Louis XVI and Marie Antoinette went into a room with a balcony overlooking the Place de Grève and greeted a multitude on the square below. Prolonged cheers welcomed them there too.[124] Somewhere during these formalities Lafayette felt a hand clasp his as if in gratitude, and he was pleased to see that it was the hand of Mme Elisabeth.[125] After Their Majesties expressed "their satis-

---

[123] *Procédure au Châtelet*, I, 197–98 (Gueroult du Berville).

[124] Lacroix, II, 190–92; Tourzel, I, 43; and *Mémoires*, II, 343. *Moniteur*, October 12 (but actually of a later date: see above, n. 101), p. 294, says that Lafayette tried to badger the king to announce that he would remain in Paris, but we have no other evidence for such badgering.

[125] *Mémoires*, II, 344.

faction over the good will that they saw reigning among all citizens,"[126] they at last were free to proceed to the Tuileries, which Saint Priest had meanwhile done the best he could to get ready to receive them. With Lafayette and the National Guard as escort, they arrived at their new home about 9 P.M.[127]

Paris now subsided, and the lights went out. At last the king and the commandant general could go to bed. Lafayette had probably not touched a bed since the morning of October 5, and it was now late on October 6. But he was to wake on October 7 to new duties, honors, and responsibilities.

The poet has taught us what often happens to the best laid schemes of mice and men. On October 5 and 6, however, if there had been any scheming at all, it had not been Lafayette's, and he had at times seemed to lose control of whatever schemes others might have laid without his approval. Yet his lack of scheme had gone anything but agley for him. His conduct on this occasion "acquired for him from all parties the appellation of the guardian angel of the day."[128] He was now Louis XVI's majordomo, a sort of shogun to an irresolute occidental mikado, and for months to come he was to be the most powerful man in France.

BIBLIOGRAPHICAL NOTES

Many legends regarding the events of October 5 and 6 have gained wide currency because they are based upon contemporary though not necessarily first-hand accounts. We have deliberately avoided relying upon the many contemporary periodicals which reported these events, for they rarely had correspondents *sur place*, and they frequently copied hearsay reports from one another. The same is true of the several diplomatic reports from foreign agents in Paris. And many of the so-called memoirs which dealt with October 5–6 are equally suspect. Some of them (e.g., the continuator of Bailly's Vol. III, Ferrière, Alexandre de Lameth, Montlosier, and Rabaut St. Etienne) are largely based not on personal recollections but on borrowings from other contemporary sources, and some on myths subsequently developed (e.g., Mme Campan and Maleissye), although others, if carefully checked against the direct contemporary testimony, may yield relevant and credible details (e.g., Dumas, Mme La Tour du Pin, Saint Priest, Miot de Melito, Thiébault,

---

[126] Lacroix, II, 192.

[127] *Procédure au Châtelet*, II, 38 (Lafayette); Weber, pp. 279–80; and Saint Priest, II, 22, 90.

[128] Short to Jay, October 9, Boyd, XVI, 5, ed. note.

Mme de Staël, and La Marck). In general, however, as has frequently been observed, memoirs are unreliable sources, suffering as they do not only from the inevitable egocentrism of the observer but frequently also from a lengthy lapse of time between observation and recollection, a lapse which brings forgetfulness of some details and embroidery of others.

The reader will perhaps wonder, therefore, why we have so frequently given credence to Lafayette's *Mémoires* in our account of October 5–6. There are several good reasons for this apparently partisan credulity. First, having frequently been able to check the data he gives against other eyewitness testimony we have been persuaded that he knowingly invented details only rarely. Second, he has left at least five separate accounts of what happened on October 5–6 (not counting casual references), all of which have a convincing consistency. Two of them were close to the events (the letter of October 6, 1789, in *Mémoires*, II, 411, and his affidavit of April 27, 1790, in *Procédure au Châtelet*, II, 36–39), but the other three (the relevant pages of his letter of January 15, 1799, in *Mémoires*, III, 235–37, his so-called "Second récit des événemens du 5 et du 6 octobre," *ibid.*, II, 346–54, written in 1814, and his so-called "Premier récit des événemens du 5 et du 6 octobre," *ibid.*, pp. 328–45, actually written after the "Second récit," *ca.* 1829) are so similar to the other two as to suggest that he consulted the earlier ones in preparing each successive account. In fact, the accounts of 1799 (*Mémoires*, III, 236–37) and 1814 (II, 347–48) are at times almost verbatim the same. Where the minutiae of these accounts differ, we have generally preferred the earlier to the later ones, not hesitating to discard all of them if we saw good reason to do so.

Mounier has also left several accounts of what happened on October 5–6 (his "Exposé" of October 26, *AP*, IX, 573–78; his affidavit of July 10, 1790, in *Procédure au Châtelet*, III, 573–78; and his *Appel* of 1791), but on the activity of Lafayette in Paris on October 5 and for the most part in Versailles on October 6 they give only hearsay evidence. Mounier's *Appel* was an effort to rebut the *Rapport* on the Châtelet investigation which on September 30 and October 1, 1790, Chabroud, having examined the nearly four hundred affidavits collected by the Châtelet in investigating the disorders of October 5–6, gave to the National Assembly as spokesman of its Comité des Rapports. The Châtelet determined that there was reason to bring Mirabeau and Orléans to trial for their alleged part in the misdeeds of the two days, but partly because of Chabroud's rebuttal the National Assembly voted not to impeach the two accused; see *AP*, XIX, 338–93 (October 1, 1790). Mounier published his reply to Chabroud's *Rapport* from exile in 1791. Thus, in a sense, by 1791 the deponents at the Châtelet had been examined by Chabroud for the defense and cross-examined by Mounier for the prosecution, fully exposing their inconsistencies, absurdities, trivialities, contradictions, irrelevancies, and fancies. And yet the question of responsibility for October 5–6 remains moot. We have tried not to avoid moot points when relevant to Lafayette, indicating those that still are moot but endeavoring in such instances to conclude what the burden of the evidence seems to require.

Marc de Villiers, *Les 5 et 6 octobre 1789: Reine Audu (les légendes des journées d'octobre)* (Paris, 1917), gives a rather sober account of the events themselves but is sometimes carelessly documented. Leclercq's footnotes still present the most extensive bibliography for the *journées d'octobre*, but unfortunately he is himself, though painstaking, far from a judicious historian. For example, on the basis of a quotation in a secondary source of a report of a statement by Mounier he twice (pp. 120–21, n. 8, and 144, n. 2) gives in his footnotes the intrinsically implausible story that the women of Paris soaked their bread in the blood of fallen bodyguards and ate it, though once (p. 144, n. 2), without repudiating the story, he wonders how (not whether) Mounier, its supposed original source, could have witnessed it since he was not present. And yet Leclercq at times refuses to believe Lafayette's direct testimony!

Battifol's article not only gives the best maps and plans of the Château of Versailles and its environs in 1789 but also usually sifts fact from fiction about the events of October 5–6, but we have been unable to discover the sources for his statements (pp. 77–79) that on three separate occasions Lafayette mounted his horse, inspected the streets of Versailles before he went to bed fully clothed, and slept for twenty minutes before the invasion of the Château. Our sources lead us to believe that Lafayette left the details of inspection to his staff and perhaps got less than twenty minutes of sleep, if any at all.

APPENDIX I

Madame de Simiane

Having been able to consult the letters of Adrienne de Lafayette to and from her husband that were discovered at the Château Lagrane-Blénau, André Maurois in his *Adrienne* gives the best account of the triangle formed by the Lafayettes and Diane-Adélaïde de Damas, Comtesse de Simiane. He maintained, we think correctly, that Adrienne knew about her husband's devotion to Mme de Simiane, was sad about it because she would have liked to inspire him with a similar devotion, but felt no resentment against either of them.[1]

Adélaïde was the sister of Charles Damas d'Antigny, whom Lafayette got to know, if not earlier, as an aide to Rochambeau in America in 1781–83.[2] He was then the Comte de Damas but was later to become the Duc de Damas, his younger brother, Roger, becoming the Comte de Damas. It is generally assumed that Lafayette met Mme de Simiane first at the Neckers' salon in 1783.[3] On the basis of the newly discovered documents at Lagrange Maurois shows that Lafayette and Mme de Simiane probably became intimate friends in September 1783, when he was at Nancy, where her brother Roger was very ill and many of the Damas d'Antigny family had foregathered. Lafayette was there on his way from the maneuvers of his former regiment, the Noailles Dragoons. That was shortly after his split with Aglaé de Hunolstein.[4]

The relations of Adélaïde de Simiane and Lafayette soon became a subject of salon gossip. Among the people who talked about them in the late 1780's and afterwards as if they were no secret were Espinchal,[5] Bertrand Barère,[6]

[1] See especially p. 117 of the Paris edition.

[2] See Gottschalk, *Close,* pp. 152–66.

[3] See Gottschalk, *Between,* pp. 16–17.

[4] See Gottschalk, *Lady-in-Waiting, the Romance of Lafayette and Aglaé de Hunolstein* (Baltimore, 1939), pp. 100–102. Gottschalk, *Between,* pp. 29–30, says that the patient at Nancy was Adrienne's grandfather, but the documents published by Maurois, pp. 147–48, show that it was Adélaïde's brother.

[5] See *Journal d'émigration,* p. 511.

[6] See his *Mémoires* [Paris, 1843], IV, 289.

Théodore de Lameth,[7] the Duc de Laval,[8] the Prince de Ligne,[9] and the author of the so-called *Mémoires de Condorcet*.[10]

If the Comtesse de Boigne[11] was not repeating idle chatter, once when Adélaïde and Lafayette were together in a box at some musical performance at Versailles, a line was sung that ran: "Love beneath laurels finds ladies kind," and the audience, discerning that the line applied to them, made plain that it approved.[12] So when in March 1788 the Comte de Simiane blew out his brains, everyone, including Jefferson, assumed that it was because he was jealous of his wife's affection for Lafayette.[13] Shortly after Morris reached Paris, in February 1789, he seems to have been regaled with "the History of Mr de La Fayette and Madame Simien [*sic*]."[14]

Maurois describes Adélaïde as "dame d'honneur de Madame"[15]—i.e., of the Comtesse of Provence—probably because she is described in the *Mémoires secrets* of Bachaumont[16] as "attachée à Madame comme dame pour l'accompagner." But that description may not be correct. The lady who is listed in the *Almanach royal* of 1789[17] among the twenty-four "dames pour accompagner Madame" is "Madame la Marquise de Simiane," and since Adélaïde's titles were "Comtesse de Simiane and Marquise de Miremont" this may not be she but Anne-Emilie de Félix, Marquise de Simiane, of another branch of the family (with whom the editor of the Comtesse de Boigne's *Mémoires* also confuses Adélaïde).[18] In any case she was not a "dame d'honneur," which was regarded as two degrees higher in rank, with "dames d'atours" in between (each of the higher ranks held by only one lady). In all events, Adélaide, as all the sources seem to indicate, was a member of the inner court circle at Versailles.

As long as Lafayette were merely a liberal noble, politics was not a cause of strain between them, and the letters he sent Adélaïde to Versailles from Paris in 1788 and early 1789 were usually frank discussions about his political opinions, actions, plans, and aspirations, sometimes mixed with words of endearment. As time wore on, she became increasingly concerned over his "Patriot" proclivities—as the above pages show—without any break, however, in their mutual affection. The imprisonment and exile which the

---

[7] P. 109.

[8] See Ste-Beuve, *Portraits littéraires* [Paris, 1862–64], II, 157.

[9] *Fragments de l'histoire de ma vie* [Paris, 1928], I, 304–5.

[10] II, 64–65.

[11] Comtesse de Biogne, *Mémoires*, ed. Charles Nicoullaud [Paris, 1907], I, 26.

[12] See also Théodore de Lameth, p. 109–10, n. 5, which says that the Comtesse de Boigne got the story from him.

[13] See Gottschalk, *Between*, p. 293 and n. 32.

[14] Morris diary, March 19, Davenport (ed.), I, 15. See also March 22, *ibid.*, p. 18.

[15] P. 197.   [16] Quoted *ibid.*, p. 174.   [17] P. 136.

[18] III, 6, n. 1, Cf. F.-A.-A. de La Chesnaye-Desbois and M. Badier, *Dictionnaire de la noblesse* [Paris, 1863–76], XIII, 625, 627.

Lafayettes subsequently had to endure (1792–99) and Adélaïde's overlapping emigration brought them all closer together, and she remained a dear friend of all the Lafayette family even after their return to France. The attachment of the two lovers seems to have lasted, though perhaps with diminishing fervor, throughout their lives, Adélaïde (d. 1835) surviving Lafayette by approximately one year.

Anecdotes about their relationship in the months which are the subject of this volume are few, and, as already indicated, those few suspect. One of them runs that early in the Revolution "Madame de Simiane was struck by an apple thrown from the upper gallery at the Théâtre français," whereupon "she sent it to her brother-in-law [sic], Lafayette, and wrote, 'Here my dear General, is the first fruit of the Revolution that has reached my hands.' "[19] The story apparently is derived from Mme de Genlis' memoirs,[20] which, however, say that it involved Mme de Biron (not Mme de Simiane) and that, Lafayette coming in soon after, she gave (not sent) him the two oranges (not one apple) thrown into her box (not at her). The so-called Mémoires de Condorcet, which seem to be Madelin's source, gives the same story as Mme de Genlis except that it also speaks of one apple instead of two oranges.[21] Somewhere about the same time Mme de Simiane is supposed to have remarked to Lafayette, after a stormy evening at the theater: "Our canaille [apparently meaning the aristocratic brawlers] are decidedly better than yours."[22]

If these anecdotes have any historical value at all, it is only to show that although the relationship of Adélaïde and Lafayette was publicly recognized, their political sympathies were not expected to coincide. Meleissye, who was no friend of Lafayette, records that upon a visit to Mme de Simiane and her uncle, the Duc de Châtelet, sometime before the commandant general brought the royal family to Paris in October, he spoke disparagingly of Lafayette but that both the lady and her uncle defended their mutual friend as acting out of loyalty to the king.[23] In 1830 Lafayette wrote to the daughter of Mme de Staël: "I lived the early years of the Revolution in close association with women who were my friends [l'intime société des amies] and especially with one friend who was very dear to me. There was continual disagreement without troubling our mutual affection."[24]

The letters in Lafayette's Mémoires which are not specified as being to a named recipient are generally thought to be to Mme de Simiane, and some of them have a tone that a leading political figure might sound in writing to a mistress interested in politics as well as in himself as a lover. But a few of

---

[19] Louis Madelin, French Revolution (New York, 1923), pp. 131–32.

[20] Souvenirs de Félice (Mémoires de Madame de Genlis), ed. F. Barrière (Paris, 1882), pp. 206–7.

[21] II, 64–65.   [22] André Le Breton, Rivarol (Paris, 1895), p. 75.

[23] Maleissye, pp. 93–95.

[24] Lafayette to the Duchesse de Broglie, October 2, 1830, Archives de Broglie (courtesy of the Comtesse du Pange).

them decidedly do not; they do not even sound as if they were written to a lady. Hence, we have at times above found it appropriate to suggest some other addressee than Mme de Simiane and even to guess who that other addressee might have been.[25]

Our conviction that these letters were not all addressed to Mme de Simiane is strengthened by the circumstances of their publication in the *Mémoires*. The Château Lagrange-Blénau, where Lafayette spent his last years, was not Lafayette's property (his having been confiscated on the grounds that he was an émigré after 1792) but his wife's. Hence until he went to occupy it after his return to France in 1799, it had no previous association with him and presumably contained no papers of his. The abundant papers that are now to be found there, if they date before 1799, were subsequently collected by him for his records. He also added similar records to those already at his birthplace in Chavaniac when it again passed into his hands by inheritance from his aunt. Somewhere in the interval between 1799 and his death in 1834 he caused to be made at least two sets of copies of letters which are designated on the cover of one set "Copies de lettres ou manuscrits du Gal Lafayette" and of the other "Extraits de lettres à Mad. de S***." These sets were probably originally at Chavaniac rather than at Lagrange, for they eventually passed, along with some other possessions of the Château de Chavaniac, into the hands of M. Emmanuel Fabius, autograph dealer of Paris, and ultimately were divided between the Bibliothèque Nationale and Cornell University. The two sets of copies are in different handwritings, one of which might conceivably be that of Mme de Simiane. The important point is that the cover of one set of copies implies (as we think correctly) that not all its contents are letters to Mme de Simiane,[26] while the other cover (which, if we are not wrong, is mistaken) says they all are.

These copies probably were the ones which the editors used for the 1837 edition of the *Mémoires*. They apparently wanted them all to be considered, to use their phrase, "lettres de famille et d'intimité."[27] Both sets of copies are now in the Lafayette Archives, Cornell University Library, Box 2, and an examination of them shows that although the editors of the *Mémoires* "emended" them only slightly, they avoided mention of Mme de Simiane studiously enough (whether or not intentionally) to render dubious to anyone who had seen the copies from which they worked their repeated reminder[28] that most of the addressees were members of the Lafayette family. Despite the reminder they left the matter open by directly naming no addressee for any of the letters in these folders. We have explained above[29] why we think that none of the letters without salutation was addressed either to Mme de Lafayette or to Mme de Tessé. Maurois, who saw many of

---

[25] E.g., p. 251, n. 77.

[26] In fact, the letter of August 7, 1785, published in *Mémoires*, II, 128–29, is plainly to *ma cousine* (as Lafayette regularly addressed Mme de Tessé).

[27] *Mémoires*, II, 232 n.

[28] *Ibid.*, pp. 49 n., 128 n., 232 n., and V, 502 n.

[29] Chap. VI, "Bibliographical Notes."

the originals of Lafayette's letters of Adrienne at Lagrange-Blénau, seems to have found among them none of those contained in the two sets of copies now in the Cornell University Library, and he assumed that, as published, the latter were all to Mme de Simiane. We have concluded, however, that a few were probably addressed to others.

As indicated above,[30] the letter addressed to on unnamed recipient and dated "ce mardi" (October 6)[31] must be considered among those not intended for Mme de Simiane. The principal reason for thinking so is that this letter is obviously addressed to someone in Paris, and Mme de Simiane would normally be in Versailles. We know that she was in Versailles on October 5–6 because the Marquise de La Tour du Pin tells us that Mme de Simiane during the attack upon the Château took refuge with an old servant who lived near the Orangerie.[32] Lafayette, therefore, would not have expected her to need to learn what was going on in Versailles from his report to Adrienne in Paris.

[30] P. 367, n. 54.

[31] *Mémoires,* II, 411.

[32] I, 230.

APPENDIX II

Hagiography and Demonography

Despite our effort to narrate every point we judged significant in the career of Lafayette from January 1 to October 6, 1789, considerations of style and of space have constrained us to omit mention of a fair number of pamphlets, songs, hymns, speeches, plays, medals, paintings, engravings, sculptures, porcelains, and caricatures pertaining to him which appeared in the interval. The reader will find more information on the pamphlets in the bibliographical works of Monglond, Jackson, and Martin and Walter (among others) and in the catalogues by Girodie, Blancheteau, and Braibant (among others) was well as in the still invaluable *Bibliographie de l'histoire de Paris pendant la Révolution française* by Maurice Tourneux (5 vols.; Paris, 1890–1913). With the aid of bibliographical guides such as these we have found more than a score of pamphlets which pertain to Lafayette but which we have not hitherto mentioned. They are not of equal importance, nor are they all, strictly speaking, independent writings, since some of them are speeches, letters, resolutions, or other extracts from the minutes of some municipal district, National Guard, or other body. Their general tenor is favorable to Lafayette but some, usually not giving his name in the title, seem to be attacks upon him—for example, "Le coucher, ou la vérité toute nue, pour servir de supplément aux quatre repas" (said to be an attack on Lafayette by Mirabeau) and "Patriote Véridique" (an attack on the municipal officers of Paris, including Lafayette, as speculators on the bread market). The titles of other pamplets—*Les Crimes de Lafayette en France* and *M. de Lafayette traité véritablement comme il le mérite*—plainly give away the nature of their contents.

For songs and verses dealing with Lafayette during this period the best guide is Pierre Constant (ed.), *Hymnes et chansons de la Révolution* (Paris, 1904), but the works of Bérenger (esp. pp. 273–87) and Rogers are also helpful. Some of the verses which appeared in January–October 1789 in the newspapers of the day were the work of now forgotten poets and probably were not sung anywhere, but that some were intended to be sung is indicated by the designation of a popular song as the melody to which they were written. If sung at all during the months of July–October 1789, they were most often sung at banquets or other celebrations of the National Guard. One verse of this period, which will serve to illustrate their general content and quality, was intended to be placed at the foot of pictures of Lafayette:

La France en liberté, l'Amerique affranchie,
Aiment dans La Fayette un héros citoyen.

Boston, pour ton salut, il prodigua sa vie,
Paris, à ton repos, il immole le sien.[1]

The verses at times also spoke glowingly of Mme de Lafayette and their children.[2]

Plays about Lafayette were still very rare during this period. The *Courrier de Versailles à Paris*[3] mentioned the fifth performance in London of one entitled *Triumph of Liberty, or the Demolition of the Bastille*, in which he was one of the characters. A manuscript in the Bibliothèque Nationale[4] is entitled "Le triomphe du patriotisme" with the crossed-out subtitle "ou l'aristocrate converti." It is described on the title page as a "comédie nationale en 3 actes et en prose," and it is "dediée et présentée à M. le marquis de Lafayette, commandant de la Guard nationale parisienne." It gives no indication of its author or the date of its composition, and it may not properly belong to this period. The Bordeaux National Guard plays a part in it.

The best guide to the iconography of Lafayette is Olivier's,[5] which should, however, be supplemented by the catalogues of exhibits such as Girodie's and Braibant's, since Olivier deals only with numismatics. Besides the similar items mentioned in the text we have, among other pictures for these months, records of several engravings of Lafayette,[6] a gilded bust,[7] a silhouette,[8] and a pen and ink sketch[9] as well as of contemporary illustrations of events in which he took part (particularly in the pamphlets and journals we have cited). The number of such pictures was already numerous for January–October 1789, but will become more so later on.

For all his popularity, Lafayette was also a frequent butt of caricature.[10] Among the caricatures that apparently belong to the first nine months of 1789, there is an English caricature bearing the date July 1789.[11] It shows Lafayette and Bailly as storks preparing to eat the frogs around them, and it is entiled "The Frogs who wanted a King." Almost the same caricature was to be published in French in 1791[12] with one major and several minor

---

[1] *Lettre à Monsieur le comte de B****, I, 364.

[2] See above, p. 298, for verses to her on September 22.

[3] September 12, pp. 200–201.

[4] Fr. 9279, fols. 261–304.

[5] See esp. Nos, 2, 3, 13–21, 26–27, 29–30, 136–39.

[6] By P.-S.-B. Divivier and P.-L. Debucourt, among others.

[7] Catalogue of the Fogg Museum exhibit of February–May 1944.

[8] By P.-E. Boutillion, described in *American Clipper*, April 1940, No. 122.

[9] John Cochrane, "Centennial of the Cincinnati," *Magazine of American History*, X (1883), 193.

[10] On this subject see (among other titles) André Blum, *La Caricature révolutionnaire* (Paris, n.d.), pp. 137–40, Nos. 359–78; Marcel Aubert and Marcel Roux (eds.), *Un siècle d'histoire de France par l'estampe, 1770–1871. Collection de Vinck* (Paris, 1921), III, Nos. 4370, 4416, 4457; 4475–76; and Bruel, II and III, *passim*.

[11] See Charavay, facing p. 272.

[12] See Fernand Laurent, p. 329.

differences, the major difference being that now the stork with Lafayette's head stands on a log with the head of Louis XVI, who is labeled "Le roi soliveau," and the title now reads "Le roi soliveau, ou les grenouilles qui demandent un roi." Another caricature shows the Duc d'Aiguillon, who supported the August decrees, intended to abolish privileges, as a half-monkey throwing his money into the fire, whence Orléans, shown as a half-lion, picks it up, throwing it over his shoulder to Lafayette, shown as a half-horse, who swallows it. The title is "D'animaux malfaisants c'étoit un très bon plat."[13]

In contrast to the animosity of these caricatures, at least one probably contemporaneous caricature not already mentioned in the text is friendly to Lafayette. It shows him defending France and triumphing over Despotism and Feudality; it is entitled "La Nation française assistée de M^r De la Fayette terrasse le Despotisme et les abus de Règne Féodal qui terrassaient le Peuple."[14] Another probably contemporary caricature may or may not be friendly. It shows a double-faced man, the left half of his body being Lafayette in military garb and the right half Bailly in civilian garb, standing in front of the Hôtel de Ville.[15] The title ("L'homme à deux faces") may be pejorative, but perhaps it shows approval of the close cooperation of the civil and military arms of the commune.

[13] See G. L. B[urr] (ed.), *Catalogue of the Historical Library of Andrew Dickson White*, Vol. II: *The French Revolution* (Ithaca, N.Y., 1894), p. 294.

[14] *Ibid.*, p. 295.

[15] See Fernand-Laurent, p. 327.

APPENDIX III

The "Round the World" Speech

Lafayette left at least three versions of the speech he claimed to have made forecasting the global circumnavigation of the tricolor. In two of these versions he quoted the supposed speech in full. In the more succinct and earlier of the two full versions, it ran: "I bring you a cockade that will go around the world, and an institution [i.e., the National Guard] which is at the same time civil and military and which condemns all arbitrary governments to the alternative of being beaten if they do not imitate it and of being overthrown if they dare to imitate it."[1] This version was written *ca.* 1815.

Unfortunately, the contemporary minutes and newspapers, which rarely missed any dramatic statement by the hero of two worlds, do not record this flourish. One wonders, too, where Lafayette found his version of the speech, since usually for other speeches that he quoted verbatim he used a contemporary journal or minutes as his source. Another version[2] was dictated *ca.* 1829.[3] Except for a few additional words it is practically the same as the earlier one.

The third version[4] is in indirect discourse. It says only that Lafayette announced "publicly" (not "to the Hôtel de Ville," as in the two other versions) that the new cockade "would go round the world." Here he does not claim that he said anything about the doom of arbitrary governments whether or not they imitated the National Guard. This version of the speech is contained in an autobiographical letter to M. d'Hennings dated January 15, 1799. A remark to the effect that the institution of the National Guard would "reduce old governments to powerlessness to defend themselves against us if they did not imitate it or against their subjects if they dared to imitate it" appears in this letter[5] very close to the brief citation of the speech but without any suggestion that it was part of that speech.

This version is much closer to the actual event than either of the other versions. It is more likely to be correct, not only because it probably suffered less from the dimming of memory but also because if the speech was given publicly rather than before a municipal body it is less difficult to explain why it failed to be mentioned in the contemporary records of the Hôtel de Ville.

[1] *Mémoires*, III, 281.

[2] *Ibid.*, II, 267.

[3] See *ibid.*, pp. 95 n., 249, n. 1.

[4] *Ibid.*, III, 228.

[5] *Ibid.*, pp. 227–28.

If this version is correct, a reconstruction of the actual course of events may be attempted. (1) Lafayette, speaking publicly on some occasion said (and probably fairly casually, for otherwise the newspapers doubtless would have picked it up) that the new cockade would go round the world. Since the National Guard was a municipal organization not yet intended to replace the royal army, he could hardly have said anything about its potential impact upon foreign countries at this time. (2) In 1799, however, when the armies of the French Republic had in fact overthrown a number of old regimes, it was easy for him to think that the National Guard had been the nucleus of its new military power and political appeal, and he said so in his letter to Hennings. (3) In 1815 these two ideas were already in juxtaposition in his mind, a juxtaposition which made them appear to him parts of the same speech, given with an official formality which he had not previously claimed for it. (4) In *ca.* 1830 he elaborated the speech a little more.

Lafayette, almost always an intentionally honest if sometimes romanticizing witness, was here apparently tricked by his memory into thinking he had made a remark which years later, after the French Republic and the Napoleonic Empire had overthrown old regime after old regime and then had themselves vanished, having temporarily planted the tricolor under almost every European sky, seemed exactly the right prognostication for him to have made in 1789.

APPENDIX IV

Did Lafayette Kiss the Queen's Hand?

The *Correspondance et souvenirs du Comte de Neuilly*[1] is one of the several eyewitness accounts which, in much the same language as Lafayette,[2] give the details of the balcony scene where Marie-Antoinette appeared alone, and yet Neuilly does not mention Lafayette's kissing the queen's hand. Rousseau[3] stated only that the queen appeared alone on the balcony (not even mentioning Lafayette as accompanying her) and was applauded. Espinchal, who was not an eyewitness, agreed in general that "Lafayette à coté d'elle semblait la protéger."[4] Espinchal appears to have got his information from an account by an unnamed eyewitness who wrote to the Comte d'Artois of these events, stating that Lafayette "kept close" to the queen "and seemed to cover her with his aegis."[5] Even this unnamed eyewitness, though describing Lafayette as the queen's protector, mentions no hand-kissing. And the account of October 5–6 in the *Moniteur*[6] (which, however, was not in existence at this time, this number being only subsequently made up), speaks of Lafayette as her "interprète et le garant des sentiments qu'elle crut alors d'avoir témoigner" but mentions no hand-kissing.

This lack of corroborative evidence induced M. L. Battifol[7] to maintain that Lafayette's account of his kissing the queen's hand[8] is incredible. That so dramatic and public an act should not have been corroborated unmistakably by some other witness among the scores who left some sort of testimony on the events of that day is indeed difficult to explain. Nevertheless, we find it even harder to explain why Lafayette, whose testimony in almost every other significant detail of the day's activities can be corroborated by some other direct witness, should in this instance have invented such an easily refutable story. Furthermore, some friendly gesture like that he described

---

[1] Ed. Maurice de Barberey (Paris, 1865), pp. 16–19.

[2] *Mémoires*, III, 341, 349.　　　　[3] Lacroix, II, 185.

[4] Espinchal Ms. 297 in Bibliothèque de Clermont-Ferrand, p. 37.

[5] L. Maury, "Une relation inédite des journées des 5 et 6 octobre 1789," *RH*, LXXXIV (1904), 301.

[6] October 12, p. 294.

[7] "Les journées des 5 et 6 octobre 1789 à Versailles," Academie de Versailles, *Mémoires de la Société des sciences morales, des lettres et des arts*, XVII (1893), 27–29 n.

[8] *Mémoires*, II, 341, 349.

would help to account for the apparent change in the mob's mood toward the queen and in the queen's own mood. Paroy says of Marie-Antoinette on the balcony: "Elle resta environs deux minutes dans cet cruelle perplexité."[9] What relieved her of her perplexity?

The earliest explicit statements we have seen that Lafayette kissed the queen's hand came in two biographies of Lafayette which were published in the 1820's by authors who probably got the story from him.[10] The revised edition of one of these, Ducoudray-Holstein's biography,[11] probably because corrected upon Lafayette's insistence,[12] left out some of the histrionic details of the earlier edition but still had Lafayette kissing the queen's hand. Although both of these biographies were published in the United States, it seems improbable that if their story of the hand-kissing were a complete fabrication, it would have gone unchallenged by all of what must have been a fairly large number of surviving French witnesses in the 1820's and 1830's, particularly those who by that time thought they had good reason to paint Lafayette in the worst possible light, for Lafayette's triumphal tour of the States in 1824–25 was closely followed in France. It appears more credible that no one else mentioned Lafayette's kissing the queen's hand because, while in retrospect it might well have seemed "un signe hasardeux, mais decisif,"[13] yet for a protective noble of the court to kiss his distressed queen's hand was no more than a becoming gesture not needing to be singled out by the observer from all the rest of "ce qu'on pouvait attendre de la circonstance et de mon devouement,"[14] and only as royalist reaction against Lafayette intensified, under the Comte de Villèle as premier, did that action, which probably appeared in its own time no more spectacular than the numerous accompanying actions, seem to Lafayette worthy of special emphasis as a service he had rendered to royalty—an emphasis which, when he finally gave it a decisive role, no one bothered to gainsay. Hence, we surmise that while Lafayette probably did kiss the queen's hand, his gallantry did not have quite the decisive, electrifying effect upon the people in the Cour de Marbre that he afterward attributed to it.

[9] Paroy, *loc. cit.*, pp. 5–6.

[10] H.-L.-V. Ducoudray-Holstein, *Memoirs of General Lafayette* (New York, 1824), p. 107, and Anon., *American Military Biography . . . Also the Life of Gilbert Motier de La Fayette* (n. p., 1825), p. 339, and cf. Gottschalk, *Lafayette Comes to America*, pp. 146–48.

[11] P. 118.

[12] Gottschalk, *loc. cit.*

[13] *Mémoires*, II, 341, written *ca.* 1829.

[14] *Ibid.*, p. 349, written *ca.* 1814.

INDEX

(Italics are used for bibliographical data.)